Joachim G. Joachim

Ioannis Metaxas
The Formative Years 1871-1922

PELEUS

STUDIEN ZUR ARCHÄOLOGIE UND
GESCHICHTE GRIECHENLANDS UND ZYPERNS
BAND 5

Joachim G. Joachim

Ioannis Metaxas
The Formative Years 1871-1922

BIBLIOPOLIS
Mannheim und Möhnesee 2000

PELEUS
Studien zur Archäologie und Geschichte Griechenlands und Zyperns
Herausgegeben von Reinhard Stupperich und Heinz A. Richter
Band 5

Die Deutsche Bibliothek - CIP Einheitsaufnahme

Joachim G. Joachim: *Ioannis Metaxas. The Formative Years 1871-1922.* Mannheim; Möhnesee: Bibliopolis, 2000 (Peleus; Bd. 5)
ISBN 3-933925-11-8

Cover vignettes:
Front Cover: King Constantine (wearing a black mourning band) and his staff during the Second Balkan War. Sitting at the table, left to right, Xenophon Stratigos, Constantine, Victor Dousmanis, Ioannis Metaxas. Standing, left to right, the King's brother Andreas, his son Alexandros, his brother Nicholas, sitting on the left, his son Christophoros.
Opposite title page: Cup by the Peithinos painter, Berlin, Pergamonmuseum (CVA Berlin 2, Taf. 61).

Gesamtherstellung: Druck Partner Rübelmann GmbH, Carl-Benz-Str. 11, 69 502 Hemsbach

BIBLIOPOLIS
D - 59519 Möhnesee-Wamel, Schulpatt 13
Tel. 02924/2781, Fax 02924/2757,
e-mail: bibliopolis@t-online.de

ISBN 3-933925-11-8

For Dorothy

Acknowledgements

I should like to express my appreciation and gratitude to several people who have given me the benefit of their experience and wisdom, during the writing of this book. My thanks especially go to Professor F. Roy Willis, Professor Richard N. Schwab and Professor William W. Hagen, all three of the University of California. My thanks also go to Professor Dr. Heinz A. Richter of the University of Mannheim, Germany, for his indefatigable efforts in seeing the book through the press.

The research for this book was carried out in several libraries on both sides of the Atlantic. The author is grateful to the Staffs of the Gennadeion and several other Libraries in Athens; the Staff of the National Library, the Staff of the Old Parliament Library, (where a special room contains the personal library of loannis Metaxas and many interesting memorabilia of the Regime of the Fourth of August). Many thanks also go the Staff of the General State Archives in Athens.

I am also grateful to the staff of the British Library in London (which was still housed in the British Museum), the Staff of the Public Record Ofce in London and the Staff of the University of California Libraries at Davis and at Berkeley.

Most of all, my thanks and deep gratitude are due to dear Dorothy, my long-suffering wife, for her unfailing love and support in this as in all my other academic endeavors.

Content

Contents

Introduction

Outside Greece very little is known about Ioannis Metaxas. Some Europeans associate his surname with a certain type of brandy. Others, the historically more versed ones, connect this name either with the Greek fascist dictatorship of the the 1930s or with the Metaxas line of fortresses covering Greece's northern frontier against attacks from the north, or, in rare cases, with both. In Greece, Metaxas is the man who said no (όχι) to Mussolini's ultimatum on 28 October 1940 and led Greece through that glorious period which is called in Greek historiography the "Έπος του σαράντα" (the epic of 1940) i.e. the successful defensive battle against the Italians in the Greek and Albanian mountains. Each year this day is commemorated; it is a national holiday. Greeks with a deeper knowledge of their history remember his military achievements in the Balkan Wars and refer to him as little Moltke considering him a military genius.

Still in the 1960s the following story could be heard: When Metaxas studied in Leipzig his professors were so impressed by his intelligence that after he had left they put the following inscription in golden letters on the tympanum of the main university building: Για το Ιωάννι Μεταξά είναι τα αδύνατα δυνατά (For Ioannis Metaxas the impossible is possible). However, even for him, being a professional soldier it was impossible to be admitted to a university.

Historiography on Ioannis Metaxas is extremely scarce. There is not one biography dealing with his whole life. There are historical accounts of his time as a dictator but they contain very little personal biographical information. This is astonishing because biographical sources on Metaxas are rather plentiful. Since his early years Metaxas kept a diary which is a mine of information about his private and public life. This diary was published between 1950 and 1960 in four volumes closely supervised by Metaxas' widow. Additionally Metaxas' notebooks which he kept over the years were printed and they, too, offer valuable information. Both sources were well known by historians and frequently used for their accounts of general Greek history or more specialized monographs mostly dealing with the period of the dictatorship. Dr Joachim is the first historian to make extensive use of these sources when he was writing the present biography.

This biography covers the life of Ioannis Metaxas from 1871 to 1922. As was usual for a member of a noble family of the Ionian Islands (in the 17th Century the Venetians had made the Metaxas family counts) was to take a military career. From 1885 to 1890 Metaxas studied at the Greek Military Academy (Σχολή Ευελπίδων). In the disastruous Greek-Turkish war of 1897 Metaxas served as a engineer officer and came into close contact with the Crown prince of Greece, Constantine. The latter discovered Metaxas' strategic talent and had him sent for additional studies to the Prussian Military Academy (Militärakademie) in Berlin from 1899 to 1903. After his return he worked in the General Directorate of the Army planning the reorganizing of the Greek army according to the German model. When the new General Staff was formed

Constantine invited Metaxas to become a member. In 1907 Constantine entrusted to him the military education of his eldest son George, the future King George II and Metaxas' co-dictator. When, after the Revolution of 1908 Eleftherios Venizelos became Prime Minister Metaxas was appointed his first *aide-de-camp*. In this position Metaxas acquired first hand insight into Venizelos' policy and often discovered fundamental differences in their views. In 1912 Metaxas was sent on an official mission to Sofia to negotiate the military convention with the Bulgarians which he signed on 30 September on behalf of Greece. In both Balkan Wars Metaxas served as third in command in the General Staff and proved his military talents. Several times he was promoted and in September 1913 reached the rank of a Lieutenant-Colonel. After the War he became Director of the General Staff and Principal of the Higher Military Academy. Venizelos and the Crown Prince promoted their successful soldier.

In the First World War Venizelos believed in the victory of the Entente whereas Metaxas was convinced that Germany would win the war and advised King Constantine accordingly. In 1915 Metaxas became Chief of the Greek General Staff. When, in the same year, Venizelos insisted on Greece's participation in the Entente's attack against Gallipoli, Metaxas resigned from his post. In the ensuing schism of Greece he became the sharpest political opponent of Venizelos. When in 1917 Venizelos with the help of the Allies emerged victorious from the domestic struggle Metaxas was among those who were deported by the French to Corsica. In 1919 Venizelos' former opponents were sentenced to death and Metaxas fearing that the French might hand him over to the Greek authorities fled to Italy where he lived until the end of 1920. At the end of the First World War Greece had emerged as one of the victorious nations. But unlike the others her war aim, the restoration of a Greater Greece, (Megali Idea) had not been achieved. Metaxas considered this idea a sheer folly. He was convinced that such an adventure would end in a disaster. Called back by the re-established Royalists he was offered the post of the Chief of the General Staff for the war against Kemalist Turkey which had just started. Metaxas refused flatly and advised the Greek Prime Minister Gounaris to seek a political way out of the dilemma. The latter did not follow Metaxas' advice and the Asia Minor Catastrophe was the result. Metaxas withdrew from the military and began a political career which led him finally to the Dictatorship of 1936.

Against this highly dramatic political background Metaxas' personal biography often seems rather petty-bourgeois. At the same time we observe the unfolding of a rather split personality with strong likes and dislikes and partly neurotic features. Joachim's biography makes fascinating reading and I can but wish him many readers and the strength to finish the second volume bringing the story to its end.

Heinz Richter

The Greek-Turkish War of 1897

Ioannis Michael Metaxas was born on 24 April 1871 on the island of Ithaca where his father was Assistant Prefect *(Eparchos).* His father recorded the event on a sheet of paper under the heading "My Yiannos". The mother, he wrote, was in labour for three days. Present at the birth were the wives of the mayor, the district treasurer and the doctor, as well as three or four other women, and the doctor himself. The father wrote: "In the rooms of the house there were various persons of every class, including young girls. Outside the house there was a great number of people of every class, age and sex. When he was born, Evdokia, Praxithea and Elpiniki dressed him." Then he added: "God grant him a long life and make him a good Christian and an honest citizen." Further down the page he wrote: "Two days later the musicians came and played outside the house for good luck."[1]

The Metaxas family had been known as "Contides", (Counts) for two centuries. Thirty years before the birth of Ioannis Metaxas, "the Noble Signor Giorgio Metaxa Anzolato" submitted documents to the Senate of the United States of the Ionian Islands which demonstrated the claims of the Metaxas family to the title of "Count" and requested on behalf of himself, his brothers and cousins, a decree reaffirming their claims. On 10 February [O.S.] 1841 the Senate, "Having seen the original decree, in virtue of which, from the year 1691, the family of the said Counts Metaxa has been invested, *in perpetuum*, by the Venetian government with the title of "Count" [and] "Considering that the said gentlemen have a just right to that title", authorized that they "continue styling themselves "Counts" [a title which] may also be assumed by the legitimate descendants of the said Counts Metaxa, *in perpetuum* ..."[2] One of those mentioned in this decree as entitled to call himself Count was Ioannis Metaxas, son of Nikolaos Anzolatos, the paternal grandfather of Ioannis Metaxas. This "noble lord", Ioannis Metaxas, married a poor girl who came from Macedonia in 1821 (perhaps a refugee as a result of the Greek War of Independence), after living with her for many years and begetting four children, a not uncommon practice among those classes.[3] One of these children was Panaghis Metaxas, the father of Ioannis Metaxas. He, in his turn, married the daughter of a small landowner from Agrinion, a town in Epirus. Thus

1 *Diary,* I. 41. Metaxas did not use his second name of Michael, but in his earlier years he would sometimes insert the middle initial P for Panaghis, his father's name. The popular version of Ioannis (or Joannes) is Yiannis. His family and close friends (e.g. Sophia, the consort of Constantine) would often affectionately call him Yiannakis, little John, Johnny, a diminutive which suited him because of his small stature. During his dictatorship the paternalist image of Metaxas, carrying a silverhandled walkingstick, was reinforced by the use of the name Barbayiannis - Father John. The French called him Jean, the Italians Giovanni, while British and American correspondents referred to him as John.

2 A facsimile of the decree in Greek, English, and Italian is printed in the *Diary,* vol. I. p. 47.

3 A similar case is that of Dionysios Solomos. Solomos' mother was a maidservant in the household of his noble father, who married her only on his deathbed. See R. H. J. Jenkins, *Dionysius Solomos* (Cambridge, 1940).

Ioannis Metaxas, although a direct descendant of a noble family, had in his veins the blood of the common people from his paternal grandmother and from his mother. When in later years the middle classes shunned his messianic fervour, Ioannis Metaxas remembered this humble side of his background and turned to the working classes in an effort to win their support. He claimed then that he, too, was a farmer's son and his publicists styled him, rather absurdly, The First Labourer and The First Countryman of Greece.

1 Ioannis Metaxas and his parents around1875.

Metaxas' father was a tall, quiet, gentle person with aristocratic manners, who took special care of his long sidewhiskers. The Metaxas title was of very little value by this time. The Ionian aristocracy had been on the decline since the end of Venetian rule; the incorporation of the Ionian Islands into the Greek state in 1863 was the final blow. The Greek Constitution of 1864 laid down that in the case of Greek citizens titles of nobility or distinction were neither bestowed nor recognized -- with the exception of the Royal Family. Titles could be used only on the Ionian Islands, but by then these were too numerous to carry much weight. The shift of power to Athens preempted any value that they might still have possessed. Still, its must have been a great comedown for Count Panaghis Metaxas to seek and accept employment in Government service at a time when such positions were neither lucrative nor held in much esteem.

While Ioannis Metaxas' grandfather had married a girl of the people from necessity, Metaxas' father married a commoner from choice. Panaghis Metaxas met and fell in love with his future wife in Agrinion, where he was working at the time. She was Eleni Constantinou Trigonis, the daughter of a local landowner, but it appears that she brought little or no property to her husband. "I was born in poverty," Ioannis Metaxas used to claim in later years. His mother was a vivacious woman with a practical and assertive bent of mind, unlike his artistic and retiring father. Ioannis inherited some of the intellectual interests of his father's class, but he also possessed a peasant's obstinacy and determination and his mother's drive and ambition. In physical appearance he took more after his mother, who was short, with homely features and, with advancing years, an inclination to stoutness.

In 1879 his father lost his position in Ithaca and returned with his family to his native island of Cephalonia. The young Ioannis-Yiannakis attended the Gymnasium at Argostoli. His conduct was exemplary; he was a good student and excellent in mathematics. Otherwise he was a lonely boy who liked to go for long solitary walks in the countryside. At fourteen he left Argostoli and went to Athens, where he registered at the Military School (Σχολή ευελπίδων) on 24 September 1885. It was his own decision: perhaps because of family tradition, perhaps because he wanted to start earning his living immediately. He chose the Engineers Corps, where two of his relations, Gerasimos Metaxas (1816-1894) and Nikolaos Metaxas (1833-1903), the future Minister of War, had already distinguished themselves. Ioannis did well at the Military School, where he was "always promoted first among his fellow students," as recorded in the School Register next to the date of his graduation in August 1890.[4] He

4 Kallonas, *Ιωάννης Μεταξάς*, p. 28. Until the Balkan Wars of 1912-1913, the graduates of the Athens Military Academy (Σχολή Ευελπίδων) belonged to a social élite and their sense of *esprit de corps* was strong. Only youths from the wealthier families could afford to study there. In these families, the eldest son would usually become a lawyer and look after the family property and, perhaps, pursue a political career. The second son would choose a military career, especially in the artillery, which was the most prestigious. In Cephalonia where, before unification with Greece, the

was then only nineteen and a Sublieutenant in the Engineers Corps. On 1 September 1892 he entered the Engineers Military School. In 1894 he was stationed at the local garrison at Nafplion, a beautiful seaside town in the Peloponnese. His father had been transferred there and John lived with the family - his parents and his sister Myrianthi. His young brother Costakis was away in Athens studying medicine.

It appears that Metaxas' paternal grandfather had squandered the family property and what Panaghis Metaxas inherited did not amount to much. Even what little remained he was forced to sell after his eldest son John was born. To continue to use the ancestral title in such straitened circumstances would have been too painful; but Ioannis Metaxas never quite forgot his noble ancestors. In 1896, he met an old ruined man of his own class; and he was moved, as he wrote, listening to that half-drunken aristocrat who spoke about his son and his hopes that the boy would grow up to gild the family name. "*It was touching to watch this man who, although ruined by drunkenness and debauchery, still retained the skeleton of the old lord, centering all his dreams of glory and fame upon his child and shed tears, tormenting himself in his anxiety, wondering whether the boy would live, whether he would reach manhood, whether he would become a real Count Logothetis. And I felt all this very strongly because, with all my democratic -- not democratic, folkish, I would say -- veneer, in the depths of my soul the aristocratic ideas always linger.*"[5]

These ideas acquired great importance during the formative years of Metaxas' life, when he met the Greek Crown Prince Constantine in 1897, and when he was a student at the *Kriegsakademie* in Berlin from 1899 to 1903 among the aristocratic Prussian officers. His sense of history was strengthened and his outlook went beyond the narrow borders of his country directly back to Byzantium. "This Greece which was born in 1821 is not my motherland," he wrote, "because as a Metaxas I belong to that race which existed before this motherland and which belonged to another, greater motherland."[6] Again he wrote, "I belong to that aristocracy which has already fought

---

scope for political activity was limited, the eldest son, more often than not, would become a doctor. Until 1913 the Athens Military Academy was modelled on the French *Ecole Polytechnique*, preparing officers mainly for the artillery and the engineers corps. After 1913 and the advent of the French mission, the Saint Cyr Academy became the model for the Greek Military Academy, preparing officers mainly for the infantry and cavalry. The meager pay made the typical officer of those days hot in pursuit not only of martial glory but also a bride with a substantial dowry. Similarly, lack of professional security made him a willing client of any scheming politician. In 1882 the School for Non-Commissioned Officers was founded for candidates of smaller means and lesser social standing. For more on the Greek Military, see the many publications of Thanos Veremis, and especially "The Officer Corps in Greece 1912-36", *Byzantine & Modern Greek Studies*, II (London, 1976).

5 *Diary*, I, p. 122.

6 *Ibid.*, p. 527.

2 *Ioannis Metaxas at the officers school in 1889. Second row, left of the rifle pyramide.*

for its King and for the State a long time before modern Greece was born. Greece was born from the struggles and sacrifices of this aristocracy."[7]

In Nafplion, on 21 [O.S.] September 1896, Ioannis Metaxas started writing his Diary, which, with some important lapses, he kept for the rest of his life. The last entry is dated 17 January 1941, twelve days before his death. The Diary is in many ways an amazing document and of fundamental value for the study of Metaxas and his role in the history of Greece. Of a restless disposition, curious, with wide interests and firm judgments, Metaxas recorded his thoughts and actions in his Diary with unusual candor and honesty. He kept it for his own use and often turned back the pages and read it again. Mainly he recorded his feelings, his reactions to life; even when he took part in the 1897 Greco-Turkish War and the Balkan Wars of 1912-1913, he avoided descriptions of battles and accounts of political developments. "I do not write political history here," he once noted, "but only paint my own picture. And therefore events are described only to the extent that they are connected with my life and my thoughts."[8] But as public affairs were his main preoccupation and as he pursued first a military and then a political career, his Diary turned out to be, to a large degree, a running commentary on the current history of Greece.

From the explicit nature of the first part of the Diary, it is obvious that it was not meant, in the early years at least, for publication. In June 1940, when he became certain that Greece was not going to be able to avoid the war, Metaxas destroyed many of his papers (and wrote his will), but preserved the Diary, although he crossed out many words with indelible ink and tore out several pages. Apparently he thought then that the Diary should survive. He must have had the idea as early as 20 August 1905, when he adopted a new style of handwriting, more clear and regular and much more legible. He wrote at that time, "Who knows? Perhaps one day this Diary may be found useful in explaining events suddenly taking place in the future, but whose causes reach far into the past, and are not known to the general public."[9]

By 1896 (when at the age of twenty-five he began keeping the Diary), Ioannis Metaxas was already disgusted with the Greek political scene. He considered politicians of all parties loathsome and political bickering degrading. Politicians were "vile demagogues, who govern the mob, which governs everything," he wrote. The wheeling and dealing of Greek politics, the haggling over benefits in exchange for political support, he despised. "It is about time for these dealings to cease," he wrote. "The King himself is party to this dirty game: this is how he will bring disaster down on his head."[10] Because of family tradition and personal temperament, Metaxas took a keen

7 *Ibid.*.
8 *Ibid.*, p. 364.
9 *Ibid.*, p. 577.
10 *Ibid.*, p. 94.

interest in the affairs of his country and followed closely every twist and turn of the political game. Everywhere around him he perceived time-serving mediocrity, hypocrisy, dishonesty. And he was distressed to discover that none of his fellow officers could comprehend "the canker which devours the nation from within."[11] While taking an afternoon walk with some other officers, Metaxas conceded that one of them "is not completely corrupt; but I detest them all because they are related to Deliyiannis; how dirty they are in their political dealings."[12] Theodoros Deliyiannis (1820-1905) was the Prime Minister of the day. Metaxas did not much like the opponents of Deliyiannis, either. They were critical of the current government only because they were out of office, he thought. There was little to choose between them. "All these people should be kicked out because they have rotted and rotten fruit cannot make jam," he noted in his Diary.[13] Even at twenty-five the course of his future career was clearly charted. But he had to be patient. He wrote in 1896: *"Of course I am uncompromising in my ideas, but I cannot apply them yet because I may harm my father and my younger brother. Let me wait. Let me do my duty now and the moment will come when I shall strike the villains, strike them down savagely, and then let me fall a martyr to my ideas."*[14]

Metaxas was born and grew up in this atmosphere of political degradation and corruption and there were many good reasons for him to hold such a low opinion of the condition of his country and the politicians of the day.

The first test of Metaxas' patriotism was not long in coming. The Congress of Berlin of 1878 had left Macedonia and Thrace under Turkish rule. Soon afterwards Bulgarian agents formed the Internal Macedonian Revolutionary Organization (IMRO), an activist group which ostensibly struggled for "Macedonia for the Macedonians." Bulgarian *comidadjis* (guerillas of the Macedonian Committee) raided the Greek villages and terrorized the rural population. Many Greeks feared that the Bulgarians would present the world with a *fait accompli* in Macedonia before Greece had a chance to stake her claims. In despair and frustration over the incompetence of the political leadership, sixty members of the Greek military founded in 1894 the "National Society" -- a secret organization whose purpose was to fight for the incorporation with the Greek kingdom of what the Greeks considered to be Greek portions of Macedonia. The *Ethniki Hetairia,* as the National Society was called in Greek, was modelled on the *Philiki Hetairia,* the Friendly Society which prepared the War of Independence. The National Society was originally exclusive to the Armed Forces, but later expanded to include many civilians; by 1896, two years after its inception, it had fifty-six chapters in Greek cities and eighty-three among the Greek communities of the Diaspora, with a

11 *Ibid.,* p. 104.
12 *Ibid.,* pp. 103-4.
13 *Ibid.,* p. 104.
14 *Ibid.,* p. 102.

total membership of over three thousand. Metaxas, who blamed Greek unpreparedness for the loss of Rumelia, became an active member of the National Society in 1896, although he was not one of its leaders, probably because of his junior rank. That same year Metaxas founded the local chapter of the Society at Nafplion, and it was probably then that Metaxas became a Freemason.

Metaxas considered the Bulgarian struggle for Macedonia a new manifestation of the ambitious designs of Panslavism. Behind the Bulgarians he saw the Russians. The Russians were preparing "to destroy Turkey and capture Constantinople and thus absorb and enslave many Greek peoples. Only the name of the tyrant will change -- he will be called the Czar instead of the Sultan."[15] "The Russians," he wrote early in 1897, "have become the greatest threat to Europe, nay, to the whole world. What will become of us the Greeks?"[16] And he worried because he thought his compatriots were not "moral, brave, energetic, patriotic ... Can it be that we are racially corrupted? Was Max Nordau right? I do not believe it."[17] His intuition told him that it would not be long before Greece was locked in an armed struggle for Macedonia. "Every probability indicates that war will be unavoidable in the spring. Enemies press us on all sides ..."[18] And he was despondent that the country was not making intensive preparations. "I, however, prepare myself: I study constantly. I hope by the spring to be ready."[19] As was his wont, Metaxas summed up in his Diary his performance and progress during the expiring year:

"1896 draws to a close ... A significant year for me: a year of [intellectual] fermentation and [spiritual] rebirth. My illness is almost cured, my body has gained strength and has been vigorously exercised, my character has been formed. My knowledge has been much increased. I have gained a reputation in the Service. I have become a member of the National Society and I myself established the local chapter here. I have been morally reformed. I have regained my brother's love. I have acquired physical and moral courage and strength for the present and the future. But most important of all, I have acquired faith in God, in the immortality of the Soul, in Morality and in Progress. Blessed be the name of Laurent. My God, protect my parents, my brother and sister, my country, all mankind and myself."[20]

---

15 *Ibid.*, I. 100.

16 *Ibid.*, p. 132.

17 *Ibid.* Max Simon Nordau (1848-1923) was a Jewish Hungarian doctor and author. His pseudo-philosophical *Entartung* was translated into many languages. The English translation was entitled *Degeneration* (1895). His other major works were *The Conventional Lies of Society* (English translation 1895) and *Biologie der Ethik* (1921). He also wrote stories, novels, dramas and critical works.

18 *Ibid.*, p. 125.

19 *Ibid.*.

20 *Ibid.*, p. 128.

In December 1896 the Nafplion chapter of the National Society, which he himself had started, elected its local officials. Metaxas was only elected one of the two Vice-Presidents. His fellow officers in the Society did not vote for him. "They do not much like me because of my superiority," Metaxas noted in his Diary.[21] He did not much like them either, and he was determined to enlist in the Society as many educated citizens as possible -- "lawyers, doctors, scientists, businessmen" -- to counteract the ideas of the officers. "The Society needs a fundamental reorganization so that the vote of the educated and experienced member is made to count more than the vote of the uneducated and inexperienced, however well-meaning ... many new, often uneducated and inexperienced army officers have a detrimental effect on the Society ... They talk too much, they are hot-tempered, they have no judgment and accurate understanding of the situation..."[22]

The National Society organized and trained Greek guerilla bands and dispatched them secretly to Macedonia. There they fought not only against the Bulgarian *comitadjis,* but often against the Turkish authorities as well. But the National Society had more ambitious plans for Macedonia. "We shall fire the cannon in the spring and perhaps to some purpose," Metaxas wrote in his Diary on 25 October 1896. "Premature, but what can be done? We have no time any more. I have a feeling we shall suffer many disasters to atone for our many sins."[23] It is indicative of the wild nationalism which gripped the country that a calculating, usually sensible man like Metaxas should desire war, even though he knew Greece was not prepared for such an adventure. It also demonstrates how weak the responsible government was if the Society so confidently planned to plunge the country into a reckless war. On 9 December 1896 Metaxas noted in his Diary: "They have decided to throw three thousand men into Macedonia in the spring, well-organized ... They will either carry the government with them to declare war or they hope to carry with them the army of Thessaly."[24]

Early in 1897 the hostility between the Christians and the Moslems of Crete reached a new level of intensity. On 4 February, returning from an electoral campaign in the country, Venizelos arrived on the hills overlooking his home city. To quote his own words: "I saw Chania in flames; it had been set on fire by the Mussulmans, who had thus started the great revolt."[25] There was a general exodus from the burning city. Ships of the British Navy in the bay were loaded to capacity with women and children refugees. Two days later Metaxas recorded the incident in his Diary: "Today the news arrived of massacres at Chania which took place yesterday and the day before. The

---

21 Ibid., p. 124.
22 *Ibid.,* p. 113.
23 *Ibid.,* p. 105.
24 *Ibid.,* p. 118.
25 S. B. Chester, *Life of Venizelos* (London, 1921) p. 35.

Cretan Turks burned the city and slaughtered the Christians, who retaliated as best they could."[26] In Crete a "Christian Defense Force" was organized to protect the lives of the Christian population. Venizelos became the leader of the Defense Force and established the headquarters of his revolutionary bands at Akrotiri, the peninsula which separates Chania from Suda Bay.

The Armenian massacres in Turkey had begun only two years earlier, and the news from Crete aroused strong emotions in Greece. Metaxas gave vent to a rare outburst in his Diary: "*If we are to lose Crete, let us perish too, and let us drag Europe into war. Let millions upon millions of men perish, let thousands of cities be razed, let whole nations be slaughtered. Let no stone stand upon stone in that immoral place which is called Europe ...*"[27]

The long, heroic struggles of the Cretans had often stirred the people of Greece and a public outcry arose in the country over the current intervention of the Powers in the island. In the Greek Parliament, Demetrios Rallis, one of the opposition leaders, accused the government of cowardice and threatened civil war. Fearing that he might lose his majority, Premier Deliyiannis announced to the Chamber that two Greek warships had been ordered to sail to Crete. A few day later the tiny Greek torpedo fleet also sailed towards the island. Then on 12 February a landing party of fifteen hundred men under Colonel Timoleon Vassos reached Crete. The following day the Powers landed troops on the island and demanded the withdrawal of the Greek forces. At the same time the Powers suggested that Crete be made autonomous, under the suzerainty of the Sultan. The Cretans, who had abundant reasons to doubt the good intentions of the Powers and the good faith of the Turks, refused to lay down their arms and proclaimed instead immediate *enosis* -- union with Greece. Whereupon, while the Turks were besieging Venizelos at Akrotiri, the Powers shelled the Cretan positions. Ships of the British, French, Russian, German and Austrian fleets took part in the operation. The Italian Navy, although present, did not fire its guns. Metaxas noted in his Diary:

"*I could write many things today but I do not have the heart to hold the pen ... The fleets of the Powers have shelled the camp of the revolutionaries at Halepa -- a moment which disgraced the Nineteenth Century. I have no wish to work or to write. I only wish for war, war to the end, a holocaust to consume the base society of Europe.*"[28]

While Eleftherios Venizelos was defending the standard of revolt in Crete, the Allied Fleets blockaded Greece to prevent Greek troops from reaching the island. In Athens the Greek government appointed General Nikolaos Metaxas, an uncle of Ioannis Metaxas, as Minister of War. On 26 March, five days after the blockade began, King

---

26 *Diary,* I, p. 136.
27 *Ibid.*, p. 139.
28 *Ibid.*, p. 145.

George I appointed Crown Prince Constantine Commander-in-Chief of the Greek Army. On 5 April the Powers handed identical Notes to Athens and Constantinople warning that they would hold responsible the country which first began hostilities.[29] After widespread agitation, Greek irregulars of the *Ethniki Hetairia*, with the full knowledge of the government, crossed the border in Thessaly on 10 April and attacked the Turkish troops. A week later war was declared by the two countries.

As the prospect of war loomed larger, most of the officers stationed at the Nafplion garrison were transferred to Athens, *en route* for the front. Metaxas' posting did not come through and, as he wrote later, he "suffered" because of this.

"*All those days I could not do any work at all. And, awakening every morning, I felt pain, a deep pain ... And then the other officers began to leave [Nafplion], one after the other. And I began to suffer. I was ashamed to be left behind. I believed that the war would break out soon. I had so often loudly proclaimed the need to take up arms for the motherland and, when the critical moment came, I was left idle. On the other hand, the necessity for me to stay near my poor family whom I was assisting out of my small pay, stifled any impulse to try for a transfer.*

One day the matter came to a head. Mother perceived the terrible inner struggle I was going through and sent father to Athens. Nikolakis [Nikolaos Metaxas] had become Minister .... I was transferred and came here. I can write no longer. My heart is clenched like a fist."[30]

In Athens Metaxas obtained a post near his uncle, the Minister of War. Yet he was still chafing to go to the front. "One evening I begged Nikolis to let me go to the frontier [in Thessaly], and he promised to do so."[31] The Minister entrusted his nephew with some secret dispatches for the High Command. This proved to be the best introduction an ambitious young officer could wish for. Metaxas did not return to Athens, but found a place for himself on the General Staff. He became an *officier d'administration*, as he wrote, was also responsible for the records, and as often as the opportunity arose, went on reconnaisance. He was not particularly happy doing clerical work; but from this key position he could observe men and affairs. More importantly, he could make the acquaintance and cultivate the friendship of Crown Prince Constantine, the Commander of the campaign and the future King of Greece. Constantine, only twenty-eight at the time, had been educated at Heidelberg University and trained at the Berlin War Academy. He had been brought up by a Romanov mother and was married to Princess Sophia of Prussia, the sister of Kaiser William II. Metaxas was two years his junior, an obscure sublieutenant in the Engineers Corps. For both men this was their first war

29 For an account of English diplomatic activity in this crisis, see George Papadopoulos, *England and the Middle East, 1896-1898* (Thessaloniki, 1969).

30 *Diary,* I. p. 148.

31 *Ibid.,* p. 150.

experience and it left an indelible mark on their personalities. Their association was destined to have far-reaching effects on the history of Greece.

The Crown Prince, tall and blond, was an impressive figure; he was also amiable and possessed a spirit of easy *camaraderie* which endeared him to the troops. Metaxas liked Constantine at first sight. His former suspicions that the monarchy was in some sort of secret alliance with the foreign Powers and in some sort of collusion with the politicians were dissipated.

"I first saw him close to and spoke to him on Great Monday evening [the Monday of Passion Week, 7 April, O.S. 1897]. Since his arrival in Larissa the ideas I had previously absorbed began to dissolve. Now I knew him. How different I had imagined him! And what pangs of regret I felt to have allowed myself to be led astray by the gossip of the world. He is the most kind and modest young man."[32]

But Metaxas thought that the Crown Prince, owing to his father's influence, was not authoritative enough and that he lacked initiative. Constantine wasted a lot of time examining each proposal put to him and "he is often led astray by the opinion of those around him when he trusts them; but this trust can be very easily won because he cannot imagine that anyone would deceive him or exploit him."[33] However, he thought that once the Crown Prince had decided on something he would carry it out unhesitatingly. His limitations were due only to inexperience. "He has not been taught to crush every disobedience and to impose his own will. The hardships of war will teach him."[34]

The campaign in Thessaly met with disaster from the very beginning. The disorderly rabble of Greek soldiers was no match for the Turkish Army, which had been modernized under the direction of General Colmar von der Goltz (1843-1916) and was commanded by German officers.[35] The Greek Army was routed, the Headquarters at Larissa abandoned, and on 25 April the Prussian General von Grumbkow Pasha, instructor of artillery to the Ottoman Army, entered the city. At one point Metaxas had suggested to Constantine the making of an artificial lake by flooding the plain, which would have shortened the front and worked to the advantage of the Greeks, whose numbers were inferior by far to the Turks. The suggestion was not adopted. From Larissa the Greek Army fell back towards the plain of Pharsala. This plain has been

32 *Ibid.*, p. 187.

33 *Ibid.*, pp. 187-8.

34 *Ibid.*, p. 188.

35 General Baron Colmar von der Goltz (1843-1916), who was given the rank of a Turkish Field-Marshal, was the Organiser of the Turkish Army between 1883 and 1895. In his book on the Graeco-Turkish War of 1897 entitled *Der Thessalische Krieg und die Türkische Armee* (1898), he severely criticized the Turkish Army. The Greeks, he wrote, had no chance of success, unless they were led by a daring and enterprising commander. In 1914, when Germany overran Belgium, General von der Goltz became military governor of that country. He often visited Turkey. He died in Baghdad during the First World War. In 1929 his son published the memoirs of his famous father.

soaked copiously in blood down the centuries. Here in 48 B.C. Julius Caesar crushed Pompey, who fled with an escort of only four men, leaving 15,000 slain, while the remainder of his army surrendered the next day. In A.D. 1082 on the same plain, the Normans under Robert Guiscard defeated the Byzantine Emperor Alexios I Commenos. In 1897 the same fate was to befall the Greek Army. Staff Officer Papavasileiou, assisted by Metaxas, prepared a plan for the defense of Pharsala which was submitted to senior Staff Officer Colonel Victor Dousmanis. The plan was never implemented. Ten days after the Greeks had abandoned Larissa, on 3 May, they were completely crushed again at Dhomokos, near Pharsala, and retreated in disorder towards Lamia, leaving Thessaly to the Turks.

Prime Minister Deliyiannis resigned and the equally incapable Demetrios Rallis took over. Both men had incurred the displeasure of the Crown Prince by demanding the removal of the Chief of Staff, the incompetent General Sapountzakis, and the appointment in his place of General Smolenskis, who was reputed to have displayed outstanding personal courage in the campaign. The Crown Prince, who resented such interference in army affairs, refused to comply until his father the King, as Supreme Commander-in-Chief of the Armed Forces, sent him a telegram ordering the replacement. It was then that Constantine uttered the revengeful, "Je m'en souviendrai."[36]

Defeated decisively on the battlefield, the Greeks placed their fortunes in the hands of the Powers. Crown Princess Sophia wrote long letters to her mother the Dowager Empress Victoria in Germany, describing the desperate situation in Greece and the predicament in which her husband the Crown Prince now found himself as Commander-in-Chief of the campaign. The Germans, who had trained and equipped the Turkish Army, were the only Power whose counsel was heeded by Turkey. However much the Dowager Empress would have liked to help her daughter Sophia, she could not appeal to her son William II, because the Kaiser was then hardly on speaking terms with his mother; instead, the Dowager Empress wrote pleading letters to her own mother Queen Victoria. The English Queen showed great interest and sympathy for the plight of the Greeks, as can be seen from her diaries and letters. Although she did not like her grandson the Kaiser, she cabled him tactfully in code (after she had shown her telegram to Salisbury for his approval) asking him to persuade the Powers to arrange a peace between the Greeks and Turks. The Kaiser's discourteous reply was in an open telegram. Any request for an armistice, he informed her, should come from Greece, who should "beg" for that favour; a *conditio sine qua non* was that Greece must recall her troops from Crete and accept the autonomy of the island under Turkish suzerainty. On 13 May 1897 the Kaiser sent a new telegram to Queen Victoria (again not in code and

36 *Diary,* I. p. 199.

one that annoyed her excessively both by its style and its content) in which he announced that after the Greek King and his Government had "begged" for his personal intervention and had accepted his conditions completely, he had instructed his minister at Athens to arrange a ceasefire. Three days later King George of the Hellenes also appealed to the Czar, who sent a personal message to Sultan Abdul Hamid, asking that the Turks cease operations. On 20 May the armistice was finally signed and subsequently the peace treaty was concluded. Greece, despite the *débâcle* she had suffered, retained Thessaly with only minor border changes; but she was forced to pay a heavy indemnity. The Powers, who negotiated the peace on behalf of Greece, established an International Financial Commission in Athens, which took over the administration of the government monopolies and the collection of harbour dues at the Piraeus as a guarantee that payments of reparations and payments of the interest on the National Debt would be made regularly.

The war was an object lesson for Metaxas. As an administrative officer responsible for the confidential Archives of the General Staff, he was able to study the conduct of military operations and the characters of the men who directed them; he was also in a position to learn a great deal about the way the politicians pursued the diplomatic aspects of the war and negotiated the peace. In his Diary he sketched succinct profiles of the leaders of the campaign in Thessaly - and his comments were not complimentary. Bitter experience confirmed his inherent suspicions.

"I have read all the important official correspondence ... what orders were issued, what orders were executed and the manner in which they were executed; what actions the Commander-in-Chief took, what actions were carried out by the officers in the field. A brilliant light illuminated everything for me and I perceived the utter rottenness of our political and military system, the ignorance and malice of many of the senior commanders and the conduct of many others, which was almost treasonable."[37]

Metaxas' contempt for all those responsible for this national disaster and humiliation was boundless; especially for the incompetent government and the fickle politicians who had failed in their duty to build up an efficient army and who had allowed Greece to plunge into a war for which she was unprepared. There must be a better way of running the country. While on campaign in Thessaly, Metaxas remembered the example of Ioannis Kapodistrias, the Ionian aristocrat who became first President of Greece, as the only one worth emulating. Kapodistrias had ignored the Constitution and concentrated all power in his own hands and had ruled like a benevolent despot. In his

37 *Ibid.*, I, p. 184. For an independent appraisal of the Graeco-Turkish War, see the Report by an English observer published as an appendix by George Papadopoulos in his *England and the Middle East, 1896-1898* (Thessaloniki, 1969).

Diary Metaxas described a talk he had with Papavasileiou as they were riding on reconnaisance:

"On the way I was talking to Papavasileiou, I was telling him about Kapodistrias' political system and I was demonstrating to him the wrong course which Greece had taken up to then by departing from his principles. I was very agitated and spoke with excitement and clarity and with strong arguments. Papavasileiou kept silent."[38]

When Metaxas became a political leader and had his own party after the First World War, he demonstrated the low esteem in which he held the politicians by purposely keeping them waiting when they called to see him. Among the first to be arrested when he came to power in 1936 were several hundred politicians, great and small, who were either put in jail or exiled to the islands.

Metaxas' contempt for the politicians also extended to the popular press, which ventilated their pretensions and inanities. The volatile press, which had often extolled "the invincibility of the Greek soldier", now sought out culprits to blame for the defeat. Metaxas noted in his Diary: "The conclusion was that the army was victorious and that the Crown Prince and the General Staff, either because of cowardice, or because of an understanding with Europe, or because they were bribed by Turkey, ordered, in the midst of victory, a sudden retreat ..."[39] The General Staff was made the scapegoat and the Crown Prince lived under a cloud. The fact that German officers of the Kaiser's army had trained the Turks did not make things easier for Constantine with his Hohenzollern connections. Metaxas felt a profound disdain for the press which, as he wrote, "inspires in me only disgust and I avoid as much as I can reading its vile products."[40] Again, "I have not read newspapers for a long time because I am completely disgusted with the things they write."[41] Later at a carnival, he was amused by the presentation of the newspaper publishers as dogs whose barking ceases each time some bones are thrown to them.[42] His opinion of the legal professional was no higher. When someone boasted about his heroic exploits in the war, Metaxas commented ironically: "His bravery was admirable ... He must, of course, have been a lawyer or at least a student of Law."[43] His contempt and disgust were also directed towards the Greek people in general. He described the national character of his compatriots as "vain, cunning, ignorant, crawling."[44] "The Greeks shout a lot and act little," he wrote.[45]

38 *Diary*, I. p. 269.
39 *Ibid.*, p. 196.
40 *Ibid.*, p. 295.
41 *Ibid.*, p. 356.
42 *Ibid.*, p. 394.
43 *Ibid.*, p. 250.
44 *Ibid.*, p. 282.
45 *Ibid.*, p. 166.

Reading through the reports of the unit commanders of the 1897 War, he found their contents to consist of "on average, self-praise, boastfulness, stupidities."[46] His verdict was damning indeed. "The Greeks are still slavish in character and have all the feelings of slaves towards their masters."[47] He had had his fill of the 1897 War. "I can hardly wait," he wrote in June of that year, "for the moment when I shall return to my home, close my eyes and ears and live mentally far, far away from Greece."[48]

The humiliating war of 1897 acted as a catalyst on Metaxas. "How I have changed!" he wrote. "I no longer recognize myself. The war has turned me from a youth into a man and, by removing my neurotic supersensitivity, it has also removed the veil which concealed the truth of things."[49] He blamed the defeat on the ineptitude of the politicians, the bad organization of the army, the warmongering of the press. He thought the Crown Prince was vilified unjustly for the mistakes of others, that he was victimized because of a situation not of his making. A way should be found to restore his reputation and secure his position as head of the army. The only way to do this was to lay the true facts before the world, to tell the whole story as it had happened and as it appeared through the informed and responsible eyes of the General Staff. For months Ioannis Metaxas worked assiduously on the writing of the official Report on the war which was to vindicate his Chief. As he sifted through the evidence, he came to recognize the wisdom of the decision to abandon Larissa. He found Nikolaos Smolenskis (1839-1921), the new Chief of Staff who replaced the disgraced Sapountzakis, "an ignorant general," who had his relatives advertising his exploits in Athens. "Many evils are revealed ... many newspaper slanders turn out to be outrageous lies."[50] An unsuccessful attempt by the new Minister of War to prevent the completion of the Report roused Metaxas to fury: "By concealing the truth the base system would have been perpetuated and the vile parliamentary and military men who caused the disaster would have continued their work."[51]

The Report was awaited with much anticipation by the whole country. But Crown Prince Constantine knew his real friends by now, the men whom he could trust, then and in the future. Metaxas, as he described in his Diary, had finished his work on the Report and was waiting to take his leave.

"At last the Crown Prince arrived. I presented myself to bid him farewell. He received me graciously. He asked me if I would like to go to Europe.[52] *You can*

46 *Ibid.*, p. 287.

47 *Ibid.*, p. 388.

48 *Ibid.*, p. 289.

49 *Ibid.*, p. 345.

50 *Ibid.*, p. 292.

51 *Ibid.*, p. 297.

52 The Greeks, like the Spanish, talk about "going to Europe" when they leave their country for the rest of the continent. Until 1913 the Ottoman Empire extended to the Adriatic and any traveller

imagine what my answer was. He told me that he intended to send me, as well as Papavasileiou and Strategos, to Germany and that now he was 'on good terms with the Emperor', we would be accepted at the Berlin War Academy. He hoped he would be able to arrange for the Greek Government to pay our expenses. He advised me to learn German. He thanked me for my work on his General Staff and for the writing of the Report. I bade him farewell. My joy was inexpressible.[53]

3 Ipp. Papavasileiou, X. Stratigos, I. Metaxas at the Kriegsakademie in 1902.

Ioannis Metaxas, the déclassé aristocrat who had suffered the humiliations of poverty and obscurity, who never liked and was never liked by the "mob", who despised the "vile demagogues" who ignored him, had finally found his liege lord. From then on, his personal life, his political career and his totalitarian regime in the Thirties were all inextricably bound up with the royalist cause. Metaxas became a royalist in 1897 and died a royalist in 1941, always more royal than the King. The War of 1897 was Metaxas' first and most formative experience, which helped to make him the man he was to become:

"In the midst of the moral and national ruins with which my soul was filled only one figure remained standing: the figure of the King and his dynasty.

to Europe by land had to go through Turkish territory. Greek efforts to build a railway and connect Athens with the railway system of the rest of Europe were frustrated by Turkey for political and military reasons.

53 *Diary,* I. p. 343. When Metaxas assumed power in 1936, he appointed Hippocrates Papavasileiou Minister of War. Xenophon (Phontas) Strategos (1868-1927) was one of the defendants at the Trial of the Six in 1923 following the Greek defeat in Anatolia in 1922. General Strategos and Admiral Goudas were sentenced to life imprisonment, while the other six defendants were sentenced to death and executed by firing squad.

And my dedication to them was increased even more. There was a moment -- only a moment -- when I hated my country, but there was no such moment for my King. I had to find support somewhere and I found it in this feeling."[54]

The Report turned out to be an apologia and an indictment. "The general impression was excellent," Metaxas noted. "The revelation of the facts amazed the world ... For over twenty days the newspapers were writing about it and the Crown Prince was venerated and admired and acclaimed as the wisest, the strongest and the bravest Greek."[55]

It did not take long for the Report to bear fruit. The Government defied the outcry of the opposition and appointed the Crown Prince Commander-in-Chief of the army. The question has often been asked whether this appointment was compatible with the Constitution. The Greek dynasty and its members were above the law, accountable to none, and therefore beyond parliamentary control or censure. Could such important duties, carrying by their very nature grave responsibilities, be assigned to them? Constantine thought that this was as it should be: the German-trained Crown Prince had Bismarckian ideas about building an army independent of other matters of State and free of all parliamentary interference; an army dedicated to the king first and last -- the King being the only tangible and lasting symbol of the nation.

Constantine's promise to Metaxas of a scholarship for further military training at the *Kriegsakademie* proved to be somewhat premature. The Greek Government decided to hold a competition in order to choose the candidates most highly qualified to be sent to Berlin. Metaxas was unable to meet some of the requirements for candidacy and approached Colonel Victor Dousmanis, who brought the matter to the attention of the Crown Prince. Constantine thereupon persuaded the Prime Minister to modify the conditions of the competition so that his protégé could qualify. It is interesting that Metaxas, who never missed an opportunity to scrutinize all actions, both his own and the actions of those around him, apparently never felt any scruples over this affair and never mentioned it in his Diary[56] While Metaxas was waiting for the results of the scholarship, he wrote and submitted for another competition, sponsored by the Commanding Officer of the Engineers Corps, a treatise entitled *Si vis pacem para bellum*. This study, the only one Metaxas wrote on a purely military topic, won the prize (there were no other entries) and was published by the Greek Ministry of War

54 *Ibid.*, I, p. 365.

55 *Ibid.*, p. 382.

56 Thanos Veremis, who mentions this incident in his book *Οι Επεμβάσεις του Στρατού στην Ελληνική Πολιτική, 1916-1936* [The Intervention of the Army in Greek Politics, 1916-1936] (Athens, 1977), p. 109, believes that between Constantine and Metaxas a typical patron-client relationship developed which survived many vicissitudes.

under a title which translates into English as *The Contribution of the Engineers Corps in a Campaign.*[57]

On 11 August 1899 the Crown Prince invited Metaxas and his two fellow-officers, who were soon to depart for Germany, to the summer palace at Tatoi. "The royal family was most kind and attentive to us," Metaxas wrote later. "I was completely at ease, though I had no desire to increase the closeness of the acquaintance. I spoke with the utmost respect. I gather from certain indications that I made a good impression."[58] In the afternoon the royal party went for a drive in horse-carriages round the magnificent estate. Metaxas sat beside Constantine. The conversation soon turned to the war of 1897. Metaxas noticed that Constantine "retained undiminished his distaste for Rallis," the Premier who had defied him during the war. "The Crown Prince does not forget easily. He will never forgive him."[59] They returned late. While the rest went to prepare for dinner, Constantine invited the three officers to his study. He spoke to them about their future training in Germany, and "how the officers should be and how they are."[60]

"And then a completely new man was revealed before us. He detested France for her ideas of equality, and he clearly demonstrated to us that the highest duty of every citizen, and especially of an officer, is his dedication to his king. 'Unfortunately, we have no government here worth the name,' [the Crown Prince observed].
And he started a philippic against the existing system -- the parliamentary regime; and he ended: 'Either one should be a king or one should not. What, to be a king just to pocket money?' It is impossible for me to give an outline of the talk, which went on for over an hour. I only record this, that I, who am never moved by words, came out deeply moved. The future king revealed himself to us and almost confessed the secrets of his heart."[61]

They went in to dinner. Metaxas was put on Queen Olga's left. "She was most gracious to me," he wrote. When the conversation came round to Metaxas' father who, as a government employee, had often been unfairly treated by the administration, the Queen "deplored the bad treatment by the [political] parties of [government] employees." She concluded, "What a wretched situation! Can the state ever make any progress like this?"[62]

---

57 The Greek title is *Υπηρεσία του Μηχανικού εν Εκστρατεία υπό Ιωάννου Π. Μεταξά.* Sublieutenant in the Engineers Corps (Athens, 1898).

58 *Diary,* I, p. 448.

59 *Ibid.*.

60 *Ibid.,* p. 449.

61 *Ibid.*.

62 *Ibid.*.

On 22 August 1899 Metaxas sent a telegram from Zakynthos congratulating the Queen on her birthday. Two days later, after saying goodbye to his family in Cephalonia, he sailed to Corfu, from where he took the ship for Trieste. At 6:00 p.m. we went below for dinner. When I returned on deck Corfu had disappeared. Metaxas noted in his Diary.

"Farewell Greece, farewell my native land! Misfortunes have taught me much. I do not intend to seek enjoyment. No! I repeat: My life shall be a priesthood."[63]

Later in his Diary Metaxas explained this religious concept of his life's mission. He wrote: "I made a vow to God that my life should be a priesthood [dedicated to the service] of all that is just and noble (Καλόν καγαθόν)."[64]

As the ship sailed up the Adriatic, Metaxas' thoughts were with his family.

"I never cease to think of the beloved souls I have parted from. A short while ago I wrote them a long letter which I shall mail from Trieste. What are they going? Is Costakis well? God must have had mercy on us: I trust in His loving kindness and I beseech Him, if it is necessary for someone to suffer, to let that one be me, but to let me know that the rest of my family are happy."[65]

In Trieste Metaxas noticed how clean the streets were, how green the many trees which were planted all over the city. At the Post and Telegraph Office he was impressed by the good order and trust of the people who collected their letters from the open pigeon - holes. After a visit to the Villa Miramar he noted in his Diary: "My pleasure is immense when I see portraits of personages whom I had previously known only from history books."[66]

Germany made a great impression on him from the first. At the border the customs official, seeing his uniform in his open suitcase, put down the lid at once. "Ja was his only remark: we were the military, therefore for him worthy of respect as demigods."[67] Order and discipline prevailed everywhere. On the train a notice in his compartment read *Rauchen verboten.* No luggage was allowed in the corridor. "Generally I felt the hand of the State present everywhere, gently but firmly guiding."[68] He did not much admire the heavy modern architecture of Berlin, which he considered to be "the expression of the German character" as it manifested itself after Germany had fought the Austro-Prussian War of 1866 and the Franco-Prussian War of 1870-71 "and imposed her iron fist everywhere with will and power inexorable."[69] Metaxas thought

---

63 *Ibid.*, p. 462.
64 *Ibid.*, p. 488.
65 *Ibid.*, p. 462.
66 *Ibid.*, p. 463.
67 *Ibid.*, p. 467.
68 *Ibid.*, p. 468.
69 *Ibid.*, p. 482.

the Berliners very inquisitive. Walking in the streets in their uniforms, he and the other two Greek officers were taken for Frenchmen and the bystanders called after them "Dreyfus! Dreyfus!" Metaxas commented in his Diary: "I do not know if it was Dreyfus himself or his sentence which they considered a blot on France."[70] As he had some days to spare before the commencement of his studies at the War Academy, Metaxas began to explore the German capital. He took long walks, he visited museums and galleries, he went to art exhibitions, he spent many evenings at the opera and the theatre.

4 Metaxas at the War Academy in Berlin in 1901. Second row, first on the right.

In the fall of 1899 Metaxas entered the *Kriegsakademie,* Prince Constantine's *alma mater*. It was at the Berlin War Academy that the cream of the German officers was educated in the science of war. Metaxas' extensive studies included military tactics, cartography, mathematics, hygiene, transportation, military history. The German officers were also required to learn either French or Russian, the language of one of their potential enemies. Metaxas began French, with which he was already acquainted, then switched to Turkish. He was a brilliant student, nicknamed by his fellow-students "Little Moltke," because of his small stature; later a legend arose that somewhere on

70 *Ibid.*, p. 486.

the walls of the Academy an inscription read "No problem insoluble to Ioannis Metaxas." He was often commended for his achievements in the presence of his fellow-students and his reputation reached as high as the Kaiser. On one occasion his instructor in tactics, General Stein (later German Minister of War), evaluated his performance in resolving a complex military problem with the words *"Ganz gut,"* as Metaxas proudly recorded in his Diary. At the completion of his studies, the Director of the War Academy presented him with the following testimonial.

"An able officer with calm, modest and polite manners. He works diligently, meticulously and conscientiously. He has a good understanding of military tactics, he is quick in taking decisions and very skilful in issuing orders. He has the qualifications of a cartographer. In 1900 he participated successfully in a three-month exercise with the Engineers Corps and in 1901 he participated successfully in a two-month exercise with the Cavalry."[71]

In 1901 Metaxas visited the munition factories of Krupp and Erhardt to see the latest in armaments. In June-July 1902 he successfully took part in the arduous exercises of the Prussian General Staff -- the *Generalstabsreise.* These exercises took him all over Germany, often on horseback.

German militarism was at its height around the turn of the century. In his Diary Metaxas gave long accounts of the rigorous training the German officers went through. The German victories in the Danish-German War of 1864, the Austro-Prussian War of 1866 and the Franco-Prussian War of 1870 were still within living memory and made the Prussian Army proud and boastful. The Germans were aware of the French pledge for *revanche* and of French vows for the reoccupation of Alsace-Lorraine. Metaxas thought friendship was impossible between these two nations.[72] He also noticed that the Germans had no love lost for the English, either. From the newspapers he followed the course of the Boer War. "The English campaign in the Transvaal excites a deep hatred here ... the officers in general express themselves openly and in harsh terms against the English."[73] Metaxas himself considered that England was in the wrong in South Africa, but he had his own reasons for approving the progress of the war, which was in favour of the English. On 3 March 1900 he wrote:

"This is the result of strategic attack "with tactical defense". "Das ist Unsinn", according to Stein. Sad, very sad for these two unfortunate peoples. And while my logical mind makes me realize the injustice of the war, I am glad of the English victories, because it looks as if two democracies are out of the way ...."[74]

71 *Ibid.*, p. 58. This passage is an English rendering of the Greek translation from the German.

72 *Ibid.*, p. 552.

73 *Ibid.*, p. 525.

74 *Ibid.*, p. 520.

The Germans envied the vast territories of the British Empire on which the sun never set. The French and the Russians too, had built huge empires in the Nineteenth Century. Historical reasons had kept the Germans lagging behind, and they were bitter and anxious to begin. In 1895 the Kiel Canal joined the North Sea with the Baltic. In 1897 the Germans occupied Kiaochow on the coast of China. In 1898 the first German Naval Law was passed, at the suggestion of Admiral Alfred von Tirpitz (1849-1930), inaugurating a program of naval ascendence. The second German Naval Law, again at the suggestion of Admiral von Tirpitz, was passed on 12 June 1900 and provided for a seventeen-year program for building a fleet "so strong that even the strongest fleet in the world [the British] would hesitate before attacking it." Such a measure and the drive towards the Near East, an area of traditional British interests, were bound to create antagonism and friction between the two nations. In 1898 the concession was secured by the *Deutsche Bank* for the Baghdad Railway, which was to transform Turkey into a virtual German satellite. The same year, while the world was shocked by the Armenian massacres, Emperor William II went on a theatrical pilgrimage to the Holy Lands, stopping at Constantinople to greet and be feted by Sultan Abdul Hamid II (reigned 1876-1909). In their Middle Eastern drive the Germans naturally wanted to include Greece. The German-trained Crown Prince Constantine, brother-in-law of the Kaiser, provided an ideal link. Metaxas and the other protégés of Constantine were warmly received everywhere in Berlin and were duly presented to the Chancellor Count Bernhard von Bülow (1849-1929) and the Chief of Staff Count Alfred von Schlieffen (1833-1933), who "was surprised by our uniforms; he thought all the Greek military wore the *fustanella*"[75] -- the white kilt -- like garment worn by *evzones*. Finally Metaxas was presented to the Kaiser himself. He described the Kaiser in his Diary:

"I was very impressed by his eyes, which are steady, penetrating, unfalteringly meeting the gaze of his visitor - but at the same time his eyes are mild and benign. He has graceful manners, unlike the wild and warlike air with which he is represented in his portraits."[76]

The military education which Metaxas received at the Berlin War Academy and the social and cultural climate of the German capital helped him to clarify his ideas and mature into a man of strong, independent opinions. What the Greco-Turkish War of 1897 had begun, Germany completed. A few months after his arrival in Berlin Metaxas learned that Crown Prince Constantine had presented the Greek Parliament with a new body of Army Regulations (known as "Οργανισμός Διαδόχου"), which would have transformed the army into an exclusive royal domain. The long standing conflict

---

75 *Ibid.*, p. 482.
76 *Ibid.*, p. 508.

between Constantine and Parliament had come to a head. It was only the beginning. In a prophetic entry in his Diary on 4 December 1899 Metaxas wrote:

"A struggle [αγών] has begun between the Crown Prince and parliamentarianism. The stage for the struggle is already the Army. But the question of "Οργανισμός" is only a phase of the great struggle which will follow. Well, I too, shall do my bit to drink a little parliamentarian blood ... The circumstances will present themselves."[77]

The stand taken by the Crown Prince against the politicians would gather together "all those steadfast, honest, determined elements, those with character who, now scattered here and there, are drowning in the ocean of Greek parliamentary corruption."[78] But Metaxas thought that Constantine must be more daring. Then, "In one battle he will win the Army and all the rest. *Audaces fortuna iuvat*."[79] Fortune favours the brave.

The Army was of crucial importance. In a country where democratic institutions were not vested with the authority of tradition and where the people, according to Metaxas, had neither the inclination nor the means to bring about any change, the initiative must come from the Army and its leaders, where actual power resided. Metaxas, a professional soldier, understood that much. If only the Crown Prince could organize the Army "really well".

"Because in questions of principle there is no middle way. Once it is proved that the monarchy, replacing parliamentarianism in the military branch, has succeeded, nothing will prevent the nation from inclining towards it in other branches also. And then the King, who would be supported by a faithful army, will really be a master and not merely a shadow."[80]

George I was not a shadow; but he was content to regulate the parliamentary game from above, without any undue eagerness to join in the mêlée. The King was aware of his constitutional limitations and was careful not to be drawn into the arena of everyday politics nor to interfere with the domestic administration of the country. Once, while visiting a remote mountain hamlet, he listened patiently to the complaints of the villagers, who asked for a bridge to ford a river which cut them off from the rest of the world for several months every winter. In his reply George I playfully suggested to his audience that they elect him as their deputy in the coming elections; then, he assured them, he would see to it that they got their bridge. As it was, he was only the king and could do very little. This incident is characteristic of George I, who was well satisfied with his assigned role in the constitutional structure, relegating all responsibility to his ministers. Every summer the King, who also believed in "the good life," would set off

---

77 *Ibid.*, p. 500.

78 *Ibid.*.

79 *Ibid.*.

80 *Ibid.*, p. 526.

on a long, leisurely vacation in the fashionable spas of Europe; it was rumored that his intimate friendships with the European royalties, almost all of whom were his relations, brought great benefits to his small kingdom. The Greek monarchy under George I, despite an occasional intervention to ensure that the wheels of the constitutional machine were turning smoothly, remained aloof from the hurly-burly of Greek politics.

The present move of the autocratic Crown Prince marked a new departure which was bound to create a political force above and beyond the parliamentary parties. Metaxas at once perceived the implications of this development.

"The monarchist party is outside Parliament, it is the Crown Prince himself. And he draws his support from those who, because of ancestry or character, are dedicated to the monarchical idea -- and these persons are few -- and from those who, having suffered, either directly or indirectly, either to a greater or lesser degree, from rampant Parliamentarianism, have turned away from it and are seeking a shelter in the Monarchy -- and these persons make up most of the Nation. Admittedly, there is still hesitation among this majority; but it is dominated by the will and the resolution of the Crown Prince, and is inexorably inclining towards the goal, which is already clearly visible. Neither will this [monarchist] party ever appear in Parliament; because precisely this is the essence of the Monarch: to be dependent upon the will and the determination of the Monarchy itself and not upon persuasion through parliamentary debates."[81]

In his Diary Metaxas noted that all the German officers at the War Academy came from noble families. The army was their career; their livelihood and social standing were bound up with it. The Emperor was the leader of the army and was often present at the military exercises and the interminable parades.[82] In Germany Metaxas remembered his own aristocratic ancestry and his title, which he had hardly ever used in Greece. He wrote:

---

81 *Ibid.*, p. 527.

82 Metaxas was not wholly uncritical of the German Army. He wrote about the shouts, the curses, the foul language that the aristocratic officers used in governing their units - "They call the soldiers names deliberately because the German peasant needs brutality to be governed, so, at least, the officers think." *Diary,* I. 562. Perhaps it should be noted, *en passant*, that Crown Prince Constantine, who had been trained at the Berlin War Academy, often used foul language with his officers in Greece. (See Αλέξανδρος Μαζαράκης-Αινιάν, *Απομνημονεύματα* (Athens, 1948) pp. 94-95). Metaxas, who was usually on campaign with Constantine, makes no mention of this. Metaxas thought a lot of time was lost at the Berlin War Academy: "Generally I found in two exercises of actual shooting practice that the cavalry is not at all trained in shooting, and that the officers show very little care for the exercise. They told me they have no time. Nevertheless, a lot of time is wasted on parades ..." *Diary,* I, 561. And again, "Those straight lines where not a single horse's head protrudes, not even a few centimeters from the line of horse's heads, proves only that the cavalry columns were trained solely for parades". *Ibid.*. It is saddening to contemplate the pathos of the gallant cavalry charges in the Great War against the relentless onslaught of machinegun fire which mowed down men and horses alike.

"I am a soldier and a nobleman, and I pledge my sword to the service of my King; I dedicate to him my life and my brains. It is of no interest to me if the King is good or bad, useful or harmful; I do not examine if his actions do good or harm to the nation; I follow him blindly in whatever he wishes; his will is my law; and I consider myself happy that I enjoy the favour of the Crown Prince, a determined and ambitious leader."[83]

Metaxas admitted in his Diary that he had not always felt like this about the Greek Royal House. "But the war [of 1897] brought me to my senses. I realized my debt as a soldier and above all as a nobleman and as a Metaxas."[84]

The fact that King George I of the Hellenes was (like King Othon before him) of foreign extraction, did not worry Metaxas in the least; his dedication to the Greek Royal House transcended the family and national background of the King of Greece. "The Greek dynasty was not born after a treaty", he wrote, but derived from the history of "a greater motherland," the Byzantine Empire, and "it sprang from the profound desire of the nation, which, during the years of its enslavement, was waiting for the moment when the life of the dynasty, which had been interrupted in 1453, would be resumed."[85] In this context Metaxas found no difficulty in pledging his allegiance to the Greek dynasty. "I dedicate myself to the King and consider him the symbol of the motherland, the past, the present and the future of the nation."[86] Metaxas was a soldier and an aristocrat. For him "the road is clearly marked. The dynasty in Greece is a continuation of that which my ancestors served. Therefore it is my duty to serve it, too."[87]

While in Berlin the news reached him that his father had been dismissed from his post. *"Thus my father's career in government service came to an end -- my kind, honest, noble, admirable father. In my country, where thieves wear decorations, where blackguards are advanced, my father retired with a pension of 200 drachmas and his property reduced by half, after twenty-five years of service."*[88]

The Metaxas family then returned to their native island of Cephalonia. Always a devoted son, John sent them a part of his scholarship grant. "I shall send them regularly 100 drachmas a month, I hope they will manage. I shall help them in all their needs, because they are the only beings in this world whom I love."[89] Even this setback helped Metaxas define his attitude towards the politicians, who had inflicted such injuries upon

83 *Diary,* I. p. 527.
84 *Ibid.*.
85 *Ibid.*, p. 528.
86 *Ibid.*, p. 527.
87 *Ibid.*, p. 528.
88 *Ibid.*, p. 499.
89 *Ibid.*, p. 501.

his family. The only man who had promoted his career and thus helped his family was Crown Prince Constantine, who had himself been unjustly treated by the politicians.

"I shall be obliged no longer to keep silent, and bow, and beg, and suffer the arrogant manners of one person or another. I am obliged to the Crown Prince only and I am pleased about this. My dedication to him will be unlimited because my convictions already drive me towards him, and because the enemies facing him are all those who have made us [Metaxas and his family] suffer." And he added his favourite quotation from Homer: 'Ελεύσετ' ἥμαρ .... A day will come.[90]

Twice a week Metaxas wrote long, affectionate letters to his family in Greece. During the four years he spent in Germany he was continually worried about the health of his younger brother Costakis, whose mental illness was steadily worsening. Metaxas' loyalty to his family was absolute, his sense of duty towards them without limit. The affliction that had befallen his brother cast a dark shadow over Metaxas' life, a deep-rooted sorrow which never really left him. There was no consolation for this kind of anguish. He wrote: "Sometimes I rebel against my fate and evil thoughts assail my mind, and evil words spring to my lips, but I choke them all back immediately; one must accept life as it is meted out to one".[91] Letters from home strove to conceal Costakis' increasing insanity and the family's despair. Metaxas could not rest for imagining the sufferings of his brother, the agony of his family. "My slumbers were very disturbed. Costakis appeared in all my dreams," he once noted in his Diary.[92] Could it be that he himself was, in some obscure way, responsible for his brother's plight?

"I spent a very bad Tuesday. I was tormented by the idea that I was not sharing Costakis' predicament; because if I had behaved towards him in a more paternal manner on every occasion we were together, if I had not abandoned him to circulate in the salons of Corfu, at other times so that I might be with Dousmanis, at yet other times in order to enjoy the embraces of R.... [his φιλενάδα in Athens] perhaps he would not have succumbed to the disease."[93]

Ioannis Metaxas was the eldest child, six years older than Costakis; his love for his brother was almost fatherly. In Germany he heard that Costakis was under the constant care of doctors, that their father often had to take him to Athens for observation and treatment and that for some time Costakis had had to be confined in a mental institution.

---

90 *Ibid.*, p. 500. In other words, a day will come for revenge, for fulfillment. Elsewhere he wrote, "When the hour comes we shall settle accounts with all these people". *Ibid.*, p. 544.

91 *Ibid.*, p. 517.

92 *Ibid.*, p. 523.

93 *Ibid.*.

"I begin to despair completely for Costakis. My life is full of bitterness and sorrow -- could I have been in some way responsible for his misfortune? Perhaps a different kind of behavior on my part could have prevented it. Unfortunately the disease cannot be cured by my self-accusations. But I fear for the others, too. Will they endure the ordeal unscathed? I am particularly fearful for Myrianthi, who has herself suffered in the past [from mental illness]."[94]

Metaxas' feelings of guilt were aggravated because he had not kept the promises that he had made on his departure from Greece; he had vowed to God that he would dedicate his life to the service of all that was "just and noble." But he was young and impulsive and often acted in ways he had resolved to eschew: his beloved Costakis ought not to suffer because of the frailties of his elder brother. *"The unhappy boy! How much he has suffered! What martyrdom, what tortures! My God, have mercy on him! I am unworthy to beseech you because I have not kept the vows which I made when I came here; but I am only human, I have sinned, let him not pay for my sins ..."*[95]

His studies at the War Academy, his social obligations and his passion for women did not prevent Metaxas from enjoying to the full the artistic and intellectual pleasures which the German capital afforded at the time. Apart from his native Greek, Metaxas knew French, Italian and German, and he read newspapers, magazines, novels and plays, as well as books on history and politics, in all these languages. Painting, sculpture and architecture interested him greatly and in his Diary he often made perceptive critiques of the works of art he had seen. But his greatest love was music. Like many an Ionian islander, Metaxas was naturally musical. At one time he had taught his sister the piano and he often remembered with nostalgia the family evenings when he had sung operatic pieces with his father. One of the works he practiced on the piano with his music teacher when he was stationed at Nafplion was Wagner's *Lohengrin.* On hearing the same opera in Berlin, he was profoundly moved. "It left an indelible impression upon me. In the old days, because of my reading of Max Nordau, I despised Wagner as a decadent, without having heard him. Now, having heard him, I admire him." Then, with a touch of Cephalonian wit, Metaxas added: "Perhaps my own decadence has increased also."[96]

Music provided solace and inspiration for Metaxas. Life was not always easy in Berlin. His work at the War Academy was very demanding and he had to compete with the élite of the German officers corps in a difficult language he had only recently learned. But he was not the man to be easily discouraged.

"Do what you should and let what will befall, was always my principle. And I felt a kind of painful pleasure in my sufferings and in the obstacles I had to overcome;

94 *Ibid.*, pp. 522-3.

95 *Ibid.*, p. 509.

96 *Ibid.*, p. 498.

because there was no doubt in my mind that I had to overcome all obstacles. I felt an enormous will inside me and every time I was faced with an obstacle, I could hear echoing in my imagination the battle cry of Wotan, or Siegfried's song of victory."[97]

Metaxas was also stirred by *Tannhäuser.* Wagner, he wrote, transported him into a trance-like ecstasy. He became obsessional ("maniacal" as he put it) about Wagner. On another occasion he attended the opera *Margarete* (possibly Gounod's *Faust).* He liked it, but the impression he gained was unexpected. "Wagner's music had rendered my ear insensitive to whatever I was not enthusiastic about. And then, how little of Goethe's *Faust* came across -- almost nothing."[98] Similarly Metaxas was not over-enthusiastic about *Don Juan* (Mozart's *Don Giovanni*), although he read the *Textbuch* before attending the performance. "My aesthetic sense, accustomed differently, does not immediately understand music of this kind ... I did not come out of the theatre [with the same emotions] as I came out after *Tannhäuser* and *Lohengrin.*"[99] But he decided to give himself another chance and listen to it once more, this time with closed eyes, because "in *Don Juan* everything is superfluous except the music."[100] Visiting the *Philarmonie* ("the refuge of that section of society which is poverty-stricken, but whose cultivated tastes are not content with vulgar pleasures"), Metaxas heard Beethoven for the first time. As he recorded in his Diary, "a certain symphony disturbed me -- it reminded me vividly of Costakis."[101]

The music of Wagner, that odd mixture of brutality and sentimentality, exercised the strongest and most lasting influence on the moral and emotional development of Ioannis Metaxas during his years in Berlin. Metaxas came to Wagner psychologically prepared. After the first two hectic years in the German capital, he was calmer and more confident. He had striven hard and he had prevailed. It had not been easy: "My fatigue was great, but also great were my endeavors to overcome it."[102] At one time he thought that he would have to abandon Grethe, his German girlfriend, to limit his intellectual interests, to consider Art merely as a diversion, "to reject the philosophical theories on the basis of which I have already begun to arrange my life; in other words, to do what Mephistopheles advised Faust to do, so that he could be transformed into a young man without the help of magic." It was, however, too late, because "the rejection of my inner life which had opened up before me would have been a fall and I did not want to fall."[103] By the second year of his stay in Berlin Metaxas had mastered the German language

97 *Ibid.*, p. 593.
98 *Ibid.*, p. 522.
99 *Ibid.*, p. 514.
100 *Ibid.*.
101 *Ibid.*, p. 523.
102 *Ibid.*, p. 592.
103 *Ibid.*.

sufficiently well to be able to compete and be placed first among all his classmates in Military Tactics and to receive the excellent grade of nine out of ten for Military History. By now he had cut down his social engagements to the minimum and he was no longer tormented by his initial frantic pursuit of women. His liaison with Grethe brought him peace of mind and he tried to remain faithful to her, although determined, as he said, not to become involved in a permanent relationship. Grethe had a cathartic and uplifting effect on Metaxas.

"During this whole period, from the autumn of 1902, I lived in a strange state of exhilaration. My sentiments had become nobler and loftier, my emotions more varied and sensitive, my intellect more keen, my sense of justice and morality stronger and more despotic over me. My religious feelings were reborn -- my faith, alas, had long since vanished -- not in the form of dogmas as in the past, but as an emotional experience."[104]

In 1902 Metaxas received better news from his family in Greece: his father, who had been ill, had recovered. His brother Costakis had resumed his medical studies and there were hopes that he might be permanently cured. The prospects of a good marriage for his sister Myrianthi were bright. Metaxas was self-assured now and viewed his occasional lapses into his old ways with more equanimity: "This is the human condition: tossed about like the waves of the sea, we descend into the grave," he reflected in philosophic vein in his Diary.[105]

It was in this state of exaltation that Metaxas heard for the first time Wagner's *Der Ring der Nibelungen*. Significantly enough, when he described the experience later, his prose, which was usually lucid and unaffected, became obscure and even muddled.

"The spiritual and moral state in which I found myself contributed to the deep impression this drama made upon me. I was emotionally prepared for this impression, first because of my character, which had undergone a natural evolution; second, because of the circumstances of my life; and finally, because of that unique tendency of my soul which had further developed during the two years I had spent in Germany. Whether I understood exactly what Wagner tried to express is doubtful; what is certain is that Wagner's works produced certain impressions on me, through which in turn I interpreted his works. Wagner's works, strangely enough, influenced my moral actions. These impressions, diffused in the moral atmosphere in which my soul lived, determined the development of my ideas towards the unique direction I have already mentioned. I became obsessional about Wagner's dramas, so much so that I neglected all other musical works and I did not follow as much as I should the contemporary dramatic movement. At all events, even the few plays that I saw,

104 *Ibid.*, p. 586.
105 *Ibid.*, p. 586.

especially some by Hauptmann, exercised a similar influence on my soul. Generally my intellectual life was activated by such impressions .... I selected my reading according to this direction, e.g. I read the books of Chamberlain on Wagner, Die Grundlagen des XIXten Jahrhunderts, and a few others.

I cannot characterize exactly here this kind of spiritual development. It was mainly a disposition of soul, in itself undefined, but taking a certain form as it gave a twist to my thoughts and actions. Only by recounting the innumerable incidents of my everyday life can a clearer notion be gained of this disposition of soul. The episode with Grethe furnishes some insight into this."[106]

During this spiritual experience Metaxas discovered two most profound "ideas." The first idea concerned "the worth [αξία] of a free and sovereign personality, which alone determines its road".[107] He continued: "I no longer accepted the ability of society to guide me morally nor the common opinion of men to be the Lydian stone of good or evil."[108] He would supply his own moral criterion. "Thus I placed myself above all others and I alone defined the rules of my conduct."[109]

The second idea Metaxas' spiritual development produced was concerned with action -- "only in action does the personality find the means for its growth and the soul its tranquillity; action is the natural and healthy state of our soul; all action can have only one aim: the good of others."[110] There are, of course, people who do harm, "but I realize that such harmful activity would be against the inclination of my soul .... As a consequence of these ideas, I considered good or evil only what I regarded as such."[111] Metaxas believed that this sense of reality posed for him a "sacred duty" and "any failure in my obligations would only harm all those for whose sake I undertook them."[112] In the same spirit Metaxas explained his "faith in the King and his feeling for the motherland, which took a strange form."[113]

"Since all nations live apart from each other, every citizen should be benevolent to his own nation. I, therefore, because I was born in Greece and because my inclination

---

106 *Ibid.*, p. 587. Houston Stewart Chamberlain (1855-1927), the author of *Die Grundlagen des XIXten Jahrhunderts*, an Englishman by birth, married in Munich in 1899 Wagner's only daughter Eva and was eventually naturalized in Germany. In this, his most important book, he propounded the racialist theories which later were to influence Hitler. The book was published in English in 1911 in two vols. under the title *The Foundation of the Nineteenth Century*. Ioannis Metaxas, although a believer in the civilizing mission of the Hellenic race, was not a racist.

107 *Ibid.*.

108 *Ibid.*. Lydian stone was a hard black stone on which the degree of purity in gold and in silver was checked.

109 *Ibid.*, p. 588.

110 *Ibid.*.

111 *Ibid.*.

112 *Ibid.*.

113 *Ibid.*.

is benevolent, must work for the good of Greece. It is inmaterial to me if Greece be the least of nations; my obligation is not to find in her virtues she does not possess, or to ignore the vices she does. My obligation to Greece does not derive from any enthusiasm or love or admiration, but from the fact that I was born a Greek and, as the need of my soul is benevolent, I therefore have to be useful to Greece."[114]

An irrational philosophy such as this, by which an individual may follow indiscriminately a good or a bad king, by which self-righteousness is happily united with blind faith and can only be expressed, in a pseudo-metaphysical sort of way, through action as a sacred duty to other, lesser people, provides the clues for a fuller understanding of the career and policies of the future dictator of Greece. If a man has decided that he is good, if he is convinced that he has a sacred duty to his fellow-men, if action alone can redeem, he must also be strong and determined. Metaxas is nothing if not candid when describing his personal transformation in this direction.

"My character, then, has been much strengthened. Especially lately, my will, my decisiveness, has acquired great power. But where have they gone, my beliefs in freedom, in virtue, in morality? Where has it gone, that solicitude that, even in my smallest actions, virtue should shine through? The world, hardships, bitterness, have made me a man of iron, but have also made me less scrupulous in the choice of the means."[115]

As the day for his return approached, news from Greece interested him more than at any other time. He had already learned that he had been appointed to the General Directorate of the Army, while the two other Greek officers studying with him had been given less important posts. During the recent Greek elections there had been violent attacks on the General Directorate. "An especially dreadful impression was made on me by the events that followed the elections, the attitude of the Athenian people, the anti-dynastic opposition .... And I was possessed by an inner rage: I was dreaming of being there, of having power, of being at the head of a good army to wipe out those demagogues."[116]

He was now ready to return home. Early in April 1903 he took the train for Rostock. He had a month at his disposal and decided to spend it travelling in Europe. From then onwards everything he saw, everything he heard, he would judge through his new insight. The time and money spent on his education at the Berlin War Academy had not been wasted. As the train pulled out from the North Station he was summing up his years in Germany.

---

114 *Ibid.*. Unfortunately, the second sheet of the fifth exercise book where these fascinating notes are continued has been torn out. These recollections from Germany were written in 1905. Metaxas tore out some pages in June, 1940: it is anybody's guess why.

115 *Ibid.*, p. 519.

116 *Ibid.*, p. 640.

"Farewell Berlin! Four years have gone by since poor, obscure, inexperienced, unhappy, with the same companions, I arrived here in a rainy autumn. Now, with the same companions, in the spring, I am leaving; but I am not the same; how much I have changed! A different man -- knowledge, education, experience of the world, life, the enjoyment of good and evil things, strengthening of character, self-confidence! And yet; something was missing [in Germany] which I had then [in Greece]; the faith in a higher Providence, and that higher morality that flows from it, had suffered a basic shock and they were lying partly in ruins. Instead of these: an unbridled will for the acquisition of power in the world."[117]

117 *Ibid.*, p. 648.

The Coup d'Etat of 1909

The general disillusionment and discontent following the disastrous war of 1897 culminated in 1909 in a military revolt, the Revolution of Goudhi. The young, mostly non-commissioned officers of the Athens garrison who staged the revolution demanded drastic changes in the Constitution and the administration of the country. The exhausted forces of the old order capitulated without a fight, almost with relief. A new era had begun. The Revolution of 1909 was the turning point in the history of modern Greece. It marked the close of Nineteenth Century Greece, a rural, peasant society, which had lived in poverty but also on beautiful illusions, and ushered in the democratic bourgeois state of Twentieth Century Greece, whose agonized search for solutions was resolved sometimes in triumph, more often in tragedy.

As soon as Metaxas returned to Greece, he joined the General Directorate of the Army and worked with Colonel Victor Dousmanis (1862-1949), another royalist officer, on drafting the new Army Regulations in accordance with the laws recently passed by the Greek Parliament. By February 1904 the long and complex Army Bill was ready and Theotokis introduced it to the Chamber. The new Bill was an elaborate exercise in military organization which transformed the Greek Army into the private army of the Crown Prince. Dousmanis and Metaxas had used the German system as a model -- the only difference being that, in place of the Emperor, the Crown Prince and not the King was to be the Leader of the Army, accountable to no one.

As soon as the General Staff was formed, Constantine invited Metaxas to become a member. While in Germany Metaxas had been promoted to Lieutenant. In July 1906 he was made a Captain Second Class and, a few months later, Captain First Class. In his position as Staff Officer Metaxas enjoyed great advantages. He had regular access to the Crown Prince and, through him, could exercise a great deal of power in the Army. He became a close friend of Prince Andrew and, through him, he could transmit his thoughts and requests to the King himself. In October 1907 he was asked to undertake the military education of Constantine's eldest son, the future King George II of the Hellenes. The young Prince had just turned seventeen and for the next two years he studied Military History and Tactics with Metaxas. The proud teacher kept a record of these studies and preserved his lesson notes.[1] Metaxas explained the Greek defeat of 1897 to his student as the result of "lack of experience, administration, education, morale: lack of character." In his report to the Prince's tutor on 9 May [O.S.] 1909, Metaxas wrote that the young Prince was wanting "in harshness and forcefulness" in issuing oral and written commands. In Military History the Prince tended to become bogged down in "details, sometimes insignificant from the military point of view." What impression Ioannis Metaxas made on his student at that time is unknown; but in 1936, a short while after his restoration to the throne, George II showed his absolute trust in

1 They are now part of the Metaxas Papers in the General State Archives Athens.

his former teacher, signing the decrees Metaxas presented to him by which civil liberties were suspended and the dictatorship was established. Metaxas' proclamations of his regime were appropriately harsh and forceful.

Many ambitious army and naval officers who had been excluded from the higher posts in the armed forces by the Crown Prince's New Army Regulations, came to believe that the national interest were being sacrificed for the sake of the personal interest of the Royal Family and the politicians. The general feeling among many young officers was that the King and his numerous relations were primarily interested in the future of the dynasty and its privileges, while the politicians cared only for their own power and the perpetuation of the notorious spoils system which they themselves had employed to get into office. If Greece were ever to avenge the defeat of 1897 and defend her honour in the face of Turkish provocation, radical changes were necessary in the social and political structure of the country and in the military leadership. In May 1909 a group of junior officers organized themselves into a secret, revolutionary society in imitation of the Turkish Committee of Union and Progress, which had been set up in the July of the previous year in Salonica. The officers of the Military League (Στρατιωτικός Σύνδεσμος), as the society was called, were aware of the chaotic state of affairs in Greece, the political corruption and misgovernment, especially the shortcomings of the Armed Forces, at a time when not only the Turks but also the Serbians and Bulgarians were reorganizing their countries and enlarging their armies.

Greek frustration was aggravated by the internal situation in Turkey. The Young Turks were vigorously pursuing their policy of "Ottomanizing" the Christian populations of the Ottoman Empire. Non-Moslem schools were closed and the official use of any language but Turkish was forbidden. Constitutional liberty, to the Young Turks, simply meant national and religious uniformity. However, making good Osmanlis out of the subject peoples of Turkey, although sometimes achieved in the past, had never been an easy task. When assimilation did not work, a policy of repression was adopted. "From the point of view of the non-Turks," wrote historian René Albrecht-Carrié, "efficient efforts at Turkification might be even less attractive than sporadic religious persecution under an inefficient and corrupt, but largely indifferent administration."[2] The Greek officers, many of whom had fought a clandestine guerilla war in Macedonia to protect the Greeks from persecution and safeguard Greek claims in that part of the Balkans, certainly had no illusions about the Young Turks and their vaunted reforms.

On 28 August 1909 the Military League staged a coup d' état. Simultaneously a revolt broke out among several naval units. The leadership of the Military League had been offered to Colonel Nikolaos Zorbas (1844-1920) who, although a mild man and

---

2 Rene Albrecht-Carrie, *A Diplomatic History of Europe since the Congress of Vienna* (New York, 1973, rev. ed.), p. 263.

not at all a revolutionary by nature, bore a grudge against Constantine and his Staff for having criticized him for incompetence in the 1897 war and for blocking his promotion. Under the command of Zorbas, 450 officers, 2,000 infantrymen and 200 cavalrymen occupied the barracks of Goudhi on the outskirts of Athens. The Military League of army and naval officers issued a revolutionary memorandum, "Addressed to the King, the Government and the Greek People," and threatened to march on Athens if their demands were not met.[3] Chief among these demands was the removal of the Crown Prince and his royal brothers from all army posts and the appointment of professional officers to the posts of Minister for the Army and Minister for the Navy. The rebels of the Military League were obviously not impressed with the work of the Crown Prince's General Staff and they now demanded the complete reorganization of the land and sea forces of the country. In the long memorandum they spelled out the steps that had to be taken to bring about the army reforms: Greek officers were to be sent abroad for further training, and foreign military missions were to be invited to assist with the reorganization. The rebels also called for specific reforms of the administration, the judiciary, education and the economy; they demanded lower taxation; they were against the spoils system in politics; they were against nepotism and favouritism in the army, which hindered their chances of promotion. But they did not call for the abolition of the monarchy or the replacement of King George I: neither did they want to establish a dictatorship, "or in any way harm the constitutional system of government." Finally the rebels demanded that Parliament be summoned immediately to ratify by vote the necessary measures of their program.[4]

Although some high-ranking officers joined the rebels of the Military League, there was little public response. Once the Revolution, as it was called, had been proclaimed, its leaders tried to organize the peoples' support. King George threatened to abdicate. His sister, Queen Alexandra of England, wrote urging him to give up the throne and to come and live in England, free from care. George replied that when he opened his bedroom window every morning in the Tatoi palace and looked out on the lovely skies of Attica and the clear horizon, he felt deeply that he could never have the strength to leave this country which he loved so much. So, on second thoughts, in order to placate the rebels, the King instructed his sons to relinquish their military commands. The Crown Prince and Prince Nicholas were dismissed outright, while Prince Andrew, Prince Christoforos and Constantine's son, the young Prince George, were given three

3 The Revolutionary Memorandum, which has been described as a *pronunciamento,* is included in General Nikolaos Zorbas, *Απομνημονεύματα ή Πληροφορίαι περί των Συμβάντων κατά την διάρκεια της Επαναστάσεως της 15ης Αυγούστου 1909* [Memoirs or Information on the Events During the Revolution of 15 August 1090] (Athens, 1925) pp. 15-22. An English translation appears in Papacosma, *The Military*, pp. 190-196.

4 For an excellent account of the Revolution of Goudhi see S. Victor Papacosma, *The Military in Greek Politics: the 1909 coup d'etat* (Kent, Ohio, 1977).

years leave to pursue military studies in Germany. Colonel Zorbas expressed surprise in his Memoirs that the government showed no signs of resistance, although it had several loyal army units in the vicinity of Athens. Premier Rallis, after trying unsuccessfully to negotiate with the rebels, stepped down, and the new Premier, Kyriakoulis Mavromichalis, who was sent for by the King, accepted all the demands of the Military League. Submitting to the will of the rebels, the King also signed a decree dismissing Captain Andreas Kallinsky from the army and placing Lieutenant-Colonel Leandros Metaxas, a cousin of Ioannis Metaxas, on the retirement list. Both these men had tried unavailingly to prevent certain army units from joining the rebels. After Constantine's dismissal as Commander-in-Chief his General Staff was disbanded. Victor Dousmanis and Ioannis Metaxas were particularly hated by the rebel officers as they were the most influential members of the exclusive clique which surrounded the Crown Prince. But Zorbas was not a Caesan, not even a Brutus. Metaxas was merely reassigned to his regiment, the Engineers Corps, at the distant garrison of Larissa in Thessaly.

5 Ioannis Metaxas and his wife Lela née Hadjioannou

His banishment came only fifteen days after his wedding and his wife, formerly Miss Lela Hadjioannou of Athens, sadly accompanied him to the distant provincial town in the plain of Thessaly. It was a distressing experience for Metaxas and his bride. At their wedding in Athens, which was solemnized by a bishop with much pomp and ceremony, the best man was Crown Prince Constantine himself; among those present were Prince Nicholas and Prince Andrew with his wife, Princess Alice of Battenberg. Metaxas was then a rising young officer, a member of the General Staff of the Crown Prince, basking in the favour of royalty, the brightest star in the Greek military firmament. The Revolution changed all this and Captain Ioannis Metaxas came under fire from the rebels, who accused him of being a lackey of the monarchy and the evil genius of the Crown Prince. But Zorbas was not a Caesar, not even a Brutus. Metaxas was merely reassigned to his regiment, the Engineers Corps, at the distant garrison of Larissa in Thessaly.

George Theotokis, Demetrios Rallis, Stephanos Dragoumis, Demetrios Gounaris and the rest of the old guard tried to prevent the government from functioning, either by filibustering or absenting themselves from Parliament. The rebels at Goudhi threatened to send army units to occupy the Parliament building. In the shadow cast by the rebels' bayonets some 163 bills were hurriedly passed in the Chamber to satisfy the demands of the Revolution. Many of these laws were quite unworkable - the German Minister at Athens described them to his government as a *Weltrekord*. But, unexpectedly, a new, energetic Minister of Finance, Athanasios Eftaxias (1849-1931) performed such a thorough job in reducing government expenditures that the budget showed a surplus for the first time in the history of modern Greece. On 9 January 1910 Premier Mavromichalis paid a visit to Colonel Zorbas and explained that, as the bills proposed by the Revolution had been passed, the Military League "had no reason for existence," and called upon the rebels to lay down their arms. The rebels, although behaving in a dictatorial manner, did not possess a dictatorial will and no strong man emerged from their ranks with the authority the Revolution so much needed. Once the initial stage was past, they were at a loss what to do next: it was then that the suggestion was made by some of the rebel officers that the Military League should invite Eleftherios Venizelos over from Crete and seek his advice. As Edward S. Forster, the historian of Greece, observed "seldom have the man and the opportunity been so well fitted to one another."[5]

Eleftherios Venizelos was already wellknown in Greece. His reputation as a patriot and nationalist was widespread throughout the Greek world as a result of his struggles for the liberation of Crete from Turkish occupation. If Greece were to make a stand against Turkish provocation, the fighter of Akrotiri was the man to rally the country. Many of the officers of the Military League were personally acquainted with him since the time they had gone to Crete to help organize the National Guard. His example of defiance against the despotic rule of Prince George, the High Commissioner of Crete, was an inspiration to the rebels of the Military League. The Cretan revolutionary had

---

5 Edward S. Forster, *A Short History of Modern Greece, 1821-1956* (London, 1958, 3rd ed.) p. 45.

a reputation for being "anti-dynastic," which appealed to the revolutionary fervour of the young officers. He was a progressive and skillful politician, who had painlessly rid Crete of Prince George. A new man, Venizelos had avoided the rough and tumble of Greek politics and his name remained unsullied.

When the 1909 Goudhi Revolution broke out, Venizelos was the first to praise the idealism of the young rebels and to offer his support to their Revolution. This gesture, coming at a time when the rebels were being vilified as traitors on all sides, gratified the leaders of the Military League and won the hearts of the young officers and their sympathisers. Venizelos declared his support in a series of articles he published in the newspaper Κήρυξ (The Herald) of Chania, Crete, which were promptly reprinted by the Athens press. The articles were published anonymously, but it was no secret who the author was. The Revolution, wrote Venizelos, came as a natural response to the demands of the Greek people for an end to the selfish tactics of the Royal Family, for an end to the discord among the political factions, for an end to Government corruption and the self-seeking activities of the plutocratic oligarchy. In his articles Venizelos advocated a National Assembly which should be convened at once in order to lay a new foundation for the whole structure of the state and determine the way the Greek people should be governed in future. Should the King prove unwilling to place himself at the head of the reconstruction movement, a dictatorship should be proclaimed for a specified period of time to prepare for the National Assembly. Venizelos' articles helped to clarify and define the aims of the Revolution for the Greek people and helped the rebels articulate their initial demands and provide the Revolution with a dynamic program.

Venizelos' answer to the invitation of the Military League was sent on 4 January 1910. This answer was the first of a number of deft political manoeuvres which were to take the Cretan leader from the limited sphere of his island to the wider arena of Greek politics. "A negative answer from me would be unthinkable", Venizelos wrote back; still, he made it clear that he could not accept the offer of the Military League until a closer study of the political situation in Greece persuaded him that acceptance "was an imperative duty imposed by the interests of the nation." In order "to study the situation" on the spot, Venizelos proposed to travel to Athens within a few days, "although I have tried to avoid the journey to the last." He requested that his trip to Athens be kept secret.[6]

Venizelos had studied Law at the University of Athens and knew the Greeks and their politics well. As an "unredeemed Greek" himself, his only political goal until then had been the liberation of his native island and he had made no commitments to any Greek political party and had never compromised his integrity. Despite his reputation, which

---

6 Theodore Pangalos, *Απομνημονεύματα, 1897-1947* [Memoirs, 1897-1947] (Athens, 1959) I, p. 108.

had preceded him, he would be a stranger in Athens, with most of the cards stacked against him. He had no political basis of his own; he was brought to Greece by the Military League, which was in open rebellion against the dynasty and the government; the Military League, which had invited him, would naturally try to dominate him; because of his revolt against Prince George in Crete, the Royal Family would regard him with suspicion; the old politicians, distrustful of an outsider, would oppose him; as a leader of the Military League, he would be forced to become a revolutionary against the Greek state. Nevertheless, Venizelos, who had learned from bitter experience that no struggle for the liberation of Crete had any chance of success as long as the Greek ship of state continued to flounder amid chaos and turmoil, considered the Goudhi Revolution a rare opportunity for national reform and reconstruction and could hardly conceal his excitement at the invitation that arrived from the Greek capital. On the day Mahmud Shevket Pasha threatened in the Turkish Parliament that if Greece did not publicly renounce all claims to Crete a million Turks would invade Thessaly, Eleftherios Venizelos set off from Suda Bay to Piraeus.

The officers of the Military League dispatched a steamship, recently renamed Goudhi, to convey Venizelos to their shores. But no sooner had the ship left Crete with her precious passenger aboard than she developed engine trouble and had to return to the island. Whereupon Venizelos transferred to the Italian steamer Singapore, which was making the regular voyage from Crete to Piraeus, and set sail once more for Greece. On 10 January 1910 at three o'clock in the afternoon the Singapore arrived at Piraeus, the busy port of Athens. Rear-Admiral Alexander Hadjikyriakos came alongside in a motorlaunch of the Royal Greek Navy to receive him. Venizelos was then forty-five years old, tall and vigorous, his short pointed beard already turning grey, his hair beginning to recede, his small gold-rimmed spectacles giving him the air rather of an academic than a fiery revolutionary. His arrival, far from being secret, was common knowledge; but the Cretan refused to address the waiting crowd or to make a statement to the assembled journalists. "I always wanted to make this trip," he confided with a disarming smile. And he advised the rebel officers to convene a National Assembly, by force, if necessary. "Only in this way can the Military League put an end to the abnormal conditions created by the Revolution."[7]

The more conservative among the officers of the Military League then voiced their fears that a National Assembly might resolve to alter the Constitution and dispense with the monarchy -- an act which was bound to cause great conflict and unrest among the Greek people. Other officers wondered aloud whether they had sufficient popularity to summon a National Assembly. Rather surprisingly, Venizelos now advised them to contact the political leaders of the country and come to an agreement with them for a

7 Zorbas, *Απομνημονεύματα* pp. 67- 68.

revisionist, not a constituent Assembly. Such an Assembly would revise specific articles of the 1864 constitution, not the fundamental articles which defined the Greek state as a crowned democracy (βασιλευόμενη δημοκρατία). Thus the King would have no reason to object to the convocation of a National Assembly.

The question then arose, who would make these contacts with the King and the politicians? Not the officers themselves, who were in open rebellion against them. Could Venizelos, the rebels pleaded, stay in Athens for a while and conduct these delicate negotiations as their representative? No, he could not, he had to return to Crete immediately -- unless, of course, they should insist, he added coyly, in which case he would be reluctantly compelled to prolong his sojourn in Athens after all. From that moment Eleftherios Venizelos, that consummate politician, was in business. Soon after, on 28 January 1910, Venizelos wrote to Colonel Zorbas, "asking permission" to request Stephanos Dragoumis (1842-1923) to form an interim cabinet. At Venizelos' insistence, Colonel Zorbas was appointed Minister of War in this caretaker government, which was sworn in on 31 January 1910.

When the King first heard that the Military League had invited Venizelos to Athens, he was greatly disturbed. "I hope Venizelos will soon be hanged from the mast of a battleship," he is reported to have remarked.[8] Venizelos was hated and feared by the Greek Royal Family; even after learning that he was negotiating with the political leaders for a Revisionist National Assembly, George I had his misgivings about Venizelos' motives. Once the Assembly met, there was no certainty as to the direction in which it could be swayed by men like Venizelos. Speaking to Sir Francis Elliot, the British Minister at Athens, the King told him that the Assembly -

".... was certain to be composed of demagogues, journalists, and numbers of officers .... [from] the League, all ready to vote for anything, including his own dethronement, which might be recommended to them by M. Venizelos, who was now master of the situation, and was actuated by personal ambitions and by hostility to himself and the Royal Family, dating from the time of his quarrel with Prince George on Crete."[9]

George Moses, the American Minister at Athens, shared the King's opinion of the potential danger to the monarchy posed by a National Assembly. "It was a National Assembly that brought me here," he observed wryly.[10] However, Venizelos was not to be deflected from his purpose and he certainly had no fear of kings. If George I did not agree to the convocation of a Revisionist Assembly, the situation would become explosive: "I shall place myself at the head of the Revolution," Venizelos threatened.[11]

---

8 Alastos, *Venizelos,* p. 65.

9 Papacosma, *The Military*, p. 123.

10 *Ibid.*

11 Ventiris, *He Hellas*, I, p. 60.

Colonel Zorbas put the troops on alert and in the afternoon of 30 January 1910 they paraded ominously through the streets of Athens with weapons at the ready. During this military demonstration the King rode by on his way to the Palace and was greatly affected by the spectacle. After a number of political manoeuvres, Parliament passed the necessary laws, King George I, accompanied by Queen Olga, entered the Chamber and addressed the members, expressing his Royal thanks for their "noble zeal and devotion" to the country and to the dynasty. The King then signed the Royal Decree for the convocation of the National Assembly and appointed S. Dragoumis head of a service government. The previous evening, acting upon an agreement reached with the King, the rebel officers announced that since "the government has carried out the mandate which it received from the Revolution," they considered the work of the Military League completed.[12] Thus the Goudhi Revolution of 28 August 1909 came to an end. On 14 April 1910, after seven tension-filled months, the King and Queen left Athens for Mon Repos, the Royal residence on Corfu. Twelve days later they were joined by Crown Prince Constantine, who had been out of the country since his dismissal from the Army the previous September.

The elections of 21 August turned out Venizelos' "Independents" the strongest force in Parliament and on 19 October 1909 the King appointed him Prime Minister. On the same day, returning to his house from the camp about noon -- he had in the meantime been recalled from Larissa to Athens -- Metaxas found a note inviting him to call on Venizelos at his hotel at 12:30 p.m. He hurried there immediately; the Prime Minister was awaiting him. In his Diary -- which Metaxas resumed that same day after a silence of four and a half years - he set down the following conversation which took place between Venizelos and himself at their first meeting.

Venizelos: *You know what a lamentable situation we are in, that we have to suffer the humiliating provocations of the Turks without being able to defend our honour. I am determined to work resolutely towards the creation of an efficient army and the application of strict discipline. I ask for your contribution in this undertaking. For this reason I offer you the position of my first aide-de-camp.*

Metaxas: *I shall make my best endeavors to assist you in the task which you have outlined. I accept.*

Venizelos: *I am telling you all this, and perhaps you can see that I am a trifle agitated, because I have not encountered from everyone the same readiness to come to my assistance ... From now onwards I shall be compelled to issue orders and not ask anyone whether they wish to cooperate or not ... The Director of Personnel will be Mr. Nider. Are you on friendly terms with him?*

Metaxas: *Certainly.*

---

12 Papacosma, *The Military*, p. 148.

Venizelos: *You will be able to work together, then."*[13]

However gratifying the Prime Minister's offer, Metaxas was less than enthusiastic about his new appointment. He wrote in his Diary:

"I wish I had had the strength to refuse, to remain outside, to accept only under certain conditions, to appear uncompromising and demand the position in the Army which my worth [αξία] deserves. And if they would not give in to my demands, that is, if I were not considered indispensable, to refuse them my assistance."[14]

It was a conflict between his stubborn pride and his overriding ambition. Why, then, had he accepted so readily? Metaxas searched his conscience for an answer. "A weakness of the will which manifested itself at the critical moment? A thirst for a return to power, of whatever kind? I do not believe so."[15] How, he wondered, could he have dictated his own terms to the all-powerful Prime Minister? Was he, in fact, indispensable? Then there was the question of his duty towards his country and "the salvation of the Army." "Venizelos' proposal found me in such a state of self-doubt that I accepted because I had not resolved the problem beforehand within myself. And then I realize that we [the Crown Prince and his followers] have been permanently defeated."[16] As he admitted, the swift rise to power of Venizelos had caught him off balance. "Let me await developments," he wrote in his Diary. "I remain faithful to my principles. What do I care about the rest?"[17] If his position became untenable, he could always resign his commission and leave the Army altogether. But could he, in fact, do so? The day after he had accepted Venizelos' offer, he wrote in his Diary: "Will I be able to find other work? ... I have made up my mind to leave the Army, but, when the hour of decision comes, will I go through with it? I vacillate in self-destructive uncertainty, the slave and not the master of circumstances."[18]

Metaxas' first reaction to Venizelos was mixed. "My impression of Venizelos is better than I had expected. But he did not strike me as a man of authority," he wrote in his Diary after his first meeting with the Cretan.[19] The following day he wrote: "I confess Venizelos does not inspire me with confidence."[20] Metaxas considered Venizelos to be an instrument in the hands of the rebel officers.

"Venizelos is not, of course, the man of strong will everybody takes him for. [At this point five lines of the Diary have been crossed through with indelible Indian ink-

---

13 Metaxas, *Diary*, II, pp. 17-8.
14 *Ibid.*, p. 18.
15 *Ibid.*
16 *Ibid.*
17 *Ibid.*
18 *Ibid.*, p. 19.
19 *Ibid.*
20 *Ibid.*

almost certainly a short time before Metaxas' death in January 1941]. I think that the remnants of the Military League still exert an influence upon him. [Some words struck out]. It is not in the interests of the King to repose complete trust in him. [More words deleted]. Perhaps he is not sincere ... Let us not forget the recent past. Undoubtedly Venizelos has formerly acted against the King, perhaps even against the monarchy itself. Now he appears a changed man! Has he really changed? I doubt it. I suspect that he has not severed all connections with the rebels of Goudhi."[21]

To the end Metaxas remained suspicious of Venizelos' motives. "We are only a shadow [window-dressing; a front]. Perhaps he only took us up in order to throw dust in the eyes of the king and the world. Indeed, the people were reassured by our appointments".[22] Metaxas never ceased to observe Venizelos with a critical eye. He continued to be wary of him and remained resentful of his sudden success. *"Therefore I am an aide-de-camp in name only. My principles, my faith in the Royal House, my place by the side of Theotokis are well known. Consequently I have the right to act and speak as I do. But what is the use? I am harnessed to the wrong chariot."*[23]

Venizelos' first impressions of his aide-de-camp are unfortunately not recorded. At that time the Prime Minister had more pressing matters to attend to than Captain Ioannis Metaxas. On the day following his meeting with Metaxas, Venizelos faced the first test of his government in the National Assembly. The 1864 Constitution stipulated that the presence of half the number of deputies was necessary for a quorum of the legislative body; the Greek party leaders, all former premiers, who resented Venizelos' rise to power, absented themselves with their followers from the sessions and thus effectively prevented the Assembly from functioning. In support of Venizelos, the university students and the Trade Guilds organized a rally in Athens over ten thousand strong and denounced the obstructionist tactics of the old politicians. Venizelos went to the Palace to tender his resignation.

That morning Metaxas slept late and had no idea of the crisis that had befallen the government. On arrival at the Ministry of War, he found a note from his friend Prince Andrew asking him to meet him at the Palace at once. At the Palace Metaxas also found Crown Prince Constantine, Prince Nicholas, and Dionysios Stephanou, the Director of the King's Political Office. Venizelos was closeted with the King in the Royal study. Prince Andrew drew Metaxas to the bay window. Metaxas said to him:

"Venizelos will be most useful and helpful if he can be detached from the lawless elements of the Military League. As long as he is powerless, he is in need of them and he will not break away from them - thus we shall be under their authority. If he becomes powerful, he will not need them; they will become not only useless, but

21 *Ibid.*, p. 20.
22 *Ibid.*, p. 21.
23 *Ibid.*, p. 25

burdensome too, and he will discard them. Therefore the King should support him in every way."[24]

Prince Andrew said that the King's inclination also was to support the Prime Minister. Prince Andrew and Metaxas then joined the others. Presently Venizelos left the Palace. The King invited the Princes into his study. Prince Andrew asked Metaxas to wait for him. After a long time he returned and related to Metaxas all that had passed. The King had refused to accept Venizelos' resignation; instead he had apparently insisted that the Prime Minister should present his government once more to the Chamber and again solicit a vote of confidence. If he were unsuccessful, the King promised to grant him a dissolution of the Chamber and a proclamation of new elections. Prince Andrew had conveyed to the King Metaxas' views. The King concurred.

When Venizelos again appeared before the House, he discovered that the old politicians, who were now present, were not prepared to give his government a vote of unconditional confidence. Theotokis declared that he was ready "to accord tolerance to the government." Mavromichalis said he would vote against the government. Rallis said he would abstain. Venizelos realized that no constructive work could be achieved by the Assembly under such circumstances; he also realized that the party politicians had discredited themselves in the eyes of the Greek people. Again he submitted his resignation, which the King now accepted, at the same time handing him the Royal Decree for the dissolution of the Assembly and the proclamation of new elections. The party leaders, resentful because the King had not invited one of them to form a government and had dissolved the Assembly without consulting them, announced that they and their parties would play no part in the ensuing elections. These elections, they declared, were unconstitutional and would ruin the country. The Athens newspaper Πατρίς wrote that, by abstaining, the politicians had committed suicide in order to escape the guillotine of the elections. The Trade Guilds and the commercial organizations supported the King's decision. All the trump cards had been dealt to Venizelos and the wily Cretan could hardly wait to play his hand.

Metaxas had not anticipated such a swift turn of events and was taken aback by the gathering momentum of Venizelos' rise to power. The Prime Minister still refused to reinstate Colonel Victor Dousmanis, the former Chief of the Crown Prince's disbanded General Staff; neither was he at all anxious to recall to the Army the other royalist officers who had been cashiered by the rebels. Two of them, Colonel Menelaos Metaxas, first cousin of Ioannis Metaxas, and Colonel Kallinsky, had been deprived of their commissions because they had tried to prevent some cavalry units from joining the Revolution of Goudhi. Kallinsky took his case to the courts. One morning Metaxas showed Venizelos two more appeals to the courts by dismissed officers.

---

24 *Ibid.*, p. 22.

Metaxas: *As you know, the decision of the courts on Kallinsky's case will create a precedent for all the others. I think it would be preferable and more dignified for the State not to appear coerced into administering justice.*
Venizelos: *You are aware, Mr. Metaxas, that I have already given the subject some thought, and as Mr. Nider must have told you, a Royal Decree will be issued recalling all dismissed officers. But don't you think such a move is premature? Would it not cause unfavourable reactions from the Army?*
Metaxas: *Reactions? What of it? But, if you will allow me, I do not consider the mere recall of these officers to be enough, because by doing only this, the consequences of their dismissal is not corrected. They will again resort to the courts to regain their seniority.*
Venizelos: *Of course, I can see that.*
Metaxas: *I propose that you cancel the decree which dismissed them from the Army.*
Venizelos: *Let me tell you this, Mr. Metaxas. I myself did not hesitate to tell the rebels that they had acted wrongly in punishing these officers. Because, after all, these officers believed that they, too, were doing their duty; only they had a different concept as to what their duty was. In actual fact, they were legally more in the right than the rebels.*
Metaxas: *Let me give you my opinion as well, Mr. Prime Minister. If I had been in the place of the rebels of 28 August, I would have immediately shot Messrs. Menelaos Metaxas, Kallinsky, and the rest ... But since I had not done this, since I had turned from a rebel into a government, I would have rewarded them: because these were the officers who upheld the law.*
Venizelos: *[Metaxas indicated in his Diary that at this point Venizelos smiled and avoided a discussion on the matter]. Come now! In Greece we consider blood to be precious.*
Metaxas: *[Earnestly, as he indicated in his Diary]. That is what I would have done. And I insist that you cancel the decree of their dismissal. But because I can see how difficult your position is and how unprofitable it might be to probe the substance of the problem now and bring it back once again, I suggest you cancel the decree of their dismissal as contradictory to the earlier decree of amnesty.*
Venizelos: *Is it possible to do so? Then there is a way out for us. I like your idea, Mr. Metaxas. We can in this way avoid all reactions and discussions. Bring the decree of amnesty to me and if it can be done, why not?"*[25]

But the Prime Minister, more sensitive to political realities than Metaxas, dragged his feet over the question of the reinstatement of the dismissed officers. Metaxas, dissatisfied, discussed Venizelos' policies with several representatives of the old regime. He

25 *Ibid.*, pp. 35-6.

saw Crown Prince Constantine, the Royalist politician Nikolaos Stratos (1872-1922) and ex-Premier George Theotokis. Theotokis said to him: "I am of the opinion that Venizelos is a demagogue of the same type as the late Deliyiannis."[26] Finally, on 3 November, Metaxas had an audience with the King himself.

The King expressed his pleasure at the meeting, greeting him with the words, "I am very glad to see you again, especially under more auspicious circumstances than last year."[27] He knew of Metaxas' distrust of Venizelos and tried to reassure him. He had confidence in the Prime Minister, the King said; Venizelos would be "good for the country."[28] Venizelos might still be hesitant to break completely with the Military League; but when he was returned in the elections with a large majority, he would impose his will and do all things necessary. For this reason, he should be assisted in the elections.

Metaxas: *There is no doubt that he will win all the votes since there is no opposition. For precisely this reason, he should now display his authority. It is the best opportunity.*

George I: *No, there is the danger that many people may abstain from the elections. He may still have his own deputies elected, but a substantial abstention at the polls will indicate a lack of confidence in him and will make his position difficult.*

Metaxas: *Be that as it may, it is imperative to us that he inspire confidence from this moment by severing all connections with the officers of the Military League. He should, from now onwards, show to the whole world that there is no association between him and them.*

George I: *This will come about, too, little by little, so as not to give rise to any adverse reactions; he will do all this when he gains the majority. He will declare this in his speeches at the elections.*

Metaxas: *Speeches have no significance, Your Majesty. He must prove by his deeds that he is not the successor of the Military League.*

George I: *You must bear in mind that we must not demand everything from him at once ... He has already done enough for a beginning. Let us be patient. All will come to pass in due course. It would be very useful if someone close to him were gradually to win his trust; he would then be able to guide him in many ways."*[29]

Metaxas left the Palace with the impression that the King in his innermost heart did not expect much of Venizelos, but that "he wanted to convince himself that there are great hopes for the future."[30]

---

26 *Ibid.*, p. 25.
27 *Ibid.*, p. 30.
28 *Ibid.*
29 *Ibid.*, pp. 30-1.
30 *Ibid.*, p. 31.

Metaxas often worried about the ethics of discussing the Prime Minister behind his back and divulging to the Palace news he had gathered as aide-de-camp to Venizelos. At one point he even suspected that Venizelos was aware of his activities and was shrewdly feeding him with the information he wanted transmitted to the King. Metaxas asked himself: "Are my actions and feelings compatible with my position? The position of aide-de-camp is confidential: but confidential to whom? The Minister of War, or to Venizelos personally?"[31] Metaxas had a ready salve for his troubled conscience. "I have my past, which I cannot renounce. Because of my past, it is my duty to remain loyal to the dynasty. Venizelos knew about this when he appointed me."[32] A single-minded soldier, Metaxas could never forgive the rebel officers who "broke their oath to the King," and could not forget that Venizelos was the expression of the Revolution of the Military League.

"Venizelos is two-faced. On the one hand, he is the Minister of War and therefore the King's adviser; he administers the Army in the name of the King; he supervises all army officers and his duty is to maintain order and discipline in the Army and ensure the Army's loyalty to King and country.

On the other hand, he is Venizelos, the product of the revolutionaries who have turned against the monarchy -- Venizelos himself has turned against the monarchy. He is the representative of the rebel officers who have broken their military oath and renounced their military duties, who have launched the policy which Venizelos continues ....

I am loyal only to the first Venizelos, the Minister of War, the King's adviser. Not to the revolutionary Venizelos, the political leader who was hatched from the Military League.

I am not two-faced ... Faithful to King and country, I serve the Minister of War faithfully; but I reserve the right of freedom of action in connection with the hidden revolutionary aspects of his activities.

Of course my position is delicate. I treat a narrow path ... Any false step makes me a spy or a traitor or disloyal ... It was a mistake for me to embark upon such a morally dangerous road ..."[33]

Venizelos chose Larissa to inaugurate his electoral campaign for a number of reasons. Larissa, the largest agricultural town in the plain of Thessaly, became the visible symbol of the national humiliation of 1897 when it was abandoned by the Greek Army, and it now lay defenseless at the mercy of the Turkish guns across the border. Furthermore, many of the social and economic troubles of the country were more apparent in Larissa than anywhere else: Larissa had the previous March been the center

---

31 *Ibid.*, p. 47.

32 *Ibid.*

33 *Ibid.*, pp. 48-9.

of violent demonstrations by the landless peasants demanding the expropriation of the chiftliks and the distribution of the land to the cultivators. The peasants of Thessaly owed no loyalty to the old political parties of the Greek oligarchy and looked to Venizelos as the new man of Greece, who expressed the ideas and the will of the Revolution of Goudhi, to assure them that their lot would be improved and their lives and possessions protected from the Turkish threat. Starting from Larissa, Venizelos campaigned indefatigably, travelling to many regions of the land, promising a modern and just administration and a strong and prosperous country which could defend her honour and be respected at the conference tables of the Great Powers. Greece had suffered humiliations because of the incompetence and corruption of the previous governments; the army was justified in its rebellion, which had set the stage for national regeneration. A British historian has described Venizelos' campaign as Midlothian; but, as Venizelos gave his campaign the character of a plebiscite, it resembled rather the electoral campaign of General de Gaulle in recent times than that of Gladstone. The old political parties did not contest the elections and exhorted their followers to stay away from the polls. Thus the only choice open to the voters was a yes or no to Venizelos. As it turned out, the old political parties had committed political harikari and were not to reappear on the Greek political scene until 1916, when the conflict between Venizelos and King Constantine came to a head.

Venizelos took the train for Thessaly on 26 November 1910. As the Prime Minister, who was also Minister of War, intended to inspect the local military units, he took his military advisers along with him. For Ioannis Metaxas the journey to Larissa was a nostalgic and often painful return to the past. Metaxas had spent one mortifying year in Larissa after being packed off there to rejoin his regiment, the Engineers Corps, by the rebels of Goudhi. Those had been bitter days and Metaxas could not fail to remember them as the train in which he and Venizelos were travelling sped towards Larissa.

Metaxas shared a compartment with the Prime Minister, and during the journey he spoke to Venizelos on military matters. The Army needed its own strong leaders, emphasized Metaxas. Venizelos replied that the Crown Prince must be reinstated in his former position. "He is the only one we can trust," Venizelos remarked. Metaxas commented in his Diary: "Does he really admire the Crown Prince? Is he really sincere?"[34] In Larissa Metaxas was in attendance when the Prime Minister inspected the troops. "I made numerous notes concerning petitions, personal or administrative complaints, etc. I know from experience that such representations come to nothing in the end."[35] Metaxas noticed how deferential to him the officers now were. "They think

34 *Ibid.*, p. 54.
35 *Ibid.*

I am powerful and they are afraid - their obsequiousness disgusts me," he observed.[36] But he found time to slip away from his round of duties and allow his mind to drift amid a host of memories of the days he had spent in Larissa with his wife.

"I hurried to our former house. My God, what emotions! Within those walls for a few months I lived life to the full. And what a life it was! Happiness, bitterness, fears, joys, eros, altercations! Underlying everything were my efforts to do my duty, to make others happy ... Our narrow street, our walks ... how Larissa united us, my Lela. Memories of you are written everywhere here and they touch my innermost soul."[37]

From the balcony of a local club, while rain fell steadily, Venizelos delivered his first electoral speech to a crowd of several thousand. His style was informal and he spoke in simple language without the rhetorical flights customary with the Greek politicians of his day. The Prime Minister spoke about the heavy taxes that weighed heavily upon the poorer classes and promised a more equitable system of taxation in which the wealthy would pay their full share. Communal institutions would soon be established to replace the old system of local government which fostered corruption and inefficiency. The gendarmerie would be reorganized so that everyone would feel secure in his house. The juridical codes would be revised and a new system of justice would assure every citizen of his rights. The Armed Forces would be completely reorganized on modern lines and for this purpose foreign missions of experts would be invited to assist. Greece, Venizelos said, should turn away from the past and look towards the future and cultivate the friendship of the peoples of the Near East - both her Balkan neighbors and Turkey. Finally, addressing himself to the farmers of Thessaly, Venizelos said that the new Ministry of Agriculture, Commerce and Industry would develop and utilize the productive resources of the country. Emigration, which deprived Greece of many of her young sons, would be discouraged, but not through compulsory measures. The relations of the peasants with the landowners would be regulated by just laws; but Venizelos made it clear to his audience that there was going to be no free distribution of land. The government would purchase the chiftliks as they became available and would then divide and sell the land to the cultivators. Venizelos believed that the right way to solve the agrarian problem of Thessaly was to distribute the land gradually, with full compensation paid to the landowners; the Government was willing to grant loans to the peasants to help them buy their share of the land. Once again Venizelos demonstrated to the Greek people that he was not the radical revolutionary he was reported to be, but a moderate liberal, cautious lest he upset the social status quo and careful not to encroach upon the privileges of the middle classes which, more than any other class, he himself identified with and came eventually to represent. The landless peasants of

---

36 *Ibid.*
37 *Ibid.*

Thessaly were bewildered and disappointed, but the rising bourgeoisie, which would benefit most from Venizelos' reform program, gave him a hero's welcome. Metaxas made no comment in his Diary on Venizelos' speech. "To convey my impressions, I would have to write an extensive psychological treatise," he noted dryly.[38]

The next stop on Venizelos' campaign trail was the Thessalian town of Karditsa. In order to avoid an anticipated confrontation with the peasants, Venizelos did not speak of the agrarian problem. After enumerating the various other aspects of his reform program, he merely added at the end as an afterthought: "We shall also promote a plan which will establish you as small landowners."

"With compulsory expropriation!" a loud voice came from the crowd.

"Voluntary," Venizelos replied.

"Compulsory! Compulsory!" shouted the peasants in unison.

"Voluntary! Voluntary!" called back Venizelos angrily in a stentorian voice, smiting the balcony rail with his fist.[39] In this town too, Metaxas found time to collect his thoughts and remember the past.

"By the evening I was alone and I could recreate in my memory an afternoon which I spent here with Lela; it's almost a year ago now. I was then persecuted, accused of treason; the recollection of that afternoon is still sweet to me, as sweet as Lela's sweet face, which comes to my mind at every step ..."[40]

Three hours later the Prime Minister and his entourage took the train for the seaside town of Volos. Soon after its departure, as the train was about to cross a large bridge, there was a tremendous crashing sound and the train came to an abrupt halt. Apparently an attempt had been made to derail the train by placing an iron bar across the tracks. Luckily the Director of the Thessalian Railways, who was at the controls for this special journey, had spotted the obstruction in time and applied the brakes, thus considerably lessening the impact. Apostolos Alexandris (1879-1961) a minister in the Venizelos cabinet, wrote in his Recollections that Ioannis Metaxas fell on him and that both of them fell on top of Venizelos. Metaxas himself wrote in his Diary that at the time of the crash he was in the washroom. However this may be, on several occasions in later years Metaxas greeted Alexandris with the words: "Do you remember how the Thessalians tried to kill us?"[41] Alexandris noticed that the only time Metaxas studiously avoided the phrase "to kill us" was in 1937, when he was dictator of Greece.

For the remainder of the journey to Volos Metaxas was expounding to Venizelos the battles of Pharsala and Velestino in the disastrous war of 1897. At dinner in Volos, in answer to a question from a local parliamentary candidate, Venizelos said:

---

38 *Ibid.*

39 Apostolos Alexandris, *Πολιτικαί Αναμνήσεις* [Political Recollections] (Patras, 1947), pp. 130-1.

40 Metaxas, *Diary,* II, p. 55.

41 Alexandris, *Αναμνήσεις,* p. 132.

"I understand the role of the King in the State to be an active one. I am of the opinion that, if one of his ministers promulgates decrees with which the King does not agree, the King may refuse to sign them, unless by so doing he would cause a political crisis. But if the government repeatedly insists on such a course, I believe that the King has the right to dismiss the government."[42]

Metaxas, who was sitting opposite Venizelos and could hear everything, commented in his Diary: "In other words, he does not recognize the principle of declared majority (δεδηλωμένη; for details pp. 62, 228). But we shall see what happens later."

The following day there were more political speeches and official entertainment in the town of Chalkis on the island of Euboia. By the time Venizelos and his party took the train back to Athens it was dark. In evocative language Metaxas described in his Diary his feelings during the long night journey.

"Evening was drawing on; the sky was overcast. It was raining and it was getting dark very fast. I had withdrawn into a corner and my melancholy thoughts strayed to my home. How will I find them? Lela's pale, sad face rose up before me ... Night had set in and I was overcome by drowsiness.

Suddenly a man's shouts awakened me. We were at Menidi and the train had stopped. A fanatic was singing the praises of Venizelos. But even in his fanatical, mad declamations, I could feel the vibrations of a hollow pretence." The Greeks are still a nation of slaves.[43]

One of the demands of the Revolution of August 1909 was for the employment of foreign military and naval missions to help in the reorganization and training of the Greek Armed Froces. This was not a new idea. In 1903 Crown Prince Constantine, on a visit to his brother-in-law the Kaiser in Berlin, asked him to send German officers to train the Greek Army. On that occasion the German Emperor declined, but a few years later his attitude was different. In 1908 King George I visited Berlin and in conversation with the Kaiser spoke about the diplomatic efforts of Greece in the Cretan Question.

William II: *Diplomacy is all very well, but you should make sure that you arm yourselves. I shall build you an Army and a Navy.*

George I: *Greece would very much like that. But you are training the Turkish Army. How can the two [commitments] be reconciled?*

William II: *That is my business.*[44]

In 1909 the Kaiser, while staying at the Achilleion, his summer palace on the Greek island of Corfu, received Premier George Theotokis. The two men came to a preliminary agreement that a German Military Mission should be sent to Greece to train the Greek Army. But Theotokis, anxious not to antagonize the other Powers, on whose

42 Metaxas, *Diary,* II, p. 56.

43 *Ibid.,* p. 56.

44 Ventiris, Ελλάς, I, p. 80.

good will the future of Crete depended, requested the Kaiser to delay the matter until the resolution of the Cretan Question. A few months later the Revolution of Goudhi broke out and the whole picture changed. Theotokis was out of power, the Crown Prince was dismissed from the Army and his General Staff dissolved. During the ministry of Stephanos Dragoumis, Colonel Nikolaos Zorbas made the first overtures to France for a French Military Mission to Greece. King George I, fearing that such a reversal of policy was bound to offend the Germans, managed to restrain the rebels and the discussions with France were brought to a halt.

When Venizelos came to power he immediately invited a French Military Mission to Greece to train the Army, a British Naval Mission to train the Navy and an Italian Mission to train the Gendarmerie. The Prime Minister acted without consulting the Palace, as tradition dictated. The Army was by far the most important branch of the Armed Forces and the invitation to the French to train the Army, a task which the Germans had already agreed to undertake, became the subject of heated dispute. The King first learned of Venizelos' invitation to the French from the French newspaper Gaulois. Writing in French on 30 April 1910 to Dionysios Stephanou, the Director of his Political Office, the King expressed his incredulity at the news and his annoyance at not having been informed. George I feared further complications from this action of his new Prime Minister: "By asking France today to give us officers for the reorganization of the Army, we commit our foreign policy to that of France and her allies, something I cannot accept."[45] The Palace was suddenly confronted by a Prime Minister with a will of his own and was uncertain how to deal with him. The King received Venizelos and tried to change his mind:

George I: *Mr. Prime Minister, I beg you not to proceed in this matter. You will cause me family problems. [The King was referring to his German daughter-in-law Princess Sophia and her husband, Crown Prince Constantine.] Then we run the risk of offending the German Emperor. I have already agreed with him to send us German organizers for the Army.*

Venizelos: *I am very sorry, Your Majesty, but the French Mission must come. I need to have a trained army of 100,000 men as quickly as possible. To achieve this I would not mind facing the displeasure not only of Germany, but of France and England as well.*[46]

When Metaxas heard about the invitation to the French Military Mission he offered his opinion as military adviser to the Prime Minister and Minister of War. "I believe the

45 The King wrote: "En demandant aujourd' hui ŕ la France de nous céder des officiers pour la réorganisation de l' Armée, nous engageons notre politique exterieur à celle de la France et de ses alliés, ce que je ne puis admettre." Quoted by Spyros Markezinis, *Πολιτική Ιστορία*, III, pp. 130-1.

46 Ventiris, *Ελλάς*, I, p. 80.

French are not the most suitable," he told Venizelos. "The Germans are the best of all," but they might not succeed because "there is a great difference between them and us."[47] As second-best, Metaxas suggested the Austrians, who "are more used to administering a variety of races, especially the peoples of Eastern Europe."[48] It was particularly painful for Metaxas to have to discuss the relative merits of foreign military experts when he believed that the organization of the Greek Army under the General Staff of the Crown Prince, of which he was a member, had been proceeding smoothly until its work was interrupted by the Revolution:

"I could not tell Venizelos plainly that the best thing is not to send for any foreign organizers at all, because I would have ended up telling him to entrust the organization of the Army to Dousmanis and myself. How could I have possibly told him this? They do not want to recognize it of their own accord."[49] Venizelos tried to mollify his aide-de-camp.

"Rest assured, Mr. Metaxas, that I, too, would have preferred the Austrians. But in the first place, the question has already been resolved by the previous government. Then the international position of Greece, Greek foreign interests, compel us to turn to the Powers of the Triple Entente - there are reasons for this which I cannot disclose to you."[50]

Regarding the Naval Mission, Venizelos thought the choice was between the English and the Americans. He would have preferred the Americans, because this would have made it easier for Greece to purchase two warships from the United States, badly needed to flank the Greek flagship Averoff, already under construction in an Italian shipyard. But the future of Crete was in the hands of Great Britain, the Prime Minister explained. Therefore the invitation for a Naval Mission was sent to London.

"The King, you know, does not want the French. He has no confidence in them. And he insists. At all events, I cannot bring in the Germans. The King worries that the Kaiser will be angry. But, after all, let him be angry! Because, very well, suppose that we do invite the Germans, what will they give us in return? On the other hand, we have the greatest interest in siding with the Powers of the Triple Entente ... The Cretan Question, Mr. Metaxas, rests entirely in the hands of the English. In addition, we are obliged, because of international considerations, to apply to the French ... The French will also help us with the loan."[51]

Metaxas remained unconvinced. He felt that the Army was being sacrificed for the sake of diplomacy. He was, of course, right in believing that wider considerations

47 Metaxas, *Diary*, II, p. 32 .

48 *Ibid.*

49 *Ibid.*

50 *Ibid*, p. 34.

51 *Ibid.*, p. 39.

played their part in the policies of the Prime Minister. Venizelos knew that France and Great Britain were becoming restive over German ties with Turkey; the Entente Powers were beginning to have second thoughts about the time-honoured postulate of upholding "the integrity of the Ottoman Empire." The Greek Premier sensed this gradual change and wanted his country to be an active participant in any developments that might ensue. His invitation to the missions brought an immediate response from France and Great Britain. But the Germanophiles in Athens remained an intractable group, unable and unwilling to follow his leadership. One day in November 1910 Venizelos probed Metaxas concerning the intention of the members of the former General Staff.

Venizelos: *Will our more able officers agree to cooperate with the French? Will those trained in Germany cooperate?*

Metaxas: *We shall do our duty. Whether or not we shall be useful to them depends on them and their ideas. It is not enough that they should be able officers in the French Army; they should have the ability to organize us here.*

Venizelos: *We run the risk that they make a mistake in selecting the right men ...*

Metaxas: *We shall always run that risk when we send for foreign experts.*

Venizelos: I hope the French will be especially careful in selecting their officers. The success of the Military Mission is of the utmost importance to them also. I shall write to our Minister at Paris instructing him to draw the attention of the French Government to this point. It is the only thing we can do."[52]

As soon as the decision to invite the French Mission was announced Metaxas went to see the Crown Prince. Constantine was disturbed about the French. Metaxas did his best to add fuel to the flames.

Metaxas: *I believe that the choice of French organizers was made, from the start, for the sole purpose of limiting any influence Your Highness has in the Army. Zorbas and his friends thought that if German officers were to come they would naturally fall under your influence and, through them you would have regained your authority in the Army. At the same time, if the Germans had been chosen, it would have been impossible to exclude us from the Army, who were trained in Germany ... It was essential for the domestic policy of the Military League to invite foreign experts, especially the French - so that the rebels could fight us, or rather, pass us over, since they themselves were not competent to undertake our work.*

Constantine: *The Kaiser is furious, he speaks in the worst possible terms about us. He has already been transformed into a wild beast over the Averoff affair, because the Kaiser had come to an understanding with Theotokis to lend us the money with which to order our ships in Germany. He also gave to Theotokis the blueprints of the ships prepared for us by the German Admiralty. Theotokis agreed. Suddenly the Revolution*

---

52 *Ibid.*, pp. 51-52.

placed the order for Averoff ... The Kaiser was beside himself; but he was somewhat appeased when the order went to Italy. Now in the matter of the French Mission he will want to kill us with his bare hands!

Metaxas: *But, after all, the Kaiser has no right to complain. Why is he angry now because we invite the French officers when he himself refused to send us Germans?*

Constantine: *In point of fact, this does not seem to be true. The Kaiser had come to an understanding with Theotokis to send us German organizers. Both of them and the King agreed on this. Only Theotokis asked that the matter be postponed until the solution of the Cretan Question.*

Metaxas: *When were these agreements made?*

Constantine: *In 1908 and 1909, in Corfu.*

Metaxas: *Well then, how did Greece dare to break the agreements?*

Constantine: *That is the question. When Theotokis learned about it he protested. The King was then in Corfu and was not aware of the discussions his government was having with France. Theotokis brought him up to date. The King was terribly angry and returned to Athens determined to dismiss the Minister of Foreign Affairs, as well as Zorbas. Ever since then the matter has remained undecided.*[53]

On another occasion Constantine confided to Metaxas that the Kaiser had cabled the German Ambassador in Constantinople, instructing him to assure the Turks that Germany would never agree to any solution of the Cretan Question contrary to Turkish interests. "He is enraged because of the French Mission", Constantine concluded.[54]

Venizelos visited the Crown Prince and tried to impress upon him that the choice of the French was made for reasons of foreign policy. Constantine replied that, from a military point of view, the choice of the French was disastrous. Venizelos, in an obvious attempt to win over the Crown Prince, promised to appoint him Commander-in-Chief of the Army. Constantine feigned reluctance to accept as long as the French were present in the country. Metaxas, who had previously been closeted with the Crown Prince and who had withdrawn on the arrival of Venizelos, now returned to the study and, to his consternation, found that Constantine was attracted and tempted by Venizelos' offer.

Constantine: *What else would you have us do? When the Prime Minister of the country puts it in this way: "The demands of our foreign policy impose the French upon us", how do you want me to respond? We must agree. The question is: as we are, in any case, going to have the French, should we not assist them?*

Metaxas: *By all means; as long as they do not attempt later to blame the Crown Prince for the failure (possible, even predictable), of the French, whom we have*

---

53 *Ibid.*, pp. 40-1.

54 *Ibid.*, p. 61.

chosen not for their ability, but for the demands of our foreign policy. And you must be very careful on this point, because you are not an ordinary citizen, whose personal sacrifice for the common good, even though unfair, is justified. You are the future King. Do not forget 1897. They sacrificed your prestige then, to patch up the needs of the moment. I ask you to examine the present problem in this light and, if it is in your interest, to agree to return to the Army. Because it is not a question of your personal interests, but a question of the interests of the future King of Greece and, therefore, a question of the wider and general interests of the land.[55]

In the early months of 1911 the Second Revisionist National Assembly passed the amendment which allowed the employment of foreign officers in the Greek state. Even before the legal arrangements were completed in late January of 1911, a French Military Mission under General Joseph-Paul Eydoux (1861-1917) arrived in Athens and set to work immediately. Simultaneously France advanced Greece a loan of 110 million gold francs for the reorganisation of the Greek Armed Forces. In late April an English Naval Mission arrived under Rear-Admiral L.G. Tufnell.

Metaxas considered the arrival of the French Military Mission a personal insult to himself and the Crown Prince's Staff, and avoided the company of the foreign officers. He wrote in his Diary:

"Then a whirl of tea parties and soirées began, to entertain the French Mission - the Athenian aristocracy took them up and did not allow them one peaceful day. Using Lela's pregnancy as an excuse, I did not go anywhere and I avoided meeting them. But Eydoux called on me at my office to make my acquaintance. I returned his visit as a matter of etiquette and that was as far as our acquaintance went."[56]

As Metaxas heard from his friend Prince Andrew, the King had said to General Eydoux that he trusted Captain Metaxas completely.[57] Yet Metaxas was not asked to participate in the reorganization of the Army and the exclusion rankled. All the work he had done as a member of the dismantled General Staff of the Crown Prince was already forgotten, while all shortcomings and errors in the Army were conveniently blamed on the ousted officers. He wrote in bitter mood:

"It does not matter, let the Army go its own way. Such has ever been the fate of all real fighters .... We opened the way, we laid the foundations ... we suffered the hostility, the abuse, the persecution. Now others come who find the ground prepared and because they do a little work they reap the praise for all that was done before .... Ξενολατρεία [admiration of all things foreign opposite of Xenophobia], jealousy

55 *Ibid.*, p. 50.
56 *Ibid.*, p. 68.
57 *Ibid.*

jealousy and flattery are qualities that do not make great fighters - or small. The future will justify me."[58]

Because they would not make use of his services he gradually abstained from any matter pertaining to Army affairs. "They want complete French domination over the Army; therefore away with us."[59] As things stood, "I have no future before me hope for promotion none. From the French the greatest possible rejection."[60]

He expected the French Mission to fail. "When the hour comes they will remember us," he wrote, and busied himself with his domestic affairs and military studies. "And I prepare myself for the future, when my hour will come again."[61] Sometimes he despaired and talked of resigning from the Army and finding some other kind of occupation. To resign would be to revenge himself on the ungrateful state which had ignored him:

"What a revenge! The state? The state does not want me and shows it by so many humiliations. The motherland? I shall never cease to serve her and when the need arises I shall serve her with my life. But I need my revenge. I know how they will take it, how downcast their faces will become: because my resignation will be a blow against the regime they have created, against their system, and against the way they have treated us."[62]

But Metaxas did not feel dejected: "Inwardly I am calm. I have a sense of my own worth and I know how to wait."[63]

The reinstatement of Constantine in the Army was no easy matter. The Crown Prince had been accused of incompetence because of the mortifying defeat of 1897. He had been accused of nepotism for installing his several Royal brothers in commanding positions in the Army. He had been accused of favouritism for surrounding himself with men like Ioannis Metaxas and Victor Dousmanis, who publicly proclaimed that they owed their highest allegiance to him alone. Constantine was impressionable and easily succumbed to persuasive arguments from advisers like Metaxas. Because of his brusque, autocratic ways, the Crown Prince had succeeded in offending many Greek officers. An admirer of his brother-in-law William II, he shared some of the highhanded and tactless manners of the German Emperor. When Venizelos first went to visit him the Crown Prince burst out into an indignant tirade against the Prime Minister.

"I regret that for so long you have thought it unnecessary to come to see me, but have waited until this official occasion to do so. You even deemed it unnecessary to

58 *Ibid.*, p. 76.
59 *Ibid.*
60 *Ibid.*, p. 76.
61 *Ibid.*
62 *Ibid.*, p. 78.
63 *Ibid.*, p. 77.

visit the King before you became Prime Minister and even then you confined yourself to signing the visitors' book. You Greek politicians continually distrust the Royal Family, or rather, you seek to represent to the world that you distrust the Royal Family to gain the support of the rabble."[64]

But Venizelos recognized the Crown Prince's military talent and wanted him to return to the Army - not in an administrative capacity, which would have caused great anxiety among the officers, but as a prestigious figurehead and an able and effective Commander-in-Chief. Constantine was a tall, handsome, imposing figure, who carried his authority well. Although impatient and abrupt with those he considered officious and self-seeking, he was also disarmingly unaffected and spoke to the men in the ranks both as fighting general and comrade-at-arms. This human touch endeared him to the soldiers, who saw in him a friend and protector from the scheming politicians and the ambitious officers. The Crown Prince bore the name of the last Byzantine Emperor and was the living symbol of the Megali Idea; in the minds of the Greek people his name was indissolubly linked to the most cherished dreams of the nation. Venizelos was well aware of Constantine's abilities and popularity and wanted him to return to the Army. To those who were inclined to question the wisdom of such a policy, he would quietly observe: "The Greek people, the soul of the Hellenic Nation, have from time immemorial desired their monarchs to be warrior-kings."[65]

On 27 June 1911 the Second Revisionist National Assembly passed an amendment creating the post of Inspector-General of the Army and bestowing it upon the Crown Prince. With shrewd calculation, Venizelos left this controversial measure for the final days of the Assembly's life. His desire to reinstate Constantine was not shared by all the delegates. During the long and heated debate in the National Assembly there were bitter attacks on the bill. A deputy pointedly warned Venizelos: "Have you ever reflected, Mr. Prime Minister, what consequences for the constitutional government and for the public life of the country might follow the return of the Crown Prince from the battlefield at the head of a victorious army?"[66] There was widespread indignation among many officers and Venizelos was accused in the Press of having sold out to the Palace. But the Prime Minister was not to be deflected from his purpose; he made this issue a vote of confidence for his Government and the amendment was passed.

Constantine was now Inspector-General of the Army, but the power and authority of Commander-in-Chief still eluded him. A few days after the passing of the amendment on 26 July 1911 Metaxas went to see the Crown Prince to offer some advice on the subject. The people, Metaxas explained, although not against the Crown Prince personally, preferred him to remain outside the Army -- in this way the country would

---

64 *Ibid.*, p. 42.
65 Ventiris, *Ελλάς*, I, p. 83.
66 *Ibid.*

not be divided by dissension. "Because the Greek people are timid and nobody wants to put himself in danger for his ideas or principles. They would rather sacrifice their principles for the sake of peace".[67] The officers distrusted him, Metaxas informed the Crown Prince; they were afraid that if he returned to the Army he would take his revenge for what he had suffered at the hands of the Military League. The Crown Prince should make an effort to win the officers' trust. He should visit the camps, talk to them, be friendly towards them and grasp the hands even of the most revolutionary.
Constantine: *Kritsas I will never greet!*
Metaxas: *You must and shall greet him, Your Highness. You are not going to become a friend of anyone; you are going to appear to be a friend.*
Constantine: *My hand ...*
Metaxas: *You can wash your hand later, if you think it has been contaminated. When you have secured the Army in your favour, you will have the people with you, too. Then later, if you have not been able in your soul to forgive certain persons, you may strike them down, but only when you are certain that they will be completely destroyed, not otherwise. And not because of the League: your excuse will be different. You need diplomacy to govern our Army; because you are not dealing with men of character, but weak, wavering men, men who care only for their own interests.*
Constantine: *I know it; these are the men I have to command. I have to take them as they are.*
Metaxas: *The attitude of the French towards you, directed as it is by the dictates of French diplomacy, makes things more difficult. French diplomacy is trying to establish its influence in the Army so that it can be used against any government not following French policy. The French Mission is an instrument of French diplomacy. Because the Crown Prince is considered the representative of German ideas and the expression of the truly Greek character of the Army, the French will try to undermine his position. There is nothing left for you but to abstain from every activity in the Army; you should avoid any friction with the French and you should not take part in their work in any way.*
Constantine: *Of course, this is what I shall do. I shall withdraw completely.*
Metaxas: *Not completely. You will perform frequent inspections. But the purpose of these inspections will be for you to come into close contact with the officers and attract them to you. You should show no antagonism towards the French; on the contrary, you should praise them, but without taking any part in their work. In this way you will often see the officers informally and make friends with them ... When you have won over the Army to your side, then you can do whatever you wish - I mean, you will not then need an official position: you will be like a leader of a Military*

67 Metaxas, *Diary*, II, p. 80.

League, but a disciplined League, under a natural authority. What government would then dare to oppose you? Then, without any rights deriving from laws or regulations, you can impose on any government whatever you desire.[68]

Then Metaxas advised the Crown Prince to appoint rebel officers to his Military Office, to dispel any lingering suspicion that Constantine still harboured any animosity towards the Revolution.

Constantine: *Do you mean to say that I should appoint none of you?*

Metaxas: *None. What do you want us for? Us you have always. If you need the services of any one of us, you have only to summon us to your side. Is it necessary to be present in your office in order to serve you?*

Constantine: *I know that.*[69]

Crown Prince Constantine listened attentively to this lesson in Machiavellian politics delivered by the sage Captain Ioannis Metaxas and promised to act accordingly.

A few months later, early in October 1911, the Greek government received reports of Turkish troop movements along the northern border. Venizelos asked his chief military advisers what action Greece should take.

Metaxas: *Immediate mobilization.*

Venizelos: *I am of the same opinion. I will on no account accept the slightest humiliation of Greece. I only regret that this has happened now; in two and a half years time we shall be ready for them.*[70]

The Prime Minister was anxious over the selection of a Commander-in-Chief in case of war. His military adviser had the answer ready.

Metaxas: *The Crown Prince.*

Venizelos: *If only Eydoux were willing to accept the command!*[71]

Metaxas was taken aback. "I marvelled at his simplicity and his ignorance of the qualities that make a Commander-in-Chief".[72] Metaxas thought that Venizelos was afraid of Constantine returning victorious from a war. Like all Greeks, Metaxas thought, Venizelos suffered from ξενολατρεία -- he too was dazzled by foreigners. "Without doubt, Venizelos is a man of great worth, of will-power and great talents, but he is no military man -- he ignores even the rudiments. And this is natural. Anyway, Venizelos has, relatively speaking, a broader range of thought of all those who are now in power and he is the least envious."[73] Metaxas acknowledged the abilities of General Eydoux, especially in the administration and training of the Army, but he did not think

---

68 *Ibid.*, pp. 81-82.
69 *Ibid.*, p. 82.
70 *Ibid.*, p. 88.
71 *Ibid.*
72 *Ibid.*
73 *Ibid.*, p. 89.

Eydoux was made of the stuff of which Commanders-in-Chief were made, "especially under the difficult circumstances prevailing in Greece."[74]

Two days later, on 5 October 1911, Venizelos invited Metaxas to confer with him again. Apparently the bilateral agreement with the French government on the French Mission forbade General Eydoux to take an active part in wartime with the Greek forces. Once more Venizelos consulted his aide-de-camp about the choice of a Commander-in-Chief. Metaxas wrote in his Diary: "I insisted that only the Crown Prince is suitable for the post. I told him that, if there is going to be war, it will be a question of life or death for the nation and that the Greek dynasty will naturally share the fate of the nation".[75] Even if it were a defeat, Venizelos remarked, but a glorious defeat, it would strengthen the dynastic position of the Crown Prince. Venizelos continued: "But I cannot suggest to the King that he appoint the Crown Prince as Commander-in-Chief. In matters like this the government has no right to make suggestions. If the King comes to that decision by himself, I shall accept it."[76] It soon became apparent that the Turks had not mobilized to invade Greece, but to protect their European province from an Italian threat after the Tripolitan War between Turkey and Italy had broken out on 28 September 1911. Still, the Turkish mobilization on the northern borders of Greece put pressure on Venizelos to make up his mind on the choice of the future Commander-in-Chief of the Greek Armed Forces. Ioannis Metaxas played no small part in helping the Prime Minister arrive at his decision.

The false alarm arising from Turkish troop movements on the northern border of Greece in the early autumn of 1911 proved beneficial to Metaxas in one respect: Venizelos came to appreciate Metaxas' military expertise, his clarity of thought in practical matters, his grasp of military strategy. The Chief of Staff was then General Sapountzakis, whose incompetence was notorious from his performance in the 1897 war; Venizelos was afraid to dismiss him because of the General's connections with the Military League. During the crisis on the northern border Venizelos ignored General Sapountzakis and relied instead entirely upon his aide-de-camp. Metaxas wrote in his Diary

"He often asked to see me and consult with me and seemed very pleased with the way I clarified matters for him and thus made it easier for him to arrive at decisions. I came to be virtually the Chief of Staff because the official Chief only came to confuse him with idle chatter. Every time we approached mobilization Venizelos talked of dismissing him; but as soon as things quietened down he abandoned the idea."[77]

---

74 *Ibid.*

75 *Ibid.*, p. 92.

76 *Ibid*, pp. 92-93.

77 *Ibid.*, p. 93.

The crisis not only proved Metaxas' value to Venizelos, it also helped Metaxas to see Venizelos in a more favourable light. Venizelos had upheld the institution of the monarchy and had worked in close cooperation with the King. Venizelos had reinstated the Crown Prince in the Army. Venizelos had restrained the radical reformers and made certain that the social status quo would not be disturbed. Venizelos, far from being a tool in the hands of the rebels, had proved to be the only Greek politician capable of controlling them and restoring Army discipline. Finally, Venizelos had demonstrated that he had confidence in Metaxas' abilities. "I became indispensable to him," Metaxas noted with gratification in his Diary.[78]

In October 1911 the Greek Parliament debated the matter of the King's lengthy summer holidays, which he spent outside the country every year. George I used to say in jest that throughout his long reign in Greece he had never unpacked the luggage he had brought with him from Denmark in 1863. Every summer he would shun the torrid climes of his adopted land and eagerly head north to seek relief in the cool, elegant spas of Western Europe where he was a familiar and popular figure among the vacationing Royal Families, all of them related to him by blood or marriage. But the Danish-born King had a natural aversion to the Germans, and when visiting his relatives in Denmark he would regularly make a patriotic detour to avoid travelling through Germany although, after the marriage of his son to the Kaiser's sister, he was occasionally obliged to visit his Imperial in-laws in Berlin.[79] In Greek Royalist circles it was claimed that the King's close ties with the crowned heads of Europe was an asset to a small improvenished country like Greece. But the deputies of the Greek Chamber who came to Athens in the wake of the elections of December 1910, the majority of them merchants and lawyers, severely criticized the King's custom of abandoning the country for several months a year and spending the tax-payers' money abroad, although Greece had provided him with a number of sumptuous palaces and villas. While the King was away the controversial Crown Prince Constantine acted as Regent and, rather than have any dealings with him, the government of the day often held back current business, preferring to wait for the King's return.

Prime Minister Venizelos spoke twice during the debate on the King's travels. Metaxas, recording his impressions of Venizelos' first speech in a letter to Prince

---

78 *Ibid.*

79 King George I felt all the bitterness of a Dane towards the Germans because of the German annexation of Schleswig, Holstein, and Lauenburg in 1864. To make matters worse, the Kaiser professed an admiration for Islam and appeared to flaunt his friendship with Sultan Abdul Hamid II, under whose despotic rule an enourmous number of ethnic Greeks lived. The Germans trained and organized the Turkish Army to fight Greece, opposed Greek claims to Crete, and never showed any concern over the persecutions of Greeks or other Christian minorities in Turkey. George I even had a grawing suspicion that the Germans wanted him put out of the way and the pro-German Crown Prince Constantine, the Kaiser's brother-in-law, installed in his place.

Andrew, wrote that the Prime Minister was not crystal-clear in his attitude towards the dynasty. "If it had been me, I would have said frankly that I was mistaken in fighting the King."[80] But when Metaxas read the Prime Minister's second speech, in which Venizelos wholeheartedly defended the King's lifestyle, all his reservations concerning Venizelos were swept away. In a long psychological appraisal of the Cretan, Metaxas shrewdly described the gradual transformation of Venizelos from a "revolutionary" to a "conservative" spokesman of the established order.

"I realized instantly that Venizelos is a great man. And I believe that he is sincere in his dealings with the dynasty. He has, of course, burned his boats. And I reproached myself because for so long, and especially in the beginning, I had misgivings about him; still, after closer scrutiny, I can see that I was not then much off the mark. Venizelos did not possess from the outset the disposition he exhibits today. He, too, began with distrust and duplicity ... Gradually the wielding of power and the daily contact with the King made him conservative; it is, after all, in his nature to be conservative and if he had not had a confrontation with Prince George in Crete, Venizelos would have been one of our most conservative politicians. This confrontation and its consequences aroused rage in him and his natural malice -- because he is malicious and harbours feelings of vindictiveness. All these feelings were exacerbated by his poverty and by a sense of injured merit, conscious as he was of his great worth (αξία) and seeing the incompetent and the undeserving enjoying the rewards of a higher social position. He was studious and still very young and was very much influenced by the radical trend of our age. As a young man he must have read widely and, like many a young intellectual, he was very radical. These youthful sentiments surged upwards ...

His life here, however, and his position as Prime Minister helped him to calm down. He met and better understood men and affairs. Getting to know the rebels, getting to know their opponents -- especially us, the younger men - illumined many things for him and he understood how slippery was his course and how impossible for him it was to build anything with the incompetent rebels and their ideas. He could also perceive that envy and hatred were dominant motives of the Revolution. He could see that the beleaguered edifice [of the old regime] had great virtues.

He therefore realized that he must rechart his ship's course -- I believe he realized this a long time ago, even before he became Prime Minister. When he did become Prime Minister, although he had already come to a decision to change course, he would not come out and say so openly and irrevocably. He was thinking that if he should fall from power he could assume his familiar role of revolutionary and thus he wanted to maintain a certain degree of contact with the members of the Military

80 Metaxas, *Diary*, II, III.

League and their ideas. However, events turned out to be stronger than him. Both obliged and desiring to rule, and to rule with a firm hand, to reform the entire structure of the state, to impose discipline upon the army, to raise the prestige of government, to raise the prestige of the army, to reorganize the army, to train the army, to reorganize the other branches of government and staff them with the right personnel; finally, obliged to and desiring to administer the country, he inevitably clashed with the demagogues and the intellectual anarchists, who criticize everything and everybody, and the undisciplined, envious, incompetent officers: but all these same officers were the vital force behind the Revolution of Goudhi; he thus clashed inevitably with the essence of the Military League and consequently with the Revolution itself.

In the beginning he chose to strike down only those individuals who opposed him and to defend the Revolution. His course was erratic and often he tacked to and fro. But these things were interconnected. Each time he struck down an individual, more rebels defected to the opposition and the more the Revolution disintegrated.

Thus Venizelos came to recognize that he had to follow definitely and unreservedly the road of the conservatives. His daily contact with the King dispelled his old doubts about a sincere and fruitful cooperation with His Majesty. On the other hand, the opposition of the rebellious elements angered him and provided him, little by little, with successive opportunities for a gradual separation from them.

This separation has, in fact, already occurred. His speech in the second debate revealed this completely. Venizelos has broken away from the Revolution and will be a strong pillar of the dynasty and a conservative and strong-willed ruler. Now it is up to the King to handle him skillfully."[81]

Metaxas was too singleminded to appreciate the many-faceted aspects of Venizelos' political personality. Venizelos was neither a revolutionary in the sense Metaxas perceived him to be, nor the conservative that Metaxas thought he was becoming. The complexity of Venizelos' character bewildered many an observer of Greek politics and often puzzled and intrigued even his closest associates. Once a friend sought the truth from the horse's mouth.

Friend: *What are you, Mr. Prime Minister? A conservative or a liberal? A reactionary or a socialist? A royalist or a republican?*

Venizelos: *My dear fellow, I am all of these things combined. I am each one of these things separately at the moment when I think I should be. I am simply a politician.*[82]

On 8 April 1912 (26 March according to the Old Style, Easter Monday for the Greek Orthodox Church) the traditional Easter Military Parade took place. Ioannis Metaxas

81 *Ibid.*, pp. 95-6.

82 Tasos Vournas, *Ιστορία της Σύγχρονης Ελλάδας, 1909-1940* [History of Contemporary Greece, 1909-1940] (Athens, 1977), p. 16.

described in his Diary how at the start of the Parade, the King, mounted on horseback in full dress uniform, was applauded by the people in front of the Zappeion, while the Crown Prince was hastening to place himself at the head of the First Regiment "amid the hysterical cheers of the crowd." The King, the Princes, the officers mounted on their proud steeds, accoutrements glittering in the brilliant sunshine of an Athenian spring day, were resplendent in their colorful uniforms and plumed helmets. Metaxas wrote:

"I myself was directly behind the King and could see everything. I saw Venizelos in morning dress, on foot, drenched in sweat, standing in line with the spectators ... which saddened me; and I hurried and, through Pallis, had the King issue an order for Venizelos to stand by his side, on his right, apart from the crowd. But then the contrast was even greater .... And I reflected that Venizelos' spirit must be mortified; because he must have wanted to be the hero of the day. And I asked myself: what is he really thinking? And I expected that something of this would erupt later."[83]

Sure enough, the day after the Parade Metaxas happened to be in the Prime Minister's office when the Foreign Minister Ioannis Gryparis called to see Venizelos on routine business. At the end of the interview Gryparis reminded the Prime Minister to attend the reception to be held that evening at the Crown Prince's Palace in honour of the Orientalists, who were then holding a conference in Athens. The Orientalists, from many countries, were scholars of the Ancient Orient -- the presentday Near East. Constantine himself was no mean student of Byzantine history on which he would converse with informed enthusiasm. The Foreign Minister then added that Crown Princess Sophia had already departed for Corfu where her brother the Kaiser was spending the summer. This news was a real slap in the face for Venizelos. The arrogant Princess so much resented what she regarded as the humiliation of her husband at the hands of the Military League that she had left Athens rather than remain and be compelled to extend an official welcome to Venizelos and shake hands with the rebel officers accompanying him. Metaxas described the Prime Minister's reaction to the news: "Venizelos was visibly enraged, the blood rushed to his face, his eyes became wild, he was bereft of speech."[84] Gryparis, on seeing this display of emotion, feigned anger himself - "I am certain that he was feigning," wrote Metaxas -- and added emphatically in French: "Ah! C'est inqualifiable! C'est inqualifiable!"[85] Finding the scene too painful, Metaxas left the room. Venizelos, as so often in his career, used the press to get even with his enemies. That same day, unknown to anyone, he asked a journalist friend named Simos to visit him. Next morning the Venizelist newspaper Πατρίς in a leading editorial lashed out at Princess Sophia. "I confess I did not expect this turn of events," Metaxas noted in his Diary. "Perhaps this is a brilliant way to

83 Metaxas, *Diary,* II, p. 105.

84 *Ibid.*

85 Ibid., p. 106

handle the matter from the point of view of party politics, but I find it cowardly."[86] The other Venizelist newspapers took up the campaign, which shocked many people. Metaxas wrote that "the whole world was scandalized by the Prime Minister's attack on Princes Sophia."[87] Metaxas, who was disposed to admire Venizelos as long as the Prime Minister supported the monarchy, immediately regarded such an unthinkable attack on the Crown Princess as the first step in the imminent downfall of the liberal leader. "The Capitol Hill is too close to the Tarpeian Rock", he wrote in his Diary, "and the twenty-fourth of March is too close to the tenth of April."[88] The Capitol was the seat of government and power in Ancient Rome and the Tarpeian Rock (no longer in existence) was a peak on the Capitoline Hill from which traitors were hurled to their death. The twenty-fourth of March was the day of the Elections when Venizelos had triumphed and the tenth of April was the day on which Venizelos had launched his attack on Princess Sophia, the day, according to Metaxas, when "the Venizelist star began to fade."[89] Metaxas discussed this incident with the Crown Prince, but neither could fathom Venizelos' motives. Metaxas suspected that the actual reason was the recent swing of public opinion towards the monarchy, "and this worries Venizelos because he has never felt the ground of royal favour firm enough beneath his feet."[90] Venizelos' thoughts, according to Metaxas, must have been something like this: "The interests of the monarchy and of the nation require that Princess Sophia extend a hand of reconciliation to all persons, male or female, who represent the regime that came out of the Revolution. In a word, she should not appear injured, but full of hope for the work he is accomplishing."[91] This was a valid thought, Metaxas conceded, but the feelings behind it "are not those of a great man ... Because Venizelos has great powers of logic, but he does not search deep within himself, or within others. He does not stand above himself. Then, he does not control himself either, and he has a temper, too. Well, he flared out!"[92]

Since her arrival in Greece as the bride of Constantine in 1889 Crown Princess Sophia had been at the center of the pro-German faction among the ruling circles of the Greek capital. She never approved of the sunny, child-like aspects of the Greek character, which she considered frivolous, but the German Princess liked the earnest Ioannis Metaxas, who spoke her native language fluently, and affectionately called him Yiannakis -- Johnny. Regal and forbidding both with those around her and with her

---

86 *Ibid.*
87 *Ibid.*
88 *Ibid.*
89 *Ibid.*
90 *Ibid.*, p. 107.
91 *Ibid.*
92 *Ibid.*

children, she was popularly known in Athens as "Frau Verboten." Sophia took a keen interest in the affairs of her adopted country and in the personal interests of Constantine, to whom she was completely devoted. Because of her ambition and the influence she exerted upon the Crown Prince, Sophia was a force that every Greek politician had to reckon with. Constantine first met Sophia when he was invited to the Imperial Palace and decorated by her father, the Emperor William I while the Crown Prince was still a student at the Berlin War Academy. For the two young people it was love at first sight and they resisted all pressures from Greece and Germany against their union. George I, who did not care for the Germans, was dismayed; Charilaos Trikoupis, the Greek Prime Minister at the time, who had been working for closer relations between Greece and England, was much chagrined. Bismarck was against the marriage because, as he pointed out to the Kaiser, Germany "had not and could never have any interests in common with Greece so long as England held the supremacy of the sea."[93] Sophia's brother the Kaiser, who had recently succeeded to the German throne on the untimely death of his ailing father, had other plans for his only sister and was outraged. Aloof and distant with his mother the Dowager Empress Victoria (eldest daughter of Queen Victoria) the young Kaiser now came into conflict with his sister. When Sophia on her own initiative adopted the Greek-Orthodox faith out of her deep regard for Constantine, the Kaiser indignantly forbade his sister to set foot on German soil, a prohibition which in later years he allowed to lapse.[94] But, as there seemed no way of keeping Constantine and Sophia apart, all the parties concerned put on the best face they could at the wedding celebrations, which took place in Athens with great pomp and circumstance, attended by many European Royalties. Sophia's mother the Dowager Empress had arrived in Athens early for the wedding. But the Kaiser sailed to Greece on his yacht only one day before the wedding and declined to use the mansion which had been specially prepared for him, preferring to stay aboad in the Bay of Phaleron. On the day of the wedding the Kaiser appeared on the balcony of the Palace (the present-day Parliament building in Constitution Square) but instead of waving to the cheering crowds like the other dignitaries, he stood stiffly at attention and saluted the Acropolis in Prussian military fashion; the Greek populace was much impressed. It was rumored that during the festivities he behaved to Premier Trikoupis with all his customary hauteur. The union of the two Royal Houses in no way caused German foreign policy to become more favourable to Greece. The Kaiser remained consistently anti-Greek, insisting during the 1897 war that Greece should "beg" for peace and demanding that an International Commission be set up to ensure that Greece paid indemnities to Turkey

93 Major George M. Melas, *Ex-King Constantine and the War* (London, 1920), p. 231.

94 It was not necessary for Princess Sophia to change her religion. The Greek Constitution required that only the issue of the Greek Royal Family be baptized into the Orthodox Church. King George I remained a devout Protestant until his death.

and also the interest on foreign loans.[95] Crown Princess Sophia exerted a strong life-long influence on her husband and could lead him in any direction that she wished.

The German Foreign Office was quick to take advantage of the position of the German Princess. In 1909 the Kaiser sent as German Minister to Athens Baron Hans von Wangenheim, the former German Ambassador in Constantinople from 1899 to 1904, a redoubtable Prussian of gigantic stature and booming voice, entrusted with the assignment of guiding and protecting his master's only sister. The Baron kept a vigilant eye on the interests of his ward, often bullying and intimidating the Greek officials in Wilhelmian fashion. It was believed in Athens that Wangenheim disliked George I intensely and wanted him removed so that Sophia's Germanophile husband would succeed to the throne. For his part, George I feared and distrusted the Baron. When the revolutionaries of Goudhi invited the French Military Mission, the King was despondent. He complained to the diplomat Kallergis: "Then there is nothing left for me to do but abdicate. What will my position be vis-a-vis the Germans? Will it be a sufficient excuse to tell them that I was not consulted? I must abdicate." Kallergis tried to play down the German reaction, but the King would not be comforted. "You do not know what Wangenheim is really like."[96] The German newspapers often violently attacked George I, reiterating that Greek-German relations would not improve as long as he was alive. These relations would only improve when Constantine succeeded to the throne, with his "German iron fist." Constantine could not be deceived by certain officers as his father had been by the rebels of Goudhi. Showing such extracts one day to a Greek minister, George I kept repeating, "You see! This is Wangenheim speaking."[97]

Sophia, egged on by Baron von Wangenheim, made no attempt to conceal her implacable hatred for the rebels of Goudhi, who had heaped humiliations upon Constantine, calling him incompetent and blackmailing his father to dismiss him from the Army. Neither could the Crown Princess ever forgive Venizelos, who had associated his name with the Revolution, becoming the spokesman for the rebels, and who was now the arbiter of her proud husband's fate. Sir Francis Elliot, the English Minister at Athens, commented on the activities of Wangenheim in his annual Report to the British Foreign Office in 1910.

"The Baron, I fear, confirms her Royal Highness the Crown Princess in her irreconcilable attitude towards the party of reform, whom [i.e. Venizelos] she identifies with the leaders of the military movement of 1909, which she cannot forgive.

---

95 Interestingly enough, the Kaiser was to become the grandfather of another German-born Queen of Greece, Frederika, mother of the deposed King Constantine II of the Hellenes and Sophia, the present Queen of Spain.

96 Pericles Argyropoulos, *Απομνημονεύματα* [Memoirs] (Athens, 1970-71), I, p. 124.

97 *Ibid.*, p. 125.

Neither she nor apparently her Imperial Brother realize the necessity for the reigning dynasty here of passing a sponge over the distasteful events of that year."[98]

The quarrel between Crown Princess Sophia and Prime Minister Venizelos in the spring of 1912 and the ensuing scandal threw into sharp relief Sophia's obdurate and unyielding personality; her hostility towards Venizelos was one of the important factors that led to the National Schism between the Liberals and the Royalists three years later.

In Corfu the Kaiser learned of the newspaper campaign against his sister; but he dismissed any suggestion that a pro-royalist newspaper should be instructed to undertake her defense; instead he extended an invitation to Venizelos to visit him in Corfu. Prince Andrew told Metaxas that the Kaiser was reported to have said that since Venizelos was the Prime Minister and the way things looked was likely to remain so for many years, it would not do for enmity to exist between Sophia and Venizelos and that it was in the best interests of all concerned to dispel any ill-feeling. Up to this time the German Emperor had ignored Venizelos; neither had Venizelos, as Constantine observed to Metaxas on another occasion, ever expressed a desire to meet the Kaiser, who was a regular visitor to Corfu. Of all the Greeks, the Emperor preferred the society of George Theotokis, the Corfiote politician and aristocrat known for his German sympathies, Georgios Streit, a university professor and diplomat of German ancestry, and other royalist politicians. From Corfu King George I cabled Venizelos, who was vacationing at Zagora on Mount Pelion in the company of Arthur Bourchier, the Balkan correspondent for the London Times. The German Emperor, said the King, wished Venizelos to be presented to him; the Kaiser, he added, would make no mention to the Prime Minister of the Averoff; this was the warship the Kaiser had wanted the German firm of Krupp to build for the Greek Navy, but which Venizelos had already ordered in Italy. The German Chancellor Theobald von Bethmann-Hollweg (1856-1921) had criticized Wangenheim to the Kaiser for his open hostility to Venizelos. The Kaiser now wished to meet the Greek Premier and, for the sake of his sister, extend an olive branch.

On 30 April 1912 Venizelos and Metaxas took the train from Athens to Patras en route for Corfu. At first the two men spoke little to each other, absorbed as they were in their newspapers. Metaxas was reading the ultra-conservative Kreuz-Zeitung. Then Venizelos sought Metaxas' advice on the military preparedness of Greece; Metaxas, in his turn, questioned the Prime Minister on the country's foreign policy. At the time Venizelos was secretly negotiating the Treaty of Alliance with Bulgaria, which was to develop into the Balkan Alliance, so his answer was general and guarded. The Prime Minister and his aide-de-camp lunched in Patras and in the evening boarded the steamship Korinthia, bound for Corfu. Venizelos had cabled in advance, requesting that there should be no official welcome on his arrival, but a great crowd had gathered on

98 Quoted by Papacosma, *The Military*, p. 224.

the quay to applaud the Prime Minister. Metaxas commented in his Diary: "When we disembarked, the enthusiasm and the cheers of the populace were most lively. But after my first impression had faded, I realized that their fervour was due more to their hatred of Theotokis than to their admiration for Venizelos."[99] Venizelos and Metaxas took rooms at the St. George Hotel in the town of Corfu. That evening King George I gave a dinner at Mon Repos, the Royal summer villa, in honour of the visiting Prime Minister. In his Diary Metaxas noted with gratification that he also had been invited. "They all lavished attention upon me. I could sense their friendly disposition towards me."[100] After dinner, according to Metaxas, Venizelos "was in no mood for sleep -- out of sheer joy because Princess Sophia had spoken to him at length."[101] So the two men went for a long evening walk by themselves. Venizelos was in high spirits. He observed: "Now, when the leaders of the Opposition hear that the Princess spoke to me for so long, they will have no other resource but to kill themselves." Metaxas assured the Prime Minister that no opposition to him existed -- his opponents had no prestige.

Metaxas: *Theotokis and Rallis are spent as public figures, while the rest are of no value at all.*

Venizelos: *What of Gounaris?*

Metaxas: *Gounaris has no authority - his head is in the clouds. He has neither the will nor the perseverance nor the merit [αξία] of a statesman.*

Venizelos: *What about Zaimis?*

Metaxas: *He has no combativité - a great limitation for a statesman.*

Venizelos: *And yet, Mr. Metaxas, I should have very much liked to have a strong leader of the Opposition, someone who would defeat me after two years, because a man in public life is vitiated by staying continually in office. He has no time left for intellectual pursuits. He must be relieved for a certain period of the burders of office and from the tasks which, in a parliamentary system, crush the spirit of a statesman in office.*[102]

The next day, after inspecting the local garrison at the Castle, Venizelos went to see the Kaiser at his summer villa, the Achilleion. This was an ugly palace built in 1890 by Empress Elizabeth of Austria and named after her favourite Homeric warrior.[103]

---

99 Metaxas, *Diary,* II, p. 117.

100 *Ibid.*

101 *Ibid.,* pp. 117-8.

102 *Ibid.,* p. 118.

103 *Ibid.* Empress Elizabeth of Austria was a tragic figure. She married Emperor Franz Josef I of Austria and was the mother of Crown Prince Rudolph, the hero of Mayerling. She met a violent end in Geneva at the hands of an Italian anarchist in 1898. In Corfu Elizabeth studied the language of the islanders and spent her time translating Shakespeare's plays from English into Modern Greek with, it must be added, considerable assistance from her literary tutor, the Greek author Constantine Christomanos. The grounds of the Αχιλλείον [Achilleion] were adorned with marble statues of Sophocles, Euripides, Plato, Aristotle and other Greek philosophers and poets. The

While Venizelos was being entertained by the Kaiser, Metaxas wandered alone through the narrow streets of Corfu, trying to recapture the two happy years he had spent there twenty years before -- "my youth", as he expressed it. Now he was a happy family man, as he described himself in the Diary -- "nevertheless, the past has a melancholy charm."[104] At 2:15 in the afternoon he went to visit his friend Prince Andrew. The Prince, his wife Princess Alice of Battenberg, her sister Princess Louise, and Prince Christoforos were waiting for him. For the next three hours Prince Andrew himself drove the party around the resorts of Corfu. During the journey from Athens Venizelos had indicated to Metaxas that his position in the coming debate on the bill for the reinstatement of the Princes in the Army would be easier if the King signed the decrees for the promotion of certain army officers. Metaxas now explained this to Prince Andrew and asked him to remind His Majesty to sign these decrees.

In the evening Metaxas met Venizelos and immediately asked him for his impressions of the Kaiser. Venizelos was presented to the Kaiser at noon and talked with him until one o'clock. At one they sat down to "breakfast." Venizelos was seated on the Kaiser's left, while Crown Princess Sophia sat on the Kaiser's right. During the meal the Kaiser encouraged them to speak to each other.

Venizelos: *I knew that he wanted to bring us together. He said to me: "My sister is interested in the preservation of forests, you should support her, and you should communicate with her on matters of that nature."*

Metaxas: *What subjects did you discuss?*

Venizelos: *Various subjects. He spoke to me at length about labour problems in Germany; then about Corfu and its inhabitants.*

Metaxas: *What about the Cretan problem?*

Empress was a fervent admirer of the German Jewish poet Heine, a statue of whom she had placed in a kind of shrine. But most important of all was a statue of the dying Achilles, wounded in the heel. When Emperor William II bought the Achilleion he at once banished Heine (the Kaiser had an aversion to the Jews) and replaced the recumbent Achilles with another statue depicting the Greek hero as a War Lord, armed with gilded helmet, shield and spear, poised triumphant in victory! The first object now to catch the eye of the approaching visitor, whether he arrived by land or sea, was the glittering Achilles. Neither Empress Elizabeth nor William II were noted for their artistic taste, and the Palace is something of an eyesore, but the views from the windows and terraces are of unparallelled beauty. The Kaiser bought the Achilleion in 1905 and spent two months there every summer. The March of 1914 was the last time that he came. The Palace has now been converted into a hotel and casino. In Michael Pratt's Britain's Greek Empire (New Jersey, 1978), Photograph No. 108 shows one of the Kaiser's houseparties at the Achilleion in 1913. Photograph No. 109 shows sailors from the Imperial Yacht "Hohenzollern" assembling the pieces of the bronze statue of Achilles, which was cast in Berlin in 1909. The statue bore the inscription: "To the Greatest of the Greeks from the Greatest of the Germans".

104 *Diary*, II, 118

Venizelos: *Nothing. Only in jest, "As you cannot annex Crete, it might be as well if Crete annexed you and sent you civil servants and army officers to conquer you. Then you could say to the Turks - "What can we do? It is not our fault; they annexed us."*
Metaxas: *What did you reply?*
Venizelos: *Thus, "As you see, Your Majesty, a beginning has been made, because I, the Prime Minister, am a Cretan." As he was being jocular, I thought I could not talk to him seriously on the subject.*
Metaxas: *Did you discuss politics generally?*
Venizelos: *Absolutely nothing.*
Metaxas: *Did he ask you about our army - did he tell you anything?*
Venizelos: *Nothing, not a word.*[105]

Metaxas gained he impression that the only reason the Kaiser had invited Venizelos was to placate him. "As the government newspapers had made so much noise about Princess Sophia's insults to Venizelos, the Kaiser invited him, entertained him, made much of him, decorated him and thus disposed of him."[106] Metaxas and Venizelos left Corfu on Friday, 4 May 1912 and arrived in Athens on Saturday. On Sunday the Kaiser entertained to breakfast Venizelos' rival, George Theotokis.[107]

Back in Athens Venizelos instructed the Public Prosecutor to order the arrest of Stephanou, the publisher of Πατρίς, for his articles attacking Princess Sophia. When he was being led to prison, Stephanou asked his captors to allow him to call at Venizelos' house as he had something confidential to impart. The police officers, who knew of the close association between Venizelos and the publisher, acquiesced. The Prime Minister was having lunch with his son Kyriakos and his secretary Klearchos Markantonakis. Stephanou explained that he was being detained because of a leading article in Πατρίς -- an anonymous article, the author of which was in fact Venizelos.
Venizelos: Ah, yes! I am sorry I neglected to inform you in time.
Stephanou: *But they're taking me to gaol!*
Venizelos: *I know, but what do you want me to do? I happen to be the Prime Minister and I can't very well go to prison myself. But don't worry. I shall make sure that the whole affair will soon blow over.*

On instructions from Venizelos, Stephanou was permitted to serve his sentence in his own house and after one month he was granted a pardon.[108]

At the close of 1910 Metaxas had reviewed the year just past: the persecution he had suffered from the Revolution of Goudhi; the difficulties of adjustment with his wife in

---

105 *Ibid.*, p. 119.

106 *Ibid.*

107 *Ibid.*

108 George Pesmazoglou, *Το Χρονικόν της Ζωής μου, 1889-1979* [The Chronicle of my Life, 1889-1979] (Athens, 1979), pp. 49-50.

the first months of his married life. But now his fortunes had improved: he had returned to Athens; he had become aide-de-camp to Venizelos; the love and understanding between him and Lela was now perfect and complete; his relations with his wife's family were improved; his sister Myrianthi had married; the friction that had existed at first between his mother and his wife was now no more and, to his great satisfaction, his mother had come to stay with them for a long visit; he had also given permanent shelter in his house to his sick brother Costakis. Finally, after the distressing episode of his banishment to Larissa, he had set up house in Athens and he and his wife had begun to receive visitors and entertain friends. Metaxas was certain that he owed all these blessings to God alone. On 13 August 1911, his first wedding anniversary, he wrote:

"This evening, lying in the orchard of my house, I reflected on my situation. My Mother's future is provided for, at least during my life-time. Myrianthi is provided for. Costakis is provided for. Even if I die, Mother and Costakis will not be destitute: Myrianthi will not allow it. I hope Lela will not allow it, either, for my sake. As far as finances are concerned, we are comfortably situated. Of course, there are still many matters in my life that are unresolved and, if I close my eyes or slacken my grip on the helm, I may be faced with many problems; but I hold the wheel steady and I keep my eyes open. I do not attribute this to my own efforts. I feel that God has protected me, and that whatever I have accomplished was from God."[109]

But life had not been easy for Metaxas; especially during the first year of his marriage when he was "persecuted" by the rebels of Goudhi, when he was banished to Larissa. Both John and Lela Metaxas possessed strong, dominant personalities and in the early days of their marriage they experienced many stressful moments. Although many lines and passage in the Diary concerning his relationship with his wife have been crossed out, enough remains to indicate some of his emotional strain and his determination to make his marriage successful.

"I was patient and persevering. From the depths of my afflictions I often raised my eyes to God. There were moments when I was transported and my soul would depart from this world and would feel God. It was as if I were passing through bright clouds and then, but only for a fraction of a second, I would feel within me the infinite: this was my prayer and God helped me to struggle and to submit. .... sometimes I would be seized with uncontrollable fury ... then, every time my soul would be withdrawn into the infinite, I would realize my mistake. I would go, seething with rage, to the church and there, rapt in solitary prayer for a few moments, I could perceive my fault. Then I would correct it. Often I erred and sinned. But on the whole, in all my actions,

109 Metaxas, *Diary,* p. 84.

I sought to do good. If my passions and my vices have not allowed me to be perfect, may God forgive me and redeem me."[110]

Now Metaxas was "a happy family man" and devoted much of his time and energy to his family. Once married, he put behind him the amorous adventures of his youth for good and remained until his death a loving and faithful husband. There were no limits to which he would not go to comfort his wife and to make her happy. His reward was the lifelong companionship of an affectionate comrade and wise confidante. His life centered around his family. All his thoughts and feelings, his disappointments and hopes, he shared with Lela. He not only constantly gave her friendly advice, but also in his turn listened to her and heeded her counsel. He had no close men-friends and, if not claimed by official duties, he always chose Lela's company. His letters to his wife are as informative as his Diary and are often useful in filling in the gaps during the periods when he neglected his daily entries. Together they went to art exhibitions, to concerts, to the theater, to cafés and restaurants. He opened his heart to Lela and had no secrets from her. Once when she was indisposed Metaxas sat by her bedside and comforted her. "The afternoon wore on as I read to her the old volumes of the Diary ... What memories! What memories! I am so happy to make my Lela a partner of my past."[111]

In mid-October 1911 Madame Metaxas felt the first signs of the imminent birth of their first child. Metaxas noted in his Diary: "A new period of our common life is beginning. It will probably be a girl. Let the child be healthy in body and mind, and it is no matter which it is."[112] On 31 October his wife gave birth to a daughter. The father suppressed his disappointment. "I had hoped it would be a son. The [dowry] settlement for a daughter frightens me. But let the child be healthy in body and mind and God is great."[113] In the evening, three hours after the birth, the proud father noted in his Diary: "My wife and my daughter are resting now."[114] It was customary to name a child after one of the grandparents. Metaxas' mother was called Eleni or Helena; but as his wife bore the same name, Lela, a diminutive of Helen, they decided to christen their infant daughter Anna, after his mother-in-law. "Will Mother be offended?" Metaxas wondered. Apparently the old antagonism between the two mothers revived, so a few days later the parents settled upon the name Loukiani or Loukia because the girl had been born on St. Luke's Day. Metaxas affectionately called her Lulu. "She looks like me," he wrote happily a few days later. "How much I could write about this child! I watch her all the time with pride. Full of life and health, she fills our home with joy and

110 *Ibid.*, p. 64.
111 *Ibid.*, p. 109.
112 *Ibid.*, p. 90.
113 *Ibid.*, p. 97.
114 *Ibid.*

our hearts with kindness."[115] In December they had the christening. It is usual for the bridegroom's best man -- his Koumbaros -- to be the first to be invited to act as godfather to the children of the marriage. Metaxas' best man was Constantine, so he thought that "if the Crown Prince were the godfather it might be useful to Loukia in the future. After much thought I proposed it to him and he accepted with pleasure, with great pleasure."[116] The ceremony took place in their house. Constantine brought along his son, Prince George, the future George II. Metaxas and Lela did not invite any relatives in order to avoid any publicity and to protect the Crown Prince from the gossipers. It was a quiet family affair. A bishop officiated at the Sacrament of Baptism. "The ceremony was most beautiful," Metaxas wrote in his Diary.[117] The little girl throve and grew ever more delightful in the eyes of her father. "My Loukia is wonderful and I am crazy about her. I waste hours on end with her."[118] During the Metaxas dictatorship Loukia became a familiar figure, marching at the head of the Girl Falangists through the streets of Athens.

Metaxas' devotion as husband and father did not lessen his devotion as son and brother. When he returned from Germany in 1903 he had gathered his family around him in Athens, where he served first with the General Directorate of the Army and then as a member of the Crown Prince's General Staff. His gentle, aristocratic father died in his arms on 8 October 1905. Six years later, on the anniversary of his father's death, Metaxas visited the cemetery in the afternoon and remained by his father's grave until 6:20 in the evening, the exact time that his father had drawn his last breath. He had wanted to do this for many years, but had been prevented by the demands of his work, by his banishment to Larissa and by army manoeuvres. Metaxas loved his father deeply and his visit to the grave was an emotional and cathartic experience.

"For a long time I lived again in memory our common life. I remembered, one after another, all the incidents during those years we lived together: our common joys, our common tribulations. I thought of the friendship which united us, his perfect courtesy, his kindness, his love for me. And I felt remorseful that during his last years I could not devote more of my time to him, and could not show him more love and more attention. Sometimes I even displayed harshness towards him. And at other times, in the distant past, I behaved to him as Peter did to Jesus. But the thought comforted me that I often gave him great pleasure and that I loved him sincerely. I remembered the moment of his death; and I was saddened by the thought that I have not sacrificed myself for Mother and Myrianthi, and I wept and wept unceasingly. I remembered all,

115 *Ibid.*
116 *Ibid.*, p. 98.
117 *Ibid.*, p. 99.
118 *Ibid.*, p. 112.

all my sins and I begged for forgiveness."[119] When Metaxas accused himself of not having "sacrificed" himself, he meant that he had not remained unmarried until after the marriage of his sister. He now vowed to redress the wrong he had done Myrianthi by providing the dowry he had promised on her marriage. And he was comforted by the reflection that he had made provision for his mother and his sick brother and that he was good to his wife and child.

"I am a mixture of good and evil, of self-sacrifice and egoism; as a man I am weak, but I fight against evil: and the good prevails within me. I do not feel proud of the good I have done because I consider it to be my duty. I feel humble because of the evil I have done. My tears and my humility comforted me. I left the graveside a better man and resolved to work for the good of my whole family."[120]

Metaxas did not fare badly in the turmoil and upheaval that followed the Revolution of 1909. After a year's banishment in Larissa, he was back in Athens and once more in favour; as aide-de-camp and chief military adviser to Venizelos, he found himself near the center of power and had a unique opportunity to observe the tactics of that masterly politician. Venizelos' primary reason for appointing Metaxas to a post near himself was to reconcile the former General Staff of the Crown Prince and the Palace with the rebels of the Military League. Metaxas was appointed by Venizelos, but he was not a Venizelos man; emotionally he belonged to the King and the Crown Prince. Intellectually he often admired Venizelos, but his heart remained steadfast in its loyalty to the Palace.

Taking advantage of his unique position, Metaxas made himself indispensable to both Venizelos and the Royal Family. As both sides wished for a rapprochment, both used him as a liason to relay messages that could not be transmitted through normal channels of communication. Known before the Revolution only as an officer on the Staff of the Crown Prince, he now became better known to a wider circle of important people, both military and civilian. Venizelos and the King alike realized his usefulness and appreciated his military talents. In January 1911 Metaxas noted in his Diary: "With Venizelos I am on the best of terms ... but what really pleases me is that I enjoy the respect of the King."

---

119 *Ibid.*, p. 94.
120 *Ibid.*

The Balkan Wars I

The massacres and other atrocities committed by the Turks in their efforts to suppress the Greek War of Independence that broke out in 1821 provoked an outcry in Europe which was often translated by the European Powers into a demand for reform in the Ottoman Empire. In time, even in Turkey, some enlightened Turks clamored for reform as the only way to ensure the survival of the Empire.

The first attempt of the *Tanzimat,* the Reform Movement, was made on 3 November 1839 by the proclamation of the Hatti Sherif de Gülhane. This firman of Sultan Abdul Mecit promised security of life, honour and property to all Ottoman subjects. It was followed, seventeen years later, by a new firman, issued on 18 February 1856 at the conclusion of the Crimean War. This was the famous *Hatti Humayun* which gave assurances, if not of brotherhood and liberty, at least of equality among all citizens of the Ottoman Empire, Moslem and Christian alike.

Behind the fine words there was neither the intention of reform nor any recognition of reality. When twenty years later the Balkan peoples revolted against their Turkish rulers the bashi-bazouks in Bulgaria alone razed to the ground 67 villages, sold into slavery the women and children and crucified all male inhabitants. This was the occasion for Gladstone's well-known pamphlet on the atrocities in Bulgaria.

The only achievement of the Reform Movement was to destroy the millet system according to which the various nationalities had been governed since the coming of the Turks several centuries before. Now that all the subjects of the Sultan were "equal citizens", they were also "Ottomans", that is Turks -- and their conversion to Islam and to the Turkish identity was the ideal towards which the Ottoman state was directing its efforts.

The Young Turks, despite their initial proclamations of universal brotherhood, proved in their attitude towards the non-Turkish peoples of the Empire to be no better than the old regime which they sought to modernize. The only difference lay in their increased efficiency and ruthlessness fostered by the new spirit of Turkish nationalism. The Adana massacres in April 1909 of thirty thousand Armenians who had protested the Turkification policies of the Young Turks had a sobering effect upon the Balkan states, as Gueshov, the Bulgarian Premier (from November 1911 to June 1913), related in his memoirs The Balkan League. Throughout the Nineteenth Century the Greeks, the Bulgarians, the Serbs, and the Romanians had been vowing to free from the Turkish yoke their "unredeemed" brothers. Now the Balkan states began to fear that if the Young Turks had their way there would be very few of their brethren left to liberate.

The ignominious 1897 War between Greece and Turkey showed the Balkan peoples the futility of their small armies challenging the might of the Ottoman Empire. Eleftherios Venizelos, the new Prime Minister of Greece, had been advocating (as early as 1886 when a young lawyer in Crete) an alliance of the Christian Balkan states against Turkey. As soon as he had put the Greek house in order, he sent messages to the Bulgarian Premier Gueshov proposing a defensive alliance between the two countries. The Bulgarians knew that Crete was a constant cause of tension between Greece and Turkey and did not want, by signing a treaty with Greece, to precipitate matters because of Crete, in which they were not interested. Instead, the Bulgarians opened negotiations with Serbia, which, like Bulgaria, was alarmed by the Turkish mobilisation in Macedonia. The Turks mobilised because they feared an Italian invasion of their territories in the Balkans after Italy had invaded Tunisia and annexed the Dodecanese.

But Greece held in her hands a card which made her indispensable in any Balkan alliance and the Greek Prime Minister often reminded the Bulgarians of this. Greece alone among the Balkan states had a navy which could effectively prevent any Turkish reinforcements from reaching Macedonia from Anatolia. On 27 April 1912 the Greek Minister at Sofia presented a draft defensive treaty to Premier Gueshov. On 29 May the two parties appended their signatures. Bulgaria signed similar agreements with Serbia.

In the summer of 1912 there was widespread unrest in the Balkans. On 21 July the Young Turks fell from power and the new Government dissolved the Turkish Parliament by force and proclaimed martial law. The Albanians rose in revolt. In the Aegean the island of Samos took up arms against the Turkish garrison. There were sporadic Turkish massacres of Serbs and Armenians in Macedonia and of Greeks in Thrace and Asia Minor. Anti-Turkish sentiment was running high. The Bulgarians asked the Greeks to admit the Cretan deputies to the Greek Parliament and proclaim the union of Crete and Greece.

Venizelos, who was the first to air the idea of a Balkan alliance, was not anxious to be the first to ignite the flames of war. Both friends and foes warned him that the moment Greece attacked Turkey, the lives and property of hundreds of thousands of Greeks in the Ottoman Empire would be placed in the gravest peril. Furthermore, the Greek Prime Minister, whose closest associates had severely criticized him for signing the treaty of alliance with Bulgaria with no reference to Greek territorial claims in the Ottoman Empire, feared Bulgarian designs on Macedonia and Thrace and hoped that some provisions for the future frontiers between Greece and Bulgaria could be made in the military convention between the two countries. In August 1912 Venizelos often discussed with Metaxas the military convention and the eventual division of the conquered territories in the case of a successful war.[1] On 25 August 1912 Koromelas, the Greek Minister of Foreign Affairs, on instructions from Venizelos, cabled Panas, the Minister at Sofia.

---

1 Metaxas wrote in his Diary: "Venizelos sends a message about Bulgaria--discussion with him on questions concerning the [military] convention and distribution [of conquered territories]. Metaxas, *Diary,* II, p. 130.

"In connection with the military convention it is imperative that we negotiate territorial matters and other benefits which each state will demand at the conclusion of the peace. But on this point, which is extremely delicate, it is possible that every understanding will break down, especially if the negotiations are conducted with the secret intention that no mutual concessions be made. Force of circumstances will oblige Bulgaria to take military action towards Adrianople, leaving as a field of action for Serbia the Kosovo vilayet. Bulgaria will make concessions to Serbia which will extend as far as Skoplje. It is necessary for us to find out if these concessions have been made, and, if so, to what extent. The same force of circumstances will leave Salonica, Monastir and Serres to Greece. Bulgaria will want us to make concessions on the questions of Thrace, Adrianople and the coast east of Kavalla, and therefore in return she will finally be prepared to agree to Florina, Vodena, Salonica and the district of Serres falling to our share. Thus the lands which are inhabited by solidly Greek populations, that is, to the west of the great curve of the River Maritza, will be exempted from the Bulgarian conquests. You are not to communicate the above to the Bulgarian government."[2]

Panas met with Premier Gueshov, who impressed upon him the gravity of the situation. On 27 August he cabled the Greek Minister of Foreign Affairs.

"I have spoken privately with the Prime Minister. The Russian Note [for peace] has been ignored by Bulgaria. Bulgaria and Serbia are determined to fight against Turkey. Gueshov assured me that Serbia is eager for the war to break out."[3]

As soon as Venizelos received this telegram he called a Cabinet meeting - on 29 August 1912. The Regent, Crown Prince Constantine, presided. The Prime Minister earnestly addressed the Cabinet:

"The Treaty of Alliance with Bulgaria is defensive and therefore we are not obliged to go to war. But Bulgaria and Serbia have decided on war and have asked us to join forces with them. If we remain neutral one of two things will happen: either the Slavic States will win and the Greek frontier will be set permanently at Melouna [the Olympus Passes in Thessaly]; or Turkey will win and Hellenism will be lost forever; not to mention that in the second case Russia will accuse us as traitors to the Christian cause ... I believe we should act, even without an agreement on future territorial gains."[4]

The Cabinet unanimously decided on war; Constantine was foremost in his support of the Prime Minister. "One could see in him the man who wanted to blot out 1897," Venizelos said later. Venizelos requested Constantine to take over as Commander-in-Chief of the Army. He also appointed General P. Danglis, a Venezelist sympathetic to

---

2 Kordatos, *Ιστορία*, V, p. 286.
3 *Ibid.*, p. 285.
4 Ventiris, *Ελλάς*, I, p. 96.

the Revolution of Goudhi, as Chief of Staff. But Constantine picked his Staff Officers himself. Prominent among them were Colonel Victor Dousmanis and Captain Ioannis Metaxas.

Later that day, while Metaxas was getting ready to write to his wife, Venizelos' carriage arrived to take him urgently to the Prime Minister. In his letter to Lela the following morning he explained the reason for this unexpected summons.

"It concerned a most important question of foreign affairs, connected with the direction of the Ministry of War and the General Staff ... I cannot write what it was all about, because if the letter goes astray, a most important matter of state is jeopardized. I shall tell you in person when I come."[5]

At once Metaxas remembered the wounds he had suffered in the past at the hands of the Military League and could not contain his bitterness. He wrote to his wife:

"They have forgotten that they expelled me from the General Staff, that they called me incompetent, unbalanced, and the like. Venizelos has now made me virtually Undersecretary to the Minister of War [Venizelos] and Chief of Staff."[6]

Metaxas immediately called in the Heads of Departments and the Staff Officers, many of them his erstwhile enemies, and issued the orders of the Minister to them. He wrote to Lela:

"Let not the idea cross your mind that all this made the slightest impression on me. I only feel like laughing at the comic side of the situation .... Well, today the Ministry is at work. Not me, of course: I supervise it from above. Calm and order ."[7]

Venizelos, in consultation with the Crown Prince, selected Metaxas to go to Sofia to negotiate the military convention with the Bulgarians. A few days later, on 5 September 1912, Metaxas wrote to his wife that he was "ordered to prepare for departure to Bulgaria ... Matters have reached the razor's edge; they have entrusted the fate of the State to my hands." Once again Metaxas made a great show of reluctance at being drawn into the center of affairs, belying his true feelings of gratification and excitement. He told Lela that he had tried to avoid the commission, that he detested honours and rewards, that the only thing he wanted from life was to be with her: "But what could I do? We have no one else to apply to. The State calls upon you. What could I do? Noblesse oblige ..."[8] Again his old grudge came to the surface: "They are all relying on me. They knew me but until this moment they did not need me; when the storm is over they will forget me again."[9]

---

5 Metaxas, *Diary*, II, p. 142.
6 *Ibid.*
7 *Ibid.*, p. 143.
8 *Ibid.*
9 *Ibid.*, p. 149.

In preparation for his journey to Sofia, Metaxas renovated his uniforms, bought new ones, had his sword sharpened, his buttons and decorations polished, bought new suits, a top hat, a soft hat, ties and gloves, patent leather military shoes, American leather civilian shoes, boots - all at public expense. He was especially happy with his new hatbox: "At last my hatbox has arrived -- exceptional! It takes the top hat, the two low-crowned hats, two uniform caps, the plume in its case and there is still some room left. You will admire my hatbox."[10] The Foreign Minister urged him to purchase everything he needed without regard for expense. He also handed him quite a handsome sum of money and advised him to cable if he should need more. "Excellent fellow, this Koromelas!" wrote Metaxas to Lela. "Perhaps the only advantage of my journey is that I shall refurbish my wardrobe without paying for it out of my own pocket."[11] On 14 September 1912 he attended a meeting presided over by Venizelos. Also present were Koromelas, Minister of Foreign Affairs, Stratos, Minister of the Navy, Danglis, the Chief of Staff and Nider, Director of Personnel at the Ministry of War. Metaxas wrote jauntily to Lela, "... my eminence explained to the rest how he is going to act. I also read them my plans and we agreed on them."[12] Two days later he was to confer again with the Foreign Minister and the Crown Prince: "As you see, I have become a great man, an important personage," he wrote dryly.[13] Further down he wrote in ironic vein, "I have become a diplomat, I should wear a monocle."[14] But he still insisted that what would really give him pleasure would be to be near his family. This was not to be, however. "Man proposes, but Young Turks, plus Old Turks, plus Venizelos, plus Bulgarians, plus ... plus ... disposes."[15]

There were several reasons for Bulgaria's sudden eagerness to conclude the treaty of alliance with Greece. Turkey, threatened by the preparations for war in the Balkans, was resigned to the loss of Tripolitania and was prepared to sign a peace treaty with Italy. This released the Turkish armies, which were now massed in Thrace on the Bulgarian frontier. On 25 September 1912, the day after Metaxas arrived in Sofia, the Turks announced large-scale military manoeuvres in the plain of Adrianople. By 5 October the military convention between Greece and Bulgaria was signed in Sofia. The convention which Panas and Metaxas negotiated for Greece provided that in the event of war with Turkey, Bulgaria would take the field with an army of at least 300,000 men and Greece with at least 120,000 (Article 1). Greece would also contribute her Fleet; the convention stipulated that "The chief aim of the Greek Fleet will be to secure naval

10 *Ibid.*, p. 153.
11 *Ibid.*, p. 148.
12 *Ibid.*, p. 151.
13 *Ibid.*, p. 152.
14 *Ibid.*
15 *Ibid.*

supremacy over the Aegean Sea, thus interrupting all communications by that route between Asia Minor and European Turkey." (Article 2).[16] Each party undertook not to conclude an armistice for more than 24 hours, nor to open negotiations, nor conclude a peace treaty, without the consent of the other (Article 3).[17] But the convention went beyond military matters. The original defensive treaty of alliance between the two countries was now extended to cover an attack on Turkey if the two contracting parties agreed. If one of the parties attacked a third state other than Turkey, the other party was bound to observe a friendly neutrality. The Greek representatives now also succeeded in modifying the limitations of the alliance concerning the Cretan Question. Article 6 of the military convention provided that

"If, after Bulgaria and Greece have mobilized or commenced a joint war, the latter country should find itself obliged to settle the Cretan Question in accordance with the wishes of the inhabitants of Crete, and, in consequence of that action is attacked by Turkey, Bulgaria undertakes to assist Greece ..."[18]

As in the case of the treaty of alliance, no mention was made of the division of the spoils of war and the future frontiers of the two countries. The convention was signed on 5 October 1912 by Gueshov and Fitchev for Bulgaria and Panas and Metaxas for Greece. Metaxas saved the blotting-paper on which the signatures were dried as a souvenir for his wife. Immediately after the signing of the convention, General Fitchev invited Metaxas to the Headquarters of the Bulgarian General Staff, where the two men conferred on their strategy for the coming war. In the evening Metaxas was at the Greek Legation. It was 2:00 a.m. when he got back to his hotel; but before retiring he sat down to write to Lela: "All concluded today. We signed. It was a ceremonious moment. I shall relate everything to you when I come."[19]

On 30 September Bulgaria, Serbia and Montenegro mobilized their armies. The same day, the orders of mobilization for the Greek Army were issued. On 1 October Metaxas wrote to his wife, who was vacationing on the island of Tenos:

"Return immediately to Athens .... otherwise you may never be able to return because the sea will be closed to civilian shipping ... It is now a matter of war on land and sea."[20] *"This simultaneous mobilization of the four states is an event of great historical significance ... A magnificent spectacle ... I, too, have played some part in this history."*[21]

---

16 Gueshov, *The Balkan League*, p. 132.
17 *Ibid.*
18 *Ibid.*
19 Metaxas, *Diary*, II, p. 172.
20 *Ibid.*
21 *Ibid.*, p. 169.

Before leaving the Bulgarian capital on 8 October 1912, Metaxas was presented to King Ferdinand. His mission was secret and when a Hungarian correspondent for some German newspapers sought him out and asked him if he were Colonel Metaxas, he laughed it off. "Unfortunately I am no such great person. I am a simple *secretaire de légation, de passage à Sofia,*" he replied.[22]

From Sofia Metaxas went by train for a short visit to Belgrade to consult with the Serbians on their military plans. It had been agreed that the General Staffs of the Balkan Allies were to act independently, but they undertook to inform each other on the movement of their troops. Bulgaria had already signed a treaty of alliance with Serbia, but Greece did not enter into a formal alliance with the Serbs. There were no conflicting interests between Greece and Serbia, and Metaxas' task in Belgrade was easier than it had been in Sofia. After Belgrade Metaxas took the train to Trieste where he boarded a ship for Piraeus.

The preparations for war in the Balkan Peninsula caused great alarm in Europe. The Great Powers were not only divided into two opposing alliances, there were also strong antagonisms within each camp. A vague apprehension was in the air that any gain made by a Balkan nation in such a war might unduly enhance the prestige of a rival Power. Austria did not want Serbia, the protégé of Russia, to be enlarged; Russia did not want Albania, the protégé of Austria, to be enlarged; Germany did not want the German-trained Turkish Army to be defeated; neither did Great Britain want Turkey to be weakened, which would leave the Straits vulnerable to Russia and threaten the legendary "route to India." Russia was resolved that no other nation should threaten Constantinople and therefore did not want Greece, the country with the most legitimate claims on the ancient Byzantine capital, to be enlarged; neither did Italy, who had just occupied the Dodecanese and aspired to an Italian Empire in the Eastern Mediterranean, want Greece to be enlarged. A pervasive fear circulated in the chancelleries of Europe that a spark in the Balkans might start a general conflagration that would envelop the whole continent -- a fear that was, alas, realized two years later. Russia, Austria, France, and Great Britain especially, attempted to prevent the Balkan states from starting a war whose consequences might lead to an incalculable and terrible sequel. At that time none of the Great Powers was ready to take the field -- except, perhaps, Germany; and, alone among them, Germany seemed to believe that a Balkan war would clear the air and bring peace and stability to the strife-ridden Peninsula.

In 1912 King George I of the Hellenes was, as usual, spending the summer in Western Europe. Venizelos cabled him, explaining the gravity of the situation in the

22 *Ibid.*, p. 167.

Balkans and requesting his immediate return. The King telegraphed back from Copenhagen on 26 September:

"Through Panas and the Bulgarian representative in Athens make every effort to stop the mobilization. Do not forget the peaceful Note from Russia. It is too difficult to consider the concentration of Turkish troops in Andrianople as provocation for war. Bulgaria should ask for explanations from Turkey on the reforms. If no such explanation is forthcoming, let Bulgaria initiate action and we shall follow later.... I am departing immediately and I shall travel via Paris and Vienna to be informed."[23]

King George was known for his pacific inclinations and Venizelos was determined that the King on his arrival should not meet any diplomatic representatives or any other persons before he himself had spoken to him. Boarding a motor torpedo boat at Piraeus, the Prime Minister sailed through the Corinth Canal to the Corinthian Gulf, where he awaited the arrival of the King. On 9 October 1912 Amphitrite appeared in the Gulf and the King and his Prime Minister met at sea on board the Royal Yacht. King George did not share Venizelos' enthusiasm for the coming war. He remembered how the Bulgarians had deceived Trikoupis in 1891; he remembered the Greek debacle of 1897. Yet another disastrous Greek adventure might well mean the end of his own dynasty. The King listened to the Prime Minister, but remained pensive.

Venizelos: Your Majesty! The Nation is ready and it is assisted by Allies. We shall win! We shall be in Salonica in fifteen days. Very soon we shall have the anniversary of fifty years of your reign. We shall celebrate it with a Greece double its present size.

George I: *Do not say that, Mr. Prime Minister.*

Venizelos: *Why not, Your Majesty? We have the military strength. I repeat, in two weeks we shall be in Salonica. We shall be the first to enter the city.*

George I: *Impossible! Austria wants Salonica.*[24]

The Prime Minister spoke with fervour and enthusiasm about the war and the benefits from it that would accrue to Greece.

George I: *But when I met the Emperor [Franz Josef of Austria] last week I promised him that it would not be war.*

Venizelos: *I am very sorry about this promise, but Your Majesty, travelling at the time, was not aware of the full details of the situation, the commitments of your Government, and the enthusiastic support of the whole Nation, for the policy of finishing once and for all, together with the allies of Greece, with Turkish misrule and freeing their brethren from an intolerable yoke.*

George I: *All right, let us go on, with God's help. I am entirely at the disposal of the nation. Put me anywhere you think I may be of service to my beloved people.*[25]

---

23 Kordatos, *Ιστορία,* V, p. 288.

24 Ventiris, *Ελλάς,* I, p. 102.

25 Demetrius Caclamanos, "Balkan Reminiscences," *The Slavonic & East European Review* 16:46

Edouard Driault, in his Histoire Diplomatique de la Grèce, alleges that Venizelos threatened King George with the words: "Your Majesty, it is either war or your crown."[26] By the time the Royal Yacht reached Piraeus, Venizelos had convinced the King that war was inevitable. The King had brought with him from Vienna the good news that the Austrians did not intend to attack the Serbs; had the Austrians attacked the Serbs, the Serbian Army would have been forced to turn northwards, leaving the whole Turkish Army in Macedonia free to fight the Greeks. Night had fallen when the King and the Prime Minister arrived at Omonoia Station, but the crowds were waiting patiently to welcome them. Standing in the dark on the Palace balcony, the elderly King with some difficulty read a simple address to his people by the flickering light of a candle held by one of his sons.

By the time Metaxas reached home from his Balkan mission the whole of Greece was under arms. As soon as the telegrams of 30 September 1912 announcing general mobilization arrived, the church bells of every town and village, every remote island and mountain hamlet rang out unceasingly, summoning the young men to join the struggle. The response of the people to the coming war took on the character of a national crusade. Within five days mobilization was complete; but still Greek volunteers from Crete, the Turkish-held Aegean Islands, Macedonia, Thrace, Anatolia, Cyprus, Egypt, from the numerous Greek communities in Europe and the New World, found their way to Greece to fight for the colors, their number exceeding thirty thousand. The mother country also summoned her young sons from the United States, and as many as fifty thousand American emigrants answered the call, many of them paying their own passage. An old photograph shows a group of Greek-American volunteers drilling in Athens in the shadow of the Temple of Olympian Zeus, still wearing the sedate dark overcoats and bowler hats in which they had disembarked after the trans-Atlantic crossing. A few patriots brought their motorcars with them and offered their services as drivers. It must have been both touching and amusing to see a colonel being transported to the field of battle by an enthusiastic Greek expatriate from Manchester or Marseilles or Chicago who could speak hardly a word of the tongue of his forefathers. A war fund collected nearly 200 million drachmas, mostly from Greeks of the Diaspora. Some of the wealthy donated one quarter of their entire property. Simple folks, with nothing else to contribute, gave their gold wedding-rings and wore steel ones instead. There were also many non-Greek volunteers, philhellenes from Italy, France and England, who were later organized into a special brigade, the Garibaldians; they wore red shirts and fought under the command of General Garibaldi, a grandson of the famous Italian leader. Twelve trains made the journey every day

(London, July 1937), pp. 115-6.

26 Edouard Driault et Michel Lheritier, *Histoire diplomatique de la Grèce de 1821 à nos jours*, V, (Paris, 1925-26), p. 76.

along the single track from Athens to the border town of Larissa, carrying men, horses and mules to the front.

Metaxas barely had time to hand over the documents of the military convention he had brought from Bulgaria, stow away his diplomatic wardrobe (including the magnificent hatbox), collect his campaign equipment, bid farewell to his family and head for the front. The General Staff had already moved to Larissa and Metaxas joined them on 17 October, the day before the Army advanced. Major-General Danglis, the Chief of Staff, was a genial, acquiescent man, who was content to leave all the real decisions to the Commander-in-Chief Crown Prince Constantine and his Staff of younger officers. The Director of Operations was Colonel Victor Dousmanis, an able and forceful officer, stocky and dour. Next in seniority came Captain Ioannis Metaxas, by all accounts the most perceptive of them all, the brains of the General Staff. When strategy was discussed it was Metaxas who surveyed the map spread out before him; when orders were issued it was Metaxas who wrote them. Also attached to the General Staff were Captain Xenophon Strategos, Metaxas' fellow student in Berlin, and Captains K. Pallis and K. Hexadactylos. Accompanying the Army were the Royal Princes: Andrew, Nicholas (not, however, in command of a regiment), Christoforos, and the young Prince George of Sparta, eldest son of the Crown Prince, who had been recalled from Germany where he was serving with a Prussian cavalry regiment.

In the first week of the campaign Constantine led an army of six divisions, to which a seventh division was added later, bringing the total number of men to over 100,000. The Greeks outnumbered the Turks two to one and had 100 cannons, while the Turks had only 60; the Greeks had a cavalry brigade, the Turks had none. The Greeks not only had numerical superiority; they also had excellent intelligence; before hostilities began 250 Makedonomachoi were secretly called up and sent into Macedonia. These were veteran guerilla fighters, who knew the terrain and the people intimately and who had established contacts with the Macedonians. During the campaign they performed invaluable service by acting as guides to the regular Army, by organizing local fighters, by cutting the enemies' lines of communication, by arranging for supplies of foodstuffs and animals. The Turks, according to Dousmanis, also used Greek spies effectively, and were often aware of the movements of the Greek Army. Later in Epirus Turkish spies once even managed to steal the maps from the Greek General Staff! Constantine, despite his enthusiasm and determination, had his private doubts about the efficiency of his Army. Writing in English to his friend Princess Paola of Saxe-Weimar on the eve of the outbreak of the war, he spoke of his apprehensions:

"We have not got what in Europe would be called a real army at all; it is rather a militia, and with that it is not easy to fight against trained troops, like those of the Turks, and especially against the Turk himself, who is the best soldier in the world, both because of his innate discipline and especially because he believes implicity in

what he is taught by his religion... The Turks, like the Japanese, have no kind of fear of death, and that is an enormous source of strength."[27]

The spectre of the defeat of 1897 hung heavily over the Greeks; this was not only a war of liberation, it was also a war of revanche. Constantine, accused of incompetence and cowardice in 1897, was resolved not to survive such another disgrace. On 1 October 1912, after describing the rosy consequences of victory to his friend Paola, he added: "... think what will happen in case of defeat, or, rather, it is best not to think of it! It would be better not to survive such a disaster! That is why I told you that if there were war it would be possible that I should not return from it."[28] The last words were underlined by Constantine himself, who meant what he said.

On 18 October 1912 the Greek Army crossed the Turkish border. There was only a small garrison there and this initial success greatly boosted Greek morale. Metaxas wrote to his wife that evening: "I am fine. Our Army has crossed the frontier."[29] The crossing was made at the Meluna Pass, most famous of the passes over Mount Olympus, where the Turks in 1897 had poured down into Thessaly, routed the Greeks and captured Larissa. These were the same mountain passes over which the Persians of Xerxes and the Goths of Alaric had marched in their invasions of Greece. The calamity of 1897 had plunged the country into the deepest gloom, and many Greeks nurtured a fatalistic presentiment that Greece would never succeed in crossing the passes to the north, but was for ever condemned to remain an insignificant, petty principality.

On the evening of 19 October Metaxas wrote to Lela: "After a battle we have taken [the town of] Elassona."[30] Next day he wrote: "Yesterday was the first battle. The bravery of the Army was outstanding."[31] The Turks, too, showed great courage. Although the Turkish Army was drawn from all over the vast Ottoman Empire, many Turks had been living in Macedonia for generations and they defended their homes heroically. At Elassona the hodja barricaded himself on the top of his minaret with plenty of ammunition and continued firing even after the Turkish Army had abandoned the town, killing and wounding many Greek soldiers. Eventually he was smoked out on to the balcony of the minaret and there, crying out in a loud voice his last prayer to Allah, he met his end in a hail of bullets. The Greek population of Elassona gave an emotional reception to Constantine, which he described in a letter to Paola:

---

27 Constantine I, *A King's Private Letters. Letters of Constantine to Paola, Princess of Saxe-Weimar, 1912-1923* (London, 1925), pp. 37-38.

28 *Ibid.*, p. 40.

29 Metaxas, *Diary*, II, p. 172.

30 *Ibid.*

31 *Ibid.*

"They were shouting out and raving like madmen. The people kissed my hands and boots. When you think what it means to be liberated from the yoke which had weighed on them for almost five hundred years, and of all the fears and torment which they were obliged to suffer, I think there is indeed cause for emotion, especially when one arrives direct from the battlefield after having routed the oppressors."[32]

The Turks chose the Forty Passes of Sarantaporo to make their stand. General Hassan Taksin Pasha, the Governor and Commander-in-Chief of Macedonia, offered a fierce resistance with 30,000 men perched strategically high above the rocky cliffs that overhung the passes. General von der Goltz, the German organizer of the Turkish Army, had predicted that Sarantaporo would be the graveyard of the Greek Army. After a day of savage fighting there was a violent storm during the night and it was impossible for either side to bring in their dead and wounded; but through the night the flying battalions of Evzones, the light mountaineering troops, scaled the mountain tops, outflanking the Turkish defenders. Next morning the Turks realized that their rear was threatened and hurriedly withdrew from their impregnable positions, leaving behind four siege guns, four field batteries, two million rounds of cartridges and thousands of blankets and greatcoats. The Greeks pursued them all the way to the town of Servia. Metaxas wrote to Lela:

"On 22 October the battle was dreadful. Nevertheless, as soon as we understood that the enemy had begun to withdraw, we ordered a general attack; in the meantime we had succeeded in sending in time through wild mountains a whole division to the enemy's rear.... The pursuit was terrible. All the way to Servia the road was covered with Turkish dead."[33]

There were at least 1,500 Greeks killed and wounded. Both in large engagements and in small skirmishes the horrors of war abounded. On the morning of 23 October the bodies of five Greeks and five Turks were found, transfixed on one another's bayonets. Constantine, in a letter to Princess Paola, described how an entire enemy unit was cut to pieces in a Turkish cemetery where it put up a stout resistance. At Servia the retreating Turks violated the women and mutilated and slaughtered the men, including the priests; but Constantine refused to allow any reprisals.

The rapid advance of the Greek Army left the supporting services far behind. Beyond Larissa there were no trains, so arms and ammunition as well as food and medical supplies had to be transported on pack animals. Long stretches of the single gravel road leading from Thessaly to Macedonia had been destroyed by artillery fire. The Commissariat was entrusted to the Territorial Reservists, men over forty, who wore their civilian working clothes and carried old rifles and cartridges strapped round their

32 Constantine, A king's Letters, pp. 66-7.

33 Metaxas, *Diary*, II, p. 173.

waists. These men, who were often the butt of jokes from the regular soldiers, led the pack animals loaded with food and ammunition. But their progress was constantly interrupted by the interminable line of bullock wagons coming from the opposite direction, carrying the wounded back to the hospitals in Larissa. The Army, including the Commander-in-Chief, had to sleep in the rain and go without food for days. Only tea and tinned milk were available. Dousmanis in his Memoirs (which he wrote in old age when half-senile and which are not always reliable) related how one evening at Servia he jokingly complained to the tense and tired Commander-in-Chief about the shortage of rations.

Dousmanis: *Your Highness, we have not eaten for three days; we are all famished and I can hardly restrain my officers. Metaxas, goaded by hunger, has told me that if tomorrow he is still deprived of food, he will go on strike.*

Constantine: *I will break the bones of any man who strikes, I will shoot Metaxas.*[34]

At Servia Metaxas received the first letter from his wife and he hastened to reply and to tell her with some pride about his part in the campaign:

"I have received your letter and kissed it. We are living here in the midst of feverish activity. As you will well understand, it is we who do the directing --Dousmanis, Strategos, K. Pallis and I. I, the undersigned, am the prime mover. How can I describe it to you! I don't have the time."[35]

The political factions in Athens tried to exploit the successes of the Greek Army. "The rumor has been circulating there that we are directed by the French. We are all very indignant. Tell everybody that it is all lies and that it is the Crown Prince and his General Staff who are directing."[36] Metaxas never wavered in his loyalty to his Chief. He wrote to Lela: "Here they all attribute the victory to us [the General Staff]; especially to the Crown Prince whose determination, bravery and steadfast spirit have been magnificent."[37]

By then Constantine's strategy was becoming apparent. It was the same one that, with some variations, he was to follow during the whole campaign. Using his superiority in numbers, the Greek Commander placed battallons of light infantry, mostly evzones, on the extreme right and the extreme left flank. These evzones, (the word means the well-girded), resembled the *psiloi* of Ancient Greece and the *succincti* (which also means well-girded) of Caesar's light troops. They wore the fustanella, the snow-white kilt, and tsarouchia, the leather shoes with turned-up toes worn by the Greek highlanders. The flying columns of evzones advanced across the mountain-tops and attacked the enemy's flanks, threatening his communications. The Turks, with a smaller body of troops,

---

34 Victor Dousmanis, *Απομνημονεύματα* [Memoirs] (Athens, 1946), p. 45.

35 Metaxas, *Diary,* II, p. 172.

36 *Ibid.,* p. 173.

37 *Ibid.,* p. 175.

could not afford to weaken their center and deploy their men along an extended front. This was a strategy which was adopted by the Greek Command after their failure on the first day of the battle of Sarantoporon to dislodge by frontal attacks the Turks from their well-defended positions. The dash and mobility of this elite band of highlanders amazed friends and foes alike. The Turks were forced to withdraw from pass after pass, often abandoning their guns and munitions.

6 The General Staff; Metaxas second from left, Dousmanis second from right

At Servia Constantine received the following telegram from Koromelas: "I believe we should exert our strength to the utmost to reach Salonica before our Allies beat us to the post."[38] The Greeks were well aware of Bulgarian aspirations to Salonica, but they expected that the Bulgarians would bring their campaign in Thrace to a successful conclusion before turning their attention to Macedonia. This had been the original intention of the Bulgarian General Staff, as they had not anticipated that the Greek Army would force its way through the passes of Mount Olympus as quickly as it did. But the latest information received by the Greek government indicated that the Bulgarians' plans had now been modified. The original source of this crucial intelligence came from a certain Nikoglou, a Bulgarian doctor of Greek extraction, who

38 Kordatos, *Ιστορία*, V, p. 292.

had been conscripted into the Bulgarian Army. At Kovana, thanks to an indiscretion from a Bulgarian Staff Officer, the doctor learned that General Theodorov, the Bulgarian Commander, had received orders to proceed by forced marches to Salonica and to occupy the city before the arrival of the Greek Army. The doctor immediately informed Souliotis-Nikolaidis, the Greek officer attached to the Bulgarian Staff, who at once cabled the news to the Greek Minister of Foreign Affairs in Athens. (Thirty-five years later Dr. Nikoglou, who had settled in Greece after the war, was belatedly decorated by the Greek Government for this service). Nevertheless, Constantine disregarded the Foreign Minister's instructions. From Servia the Greek Army crossed the Haliakmon [Vistritza] River and headed north-west, where, on 25 October, it occupied the town of Kozani. In their haste the Turks abandoned their munitions, 14,000 bags of flour and a well-equipped hospital of 500 beds. The Crown Prince was determined to pursue the enemy as far as Monastir where a large Turkish force was concentrated, and only then, after all threats to his rear had been eliminated, turn east towards Salonica. Constantine and his Staff had been taught at the Berlin War Academy that an army should not fight "a geographical war," but should have as its objective "the destruction of the enemy." The Greek Government, for its part, was anxious that the Army should enter Salonica before the prize city of Macedonia fell to the Bulgarians.

"In Athens Venizelos was on tenterhooks. He cabled the Crown Prince: I expect you to inform me of the future direction which the Army of Thessaly will follow. I only beg you to bear in mind that, for important political reasons, we should arrive as soon as possible in Salonica."[39]

Constantine's reaction to the Prime Minister's telegram was brusque; in military matters the Crown Prince would not accept advice from the politicians. He fired back:

"The direction of the enemy's retreat and their future intentions will determine the advance and the direction of the Army under my command.... From now on, the Government should abstain from proffering opinions which are not within their province and from meddling from a distance in the military operations."[40]

When Venizelos received this telegram he almost had apoplexy. He drafted an angry reply ordering the Crown Prince "to surrender the command of the Army to the Chief of the General Staff, Major-General Danglis, as soon as the present communication is received and to proceed immediately to Athens, placing himself at the disposal of the Minister of War."[41] But Venizelos, characteristically, did not send this telegram, but went instead to the Palace to show it to the King, the Supreme Commander of the Armed Forces under the Constitution. George I managed to convince the Prime Minister

---

39 Theodoros Pangalos, *Απομνημονεύματα, 1897-1947* (Athens, 1950, 59), p. 182.

40 *Ibid.*

41 *Ibid.*

that no such drastic action was necessary and informed him that he himself would set off instantly for the front and personally ensure that the Crown Prince carried out the government's instructions. Venizelos, whose initial fury, real or staged, had by now subsided, enquired of the King how long he proposed to stay at the front.
George I: *I do not know, perhaps a fortnight.*
Venizelos: *I think Your Majesty has an idea of returning by ship from Salonica.*
George: *You are always optimistic, and this time I believe you are right.*[42]

The King, after crossing the Greek border, travelled for security reasons in a motor convoy and arrived at Kozani at four-thirty in the afternoon of 27 October. Constantine and his Staff came out of the city to welcome him; the Metropolitan, accompanied by his clergy, was at the gate of Kozani to receive the King. The whole population turned out, waving Greek flags, and followed the royal procession to the Cathedral, where a Te Deum was sung. Afterwards the King received the General Staff and congratulated them all, especially singling out the Crown Prince and Colonel Dousmanis. Captain Metaxas, sour because he had not been included in this special royal praise, wrote to Lela that evening: "These things do not impress me. I shall do my duty, but I cannot wait for the moment when I shall return to you to start our quiet life anew. I myself desire neither triumphs nor anything else."[43]

After the King's visit, Constantine, having dispatched the Fifth Division to the north-west to guard his left flank, duly turned north-east with the main army, en route for Salonica. In the meantime, on 28 October, the Seventh Division, which was on the right wing of the Greek advance, occupied the town of Katerini on the Termaic Gulf, where an advance naval base was established only forty miles from Salonica. On 30 October the Army reached Veroia, the city mentioned in The Acts, where Saint Paul went with Silas after receiving a troubled reception in Salonica and where local tradition still points to the spot where he addressed the inhabitants. Some Greek engine-drivers employed on the Macedonia Railways now drove their locomotives into Greek-occupied territory; supplies were thereafter transported by sea as far as Eleutherochori, near Katerini, and from there transferred to the nearest railway line. At Veroia Constantine received a new telegram from Koromelas, relaying to him verbatim a communication he had just had from the Greek Minister at Berlin, Nikolaos Theotokis. According to Theotokis, Jules Cambon, the French Ambassador at Berlin, had just told him:

"I strongly advise you to enter Salonica as soon as possible, otherwise the chances are that they [the French Ambassador clearly meant the Balkan Allies and, possibly, the Great Powers as well] will make you stay in your present position permanently."[44]

---

42 Lieutenant-Colonel Sir Reginald Rankin, *Inner History of the Balkan War* (London, 1914), p. 335.
43 Metaxas, *Diary,* II, p. 173.
44 Kordatos, *Ιστορία,* V, p. 293.

But Constantine, better acquainted with the realities of the campaign, once again ignored this warning. From Veroia direct to Salonica was fifty miles by train, but as the Serbian forces were still too far from Monastir to pose any serious threat to the Turkish Armies in Western Macedonia, the Greek position was vulnerable and Constantine chose to march forty miles north and occupy first Naousa and then Vodena [Edessa], cutting off the army of Taksin Pasha, which had entrenched itself at Janitsa, from the Turkish forces at Monastir.

The city of Janitsa is situated to the west of the River Vardar, only a short distance from ancient Pella, the capital of Philip II of Macedon and the birthplace of Alexander the Great. Taksin Pasha could have chosen a strong strategic position on the east bank of the Vardar to make his final stand, thus placing the wide and fast-flowing river between his troops and the Greeks; instead he chose to defend the city of Janitsa, keeping the river at his back to prevent his men from taking to flight, as some thought. Other observers suggested that the reason for the Pasha's strange decision was different: Janitsa was regarded as a holy city by the Moslems, and the Turkish soldiers would fight to the death to defend it. There were about 33,000 Turks defending the city, while the Greeks numbered over 50,000 and had 60 cannons to the 30 cannons of the Turks. Moreover, the Greeks had 100 motor vehicles, 60 of them lorries. Both sides were accompanied by foreign military observers and by war correspondents from the European press. The Greeks, expecting the Turks to be entrenched on the farther side of the river, were advancing confidently towards Janitsa when they suddenly found themselves under heavy artillery fire from all sides. This time, unlike at Sarantaporo, the Greek artillery was deployed to good advantage and superiority of numbers and the enthusiasm of the conquering Greek Army won the day. The Creusot cannons used by the Greeks gave a far superior performance than the Krupp cannons of the Turks which, as may be imagined, became the subject of endless debate among military circles in Europe. The battle was fought in heavy rain during the day of 2 November 1912. During the night a thunderstorm broke, accompanied by hail and sleet, and the Greek soldiers had to lie, soaked to the skin, on the flooded plain. Their transports could not keep pace with the troops and no food had reached the Army for days. The battle was resumed with renewed violence the next morning, but by evening the Turkish Army had evacuated Janitsa in panic. The Greeks, who had fought this fierce battle in bad weather after a hard march of several days, lost 1,500 killed and many more wounded. They failed to exploit their victory and did not pursue the retreating enemy. The Turks crossed the bridges over the River Vardar and headed towards Salonica. A day later, realizing that they were not being pursued, they returned and blew up the bridges they had previously crossed. The harsh Macedonian winter had set in early, the Vardar was flooded, and it took five days for the Engineers Corps to repair the bridges and the Greek Army to cross the river. The Turkish Commander, Hassan Taksin Pasha, later acknowledged that the Battle of Janitsa had sealed the fate of Salonica.

As soon as the battle was over Metaxas wrote to his wife. "I am doing famously.... The moment I can get hold of a motorcar I shall send you a word or two. Here a great new victory."[45] Next day he wrote to her: "I have very little time available, because -- you will not believe this -- almost the whole direction [of the campaign] has fallen upon my shoulders. The plan of the Battle of Janitsa is my work. It was a dreadful battle!"[46] Then he described the engagement and gave an account of the casualties. There were no telegraphic communications by which to cable Lela and he had not been able to spare a moment to write to her earlier. "Can you imagine what a terrible responsibility I bear, what decisions I have to make, what work I have to carry out?.... When I return I shall have so many things to relate to you."[47] Metaxas, who always appreciated good and regular meals, complained about the food, although he told his wife that he was in excellent health. "The things you gave me came in very useful: the spirit-stove, the coffee and sugar.... I even gave some the others, even the Princes drank my coffee."[48] And again he tried to reassure Lela of his personal safety. "Do not worry about me. They look after me as though I were the apple of their eye ... they are all solicitude, from the King to Prince Christoforos. But I have had enough."[49]

By 7 November the last of the Greek columns had crossed the River Vardar and camped at Topsin, twenty miles from Salonica. For thirty-six days the men had marched over mountain tracks and passes, often wet and hungry and in bitter winter weather. They had covered more than five hundred miles on foot and had fought two hard-contested battles at Sarantoporo and Janitsa. During the campaign the Greeks captured 37,000 prisoners, 106 cannons, 75,000 rifles and enormous quantities of stores and ammunition. Their total losses amounted to 3,752 killed and 9,542 wounded. The correspondent of the London Daily Telegraph reported to his paper:

"I can give a better idea of what I went through by mentioning that during the days I followed the army I twice went thirty-six hours without food, my best bed was in a barn, and I had to pass several nights in the open near a camp fire. We experienced ten degrees of frost at Kardjalar, and torrential rains such as are usually only encountered in tropical Africa. Many died of exposure. The percentage of sick reached a climax at Vodena. Still the spirit of the men was unimpaired."[50]

The endurance and resolution of the Greeks made a deep impression upon the military observers and foreign journalists. The correspondent of the London Daily Express described how at Topsin the Greek Army *"had camped for three days in pouring rain.*

45 Metaxas, *Diary,* II, p. 174.

46 *Ibid.*

47 *Ibid.*

48 *Ibid,* p. 176.

49 *Ibid.,* p. 174.

50 Rankin, *Inner, History*, p. 343.

The ground was a swamp, and it was impossible to erect tents amid great pools of water. A bitter north wind was blowing, the mountains were snow-clad, and the bread convoys had not arrived. The army was cold and wet, with empty stomachs. But the men remained cheerful in this depressing bivouac at Topsin. Four miles away we could see the faint lights of Salonica. Across the bay, the cold inquisitive electric flashlight of Kara Bourun blinked at us for the last time in the Turkish interest."[51]

Because of the rapid advance of the Army, the commissariat was left far behind. It was impossible for such a large body of troops, constantly on the march, to live off the land and the men often went hungry. Once, when a mutiny broke out, the Crown Prince rode over to the rebellious Damianos Division -- the Greek Divisions were known by the names of their Commanding Officers -- and addressed the men himself. "Bread! Bread!" the soldiers chanted. "If you want bread," Constantine shouted back, "there is Salonica -- go and get it!" The soldiers, disarmed by the heroic mien of their Chief, responded with jubilant cries of "Zito! Zito!" -- the Greek version of "Hurrah." Not only the commissariat was left far in the rear; the problem of transportation of war materiel was equally serious. When the Greeks had to cross the Vardar, the bridge-building equipment had only reached Kozani, one hundred miles behind. The French military advisers had replaced the horses, traditionally used to draw the supply and ammunition wagons, with buffalo and oxen which, although efficient enough for the plains of France, were completely unsuited to the mountainous terrain of the Balkans. According to Dousmanis, one of the reasons the Greeks hastened their advance on Salonica was because it was necessary to replace their lines of communication on land by the sea-route from Piraeus.

While the Greek Army was crossing the Vardar, Constantine was bombarded with telegrams from Athens, urging him to press on to Salonica. On 6 November 1912 Koromelas cabled the Crown Prince, asking him to expedite the capture of Salonica before the Bulgarian cavalry, which was then only as short distance away, could reach the city.

"... the most important of all is that the Bulgarians seem to have given orders to the Army at Nevrokopi to occupy Serres and from there to hasten towards Salonica in order to enter the city before it is captured by the Greek Army, or at least to enter Salonica at the same time. Serres has already been occupied by the Bulgarian Army, which most probably is advancing towards Salonica."[52]

At the same time the Greek Government forwarded a copy of this telegram to King George, who was travelling in the wake of the Army and was then staying at Gidas, a town near Janitsa. When Venizelos received no reply from the King, he telephoned him

---

51 *Ibid.*, p. 345.

52 Kordatos, *Ιστορία*, V, p. 294.

in the middle of the night. The King's aide-de-camp answered the call and stated that His Majesty was asleep and that he could not disturb him. Once more Venizelos exploded: "The Prime Minster gives orders that he shall be awakened and that the following message shall be communicated to him with the request that the King transmit it to his son, adding also his paternal advice."[53] The shaken aide-de-camp obediently woke up his royal master and handed him the Prime Minister's message, which was addressed to Constantine: "I hold you personally responsible for the tardiness with which you are carrying out operations, which is incurring the risk of bringing the Bulgarians into Salonica first."[54] The next day, 7 November, Koromelas telegraphed the Crown Prince:

"According to information from the Minister of War the Bulgarians are today entering Serres. This very moment we have learned that the Serbs have routed the Turks, not in great numbers, at Demir-Kapou, but because of the great distance, we calculate that they will reach Salonica after the entry of our Army into the city."[55]

At 4:20 p.m. the Consuls-General at Salonica of Great Britain, France, Germany and Austria-Hungary, accompanied by General Sadek, the Commandant of Salonica, and delegates from the Commander-in-Chief of the Turkish Army, Taksin Pasha, arrived at Villa Modiano, the Greek Army Headquarters in Topsin. Salonica was a cosmopolitan city and the foreign representatives, whose primary concern was the safety of the lives and property of their nationals, with one voice implored the Crown Prince not to shell the city. Constantine's response was curt and to the point: "My paramount duty is to render the Turkish Army innocuous."[56] If the Consuls were interested in saving Salonica, he observed, they should appeal to the Turkish General who was defending it. The Turkish delegates then offered to surrender the city upon certain conditions, chief among these being that the Turkish Army of Salonica, while undertaking to remain neutral until the end of the war, should be permitted to retain its arms. Constantine made the surrender of arms a *conditio sine qua non,* but conceded that their weapons should be returned to them at the conclusion of hostilities. Constantine also demanded the surrender of Kara Bourun, the fortress which guarded the entrance to the port of Salonica. He gave the Turks until six o'clock the following morning to reply. When it was learned in Athens that the Turks had offered to surrender Salonica, Venizelos, signing the telegram in his capacity of Minister of War, cabled the Crown Prince: *"You are instructed to accept the surrender of Salonica which has been offered to you and to enter the city without loss of time. I shall hold you responsible*

53 *Ibid.*, p. 295.

54 *Ibid.* As related by Venizelos in Parliament on 26 August 1917. Also in Ventiris, *Ελλάς,* I, p. 166.

55 Kordatos, *Ιστορία,* V, p. 294.

56 Ventiris, *Ελλάς,* I, p. 117.

for even one moment's delay."[57] Constantine bided his time until the negotiations for the surrender of the city were completed before responding to this telegram.

Early in the morning of 8 November the Commandant of Salonica returned, accompanied by the Turkish Diplomatic Agent -- a certain fez-wearing Karapiperis of Greek descent -- with counter-proposals. The Turks would surrender their arms, with the exception of 5,000 rifles, which they claimed were needed for the instruction of recruits. When this request was refused, the Turkish delegates departed, having obtained a further delay of two hours. As they had not returned by the time stipulated, Constantine ordered the troops to move forward, which they did at nine o'clock in the morning. At three o'clock in the afternoon, when the Greek Army was only a few miles from Salonica, a messenger brought a letter from General Theodorov, the Bulgarian Commander-in-Chief, notifying the Greek Command that he was marching with the utmost speed to join the Greeks in the siege of Salonica. At that moment the Bulgarians were thirty-two kilometers away and Constantine immediately wrote back to General Theodorov, informing him that Salonica would be occupied within hours by the Greek Army and that the Bulgarian troops would be more usefully employed elsewhere. At four-thirty, when the Greek columns were approaching the enemy's advance posts, a letter arrived from Taksim Pasha in which he accepted Constantine's terms of surrender. Thereupon Constantine halted the advance of the Army and sent Dousmanis and Metaxas to meet with the Turkish Commander and draw up the protocol for the surrender of arms and the capitulation of the city.

Victor Dousmanis has described in his Memoirs how he and Metaxas, on horseback, accompanied by four cavalrymen, followed the Turkish messenger, who led them to the village of Daoud-Bali. But when they got there they found that Taksin Pasha had already left for Salonica, leaving no instructions behind, so the Greek officers asked to be conducted there. It was pitch-dark and raining steadily. They found Taksin Pasha "very downcast, but not agitated." Dousmanis told him that the surrender must be made unconditionally and a Turkish Staff Officer drafted the protocol. Taksin Pasha spoke fluent Greek and the following exchange ensued.

Dousmanis: *My Pasha, my Chief the Crown Prince, appreciating your bravery and the bravery of your officers in your struggle for the defence of Salonica, has ordered me to inform you that, as a mark of his respect for you, he allows you to keep your swords.*

Taksin Pasha: *In the state we are in at present, what use are swords to us? He may as well take them.*[58] Taksin was in a state of great depression, but he asked Dousmanis to convey to Constantine his appreciation and that of his officers for the courtesy. The

57 *Ibid.*, p. 116. Also in Dousmanis, *Απομνημονεύματα*, p. 51, and in Kordatos, *Ιστορία*, V, p. 296.

58 Dousmanis, *Απομνημονεύματα*, p. 57.

protocol was signed at 1:30 a.m. on 9 November, or 27 October, according to the Old Calendar, which was then observed; but, at the request of the Greeks, the protocol bore the date of the previous day, 26 October, when the offer of surrender had been made. In the Greek Orthodox hagiology, 26 October is Saint Demetrius' Day, the warrior patron saint of Salonica. Taksin then requested that the Greek Army should be informed of the ceasefire immediately, as he himself had informed the Turkish troops. Dousmanis assured him that as soon as the Crown Prince received the protocol he would issue the necessary orders for the cease fire. To this Taksin replied, "My tzane [in Turkish, dear], I fear that you may not reach the Crown Prince in time and Turkish soldiers may be killed unnecessarily. You should issue the order yourself."[59] Dousmanis did so and dispatched the order for the ceasefire by one of his men, who set off a once with a Turkish escort. A few hours after the Greeks had departed, Bulgarian representatives arrived and demanded the surrender of the city. Taksin Pasha replied that he had already surrendered to the Greeks. The Turkish Commander had been eager to surrender to the Greeks rather than to the Bulgarians, because of the humane treatment the Greeks accorded their prisoners, in striking contrast to the vengeful behaviour of the Bulgarians. Earlier that night, at eleven o'clock on 8 November 1912, the first battalion of evzones had already entered the city and established a Greek presence there.

Dousmanis and Metaxas, after having tried unsuccessfully to get a meal in a restaurant which had run out of supplies, rode back to Greek Headquarters where they arrived at five o'clock in the morning of 9 November. Constantine at once sent them back to the Turks to complete the negotiations for the transfer of administrative powers to the Greek authorities. Along with Dousmanis and Metaxas went Ion Dragoumis, the son of Stephanos Dragoumis, diplomat and intellectual, who was at this time serving in the Army. The Greeks insisted that Kara Bourun be included in the terms of surrender.
Taksin: *Kara Bourun is a fortress which you have not conquered and therefore I cannot surrender it without a fight.*
Dousmanis: *My Pasha; I am a soldier and you are a soldier: can you tell me, is it not possible for me to attack the fortress from the land? How large a garrison have you there? When our Army enters Salonica, I shall send one or two or even more divisions and lay siege to it; the strong coastal defenses of the fortress are powerless against a land army and its garrison altogether inadequate. The result would be that because of your unreasonable insistence many Turkish and Greek soldiers would lose their lives and you would bear the responsibility for such unjustifiable bloodshed.*[60]

The Turkish Commander finally gave in and by midday the negotiations for the surrender were completed. Immediately Greek Army units entered the city and occupied

59 *Ibid.*, p. 58.
60 *Ibid.*, p. 60.

its key positions. Dousmanis then hurriedly sent a train to Topsin to bring the Crown Prince to Salonica before the Bulgarians reached the city; but as the train drew into the station, it was not the imperial Constantine who alighted but the short, undersized figure of the amiable Chief of Staff, General Danglis.

Dousmanis: *Mon general, where is the Crown Prince?*

Danglis: *He is at Topsin.*

Dousmanis: *Why did he not come, why did you come all by yourself?*[61]

With ineffable simplicity Danglis replied that when he had seen a train arrive at Topsin which was about to make the return trip to Salonica, he was possessed by curiosity to see the Macedonian capital and also by a desire to take advantage of the occasion to buy some cakes, which he intended to offer to the Crown Prince at dinner that night! By the time Dousmanis and Metaxas arrived back at Topsin it was after sunset and Constantine, who wished to make a triumphal entry into the city, postponed his departure until the following morning. But during the night a Greek messenger woke him up to tell him that the Bulgarians were themselves preparing to enter Salonica in the morning. At once the Crown Prince and his Staff arose and travelled by train to the coveted port of the Balkans, where they arrived at four o'clock in the morning of 10 November. It was still dark; rain was falling; the streets were deserted. Hailing a horse-carriage, Constantine and some of his officers -- revolvers at the ready -- drove to the Government Building, where they speedily installed themselves.

The hour had now arrived for the Crown Prince to be revenged on Venizelos. In his own hand Constantine wrote a telegram and dispatched it to the Prime Minister in Athens. When issuing messages and orders Constantine always used the cheap writing-pads provided by the Greek Telegraph Company, on which he wrote in large, firm characters with a lead pencil.

"I am entirely sensible of the responsibility that I bear and I beg that, from now onwards, you will not remind me of it on any occasion. Whether or not I should have accepted the surrender of Salonica, I was the only person qualified to judge, as I was in situ and it was I who was imposing the terms of surrender. Proof of this is in the result accomplished."[62]

That morning a Te Deum was celebrated by the Metropolitan of Salonica, assisted by the Metropolitan of Athens, who had accompanied the troops during their advance. The service was held at Saint Menas' Church, because the beautiful Byzantine Church of Saint Demetrius, the patron saint of Salonica, had been turned into a mosque. Soon afterwards it was reconsecrated as a Christian church. After the Te Deum the Bulgarian General Theodorov appeared before Constantine and claimed the *droit d' alliés* to send

---

61 *Ibid.*, p. 61.

62 *Ibid.*, p. 51.

two battalions into the city. Constantine refused to share his authority with anyone and made it clear that the Greeks had been the first to enter Salonica and intended to stay. But he granted permission for two Bulgarian regiments, which had been on the march for days, to come in and rest for a while. That night a whole Bulgarian division slipped into the city.

Salonica had been captured by the Turks on 1 May 1430 despite the desperate resistance of the citizens. The Committee of Union and Progress of the young Turks had its headquarters here. Salonica is the birthplace of Kemal Attaturk, whose mother and sister fled the city in 1912 and went to Constantinople with the rest of the Turkish refugees. The city has an excellent port at the mouth of the River Vardar -- Axios to the Greeks. A railway passing through the Vardar Valley connects the Danube Basin with the Aegean and Salonica with Central Europe. At the time of its capture by the Greeks in 1912 it had a population of 121,600 of which 60,000 were Jews of Spanish origin who had fled there after their expulsion from Spain by Ferdinand and Isabella in 1471. There were also about 20,000 Moslems then living in the city. The remaining 40,000 were ethnic Greeks. A week before the Greek Army entered Salonica, Commodore Nikolaos Votsis -- whose statue now stands on the corniche near the White Tower -- braving the mines, sailed into the harbour under cover of darkness and torpedoed the Turkish warship Fethi Bulend, which went down with most of her crew. Also anchored in the harbour at this time were the French Bruix, the British Hampshire and the German Goeben. The foreign warships had come to stand by to evacuate their nationals if the necessity arose. As the Greek Army approached, the deposed Sultan, Abdul Hamid II, who had been banished to Salonica in 1909 by the Young Turks, was hurriedly ushered aboard a German man-of-war, together with his thirteen wives, and taken to Constantinople, where he died six years later.

King George I arrived in Salonica on 11 November and received an enthusiastic welcome from the Army and the people. In the triumphal procession a few days later the King rode a large chestnut horse and was followed by Crown Prince Constantine. Then came Prince George of Crete, Prince Andrew and Prince George of Sparta, Constantine's eldest son, the future George II. Prince Nicholas, who was suffering from severe phlebitis, rode in an open carriage with Princess Alice of Battenberg, the wife of Prince Andrew. This English Princess, sister of Prince Louis of Battenberg, whose family assumed the name of Mountbatten after the First World War, had followed the advancing Army as leader of a mobile nursing unit. Behind the royal train rode the General Staff, Captain Ioannis Metaxas prominent among them. Not only the Greeks of the city but also the Jews and Moslems turned out to watch the procession. The London Daily Express correspondent wrote that "Behind the troops were packed a population of red-fezzed heads looking like rows of closely-packed poppy blooms."[63] The entry of four battalions of Greek troops was received with jubilation by the Greek onlookers. The English Lieut. Colonel Reginald Rankin, in his Inner History of the Balkan War, observed that, "Amongst these troops were many American and English volunteers, and for the first time the sound of an English cheer or an Americal college yell struck upon many a Greek, Jewish, and Turkish ear."[64] The correspondent of the Daily Express, who entered Salonica in a carriage with a wounded Greek colonel, described the scene for his readers:

"Our entry was a triumphant progress. The streets were packed and the Pioneers' Regiment were obliged to force a way with the butts of their rifles. The Greeks of Salonica, whose tongues had been muzzled for weeks past, gave free vent to their joy at seeing the Greek uniforms. The Turks scowled in solemn silence. The balconies on the Marina were crowded with ladies, showering flowers on us and cheering the mud-splashed uniforms.

After us came battalion of Evzones (Highlanders), long-limbed mountaineers in khaki greatcoats hiding their no longer white kilts -- simple men from the highlands of Greece who could not hide their satisfaction at their reception, letting out yell after yell in response to the cheers of the people, and at the same time hoisting their little tasselled skull-caps on their bayonets, and waving them to the girls in the balconies. The mitrailleuse batteries were especially noted, and tired mules carrying them received many a cheer of encouragement and praise."[65]

Metaxas was housed at the Splendid Palace Hotel, where he shared a room with Dousmanis and another officer. Accommodation in Salonica at the time was so scarce that some of the Greek soldiers had to be billeted in the local brothels, after turning out "those ladies," as the Crown Prince coyly referred to them in a letter to Princess Paola. On the morning of 11 November, after the first good night's rest he had enjoyed for many weeks, Metaxas wrote a long letter to his wife in Athens, describing the trials and tribulations he had experienced during the past few days and the part he had played in the capture of the Macedonian capital.

"You cannot imagine what I have gone through these last few days. On 7 November we left Kirthzalar [the Headquarters of the Greek General Staff during the battle of Janitsa] from where I sent you a letter. In the evening we were at Topsin while the Army crossed the River Axios [Vardar]. The difficulties were great, but we overcame them all.

In the evening Turkish delegates arrived at Greek Headquarters, offering the surrender of their Army and the city. The Crown Prince entrusted Dousmanis and

---

63 Rankin, *Inner History*, p. 348.

64 *Ibid.*, p. 343.

65 *Ibid.*

myself with the negotiations. We further demanded that the Turks should give up to us the fortress of Kara Bourun. They did not accept this, and the next day we began to advance for battle. I had already written the battle orders and by the evening of the 7th we had them encircled.

But before the firing began the Turks again sent delegates and accepted all our terms. At night Dousmanis and I rode to Salonica and negotiated with the Turkish Commander-in-Chief the surrender of his Army, the city and Kara Bourun, and we signed the protocol. It was a moving moment! We returned immediately the same night.

Next day the two of us again entered Salonica and completed the arrangements for the surrender. On the afternoon of 9 November we brought in the Army. On the morning of 10 November the Crown Prince entered the city and we with him, followed by the First Division. The whole world went mad with joy! I had been without sleep and almost famished for three days in torrential rain, almost continually on horseback, but we took Salonica, Kara Bourun, and 30,000 prisoners.

The Bulgarians, with a small army, hurried, too, but they were not in time. In fact, I was sent to stop them, but they pretended not to see me and began firing, the bullets whizzing all around me so much that I was obliged to return. At last we did stop them, but they are oozing venom from every pore. [In Greek, venom is dripping from their noses.]"[66]

But even in the moment of triumph Metaxas was not satisfied. Perhaps he wanted to head the parade, singled out from and raised above all the Army. His jealousy of Dousmanis was deep, his sense of self-importance strong, his vanity boundless. Did he want, even then, to play "the great dictator"? In his letter to his wife he talked of resigning his commission and taking up some kind of work in civilian life which he had apparently discussed with Xenophon Strategos.

Three days later Metaxas was back in the saddle, bound for a new campaign in Western Macedonia. The Fifth Division under the command of General Mathiopoulos, which Constantine had assigned to Western Macedonia to protect the rear of the Greek Army, had been trapped in the mountain passes and completely cut to pieces. Metaxas wrote to Lela, "Just imagine, he had 10,000 infantry and 20 cannons and he was defeated by 8,000 enemy troops with 12 cannons!"[67] The reason for this disaster, Metaxas explained, was that the Greek soldiers had been spread out too thinly, as in 1897. "But what do you expect from Mathiopoulos?" The Turkish general who annihilated the Greek Division at Sorovits was Djavid Pasha, a renegade Jew in the service of the Sultan. The Greek Army now set off on a long march to clear enemy

66 Metaxas, *Diary,* II, pp. 174-5.
67 *Ibid.,* p. 176.

forces out of Western Macedonia. On 19 November they took the city of Florina, 150 miles from Salonica. The Turks in their retreat had to spend one night there; snow was falling heavily, but the Turkish soldiers bivouacked in the shops along the main street without disturbing the Greek inhabitants of the city -- by order of their Commander Djavid Pasha, as Pangalos testifies in his Memoirs. In another town a Turkish sergeant with half a dozen men occupied a local tower and refused to join his comrades in the retreat. He and his small band killed fifteen Greek soldiers before a cannon was brought in to demolish the tower. General Pangalos, who was present, wrote with soldierly admiration: "The heroic Turkish sergeant and his companions were found blown to pieces by the shells. He fell gloriously for his Fatherland and if the Koran speaks true, he will find a special place with the houri of Paradise."[68]

One night on campaign Metaxas sat down "with a lead pencil, by the light of a candle" to write to his wife: "This operation too, from Salonica up to here, you can guess whose concept it was and who wrote all the orders."[69] But despite the satisfaction he felt as a professional soldier for a job well done, he was never complacent about the horrors of the war. "How many are gone, my Lela! How many have been killed, how many have died! My heart bleeds for the friends and acquaintances I have lost, for the terrible things I have seen. War is an awful thing ..."[70]. From Florina the Greeks set out for Monastir, but they were twenty-four hours too late; the Serbs had entered the city the previous day. The Commander of the Turkish Army, Fethy Pasha, had been killed in action. The Turkish forces were then split in two, one half marching round Lake Presba and making their way to Ioannina in Epirus. The other half surrendered in small detachments to the Greeks in Western Macedonia after some fierce skirmishes.
Metaxas wrote:

"We have had a magnificent campaign from the military point of view through Vodena and Ostrovo towards Monastir; because of this the Serbs managed to capture Monastir. The retreating Turks fell into our hands and we dealt with them as was fitting. They were completely routed. We captured their artillery, their ammunition and their supplies."[71]

Metaxas accompanied the Crown Prince into Monastir, where Constantine paid an official courtesy call on the Serbian Crown Prince, who had just taken the city. The Greek population gave Constantine a tumultuous reception, but he diplomatically left the same day, leaving the city to the Serbs. In Monastir Metaxas bought two furs of local renard blanc for Lela -- a souvenir, as he wrote. But even then Metaxas expressed his disenchantment with the Army:

---

68 Pangalos, *Απομνημονεύματα*, p. 232.
69 Metaxas, *Diary*, II, p. 176.
70 *Ibid.*, p. 177.
71 *Ibid.*

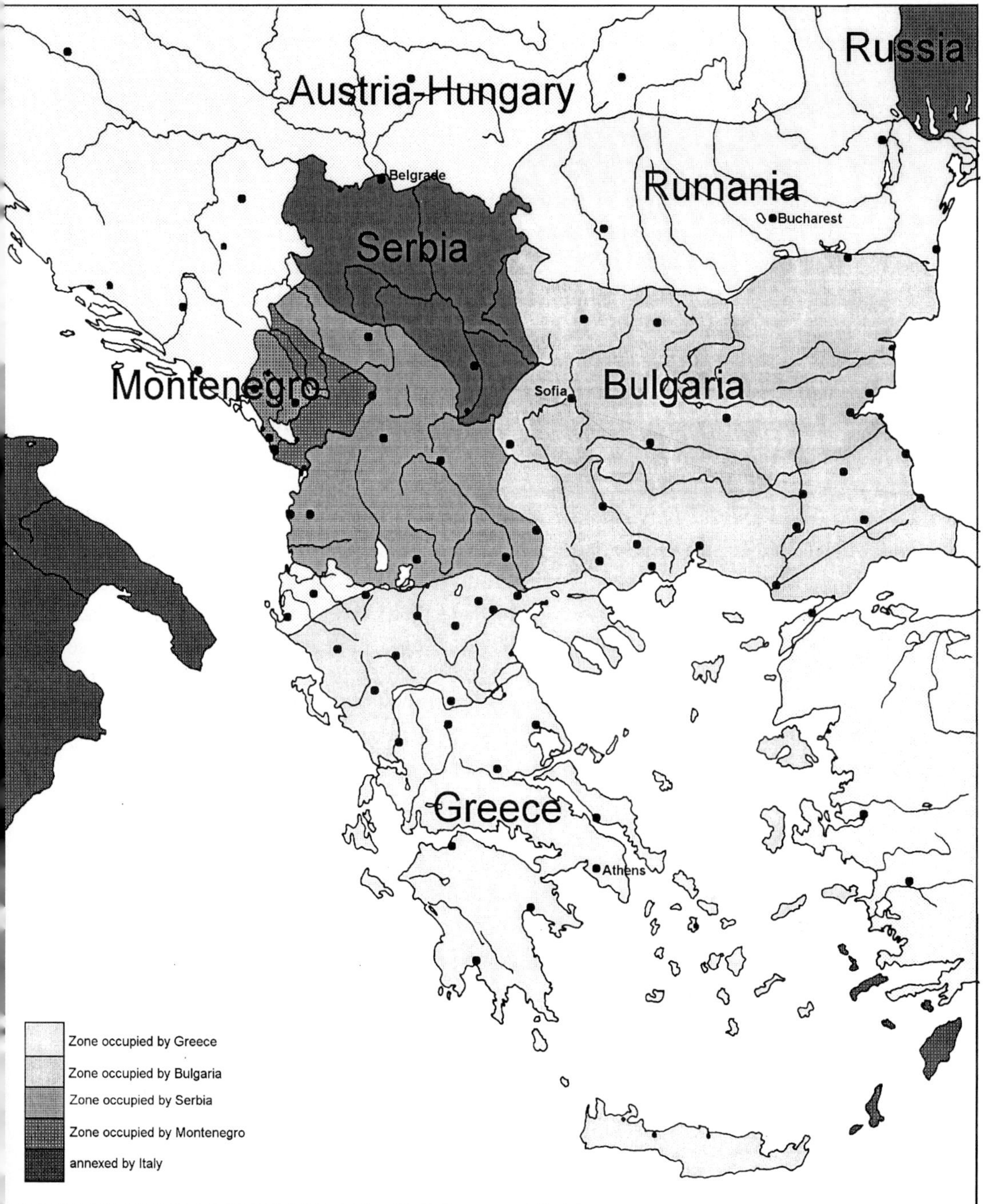

Map 1: Territorial changes caused by the First Balkan War

"I cannot wait for the moment when I shall be with you, but when? This is my dream, I sleep with it, I wake up with it ... This war is killing me, I am fed up; the glory, the successes, the victories, are beautiful, but most beautiful of all is to come back to you."[72]

It was not the war that was killing Metaxas, but the resentful envy and bitter discontent which were gnawing at his heart. He was still only a captain, firmly relegated to the background, while all the honours were divided between Colonel Dousmanis, Constantine's favourite, and Lieut. General Danglis, the Venizelist Chief-of-Staff.

The Turks could spare only 50,000 men to put against the Greeks because they were keeping 200,000 soldiers in Thrace to protect Constantinople against Bulgaria and had dispatched 100,000 men up the Vardar Valley against the Serbs. It was an unequal contest. As in the case of the Greeks, the Serbs and the Bulgarians possessed an overwhelming numerical advantage. The Bulgarians, after failing to capture Adrianople, pressed forward and on 22 October defeated the Turks at Kirk Kilisse (The Forty Churches) and a week later again at Lule Burgas. The Turks withdrew to the Chataldja Line, twenty miles from Constantinople. Only a month after the outbreak of war the inhabitants of the Ottoman capital could plainly hear the distant thunder of enemy guns. Around the world there arose a sudden concern that Constantinople might be sacked and the Straits, one of the most important waterways on the face of the globe, become the battleground for an international conflict. The Turks, who were at a disadvantage directing an offensive on a long front against the Bulgarians, displayed great tenacity fighting behind the fortifications of the Chataldja Line which guarded their capital. The fierce attacks of 17 and 18 November, which cost the Bulgarians between ten and fifteen thousand men, were repulsed.

The Serbians crossed into Macedonia on 19 October and five days later defeated the Turks at Kumanovo. The next day, 26 October, the Serbian Crown Prince Alexander who, although only a colonel, was Commander-in-Chief of the Serbian forces, entered Skoplje, the ancient capital of Serbia, where in 1346 Stephen Dushan was crowned Czar of the Serbs. Then they defeated the Turks at Prilep and advanced towards Monastir and Ochrid. By 30 October the sanjak of Novibazar was under Serbian and Montenegrin occupation. But they did not press their advantage and march against Monastir where the main Turkish forces were concentrated; instead they turned westwards and, assisted by the Montenegrins, overran Northern Albania, occupying on 10 November Durazzo (modern Durëss) on the Adriatic. An acute international crisis followed after Austria-Hungary announced her opposition to Serbian access to the Adriatic. Russia supported the Serbs. France promised Russia support in the event of war with Germany. Italy supported the Austrian position, while Germany promised

72 *Ibid.*

Austria support in the event of a Russian attack. In late November and early December 1912 Austria and Russia began to mobilize. However, the crisis subsided when Russia realized she was unprepared for war and abandoned the Serbs. On 18 November the Serbians won a great victory at Monastir, due in large measure to the approach of the Greek Army to the south of the city, which drew off strong Turkish contingents. Retiring from Monastir, the major part of the Turkish Armies headed for Epirus, where they joined the defenders of Ioannina. The Montenegrins took Plava, Gousine, and Ipev. At the end of October they laid siege to Scutari with the assistance of the Serbs.

On 4 November 1912 the Grand Vizier requested the ambassadors of the Great Powers at Constantinople to arrange an armistice between embattled Turkey and the Balkan states. At the same time the Turkish diplomatic representatives accredited to the European capitals asked for European mediation for peace. But precious time was lost while the Entente Powers and the Powers of the Triple Alliance tried to agree among themselves upon the right procedure. On 11 November the Ottoman government enquired of Mr. Rockhill, the American Ambassador at Constantinople, whether the United States would be willing to act as mediator if the Great Powers were reluctant to undertake the task. Rockhill advised direct negotiations between Turkey and the Balkan Allies; but it was the British Ambassador at Constantinople who, on his own initiative, arranged for direct talks between the Turks and their adversaries. Not only the Turks but the Bulgarians, too, were anxious for a ceasefire. Strategic reasons alone had obliged them to march against Constantinople, which they knew they would never be allowed to keep, even if they should succeed in occupying it. The Bulgarian political objectives lay to the west in Macedonia, and the Bulgarians now wanted to disengage their armies from Thrace and transfer them to Macedonia before the whole province was taken by the Serbs and the Greeks. The Serbs, who had already occupied all the districts they coveted, also desired peace and asked the Bulgarians to represent them and to sign the ceasefire on their behalf. So did the Montenegrins. When Panas, the Greek representative, arrived at Chatalja he found that the terms of the armistice had been agreed upon in his absence. He referred these terms to Athens, but the Greek Government refused to accept them. Greece could not sign an armistice while Ioannina, the capital of Epirus, was still holding out; neither would Greece agree to lift the blockade of the Asiatic coast, which would have allowed Turkish reoccupation of the just liberated Aegean islands. In a lengthy appeal to her Allies, Greece exhorted them not to take any course which would endanger the Alliance. However, the armistice between Turkey on the one hand and Bulgaria, Serbia and Montenegro on the other, was signed on 3 December 1912. The Greeks felt that they had been betrayed by their Allies, while the Turks believed that Greece had abstained from signing because of a secret understanding with her Allies, who wished to benefit from the ceasefire and transfer troops to Macedonia, but still wanted the Greek Navy to prevent any Turkish troops from Asia Minor being transported to Western Thrace and Macedonia.

Notwithstanding, Greece, although still in a state of war with Turkey, was invited to join the peace negotiations in London, which were to begin on 13 December 1912.

The single most decisive factor accounting for the Allied successes in the Balkan Wars was the effective blockade of Turkey which the Greek Fleet imposed as soon as the war broke out. Thereafter no troops could be transported from Anatolia to Macedonia and Turkey had to fight the war with only the soldiers from the local garrisons and the armies she had mobilized just before the outbreak of hostilities. When the Bulgarians pressed on with their advance in Thrace they knew that no Turkish armies could be landed in Macedonia to threaten their rear. The Greeks and the Serbs knew the enemy strength they had to reckon with, and had no fears of fresh troops and new supplies reaching their foe. The Greek blockade also interrupted the flow of all kinds of materiel from overseas on which Turkey depended for her war effort; the interruption of supplies of imported coal paralysed the Turkish railway system, and the Turkish infantrymen from Asia Minor reached the front in Thrace weary and footsore after long and exhausting marches.

Although Greece had refused to sign the armistice which her Balkan Allies concluded with Turkey on 3 December 1912 and continued to wage war on both land and sea, a large Greek delegation was sent to London, where all the belligerents had been invited by Sir Edward Grey to negotiate the peace settlement. On 6 December the Crown Prince asked Metaxas if he would like to attend the Peace Conference as Military Adviser to the Greek delegation. Major General Danglis was also attending. Metaxas at first declined, as his wife was expecting their second child and he wished to be near her. Constantine enquired when the baby was expected. In ten to fifteen days, replied Metaxas. In that case, the Crown Prince assured him, he would have time to go to Athens, stay with his wife for the birth, and then proceed to London; it was absolutely essential that he should attend the Conference. Then, with his customary spirit of camaraderie, the Crown Prince asked if Metaxas' wife was being attended by Dr. Louros, who had been obstetrician to the Crown Princess at the births of his own children; no, Metaxas replied, his wife had consulted another doctor. "In any case, after the birth, you must go," Constantine told him firmly.

As it turned out, Metaxas was obliged to leave Greece before his child was born. In his next letter, which he sent from Paris on 10 December 1912 on his way to London, he described the journey and his colleagues in the Greek Delegation. Some of them had brought along their wives and Metaxas was sad that Lela could not be with him. "I am tired of travelling. I have changed a lot; I cannot wait for the hour when I can rest from this life of a Wandering Jew, and enjoy my life with you and our children. I was not cut out to be a great man."[73] He was anxious about Lela's confinement. When he opened

73 Metaxas, *Diary,* II, p. 179.

his trunk the first thing that caught his eye was the tiny shoe of his baby daughter Loukia; it had been filled with jasmine by the loving hands of his wife, and Captain Metaxas kissed all the flowers and her letter, too. He commented: "What a prosaic thing to do in Paris, a mondaine of Athens would say. And yet, this is happiness."[74] The Greek Delegation arrived in London on 16 December 1912. Leading them was the Prime Minister himself, assisted by Stephanos Skouloudis, a Turkish speaker; John Gennadius, Greek Minister at London (whose valuable collection of rare books later formed the nucleus of the Gennadius Library in Athens); Nikolaos Politis, Professor of International Law at the Sorbonne; George Streit, Greek Minister at Vienna; Major-General Danglis; Captain Ioannis Metaxas, and another member of the Greek General Staff, Captain Athanasios Hexadactylos. The Delegation stayed at Claridges. Leading the Turkish Delegation was Reshid Pasha, Minister of Agriculture and Commerce, assisted by Osman Nizami, Ottoman Ambassador at Berlin. Dr. Danev, Speaker of the Sobranie, headed the Bulgarian Delegation; Stoyan Novakovits led the Serbians and L. Mouscovits the Montenegrins. The British Government put St. James' Palace at the disposal of the Conference. British Prime Minister Asquith, welcoming the delegates at Guildhall, spoke optimistically of the speedy and successful conclusion of their deliberations.

However, even before the St. James' conference was officially opened, the Great Powers launched their own parallel Conference on 12 December 1912 at the British Foreign Office under the chairmanship of Sir Edward Grey, the British Foreign Minister. The Balkan Alliance had taken the Great Powers by surprise; the victories of the Balkan states had astonished Europe. On the eve of the outbreak of war the Powers warned that they would not allow a change in the status quo in the Balkan Peninsula. Faced with a fait accompli, they now tried to accommodate themselves to the new realities. At the suggestion of Great Britain and Germany, the Austrian, French, Russian and Italian Ambassadors met under the chairmanship of Sir Edward Grey to discuss the progress made by the Balkan delegates and to decide what action should be taken if the St. James' Conference should break down. The Ambassadors' Conference, as it was called, began on 4 January 1913. Vital European interests were at stake and the Great Powers, who had not been able to prevent the outbreak of the Balkan War, were determined at least to direct its conclusion and dictate the peace settlement.

Germany was taken aback to find that the German-trained Turkish Army had proved inefficient; that the Bulgarians had threatened the Straits; that the Greeks had captured the Aegean islands off the Asiatic coast; and lastly that the German Krupp guns used by the Turks had proved inferior to the French Cruezots used by the Balkan Allies. The developments in the Balkans were also very disturbing to the Dual Monarchy. The

---

74 *Ibid.*

Austrians and the Magyars, who lived in constant fear of the Russian armies beyond the Galician frontier to the north, were none too happy to witness the rising power of the Slavic Balkan states to the south. To allow the Serbs passage to the Adriatic, the only sea accessible to the Habsburg Empire, would be to put the fate of the Empire into the hands of the Slavs.

Italy, who had occupied Libya and the Dodecanese the previous spring, would not tolerate any rival in the Mediterranean and strongly opposed the Greek annexation of the Aegean islands and the Greek occupation of Epirus. With disarming frankness, the Marquis di San Guliano, the Italian Foreign Minister, declared on 22 February 1913 that the intention of Italy was to intensify her activities in the Adriatic and Mediterranean and to assert herself as a Great Power in any future territorial changes that might take place in those waters.[75] The Russians, too, were against the Greek occupation of the Aegean islands, which had brought the Greeks closer to the Straits and Constantinople. Britain, on the other hand, feared that the threat to the "integrity of the Ottoman Empire" which the Balkan War had occasioned would open the way for Russian penetration in the Mediterranean and endanger Suez.

Above all else, foremost in the minds of the Powers was the threat to their extensive financial and commercial interests which the new conditions in the Balkans had brought about. Germany had a very large stake in Turkey; France both in Turkey and the Balkan states; Britain was chiefly interested in the Turkish territories in Arabia, while France was interested in the Turkish territories of Lebanon and Syria. Finally, all the Powers were anxious that the repayment of the enormous Ottoman Public Debt should be continued. Turkey had indicated that if she were to lose her European possessions she would be unable to pay the Debt. The financial settlement after the War was of as much interest to the Triple Entente and the Central Alliance as were the territorial arrangements. If Turkey were compelled to pay a war indemnity, it would be the financiers of Europe who would have to come up with the money. The Turks, who knew from long experience that the goodwill of Europe was controlled by its purse-strings, dispatched Hakki Pasha to London with his diplomatic briefcase stuffed with enticing economic deals for all friends of the Ottoman Empire. To the British the Pasha offered concessions concerning the extension of the Baghdad Railway to the Persian Gulf and concessions affecting the future status of Kuwait, control over which Britain had acquired by an agreement with the local sheik on 23 January 1899. To the Germans he offered the concession to the Deutsche Bank for the Tunnel Railway from Istanbul under the Golden Horn to Galata. And lavish promises were distributed all around, to the French, to the Italians, even to the Russians.

75 Rankin, *Inner History*, p. 496.

At last the Great Powers came into their own and established themselves as arbiters of the Balkan Conference. Even before the Turkish and Allied delegates confronted each other across the bargaining table, the Balkan representatives had to present their separate claims to the Great Powers. The Greek claims included Salonica, the Aegean Islands, and Epirus. Salonica was also coveted by Bulgaria; the Aegean islands, with a predominantly Greek population and occupied by the Greek Fleet, were not contested by any other Balkan Ally -- but Turkey adamantly refused to consider relinquishing them. In Albania, Greek claims extended as far as Valona (Avlona). Serbian claims in Albania extended as far as Durazzo. Austria and Italy threatened war against Greece and Serbia if either of those Balkan countries occupied what Austria and Italy considered to be the Albanian coast. The historical and ethnological grounds upon which Greece based her claims were hardly ever the decisive factors as far as the Great Powers were concerned. To the idealistic Greeks, who often lived in the past rather than the present, the pragmatic approach of the Great Powers came as something of a shock. In London Metaxas was treated to a brief lesson in international diplomacy. In a letter to the Greek General Staff he described the Greek Delegation's negotiations with the Powers, somewhat exaggerating his own importance:

"The Protecting Powers of Greece [Great Britain, France and Russia] demanded strategic, geographical, commercial and generally economic reasons in support of our claims. The ethnological aspect was of secondary importance to them. And I found such reasons! I am even surprised myself how I managed to do it. Because these are the only acceptable arguments for them. One almost despairs of the European diplomats."[76]

The St. James' conference was formally opened by Sir Edward Grey on 17 December 1912, the day after the Greek Fleet won the naval battle of Cape Helles. The next day the Turkish representatives declared that they could not negotiate with the Greek representative because Greece had not signed the armistice and was still fighting. New instructions from Istanbul cleared up this difficulty, but the Turkish representatives were in no hurry to relinquish their European provinces and conclude a peace. Adrianople in Thrace, Ioannina in Epirus, and Scutari in Albania were still holding out, and the Turks hoped to strengthen their defenders; there had already been signs of falling-out between the Balkan Allies, and the Turks expected that an armed conflict between them would not be long in coming. In that event, the Turks hoped that their fortunes in the Aegean might improve and that they would then be able to reoccupy the islands. The haste with which the Bulgarians had signed the armistice provided the Turks with the opportunity to build up their Army in Thrace with fresh contingents which arrived overland from Anatolia. Metaxas wrote to his wife:

---

76 Ventiris, *Hellas*, I, p. 127.

"Because of the foolishness of the Bulgarians, the Turks have revived, and it is rather unlikely that they will submit to the peace terms .... The Bulgarians, who have destroyed what we had accomplished, will not enjoy the fruits of their perfidy. Gradually the political climate is becoming unfavourable to them."[77]

The Turks were playing for time. The first six meetings were spent discussing various points of procedure put forward by the Turkish Delegation and rejecting a series of unacceptable Turkish proposals. During the tenth session on 6 January 1913 the Balkan Delegates walked out of the Conference because the Turks continued to insist that they should retain the vilayet of Adrianople and that the Aegean Islands should be restored to them.

At this time Metaxas spoke "only ten words" of English. When he could not make himself understood in London, he would revert to French or German. Perhaps for this reason he did not enjoy the English theater. "Only music entertains and satisfies me; it reminds me of so many beautiful things: a life filled with devotion and work, of great endeavor to become good, but also with many mistakes and sins."[78] He went alone to hear Handel's "Messiah." And to his great joy he found that a Wagner concert was being given in London. It was held in a vast auditorium [the Albert Hall?] which accommodated five to six thousand people. The orchestra was one hundred and ten instruments strong. "The execution was excellent and most faithful. But where was the feeling with which the Germans play Wagner!"[79] But neither music nor company nor any of the fascinating panorama of London life could make him forget the little family he had left behind in Greece. He wrote to Lela: "All around is the sea of London and I am sitting on a little island with you and our child. Everything else is lost in the fog." The teeming life of London made him feel even more lonely. "I have changed very much, my Lela: I am not the same man as I was years ago, before I married you, when I desired to be as free as a bird, when I wanted to see the world... No I only want our little home, I want you and our children: because the small private world we have created is far superior to the great world outside.[80]

In London on 16 January 1913 Metaxas received the following telegram from Colonel Dousmanis:

"We [the General Staff] are departing for Epirus. Therefore leave London and join us immediately. Arrange for necessary campaign equipment from Athens to reach you en route."[81]

77 Metaxas, *Diary,* II, p. 180.
78 Metaxas, *Diary.,* p. 189.
79 *Ibid.,* p. 187.
80 *Ibid.,* p. 188.
81 *Ibid.,* p. 197.

In Epirus the war against the Turks had reached a stalemate and the Greek Government insisted that the Crown Prince should go there with his Staff and assume the command. In consequence Major-General Danglis and Captain Metaxas were at once recalled home. It was Colonel Dousmanis who, out of malice, had often succeeded in excluding Metaxas from the counsels of the Crown Prince. He was a dour and more experienced officer, the longtime personal military adviser to Constantine, and he both hated and envied his younger and better educated colleague, whom he usually managed to keep in the background. Metaxas had written the orders for the battle of Sarantaporo, conceived the plan for the battle of Janitsa, planned the campaign in Western Macedonia. But Dousmanis, the Director of Operations, had presented all Metaxas' brilliant work to the Commander-in-Chief as the combined effort of the General Staff. Metaxas was aware of this and resented it keenly. Should not the Crown Prince have realized this fact and singled him out for warm personal commendation? As it was, the man who, as Metaxas saw it, had planned the whole campaign had not been promoted and was still only a captain. Yet not once did the loyal Staff Officer allow any word of complaint against his Chief to escape his lips. Instead he stored it all away in his heart and, as he wrote to his wife, "suffered" because of it. "Florina: it was there that the campaign against me began, because they thought that the campaign against the Turks had ended."[82] Now the Commander-in-Chief needed him once again and once again Metaxas answered the call. "I am going to do my duty, but no longer with much enthusiasm," he wrote to his wife.[83]

Before Metaxas left London Venizelos confided to him: "I shall feel much easier knowing that you are down there [at the front in Epirus]."[84] It was true. The state knew of Metaxas' services and when the need had once more arisen the state had sent for him. To Metaxas' egocentric way of thinking, all the country's war effort, all political and diplomatic activity, all the generals and all the armies would have come to nought without the benefit of his exceptional contribution. Despite his disclaimers, Metaxas was the most ambitious of men and it hurt his proud spirit to be treated as a mere instrument, carrying out policies which others had devised and for which others received recognition. One day all ambition was to be fulfilled, and as dictator Metaxas would demand in no uncertain manner the gratitude and adulation of his fellow countrymen. Until then he harboured a deep-seated grudge against the state for failing to recognize his outstanding abilities and reward his inestimable services.

82 Ibid., p. 268.
83 *Ibid.*, p. 198.
84 *Ibid.*, p. 195.

The Balkan Wars II

From London Metaxas wrote to his wife, "If you have returned the camp-bed I used on campaign, buy me another from the Military Union, because I cannot get one here: they are too heavy and anyway, there is not the time. Also buy me two heavy woolen blankets; or, even better, write to Nider to send you two army blankets and I shall give him a receipt -- they are superior by far. Also get someone to clean my saddle, the old one, and have it ready for me. You know the other necessaries for a campaign."[1] And, as a considerate husband, Metaxas assured his wife that there was no cause for her to worry, that he was going to take care of himself and return to her safe and sound. "Did you not see how well the war went in Macedonia and how I looked after myself, and how good my health was all that time?" He also asked Lela to request Nider, the Director of Personnel at the Ministry of War, to find him a suitable batman to accompany him to Epirus.

In London while attending the Peace Conference with the Greek Delegation Metaxas advised Venizelos not to sign the armistice with Turkey yet; it was only a matter of time before Ioannina, the capital city of mountainous Epirus, would fall to the Greeks. But the military situation in Epirus was far from satisfactory. The Greek Army had been under the command of General Sapountzakis, the Chief of Staff at the time of the disastrous defeat of 1897. Metaxas was in Sofia when he first heard that Sapountzakis had been appointed Commander-in-Chief of the Army of Epirus, and he was furious. He wrote to his wife: "That man can't even ride a horse. What the devil will he do?"[2] Sapountzakis failed to press on to the north and capture Ioannina, the principal objective of the Epirus campaign, although the Greeks performed a series of heroic exploits in spite of the hardships of the severe winter of 1912-13.

Many outside observers followed the advance of the Greek Army and gave vivid glimpses of the fighting men. The populations of the camps were at once colourful and diverse. Much admired were the Greek Highlanders, the tall *Evzones,* with their snow-white foustanellas, braided boleros and full, hanging sleeves, their small red caps with the long black tassels and their *tsarouchia* -- the mountain shoes, the turned-up toes trimmed with large black tufts. Fiercest of all were the Cretans, who wore black topboots and flowing pantaloons of dark blue and who were distinguished by their characteristic proud, long-striding gait and lordly manners. The leader of these Cretan irregulars was the dashing Constantine Manos, an Oxonian from Balliol, son of a famous Cretan family, who was later killed when his plane crashed during a reconnaissance mission. The foreign volunteers of the Garibaldian Regiment wore red shirts. Equally picturesque were the Greek volunteers from overseas; a Greek actor from Paris recited *tirades* from Racine in the evenings, to the amazement of his simple comrades.

---

1 Metaxas, *Diary,* p. 198.

2 *Ibid.*.

Psacoff, a Russian of Greek extraction, flew at a height of only 2,000 feet over the enemy trenches at Fort Bizani in his own plane and returned with the wings riddled with bullets.

By the middle of November the Greeks had established a loose blockade around the city of Janina, but they failed to prevent re-enforcements from reaching the Turkish defenders. Ali Riza Pasha, retreating from Monastir where he had been defeated by the Serbs, and Djavid Pasha, retreating from Korytsa where he had been defeated by the Greeks, joined forces with Essad Pasha in Ioannina. Djavid Pasha even succeeded in hauling over the mountains the cannons he had captured earlier from the ill-fated Greek Fifth Division, although abandoning his own cannons to his pursuers. The 12,000 men of the garrison at Ioannina were thus increased to 35,000. Unlike Macedonia, in Epirus the Turks had superiority of numbers in both men and guns. The Greeks were only about 20,000 strong and had only 30 cannons compared to the 100 cannons of the Turks. But the worst enemy with which the Greek invaders had to contend was the bitterly cold winter, and many men perished from frostbite and exposure. Sometimes the Greek and Turkish soldiers confronting each other in the front line positions would come to an agreement that no night attacks would be launched, and fires against the piercing cold would be lit on both sides. Fraternization between the Greek and Turkish soldiers was not uncommon -- it was on one such occasion that Fonat Bey, the Commander of Fort Bizani, learned from the Greeks of the assassination in Constantinople of Nazim Pasha, the Turkish Commander-in-Chief. Inside the beleaguered city, Essad Pasha -- who was not related to the Turkish commander of the same name who led the defenders of Scutari -- defended his home-town of Ioannina with great skill and resolution.

Metaxas arrived in Epirus on 24 January 1913, after having visited Athens to see his family. In his first letter to his wife from the front he told her that "the position will be conquered slowly, step by step."[3] Constantine had only assumed command after the Greek government agreed to dispatch a new division from Macedonia to Epirus at the risk of weakening the defense of Salonica against the Bulgarian threat. In mid-winter a great part of the Greek Army, along with their guns, horses, and thousands of pack animals, was transported by sea through the Corinth Canal from Salonica to Epirus, while other units marched from Western Macedonia over the Pindus Mountains to join the Army in Epirus. Constantine transferred the Army Headquarters from Preveza to Philippias and consigned the incompetent General Sapountzakis to services in the rear. The General Staff of the Crown Prince were hailed by the Army as saviours. The lack of ability and the mismanagement of Sapountzakis had resulted in enormous casualties. Thousands of men and animals died in the snow from frostbite and starvation. On 2

---

3 *Ibid.*, II, p. 199.

February Metaxas wrote to Lela: "This war has been dreadful, especially for Greece. Since 3 October, while the other Allies observed an armistice, we continued fighting. What the Army has suffered in Epirus is beyond description."[4] Provisions had been piling up at the port of Preveza, but only a trickle reached the suffering soldiers 50 miles away. The supporting services had to be reorganized; lorries and mules from Preveza and barges on the River Louros carried tents and blankets and warm woollen underclothing and socks against the cold; the men at the front now also received an issue of brandy every morning and a hot meal with meat every day, plus a daily ration of raisins. Metaxas wrote: "Now they all have enough to eat, they can rest, not so many freeze to death. Of course, some are killed and some are wounded and some fall sick -- that is war, but not as it was before."[5] The chaotic conditions prevailing in Epirus under Sapountzakis were bound to arouse the impatience and anger of an efficient and conscientious officer like Metaxas. The confusion extended to the whole strategy of the campaign. Metaxas wrote:

"There have been many proposals and many plans, but they were all general, none of them paid any attention to details; and details are almost everything. We found many plans, but no provision for ammunition, for engineering equipment, for food supplies, for fodder, for transportation, for tents, nothing ..... The important thing is not the plan, but the diligence and methodical manner of its execution ...."[6]

Metaxas toured the front lines and the positions in the rear to see for himself the true state of affairs.

"I studied the whole situation very carefully and then we [the General Staff] began working out everything methodically from the beginning; but because of the prevailing disorder, it will take time and, unfortunately, blood."[7]

The former Staff of General Sapountzakis had discussed several plans without consistently pursuing any one of them. Troop movements were executed without purpose, battles were fought without definite objectives. "This chaos had to be organized. We had to estimate what had succeeded, what had failed, and draw up the balance; to decide what to keep, what to discard. Then establish a basic strategy and go forward from there."[8]The enemy positions had to be determined; the artillery moved up the precipitous mountains; the infantry moved cautiously to new positions; munitions and provisions were distributed. It was apparent that the siege would take time -- but not more than a month, as Metaxas wrote. And in his self-centered manner, he wrote to Lela as though he were the Commander-in-Chief, that all depended on him,

---

4 *Ibid.*
5 *Ibid.*, p. 202 .
6 *Ibid.*, pp. 199-200.
7 *Ibid.*, p. 200.
8 *Ibid.*, p. 203.

that he would make sure that the correct course was followed. "I am not going to gamble with Ioannina -- *pile ou face*. Until success is certain, I do not intend to make the attempt. If the Athenians are impatient, let them come and take over .... But as long as I am here, I will not allow any follies to be committed."[9] The amateur strategists in Athens would, perforce, have to possess themselves in patience. As Metaxas wrote to Lela:

7 Epirus Campaign. Prince Alexandros, General Danglis, General Moschopoulos. Standing between the latter and Constantine, Prince Christophoros (standing), Prince Andreas, General Dousmanis, Metaxas, Prince George.

"How long did it take to capture Plevna? How long Strasbourg? How long Metz? How long Sebastopol? How long Port Arthur? Well then, why should we, being at a greater disadvantage, expect to capture Ioannina in a shorter time? Or, on the other

---

9 *Ibid.*

hand, why should we not accomplish as much as all these others have accomplished?"[10]

The northward advance of the Greek Army towards Ioannina was checked by a formidable natural barrier: fifteen kilometers south of Ioannina the solid mass of Mount Bizani brooded 864 meters above the mountain passes, effectively blocking all approaches to the city. The intricate system of fortifications at Bizani had been constructed under the supervision of the German Military Mission in Turkey. Cement tunnels inter-connected the heavy Krupp batteries and the trenches. The surrounding semi-circular range of mountains was also fortified with guns and cement battlements. Fort Bizani appeared to be impregnable and many experts considered that the attempts of the Greek Army were suicidal. Around the country murmurs began to be heard that an inordinate number of young men were being sacrificed in vain. As soon as Venizelos returned from London (where the peace negotiations had reached an *impasse*) he visited the front on 23 February 1913 to learn from personal observation whether the campaign should continue or the Greek Army be withdrawn. Metaxas was instantly suspicious of the motives behind the Prime Minister's visit. He wrote to Lela: "Tomorrow Venizelos is coming here. Why? I can imagine how much they must be blaming us for the delay if Venizelos himself had to come here."[11] Victor Dousmanis wrote in his *Memoirs* that at one point Venizelos took the General Staff aside and asked them, point blank, if Bizani were assailable. Because if it were not, he, as Prime Minister, would order the ceasefire and take all the blame to save the face of the Crown Prince and the Army. Dousmanis and Metaxas assured the Prime Minister that Bizani would be conquered soon. Venizelos asked to see the front and Constantine and the General Staff took him on a tour of the advance positions. The Turks, observing through their binoculars the civilian figure of Venizelos on the opposite hill, suspected that something unusual was afoot and fired a random cannonade, killing some of the Greek officers who were standing with the party of distinguished visitors. Paraskevopoulos, the Artillery Commander, immediately ordered by telephone a sharp shelling of the Turkish positions from the surrounding hills, which diverted the enemy's attention. The Turks had almost succeeded in wiping out the Greek Prime Minister, Crown Prince Constantine, Prince George of Sparta, the future George II, and the whole General Staff with a single shell! Later, when a prisoner-of-war, General Essad Pasha chivalrously avowed that had he known of the presence of the Greek Prime Minister and the Crown Prince he would not have permitted the cannonade. Metaxas did not mention such perilous incidents to his wife, so as not to alarm her. Instead he wrote: "Venizelos came and lavished great compliments on the Crown Prince and all of us: it was not at all what

10 *Ibid.*, pp. 201-2.
11 *Ibid.*, p. 208.

I feared and wrote to you about; he only came to help us out. .... I cannot write to you further. I shall tell you when I return. He left full of enthusiasm."[12]

8 General Essat Pasha, the heroic defender of Ioannina.

The storming of Bizani is perhaps the most brilliant military achievement in Modern Greek history and, as is natural, many have claimed credit for the original plan of attack. Xenophon Strategos, who was on the General Staff, once testified at a court-martial that the plan was actually based upon one prepared by a civil engineer named Mineïkos, who proposed that the Greek attack should concentrate on the enemy's right flank among the western precipices of the fortress. According to Strategos, both Danglis and Metaxas agreed with the basic concept of this plan. The Venizelist

12 *Ibid.*

historian Ventiris reported that it was a Staff Officer, Kalogeras of the Fourth Division, who was actually responsible for the success of the siege because he insisted that his plan, similar to that which was finally adopted, should be followed. Apparently several officers put forward plans like the one which was finally successful. General Pangalos and other military writers all agree that it was Ioannis Metaxas who devised the tactical manoeuvres by which the fortress was captured. Metaxas himself in his letters to his wife related how, on the bleak afternoon of 22 February, while the rain was driving down and the wind was blustering outside, he and the four other officers of the General Staff sat around the fire in Philippias, discussing the difficulties involved in an attack. All earlier plans for storming the Fort by an attack on its right had always been turned down because the western face of the mountain formed a natural unassailable wall of rock. Pallis, one of the Staff Officers, again mentioned the western heights of the mountain and remarked: "What a pity we have concentrated our forces on the eastern slopes and the attack cannot be made." Metaxas continues the story in his own words: "Then I had an inspiration. 'It can be made!' I exclaimed and I began calculating the movements of the regiments, the movements of the mountain artillery, how to withdraw them from the right [of the Greeks], how to concentrate them on the left [of the Greeks]. ... I was filled with enthusiasm."[13] The Staff discussed Metaxas' ideas and agreed upon them. For the next five days Metaxas worked furiously far into the night, calculating and putting down in writing all the orders for the necessary troop movements. None but the five Staff Officers knew what was happening. Neither Constantine nor Venizelos, whose visit to the front took place the day after Metaxas' "inspiration," were informed. The orders were worded in such a way as to deceive even the unit commanders, some of whom had made friends among the camp-followers and could not be trusted. On 28 February a detailed plan and the relevant orders were submitted to the Crown Prince the Commander-in-Chief, who gave them his approval. Next day the orders were issued to the unit commanders individually, so that each one thought he was being used as a decoy to deceive the enemy. All communications of every kind between the Army and the local population were cut off and the nearby towns were put under a strict twenty-four hour curfew.

On the eve of the attack Metaxas could not rest. At three o'clock in the morning he woke up Dousmanis, as reported by the latter in his Memoirs:

Metaxas: *It is raining heavily. Can you hear the rain?*

Dousmanis: *Yes, I can hear the noise of the water in the gutters of the road.*

Metaxas: Yes, but it is raining heavily and it is questionable whether the troop movements we have ordered can be executed.

Dousmanis: *Let me sleep. There is still time before tomorrow morning.*

13 *Ibid.*, p. 207.

Metaxas: *No, there is no time. It is three hours past midnight and if we send word now countermanding our orders, the message will arrive only just before the troops begin to move out.*
Dousmanis: *And if the troop movements should be postponed today, when do you think they could be carried out?*
Metaxas: *It would take 15 days or more.*
Dousmanis: *I myself cannot suggest such a postponement to the Crown Prince. And I will let his orders be carried out.*[14]

Dousmanis mentions this exchange in an attempt to show that Metaxas was timid. According to General Pangalos, Dousmanis was jealous of the younger and more junior officer because it was Metaxas who "had drawn up the plan and composed all the orders for the general attack."[15] Metaxas was neither timid nor cowardly, but a levelheaded and responsible military tactician, who would not take any unnecessary risks and who cared about the lives and wellbeing of his men. Before the arrival of the Crown Prince's General Staff the Epirus campaign had abounded in exploits as heroic as they were ineffectual. Thousands of men lost their lives in ill-judged engagements which, while they earned the empty dithyrambs of the Greek press, did not bring the capture of Ioannina any nearer. At 5:00 a.m. the same morning Metaxas and Dousmanis set off for the Han [Inn] of Emin Aga, from where they watched the troops move to their new positions. Twenty-four *tagmata*, amounting to 20,000 soldiers, trudged over mountains covered with snow two feet thick, and twenty-four mountain cannons were hauled with great difficulty from one mountain peak to another. Within three days the movement of the troops was completed without the enemy getting the slightest wind of it.

On 4 March 1913 at 8:30 in the morning, just before riding off to the battle with the Crown Prince, Metaxas wrote to his wife:

"Today the artillery begins the bombardment and tomorrow the general attack begins. I could not leave here without sending you and our children one thousand kisses, my precious, my beloved. I hope everything will turn out well and then I shall cable you from Ioannina. Yesterday and the day before yesterday I was in the front line with Dousmanis and we checked everything, so all is prepared as it should be. We have all done our duty. Now may God help us!"[16]

The battle began with a heavy bombardment of the enemy positions. On the first day of the attack 30,000 shells pounded Bizani, which lay under a thick cloud of smoke and dust. It was the heaviest bombardment in world history up to that time. Throughout the night the shelling continued intermittently. At the same time passes were blasted

---

14 Victor Dousmanis, *Απομνημονεύματα* (Athens, 1946), pp. 85-86.

15 Pangalos, *Απομνημονεύματα*, p. 265.

16 Metaxas, *Diary*, II, p. 205

through the surrounding mountains so that the cannons could be dragged up to the summit. The following day, 5 March, the general attack was launched, while Greek aeroplanes bombed any fortifications still left standing. By evening the chief Turkish positions had been over-run. Again during the night the bombardment continued at regular intervals. At three o'clock in the morning of 6 March Essad Pasha, who had been fighting bravely in the front lines and had only narrowly escaped capture, sent his brother Colonel Vehit Bey and the Suffragan Bishop of Ioannina to negotiate the surrender of the Fort and the city. Vehit Bey, who had been under heavy fire for two days, was tense and nervous. "Will this cannonade never stop?" he kept asking. The Greeks insisted upon unconditional surrender and Dousmanis told Vehit Bey that the shelling would continue until this took place. By daybreak the Turkish colonel was worn down and agreed to the Greek terms. At once the order was given for the bombardment to cease and Metaxas and Strategos rode to Ioannina and signed the protocol of surrender. Metaxas wrote to his wife: "I spoke for a long time with Essad Pasha and Vehit Bey. They are the most courteous of men, educated in Europe."[17] Both Essad Pasha and Vehit Bey, as well as the majority of the twenty officers on the Turkish General Staff, had been students, like Metaxas and Strategos, at the Berlin War Academy. It was almost on Old Boys' reunion. But it was not necessary to use German as the language of communication because Essad Pasha the Turkish Commander who came from the renegade Epiriot family of Glykis, spoke excellent Greek -- he was a graduate of the local Greek Gymnasium. It should be added that the Suffragan Bishop, assistant to the Archbishop of Ioannina, who accompanied Essad's brother Vehit Bey, was their nephew! Ties of blood did not lessen the fierce loyalties of either side; such unexpected family connections throw an interesting light on the social patterns prevailing in the Ottoman Empire. Colonel Vehit Bey was visibly moved as he approached the Commander of the Greek Cavalry who was awaiting him outside the city to accept the surrender.

Next day, 7 March, the Greek Army made a triumphal entry into Ioannina. The Crown Prince rode at their head, with Danglis and Dousmanis behind him; then came the Royal Princes, followed by the Section of Operations of the General Staff led by Ioannis Metaxas. It was a beautiful spring day. The surrounding mountains were covered in snow, the Lake of Ioannina sparkled in the sunlight. The city itself had not been shelled and had ample stocks of meat and maize, so the civilian population had not suffered. There was a delirium of enthusiasm on the entry of the Greek Army which has been described in many contemporary accounts. In a long letter to his wife in which he described the recent battle, Metaxas wrote:

---

17 *Ibid.*

"The entry was a real apotheosis. And what do you suppose I was thinking about then? That, rather than these theatrical events, I would have much preferred to be with you, the two of us taking a beautiful walk."[18]

9 Constantine and his staff in Ioannina, Metaxas, second from left wearing his sword.

In this letter Metaxas enclosed the plan of battle, marking the positions and movements of the Greek Army. Beneath the plan of battle he had sketched he wrote: "For my Lela. Ioannina, 25 February, 1913, Yiannakis." In the accompanying letter he continued;

"I wanted to write to you about many things, but drawing the plan of battle for you took me a long time. Still I had to send you the plan. You are the first to know how the

18 *Ibid.*, p. 206.

battle was fought; neither the princes nor the government know it yet, only the broad outlines. But my Lela should be the first to learn of it."[19]

A few days later the Crown Prince -- who had an eye for the ladies -- invited some of the female campfollowers to join him in an excursion to Bizani. Metaxas happened to be present and Constantine asked him to go along. " I therefore went, too, in the company of persons not very agreeable, whose habits and caprices were not in accordance with my way of thinking."[20] On this trip Metaxas found that he was "the object of general curiousity. Another man might have preened himself; I was disgusted."[21] Up on the mountain he fell into a reverie of home and detached himself from the company. One of the ladies broke in upon his thoughts. "What a pity your wife is not here. We would have spent a pleasant time together." Metaxas replied that had it not been for their infant daughter, his wife would certainly have been there. He wandered alone through the devastation of the fortress, looking for some memento to send his wife. Among the smouldering ruins he found a few blue and white flowers -- the Greek colours -- and gathered them for Lela "to keep the flowers I sent you from Sarantaporo company."[22] Some of the ladies asked him for whom the flowers were intended. "I told them, 'for my wife.' I assure you, not one of those vulgar women laughed. On Bizani, where death still hovers, even they do not laugh at sacred feelings. At worst they are jealous."[23] Neither the shallow cynicism of the society women from Athens nor the capricious inequities of a bureaucratic state could, even for a moment, erase from his mind the overwhelming sense of his *αξία* and the knowledge of the decisive role he had played in the victorious campaign. In the middle of his description of his trip to Bizani he suddenly burst out:

"I forgot to tell you about the promotions. It is monstrous; almost all those who bungled things in the war have been promoted. They say they will promote us later. I don't care tuppence. Whether captain or major, I led an army."[24]

In Ioannina Metaxas bought as souvenirs a belt of silver and gold-plated filigree of Turkish craftsmanship for his wife and brooches for his two daughters.

The liberation of Ioannina in 1913 after 583 years of Turkish rule was achieved at the cost of many lives. One hundred and fifty years earlier Father Kosmas Aetolos (1714-1797), a famous itinerant monk who preached the "resurrection of the Greek Nation," had prophesied that one day Preveza would awaken and find herself free, while "the young bull would swim in blood" before Ioannina was liberated. And so it proved

19 *Ibid.*, p. 208.
20 *Ibid.*, p. 209.
21 *Ibid.*
22 *Ibid.*, p. 210.
23 *Ibid.*
24 *Ibid.*

to be. During the four-month siege of the city the Turks lost 7,500 men. Greek losses were heavier by far. The Epirus campaign cost the Greeks 15,000 killed and wounded. 430 Turkish officers and 38,000 Turkish soldiers became prisoners of war. The Greeks also took 109 guns, but little ammunition was left to capture; the Turks fought to the end. In his *Memoirs* Paraskevopoulos, the Greek Artillery Commander, expressed his *"admiration for the courage, the tenacity and persistence of the garrison which defended the complex fortifications of Bizani during the siege. The Turks, although they knew that they were surrounded on all sides, isolated from the Turkish State, with no expectation of any assistance, and fully aware from our preparations that an attack was imminent and our success certain, nevertheless did not lose heart, but took all possible measures to stretch to the utmost degree their remaining material and moral strength...."*[25]

According to Paraskevopoulos, Colonel Vehit Bey who commanded the garrison of the city was "a clever, energetic, courageous leader, who knew his duty perfectly well and would not be deterred by any obstacle."[26] After the capture of Ioannina, Paraskevopoulos was travelling from Preveza to Piraeus on the same ship on which Essad Pasha and Vehit Bey and about twenty Turkish Staff Officers were being transferred to Athens as prisoners of war, and he had an opportunity to become more closely acquainted with them. The Turkish officers, who were "*libres penseurs,*" according to Paraskevopoulos, attributed the present state of decay in the Ottoman Empire to the outmoded ideas and traditions of the old regime, which they were determined to rejuvenate. When at dinner Paraskevopoulos toasted the Turkish Army for their brave defense, Essad Pasha replied that it was not the Greek Army which had been the victor but civilization, and he expressed his admiration for the Greek soldier and the humane way the Greeks had treated the Turkish inhabitants.[27] Years later, Essad Pasha and his brother Vehit Bey, on a private visit to Greece in connection with a settlement of their property rights in Epirus, paid a courtesy call on General Pangalos, who had been their adversary at Ioannina. At one point in the conversation Vehit Bey remarked: "We fought only for the honour of our arms because, cut off from Turkey as we were, we knew that there was no hope."[28]

After the fall of Ioannina the Greek Eighth Division advanced north and cleared all Epirus, including Northern Epirus, now Southern Albania, of the remnants of the Turkish forces. Metaxas travelled 240 kilometers by motorcar to Argyrokastro which, he wrote to Lela, was "built on high rocks and had a completely medieval character."

25 Leonidas Paraskevopoulos, *Αναμνήσεις, 1896-1920* [Recollections: 1896 - 1920] (Athens, 1930), p. 147.

26 *Ibid.*, p. 150.

27 *Ibid.*, p. 155.

28 Pangalos, *Απομνημονεύματα*, p. 258.

Everywhere the Greek Army went it was given an enthusiastic welcome by the Greek inhabitants of the liberated towns and villages. The main body of the Greek Army, with no opportunity for rest, was ordered aboard the Greek ships waiting at Santi Quaranta and Preveza and transferred via the Corinth Canal back to Salonica, where the Macedonian capital was threatened by the Bulgarians. Charilaos Trikoupis, during whose term of office the Canal was opened, must be given some of the credit for the success of the Greek arms in the Balkan Wars. Several other Greek regiments, after long and arduous marches through the steep, snow-clad mountains of Pindus on their way to join the Greek Army in Epirus, received the news of the Greek victory only when they were within a few miles from Ioannina; there was no time for these regiments to enter the city and rest -- they were immediately ordered to retrace their steps over the mountains and return to Salonica. As for Metaxas, he returned to Athens to see his family.

At Ioannina, in the moment of his greatest triumph, the Crown Prince received the news that the King his father had been assassinated in Salonica. George I had taken up residence in Salonica three days after the capture of the city by the Greek Army and had vowed not to leave until peace was signed and the Greeks' possession of Salonica secured.

The late king, painfully aware of Constantine's limitations of character, and fearful of what the future might hold for his country and his dynasty, bequeathed his final advice to his son and heir in an eloquent Political Testament. In this document King George urged Constantine to love wholeheartedly his "dear little country," to give his children a good Greek education, "for they must be Greeks and nothing else," and to serve his people with courage and patience.

"Let the night pass before coming to a decision. Never let the sun go down on your wrath. Be calm and never forget that you are reigning over a southern people who are easily roused and may in a moment do and say many things which they will probably forget a few hours after. For this reason never fall into a passion and never forget that it is often preferable that the king should suffer rather than his people. Do not lose sight of the fact that the interests of the people must be placed before all other interests, and God will help you in your heavy task."[29]

On 18 March 1913 Crown Prince Constantine, who had triumphantly redeemed his reputation as a field commander in Macedonia and Epirus, duly succeeded to the throne as King of the Hellenes. His encomiasts hailed him as Constantine XII, the successor of Constantine XI, the last of the Paleologues of Byzantium. However, the new King, when appending his signature did not style himself as the twelfth of his line, but simply wrote his name, adding the letter B after it -- the first letter of *Βασιλεύς*, the Greek

29 Rankin, *Inner History*, p. 388, (From the London Times, 14 April 1913).

word for king. During the enthronement Constantine took the customary oath to observe the Constitution.

10 Constantine and Venizelos

After the ceremony the new King remarked to Venizelos, "Apart from the official promise to observe the Constitution which I gave a short while ago, I wish to assure you personally, Mr. Prime Minister, that I will in all things follow the policies of my father." Well pleased, Venizelos spoke a moment later to his Minister of the Interior, Emmanuel Repoulis.
Venizelos: *Constantine has declared, and I believe his words, that he will imitate his father in everything.*
Repoulis: *I am not as certain as you are that Constantine will easily keep to all that he has promised you, Mr. Prime Minister. Let us wait and see, or rather, let us pray that it may be so.*[30]

---

30 Kordatos, *Ιστορία*, V, pp. 315-6.

The Bulgarians considered themselves the most aggrieved of the Allies. Owing to her geographical position Bulgaria was compelled to march eastwards towards Constantinople to prevent the Turks from invading her territory. But the Bulgarian national objectives lay to the west in Macedonia and the Bulgarians had taken it very hard that the Greeks had beaten them to Salonica and the Serbs had beaten them to Monastir. When Venizelos was in London for the Conference he often tried to discuss the question of the future Greco-Bulgarian boundaries, but Dr. Danev, the Head of the Bulgarian Delegation, always evaded the issue. On one occasion, 19 December 1912, Danev called by himself on Venizelos to discuss the problems which had arisen at the Conference from the endless prevarications of the Turks. When the meeting was over, Danev rose and immediately prepared to leave. The Greek Prime Minister caught up with him at the door.

Venizelos: *Now we are alone, let us talk about Salonica.*

Danev: *This is hardly the moment.*

Venizelos: *We still have a little time in which to plan a foundation for our future discussions.*

Danev: *I have received no instructions from my Government; I know nothing about this.*

Venizelos: *Let us have a serious talk and try to arrange matters.*

Danev: *With pleasure; but at this moment Salonica is in the hands of the [Allied] Armies. Politics have nothing to do with it at present; we will speak of it after peace has been signed with Turkey.*

Venizelos: *Salonica is not in the hands of the Allies, but under the Government of the King of the Hellenes. Salonica belongs to Greece by historic right and by the right of conquest. And I can tell you this: Greece will consent to any other sacrifice in order to maintain the Balkan Alliance, but give up Salonica -- never, never!*[31]

The Bulgarian representative left without another word. That evening Venizelos cabled the Greek Foreign Minister Koromelas in Athens, who was at that time acting as his Deputy: "I declared to Danev that no Greek king and no Greek government could be found who would agree to yield Salonica, unless it were after an unfortunate war."[32]

Greece was prepared to fight for Salonica. The next day, 20 December 1912, Ioannis Metaxas wrote to the Greek General Staff:

"The last meeting between Venizelos and Danev took place yesterday. Venizelos stated quite categorically that he considered the issue of Salonica to be a question of war between Greece and Bulgaria and only if Greece were to be defeated in such a war, would she yield on this question. By Salonica Venizelos also meant a territorial

---

31 C. Kerofilas, *Eleftherios Venizelos: His Life and Work* (London & New York, 1915), pp. 102-103.

32 Ventiris, *Ελλάς*, I, p. 126.

zone around the city, to the north and to the east, extending for a considerable distance, so that not only the economic survival of the city, but also its security from a military point of view, would be secured. I should add that, if Bulgaria should be implacable, Greece would accept the arbitration of the Triple Entente -- France, England and Russia. Danev said that he would refer the matter to his Government and gave no response to Venizelos' words. Under these circumstances it is advisable that you should take all precautions down there, in case the Bulgarian Army, now stationed in Salonica, makes some sudden move in order to present a fait accompli, should the Bulgarian Government not give in."[33]

In the first week of March soon after his return from London Venizelos visited Belgrade and Sofia in an attempt to resolve the differences among the Balkan Allies. Nekludov, the Russian Minister at Sofia, who was very much interested in the peaceful resolution of the Macedonian problem, asked to see the Greek Prime Minister and later recorded his impressions in his *Diplomatic Reminiscences*.

"I have rarely seen a man who, at the first meeting, has produced such a favourable impression on me as M. Venizelos did. An astonishing simplicity, an absolutely frank and open way of expressing his opinions and convictions -- which one feels to be deep-constituted and still constitute the strength and prestige of this true statesman. I felt at once that I was in the presence, first, of a perfect gentleman, and then of a scrupulously honest politician. No phraseology, no desire to deceive his questioner were apparent in the clear, precise, and modest expression of his thoughts. The very fact that he, promptly and without any preamble, broached the principal question -- that of Graeco-Bulgarian demarcation -- predisposed me enormously in his favour."[34]

Map in hand, Venizelos demonstrated to the Russian Minister why Salonica and its hinterland, including the Chalcidice Peninsula, should go to Greece. Venizelos told Nekludov:

"What is bad and what makes me anxious, is the fact that nothing on earth will induce the Bulgarians to enter into negotiations with us, as we have repeatedly suggested they should do. They always elude the subject, as if they were on the watch for fresh occurrences or some new situation; and yet amongst us public opinion is very much excited over the tone of the Bulgarian press, which even disputes our possession of Salonica!"[35]

The Russian Minister discussed Venizelos' views with Premier Gueshov and found him in perfect agreement. But Gueshov was heading a coalition government and his

---

33 *Ibid.*, pp. 126-7.

34 Anatoli Vasilevich Nekludoff, *Diplomatic Reminiscences Before and During the World War, 1911-1917* translated from the French by A. Paget (London, 1920), p. 139.

35 *Ibid.*, p. 140.

hands were tied by the warmongering Danev and the Bulgarian war party, which included the General Staff and King Ferdinand himself.

In Salonica relations between the Greek and Bulgarian soldiers were rapidly deteriorating. The greater part of the Bulgarian Army, which had been allowed into the city by Constantine, had been transferred to Dedeagatch by the end of November 1912 by a massive effort of the Greek Navy in which 42 transport ships were used; but enough Bulgarian troops remained to bolster Bulgarian claims and to provoke the Greeks. Visiting Salonica, King Ferdinand remarked to Constantine, then still the Crown Prince: "To the Bulgarians Salonica is what Mecca is to the Turks."[36] Constantine made it clear to the Bulgarian King that the Greeks were in Salonica to stay. When the late King George had observed to the visiting Ferdinand that the armistice was a mistake and pointed out that it gave the opportunity to the Turks to receive a great quantity of arms from Germany through the Romanian port of Constantza, Ferdinand replied: "The bloodshed was dreadful, I could not bear it."[37] The official visit of the Bulgarian king was amicable enough, but there was bad blood between the two countries and each regarded the other as the "hereditary enemy." The recent guerilla war which the Bulgarian *comitadjis* and the Greek *antartes* had waged against each other over Macedonia revived the ancient hatreds that went back through many centuries. A series of ugly incidents which took place in Salonica was an ominous reminder of the bitter hostility of the past. The correspondent of the London *Daily Telegraph* reported how one day a Greek soldier on entering a tram-car brushed against a Bulgarian soldier; whereupon the Bulgarian seized hold of the Greek's cap and trod it underfoot. The Greek soldier drew his bayonet and killed the Bulgarian on the spot. The alliance between the two rival Balkan nations was to prove only a brief, uneasy interlude.

It was not only Greece who was having problems with Bulgaria but Serbia as well. The Treaty of Alliance between Serbia and Bulgaria had provided that Serbia would retain her conquests on the Adriatic while Bulgaria would occupy the so-called contested zone in Macedonia. Serbia, however, who had been deprived of her conquests in Albania and on the Adriatic coast, was reluctant to give up to Bulgaria the contested zone which she had already conquered, and now demanded that the Serbo-Bulgarian Treaty be revised in order to compensate Serbia for her losses on the Adriatic coast. Bulgaria would not hear of any such adjustments to her treaty with Serbia. The Bulgarians, who in Thrace had been forced to combat the main part of the Turkish military might alone, considered themselves to have been cheated of Southern Macedonia by the Greeks and of Northern Macedonia by the Serbs. In brief, Bulgaria

---

36 Kordatos, *Ιστορία*, V, p. 306.

37 *Ibid.*

demanded Salonica from Greece and Monastir from Serbia. This common threat to their newly acquired territories brought together Greece and Serbia.

On 26 March 1913 Adrianople fell to the Bulgarians and the Bulgarian Army was then free to turn to Macedonia. The unfortunate Bulgarian troops, who had endured great dangers and hardships during the past six months of campaigning, were told as they boarded the trains that they were being returned home for demobilization. It was harvest time and these peasant soldiers were anxious to return to their villages and farms. Instead, to their dismay, they were transferred from Thrace to Macedonia and immediately put to digging trenches in preparation for a new war against the Greeks and the Serbians. The Bulgarian soldiers resented being ordered to take up arms against the allies with whom they had been fighting side by side only a month before. Several sporadic mutinies broke out in the ranks and there were many desertions; the Bulgarian High Command began to fear that unless hostilities began soon their Army might disintegrate. In the meantime, General Hassapchieff, the Commander of the 2,000 Bulgarian troops in Salonica, who had announced on 26 April that he expected to pull out his men in a day or two, received last minute orders to stay in Salonica. The negotiations between the Greeks and the Serbians for a defensive alliance were resumed with a new sense of urgency.

Metaxas, who had returned to Athens at the conclusion of the campaign in Epirus, was kept informed of the negotiations with Serbia. When the protocol between the two countries was about to be signed, he was sent to Salonica to meet with two Serbian officers and negotiate a preliminary military convention. After an irksome voyage because, as he wrote, "of the crowds which jammed the ship," he arrived at Salonica early in the morning of 4 May 1913. That afternoon he called on Prince Nicholas and the two men visited the fortress of Kara Bourun. In Salonica Metaxas stayed in a beautiful "cottage", lent by a local resident, which stood in the middle of a spacious garden leading down to the sea. It was the same villa on the outskirts of the city in which "the late King of blessed memory" had lived for the four months before his assassination. On 5 May 1913, after two months of negotiations, an initial protocol for the Greco-Serbian Treaty of Alliance was signed in Athens by Koromelas and Mathias Boskovitch, the Serbian Minister. In this draft treaty Greece and Serbia agreed to divide between them all the territory west of the River Vardar and to maintain a common frontier. Greece undertook to accord Serbia commercial facilities in the port of Salonica.

But Metaxas was unable to conclude the preliminary military convention attached to the protocol because, to his chagrin, the Serbian representatives had not arrived in Salonica. Why, then, had he been dispatched post haste to the North? His darkest suspicions were immediately aroused. He wrote to his wife, using his host's expensive stationery:

"Therefore why have they packed me off in such a hurry, Messieurs Koromelas and Dousmanis? Perhaps to get me out of Athens? Especially now that the new Crown Prince is going to Epirus? God only knows! I am merely amused at such pettiness. First, because we have our own lives to live and, secondly, because I don't care tuppence -- honestly, I don't care tuppence."[38]

Metaxas had been hoping that Crown Prince George, his former pupil, who had always lent an attentive ear to his opinions, would invite him to accompany him to Epirus, and suspected that his "enemies," out of jealousy, were trying to keep him away from the future king. If this were the manner in which he was being treated, Lela wrote back, he should abandon everything and return to Athens. "How can I return now I am involved in this mad affair?" Metaxas replied. "Because you cannot imagine with what superficiality they dealt with this matter in Athens."[39] As the Serbian officers had not arrived, Metaxas used the time to see something of the life of the city and to explore the surrounding countryside in the chauffeur-driven motorcar provided by the Government. On these trips he carefully studied the terrain from a military aspect to determine where and how Salonica could best be defended if the need arose. The center of social activity for the numerous foreign residents of this cosmopolitan city was the Club. Invited there one evening, Metaxas was surprised to find many ladies present. "The foreign ladies here are in the habit of going to the Club with their husbands!" he reported to Lela.[40]

The first serious incident between the Greeks and Bulgarians took place on 8 May 1913 when the Bulgarians unexpectedly shelled Nigrita, a town of mixed Greek and Bulgarian inhabitants already occupied by Greek troops. The next day, on 9 May 1913, the *Sobranie* voted a new war credit amounting to 50 million francs. At the same time the Bulgarians moved their forces at Doiran and Kilkis [Kukush] southwards. The Greek Army watched and waited and prepared for the worst. Metaxas had the gravest apprehensions over these incidents. On 11 May he wrote to his wife:

"Fortunately we are prepared. And I am pleased that, in this instance, too, I have done my duty. Because, if I had allowed myself to wallow in my original resentment, or if you had been an ambitious kind of a woman who had fanned the flames of my resentment, what would have happened?.... The business of Greece would not have been promoted so well and so swiftly."[41]

Finally the two Serbians arrived. Also in Salonica at the time was the Bulgarian General Ivanof, who had come to arrange for a neutral zone between the Greek and Bulgarian Armies. Meeting Colonel Pesits, one of the Serbian officers, Ivanof enquired

38 Metaxas, *Diary*, II, p. 212.

39 *Ibid.*, p. 214

40 *Ibid.*, p. 213

41 *Ibid.*, p. 214.

suspiciously, "What are you cooking up here with the Greeks?"[42] After that Metaxas was obliged to meet the Serbian representatives in secret. But, even while negotiating the Greco-Serbian military convention in preparation for a war against Bulgaria, Metaxas was at heart against this war, as he had been against the first Balkan War while he was negotiating the military convention with Bulgaria in Sofia. On 13 May 1913, waiting for the Serbian officers to arrive at his villa, he wrote hastily to Lela:

"The situation is very critical and may God protect us from a new campaign, although the whole Army is enthusiastic and eager to set about the Bulgarians. I myself find it not to our advantage. The Serbians are expected at any moment. I therefore close my letter and send you and our children one thousand sweet kisses."[43]

A few days later, on 17 May, Metaxas signed the military convention *ad referendum* on behalf of Greece. Colonels Toufektief and Pecits signed for Serbia. The Serbian representatives wanted the convention to provide guarantees that Greece would come to the assistance of Serbia if Serbia were attacked by any third Power. The Serbians sought guarantees not only against a threat from Bulgaria, but also against a threat from Austria. Metaxas -- and the Royalist faction surrounding the King -- did not want Greece ever to be drawn into any camp that was opposed to Austria and, inevitably, to Germany. For this reason the military convention which Metaxas signed on behalf of his country only provided a guarantee that Greece would assist Serbia if Serbia were to be attacked by Bulgaria. This military convention was not accepted by the Serbian Government, which insisted that Greece should undertake to come to the assistance of Serbia in the event of an attack upon her by Bulgaria or by *any other Power*.

On 22 May, after the Bulgarians had attempted to cross the Voultsista Bridge at the foot of Mount Pangaion (site of the silver mines of ancient Athens) and to enter the Greek zone, a fierce conflict ensued, extending over an area of 45 miles. As many as 20,000 Bulgarian troops took part in the attack. The next day, 23 May 1913, Sophia, the new Queen of Greece, cabled her brother the Kaiser that Bulgarian troops were encroaching on the neutral zone which had been established between the Greek and Bulgarian Armies; the situation was critical and the Queen feared that a new war might break out. The Kaiser discussed Sophia's telegram with the Czar of Russia and the King of England, who then happened to be in Berlin for the wedding of Princess Victoria Louise to Duke Ernst August of Braunschweig and Lüneburg.[44] The three monarchs had little liking for the King of Bulgaria. Czar Nicholas, in agreement with William II and George V, sent a telegram to King Ferdinand, warning him that if war broke out because of the Bulgarian invasion through the neutral zone, the responsibility would rest entirely with Bulgaria. The Czar requested the Kaiser to send a similar

---

42 Kordatos, *Ιστορία*, V, p. 327.

43 Metaxas, *Diary*, II, p. 214.

44 Helmreich, *Diplomacy*, p. 330.

telegram, which he did the following day. These representations had little effect on the Bulgarians. Incidents between Bulgarian and Greek soldiers continued to occur. On 26 May the Bulgarian coastal batteries heavily shelled some Greek war vessels sailing past the town of Kavalla.

On the same day, 26 May 1913, the Serbian Prime Minister Nikola Pasic declared that the Serbo-Bulgarian Treaty of Alliance no longer existed and that the captured territories of European Turkey must be divided according to the principle of conquest. In a speech in the *Skupshtina* (Serbian Parliament) a few days later Premier Pasic argued that his country was no longer bound by the Treaty with Bulgaria because the conquered territories were to be divided between four Allies instead of two; that the war had been prolonged to enable Bulgaria to take Adrianople and because of this Serbia had put into the field another 100,000 men; finally, that Serbia had not been allowed an outlet to the Adriatic as was promised her by the Serbo-Bulgarian Treaty, and was therefore entitled to seek compensation elsewhere. The Serbian declarations caused alarm in Europe. Austria hastened to assure Bulgaria of her support in the event of the outbreak of another war. Serbia would then find herself between two enemies, each of them stronger by far than herself. Once again the Serbs urged the Greeks to accept the Serbian terms and conclude a Greco-Serbian Treaty of alliance.

In Athens Venizelos was greatly excited by the Bulgarian threat to Salonica and by the unwillingness of the King's men to make common cause with Serbia. Some officers on the General Staff had even assured him that the Greek army, because of the high state of its morale due to the recent Greek victories, could take on Bulgaria alone. The Greek Prime Minister was not so confident. One of those whose opinion he sought was General Pangalos, then in Athens on leave.

Venizelos: *What is your opinion? Can we stand our ground in case of a war with Bulgaria?*

Pangalos: *I am surprised at your question, Mr. Prime Minister, because I believe there is no one, not only no military man, but no one possessing simple common sense who believes that Greece can confront Bulgaria alone. I am of the opinion that our defeat would be swift, crushing and inevitable. Do not forget, Mr. Prime Minister, what the condition of the Greek Army was when you arrived in Athens only two years ago. In spite of the efforts of the Revolution of General Zorbas and the really valuable work of the French Military Mission, it was not possible within one year to build from scratch an army worthy of the expectations of the nation.*

Venizelos: *And yet there are some, including some distinguished officers, who hold the opposite opinion, supported by the enthusiasm and high state of morale which the Army has exhibited in the Greco-Turkish War which has just ended.*

Pangalos: *Such views are fallacious, Mr. Prime Minister, because in the Turkish War we did not encounter a serious enemy. Without question, our Army displayed remarkable bravery, but it must be taken into account that we were always four times their number and that we had a great advantage over them in artillery and war materiel. As I see it, the Turkish War was a stroke of good fortune for Greece, because it provided a training ground for our Army, which is deficient in military training and combat experience.*

Venizelos: *What then, is your opinion, in case of war with Bulgaria, of us and the Serbs joining forces against Bulgaria?*[45]

Pangalos assured Venizelos that in that case he was completely optimistic and he also expressed the view that such a war should be waged quickly, "otherwise we shall never be able to rest easy because of the Bulgarian danger."

Venizelos called a cabinet meeting and requested King Constantine to preside. The Prime Minister spoke first, explaining the treat posed by Bulgaria and insisting that Greece had no choice but to accept the Serbian terms and sign the treaty with Serbia immediately. Constantine expressed fears for the consequences of such a step. Greece would be exposed to grave dangers if she were to sign a treaty, albeit a defensive one, against a Great Power such as Austria. The Greek king was reluctant to conclude a treaty against an ally of his brother-in-law the Kaiser. But the Bulgarian threat in Macedonia was too real to be ignored. Venizelos argued convincingly:

"This is an emergency. We either lose Salonica or we agree to face the remote danger of a general confrontation ... A localized Austro-Serbian clash is unlikely. It would mean a European war, because Russia would not abandon Serbia. Behind Russia is France. Greece would then be the ally of the whole Triple Entente, France, England, Russia, with whom the wider interests of Greece coincide."[46] King Constantine, pressured by the critical situation, was obliged to consent: *"It is obvious that I have to sign, but, if through some unlucky chance the circumstances should arise, something which I fear, and Greece should stand in mortal danger, I pray that God may forgive me [i.e., if I do not honour my signature]. If this is perjury, I undertake the responsibility; I personally take upon myself this obligation towards my country."*[47]

The King rose as a signal that the meeting was at an end. At that moment the following exchange took place between the Minister of Naval Affairs Nicholaos Stratos, and Constantine.

Stratos: *If the worst comes to the worst, we shall have to commit the dishonour of trampling this treaty underfoot.*

Constantine: *It is I who will be the first to commit this dishonour.*[48]

---

45 Pangalos, *Απομνημονεύματα*, p. 282.

46 Kordatos, *Ιστορία*, V, p. 324-5.

47 *Ibid.*, p. 325 footnote.

48 *Ibid.*, pp. 324-5.

Venizelos listened in silence. Coming out of the Palace, he observed dryly to Repoulis, the Minister of the Interior, "Did you notice how much respect he has for his signature?"[49]

Venizelos at once instructed Koromelas and the Greek Minister at Belgrade Alexandropoulos "to hasten, because the situation does not permit any delays." A new military convention had also to be agreed upon; but this time the services of Captain Metaxas were not employed, as he himself had made it clear that he could never sign a convention which would bring his country into a camp hostile to Austria and therefore to Germany. Accordingly, the Greek Prime Minister sent Xenophon Strategos to Belgrade to work out a new military convention. While the negotiations with Serbia were proceeding, the Turkish representatives in London signed on 30 May 1913 at St. Jame's Palace the Treaty of Peace with the Balkan Allies. Thus the Bulgarians, secure, as they thought, in Thrace, were now free to turn all their attention to Macedonia. That same day, 30 May 1913, Venizelos, anxious because the negotiations with Serbia were not progressing quickly enough, sent a telegram to Premier Pasic, asking him to dispatch the Serbian Minister Boschkovitch from Athens to Salonica, whither Venizelos had already urgently summoned Alexandropoulos and Strategos. Venizelos then hurried to Salonica and personally took charge of the negotiations until agreement was reached ten hours later. The Treaty was signed in Salonica on 1 June 1913 by the Greek Minister at Belgrade Ioannis Alexandropoulos and the Serbian Minister at Athens Mathias Boschkovitch. At the same time the Greek and Serbian Staff Officers Strategos and Pesits signed the military convention. Up to the last moment the Serbian representatives argued that Austria should be mentioned as one of the countries against whose attack Greece undertook to assist Serbia; but Venizelos insisted that Austria should not be mentioned by name in the Treaty, so that Greece and Serbia would not be open to the accusation of conspiring against any of the Great Powers. The Greco-Serbian Treaty was ratified in Athens on 21 June 1913.

The Graeco-Serbian Treaty of Alliance is of primary importance for the study of the National Schism, which divided the Greek Royalists and the Greek Liberals during the First World War; when Serbia was attacked by Austria at the outbreak of the Great War she immediately called upon Greece to come to her assistance according to the terms of this Treaty. The Greeks, who had signed the Treaty under the threat of a Bulgarian attack, were divided in the interpretation of those terms which defined their obligations. The pro-Entente Liberals believed that Greece was obligated by the Treaty to assist Serbia. The Greek Royalists, who felt that they had been blackmailed by circumstances and, in an obscure way, by Venizelos, into siding with the enemies of the Central Alliance, argued that the Greco-Serbian Treaty referred only to Balkan affairs

49 *Ibid.*, p. 325.

and did not apply in any situation in which a Power outside the Balkan Peninsula was involved. Venizelos and Metaxas hotly debated the terms of the Greco-Serbian Treaty in the Athens newspapers twenty-one years after the signing of the Treaty. When it was being negotiated both men clearly realized that if Serbia were attacked by Austria, Germany would back Austria, while Russia would support Serbia, and that this would mean a general European conflagration. Metaxas wanted Greece on the side of Germany and refused to sign a military convention that would have committed his country to the Entente camp. Venizelos wanted Greece on the side of the western democracies and was anxious that the Treaty with Serbia should become operative. When the First World War broke out the German Minister in Athens asked the Greek Prime Minister to repudiate the Greco-Serbian Treaty. It was all very well for a Great Power like Germany to speak contemptuously, as she had, of treaties as mere scraps of paper; Venizelos, with the comments of King Constantine when signing the Greco-Serbian treaty the year before still fresh in his memory, retorted sharply to the German Minister: "Greece is too small a country to commit such dishonour."

After negotiating the abortive military convention with Serbia, Metaxas returned to his family in Athens. Then days later, on 27 May 1913, as war with Bulgaria was now expected to break out at any moment, he accompanied King Constantine back to Salonica. Metaxas was greatly impressed by the motor torpedo boat on which he made the voyage this time. From Chalkis to Salonica took only seven and a half hours, while by steamer the journey usually took as long as twenty hours. "The sea was calm and *Panther* cleaved the waves, leaving in her wake a mountain of foam," he wrote.[50] He spent his first night in Salonica at a hotel and then moved into General Headquarters where Dousmanis and the other Staff Officers were already living. For the past year Metaxas had been travelling continually in the service of the State and this peripatetic life held little appeal for him. "I have become a nomad, a kind of gipsy. Sometimes here, sometimes there; from Athens to Sofia, from Belgrade to Elassona, from the comforts of my home to Kirtzalar, from Florina to London, from London's Claridges Hotel to Philippias, and so it goes."[51]

The Bulgarians were reinforcing their positions in Macedonia unceasingly, and the Greek General Staff made preparations for any eventuality. As usual, the onus of the task fell on Metaxas. Metaxas ensured that the Greek Army was well provisioned and well equipped, supervized the master-plan of the Greek defense, worked out a comprehensive campaign strategy, and wrote out the detailed orders for the deployment of the Army. On 26 May he wrote to his wife: "You cannot imagine how much work I found which needed to be done. ... Problems and responsibilities all day long. In the

50 Metaxas, *Diary,* II, p. 215.
51 *Ibid.,* p. 216.

evening the telegrams begin to come in and they continue far into the night."[52] As was to be expected, Metaxas secretly relished the responsibilities laid upon him and at the same time, despite his occasional disavowals, bitterly resented his subordinate position on the General Staff. On 30 May he wrote to his wife: "They need me now and they are making much of me.... But such things do not interest me any more. The period when I was either piqued or flattered is long past. I have seen it all. Now I am inwardly at peace."[53] Even the dour Victor Dousmanis went out of his way to be civil to him now -- "At least as long as the crisis lasts, but I don't care tuppence. And thus, by being indifferent, I have found peace of mind."[54] The work Metaxas had to perform was intricate and demanding. "Even I do not know myself how I find the time to write to you, I am constantly under pressure... As though the Bulgarians were not enough, I have to put right our own blunders."[55] Not only did he perform his own duties punctiliously; he also made certain that both his superiors and his subordinates were kept up to the mark. He wrote to his wife:

"Today the king leaves for Athens -- he is bored, it seems. Dousmanis was ready to follow him with the Staff, just at the moment when they should not. Because, imagine, it was only the day before yesterday that we gave the order for the taking up of new positions by the whole Army and the change will begin tomorrow. And this is such a delicate matter that all possible care and diligence are required. I read Dousmanis a lecture and he felt obliged to cancel the Staff's departure. The king will return here on Wednesday, I suppose he feels ashamed, too."[56]

Amid all the feverish preparations, Metaxas privately hoped that war could be averted even at the eleventh hour.

"I hope that war can be avoided -- although I said the same thing last time in Sofia and war still broke out. But we are preparing as though war were about to begin: because the best means of avoiding war is to prepare for it. What would have happened to Greece if this methodical and meticulous mind of mine had been missing?"[57]

His conceit had reached such a degree as to be almost disarming. And, never too modest to underrate his own achievements, Metaxas wrote long letters to Lela, revealing his thoughts and describing his work. At times this work was difficult, but it was effective.

---

52 *Ibid.*, pp. 215-6.
53 *Ibid.*, p. 216.
54 *Ibid.*
55 *Ibid.*
56 *Ibid.*, p. 218.
57 *Ibid.*

"The Bulgarians intended to launch an attack, but they were not in time and now it is too late. ... When the troop movements that we have ordered have been executed and the fortifications completed we shall feel more at ease."[58]

When Metaxas felt assured that the work of preparing the Army for imminent hostilities was proceeding smoothly, he would sometimes escape from his office and in the evenings visit an open-air cafe with some officer friends. In the garden of this place was a cinema, which Metaxas always enjoyed. He wrote to Lela: "The garden is packed with officers and *demi-mondaines* of the lower class."[59] But his heart remained always with his family. On 27 June 1913 he wrote to Lela, again displaying his natural literary skill; he possessed, without conscious effort, a novelist's eye for detail and a poet's talent for evoking emotion.

"Today I received your letter with the gardenias. How beautifully formed they are and how large they grow! Their perfume does not last; they are not like jasmine or roses. But the shape also has its own grace. All these are symbols: our memories resemble these flowers. Some return to us, fresh and beautiful, their forms lost, their outlines blurred, only one delicate, piercing fragrance survive s.... The sum of all our memories makes up our life.

It is raining. The sky is overcast. How many things come to mind ... What would you, perchance, be doing at this moment? If it is raining with you, perhaps you are in our study and there I feel you close to me."[60]

Madame Metaxas, always anxious about her husband's safety and fidelity, made constant claims on his time and attention. She had no cause to worry. Metaxas wrote to her: "You were not in my thoughts? Then why did I cable you twice every day?"[61] Despite the importance of his work, his greatest desire was to be with his family on the island of Tenos in the Aegean. On 24 June he wrote to his wife: "I cannot wait for the moment when I shall be able to come to Tenos to rest, to collect our thoughts. I am tired of worrying about the Balkans, the Triple Entente, the Triple Alliance, and all such nonsense."[62]

On the eve of the Bulgarian War Metaxas was at last promoted to the rank of Major, but not, however, for merit. He wrote to Lela: "Today I was promoted -- on grounds of seniority, naturally. Anyway, the whole world has been promoted. I do not know if you will be pleased about this, on me it made no impression whatsoever."[63] A few days later he reverted to the subject. "What did you think of my promotion? I myself was not

58 *Ibid.*, p. 219 .
59 *Ibid.*, p. 218.
60 *Ibid.*, p. 221.
61 *Ibid.*, p. 217.
62 *Ibid.*, p. 220.
63 *Ibid.*, p. 217.

impressed at all: I am only pleased that we shall receive an extra 120 drachmas a month."[64] And he added with mock gravity, "I shall, of course, be put to some expense to change the badges -- even from here I can see you smiling."[65] At the same time Metaxas was appointed Director of Operations, replacing Dousmanis, who was promoted Chief of the General Staff. Danglis, the former Chief of Staff, was, to his own dismay, left behind at Ioannina as Commander-in-Chief of the Army of Epirus. Constantine thus painlessly rid himself of the only Venizelist officer on his Staff and surrounded himself with the so-called "German" officers. Metaxas wrote to his wife: "I am now Director of the Section of Operations -- only until the storm is over, you understand. Then I shall retreat into obscurity, but this time I shall make the decision myself, before Dousmanis has the chance to make it for me."[66] From Athens Lela sent her congratulations on his promotion. Metaxas replied: "You write that I shall become a Lieutenant-Colonel. Many people have told me so, Dousmanis included, also the King. Do you believe that? I don't! It would be to their own advantage to promote me even higher, but in the end envy will prevail."[67]

Metaxas found working directly under General Dousmanis no easy matter. An older man at the peak of his career, Dousmanis feared a potential rival in the junior but better educated Metaxas. Early that same year Metaxas had written to Lela from London: "I have some vague indications that Dousmanis is working against me, but I am confident that I shall get out of this mess. I have been through so much."[68] On 24 June he wrote to his wife from Salonica: "Do not expect any kindness from Dousmanis. ... He needs me. He does not wish my good, because even my slightest advancement overshadows him."[69] Dousmanis had over the years assiduously cultivated the friendship of Constantine and as a result enjoyed the full confidence of the new King and Commander-in-Chief. Close to Constantine as he was, the new Chief of Staff often succeeded in shutting out the efficient and ambitious Metaxas from the King's counsels. On 26 June 1913 Metaxas wrote to Lela: "I never see the King, but I have the impression that he hears more about me than is to the advantage of Dousmanis."[70] Two days later Constantine, who had gone to Athens unaccompanied by any Staff officers, asked the Chief of Staff to send him someone from the section of Operations to brief him on the new positions just taken up by the Army. Dousmanis sent Captain Pallis and not Metaxas, who was the Director of the Section of Operations. Metaxas wrote to

---

64 *Ibid.*
65 *Ibid.*, p. 218.
66 *Ibid.*
67 *Ibid.*
68 *Ibid.*, p. 189.
69 *Ibid.*, p. 220.
70 *Ibid.*

Lela: "It is true that I cannot be spared from here because the Army needs me; but is that the only reason? Do not betray your feelings. Your face and manner *impénétrables*, until my hour comes."[71] The Chief of Staff was jealous "to a disgusting degree."[72] Metaxas admonished Lela to be "very correct" and diplomatic with Madame Dousmanis. On 29 June, the night war with Bulgaria broke out, Metaxas again urged his wife to display no animosity towards the wife of the Chief-of-Staff or anyone else. "Leave it to me, when my hour comes."[73]

The next day 31 June 1913 Demidov, the Russian Minister at Athens, reported to Sazonov:

"Owing to simultaneous Bulgarian attacks on the Serbian and Greek frontiers, the King [Constantine] is starting for Salonica to take command of the Greek army. The fleet has received orders to start at once for Elefteris, where according to official information, the Greek troops have cut off the advancing Bulgarian forces. M. Venizelos thinks that although war is not declared, the Greek Government is bound to take the necessary measures for defence. He is ready to conclude an armistice if the Bulgarian Government officially declares that the advance of the Bulgarian troops is due to a misunderstanding."[74]

Russia exerted some diplomatic pressure at Athens and Belgrade in an attempt to restrain the Greeks and Serbs, but no avail. On 1 July 1913 Demidov telegraphed the Russian Minister of Foreign Affairs:

"The Minister [Venizelos] regards the forward march of the Bulgarian troops as an attempt to produce an accomplished fact, and to consolidate by violence the Bulgarian right to occupy Greek territories.

Under these circumstances, it is impossible for him to start [for St. Petersburg] without receiving from the Bulgarian Government a formal repudiation of its last acts: the Bulgarian troops must retire to the line of demarcation, established by protocol, and Bulgaria must officially announce that she is willing to accept an obligatory arbitration, if not conjointly, at least simultaneously with the Serbo-Bulgarian arbitration. The situation is critical."[75] The Second Balkan War had begun.

The sudden Bulgarian attack on the evening of 29 June 1913 against the Serbian and Greek positions extended along a front of 300 miles. The next day and the following day the Greeks rounded up the Bulgarian soldiers stationed in Salonica. First to go was the Bulgarian Commander, General Hassapchiev, who was allowed to depart by train from Salonica with his Staff. General Kallaris, Commander of the Second Greek

---

71 *Ibid.*, p. 221.

72 *Ibid.*, p. 223.

73 *Ibid.*, p. 221.

74 Gueshov, *The Balkan League*, pp. 100-1

75 *Ibid.*, p. 101.

Division, informed the remaining Bulgarians that they were to leave the city within an hour by a special train made available to them. Kallaris demanded that the Bulgarian soldiers give up their arms, but their officers were permitted to keep their swords. The Bulgarians refused to go and fighting continued throughout the night. Next morning, 1 July 1913, 1,350 Bulgarian soldiers and 20 officers surrendered. 75 Bulgarians were killed or seriously wounded. At nine o'clock that evening Metaxas wrote to his wife: "Yesterday and today we cleared out the Bulgarians from Salonica. Tomorrow the war begins and we shall probably fight a major battle. May God be with us!"[76]

The Greeks and Serbs, surprised by the unexpected attack, fell back despite their preparations. By the third day, however, the Allies were standing their ground and by the fourth day they had launched a fierce counter-offensive. On 4 July a pitched battle was fought between the Greeks and the Bulgarians at Kilkish-Lahana which lasted three days. The Bulgarians had established themselves in trenches and had to be forced out of them at bayonet point. Metaxas wrote to his wife: "*The frightful battle is over...... We have utterly crushed the Bulgarians. But we, too, have lost many men. I do not know exactly how many. At least seven to eight thousand dead and wounded; among them many officers. What can one say....*"[77] The Greeks pursued the Bulgarians towards the River Struma and defeated them again at the battle of Doiran, then at Demir-Hissar. Metaxas wrote to Lela to tell her that the plan of campaign had been entirely his own. "I am exhausted, but also exhilarated. It is like a dream!"[78] During the campaign he could write only a few hasty lines, but he never failed to emphasize the major part he was playing in the war: "Despite all the victories and the triumphs, I am in a state of collapse. You cannot imagine how much I have suffered in order to push this [war] machine forward. But with what results!"[79] And he hastened to reassure his wife that, along with the other members of the Staff, he had been inoculated against cholera, which was then ravaging Macedonia. Seven days later he received the second inoculation, but again experienced no adverse reaction. A Staff Officer named Kallergis refused the inoculation and, stricken down by the disease a few days later, died miserably. Metaxas wept for Kallergis, but he was even more distressed by the death of another officer, Nastas, a friend of the family. "He was almost like a son", he wrote to his wife.[80] Although Metaxas himself had been inoculated and there was no cholera in Athens, he could still be a carrier of the disease, and so in the same letter he strongly urged Madame Metaxas to have the whole household in Athens inoculated, including

76 Metaxas, *Diary,* II, p. 222.
77 *Ibid.*
78 *Ibid.*
79 *Ibid.*, p. 223.
80 *Ibid.*, p. 224.

the servants; otherwise he would be unable to return home and would be obliged to remain in quarantine for thirty to forty days.

The Greek Army pressed on with its forward drive, routing the Bulgarians everywhere. During this operation the Greeks advanced 200 kilometers. On 9 July the town of Strumitsa (later to be returned to Bulgaria at the peace negotiations) was occupied. The same day the Greek Fleet captured Kavalla, the Neapolis of antiquity and the port of ancient Philippi. On 11 July the town of Serres was taken and on 14 July the town of Drama. Between the 21 and 22 July a ferocious three-day battle was waged among the Kresna Passes, the formidable gateway to the central Bulgarian plain. On 25 July the Greek Fleet occupied Dedeagatch. On 26 July the town of Xanthi was taken and, on 29 July, Komotini (Gioumoultzina). Thus all Southern Macedonia and Western Thrace south of the Rhodope Mountains passed into Greek hands.

The war between Greece and Bulgaria, which lasted for a period of four weeks, was particularly bitter and was fought with obstinate ferocity by both sides. The Greeks won every battle, taking over 6,000 prisoners, but the price of victory was high; 165 officers and 2,400 men were killed and the number of seriously wounded amounted to more than 22,000. The toll on officers was especially heavy and their loss was to be keenly felt during the campaigns in Anatolia a few years later. In their retreat the Bulgarians destroyed the bridges, contaminated the wells and rivers by casting into them the corpses of their soldiers who had died of cholera, and razed to the ground the towns and villages through which they passed. In Serres, Nigrita and Doxato the Greek inhabitants were massacred and the towns set on fire. Most of the atrocities were committed by the Bulgarian *commitadjis*, not by the regular Army. In retaliation for the Bulgarian atrocities, the advancing Greeks in their turn drove out the hapless Bulgarian villagers and burned down their homes. The Bulgarian Army stubbornly disputed every inch of the way and when the battle-ground shifted to Old Bulgaria almost succeeded in tipping the scales of victory in their favour. On 3 August Metaxas wrote to his wife: "I cannot describe what crises and what agonies we have gone through. And the whole weight of the enemy's onslaught, plus Dousmanis' carpings, fell upon my shoulders. We emerged victorious. But what a struggle! And, at the last moment, the Bulgarians contested our victory."[81]

Metaxas blamed the Serbs for failing to follow up their initial successes over the Bulgarians and thus allowing the common enemy to concentrate all his forces against the Greeks. After a fierce four-day battle at Bregalnitsa which cost them 6,000 dead, the Serbs entered Ishtip. But they halted their advance at Egri Palanka, allowing the First Bulgarian Army Corps to be transferred from North Macedonia to South Macedonia and join the Second Bulgarian Army Corps in preventing the advancing

81 Metaxas, *Diary,* II, p. 224.

Greeks from marching on Sofia. The Greek General Staff expected the Serbs to cross over to Keustendil and reach the plain of the Bulgarian capital. The Serbs, once they had occupied the lands they coveted, saw no reason to continue their advance into Old Bulgaria. Furthermore, the Serbs had no desire to crush Bulgaria totally, which would have upset the balance of power in the Balkans and would have allowed the Greeks to expand into Western and Eastern Thrace and even threaten Constantinople. The Serbs were also under pressure from Austria and Russia to stop the fighting. Their border with Austria was extremely vulnerable; neither did they want to offend the Russian Czar, who had recently abandoned the Bulgarians and showed favour towards them.

The task of the Greek Army was more arduous by far than that of the Serbs: not only was the main thrust of the Bulgarian Army directed towards Salonica, which the Greeks had to defend; the Greeks now felt it expedient to drive out the Bulgarian troops from the Macedonian littoral, which the Bulgarians had occupied in the First Balkan War and whose population was predominantly Greek. Unlike the Serbian General Staff, the Greek High Command believed that the only way of bringing the war to an end was the total annihilation of the enemy forces. For these reasons the Serbian contribution, which had been considerable, fell short of the expectations of the Greek General Staff. Metaxas wrote to his wife from the front: "The demands of the Bulgarians are great because the army with which they fought the Serbs was not annihilated. The Serbs did not help us at all."[82] Metaxas himself underlined the last sentence.

But Bulgaria's problems did not end with the Greeks and the Serbs. To the north, Romania was not at all happy with the Treaty of London of 30 May 1913, which awarded all the Turkish territories in Europe west of the Enos-Media Line to the Balkan Allies and, in effect, gave the lion's share to Bulgaria. Romania (which at the time was confined to the provinces of Moldavia and Wallachia -- Transylvania was acquired after the First World War) did not relish the prospect of an enlarged Bulgaria on her southern border. As Italy could not tolerate a Greater Greece, as Austria could not tolerate a Greater Serbia, so Romania could not tolerate a Greater Bulgaria. As a reward for their neutrality during the First Balkan War, the Romanian politicians demanded part of the district of Dobrudja, which had come into the possession of Bulgaria after the Congress of Berlin. Austria, who professed friendship for both Bulgaria and Romania, urged Bulgaria to make some minor concessions to the Romanians, but without success. On 3 July, three days after the outbreak of the Second Balkan War, Romania mobilized an army of 400,000 men. On 10 July she declared war on Bulgaria and the Romanian armies crossed the Danube and next day captured Silistria. A day later the whole of the Dobrudja quadrilateral was occupied. Thereafter

82 *Ibid.*

the Romanians, encountering no serious resistance, marched towards Sofia. By 31 July they were within 40 miles of the Bulgarian capital.

Finally it was the turn of the Turks to join in the *melée*. On 12 July Turkey joined the attack against Bulgaria and, taking advantage of the weakened Bulgarian defenses, retook Adrianople under Enver Pasha, an easy victory which the Young Turks exploited to pose as saviours of the Ottoman Empire. As the Turks overran the Bulgarians in Thrace they wreaked vengeance upon the Christian populations for the humiliations they had suffered in the First Balkan War. An unprecedented exodus of thousands of Greeks began as they fled before the advancing Turkish Army. Those left behind were massacred *en masse* and their towns and villages put to the torch.

When King Ferdinand realized the enormity of his blunder he sent General Patrikov to Nis (ancient Nyssa, the birthplace of Constantine the Great) to plead with the Serbians for a ceasefire, but to no avail. Neither were the Greeks much inclined to heed any such overtures. On 10 July the Russian Government called upon all the belligerents to lay down their arms. Next day King Constantine cabled from the front to his Government in Athens that "the peace should be signed on the battlefield."

"Our great advantage today is that we shall be able to enjoy a respite from Bulgaria for several generations. This advantage must not be lost. On no account should you agree to an armistice before consulting me. Ceterum censeo Bulgariam esse delendam."[83]

Besieged on every side, the Bulgarian representatives knocked at the doors of the chancelleries of Europe, seeking the intervention of the Great Powers to end the war. Stanchev, the Bulgarian Ambassador in Paris, pleaded with Poincaré; "It is the grandson of a King of France who is beseeching you!"[84] Queen Clementine, the mother of King Ferdinand, was a daughter of King Louis Philippe. But the French Premier remained unmoved.

But the greatest disappointment for Bulgaria was the attitude of the Dual Monarchy. Early in July Austria had informed Germany that should Bulgaria have a decisive success, and Russia were to intervene on behalf of Serbia, Austria would then occupy Belgrade. The Kaiser, referring to the possibility of a general European war, commented: "Completely crazy; so war after all!"[85] The question now was -- would Austria, who had incited the Bulgarians to war, come to their rescue? As it turned out, Bulgaria did not win any victories and there was no occasion for Russia to intervene

83 This last sentence reads in English: "For the rest, I am of the opinion that Bulgaria must be destroyed". It is a variation of Cato's famous dictum on the necessity for Rome to destroy Carthage, with which he concluded each of his speeches in the Senate. Driault, *Histoire Diplomatique*, V, p. 127.

84 *Ibid.*, p. 332.

85 Luigi Albertini, *The Origins of the War of 1914* (London, 1957), I, p. 454.

on behalf of Serbia. So the Austrians were forced to moderate their previous advice in their reply to the latest importunities from Bulgaria. On 15 July Berchtold, the Austrian Foreign Minister, suggested that the Government of Bulgaria should be placed in the hands of men who understood "the parallelism between the interest of the [Dual] Monarchy and those of Bulgaria."[86] King Ferdinand, in a desperate attempt to save his country, had already done this that very day by dismissing Premier Danev and appointing Vasil Radoslavov in his place. Still Austria made no move to save Bulgaria. On 18 July Ferdinand summoned the Austrian Minister at Sofia and asked him bluntly: "How is it possible that Vienna does not seize this chance to make an end of Serbia?"[87] Instead of going to war on behalf of Bulgaria, Austria strongly advised the Bulgarian King to approach King Carol of Romania directly and sue for peace.

Accordingly, on 21 July 1913, Ferdinand addressed a personal appeal to Carol, seeking peace and requesting his mediation with Greece and Serbia. The Romanian King accepted the role of peacemaker and proposed an armistice to Bulgaria, Serbia, and Greece. He cabled King Constantine, reminding him that the balance of power in the Balkan Peninsula should not be too greatly disturbed and that the Great Powers would not allow any further diminution of Bulgaria. *"Toute nouvelle effusion de sang ne pourrait qu'empirer la situation."*[88] Constantine cabled back to King Carol to assure him that he neither wished to disturb the balance of power in the Balkans nor to greatly diminish Bulgaria; but the Greek king had had *"une trop amère expérience de la mauvaise foi bulgare,"* and he refused to consent to an armistice before his preliminary conditions had been met.[89] However, Greece agreed, under some pressure from Serbia, to send representatives to Bucharest to discuss the peace.

The Treaty of Bucharest was signed on 10 August 1913. Romania received the Silistria-Balchik region of the Dobrudja, including Dobrich. Serbia won North and Central Macedonia and the Vardar Valley as far as Ghevgheli. Thus Greece and Serbia now shared a common frontier. The *sanjak* of Novibazar was divided between Serbia and Montenegro. But Serbia was not given a corridor to the Aegean, as the Greco-Serbian Treaty had provided; instead Greece granted Serbia special commercial privileges at the port of Salonica. Considering Bulgaria's perfidy in the Second Balkan War, the Allies treated her generously, allowing her to keep a small portion of Macedonia and the whole of Western Thrace, with sixty miles of the Aegean coast, including the port of Dedeagatch. The Bucharest Conference therefore called upon Greece to withdraw her forces from Western Thrace, which she had just conquered. Some regions of Western Thrace, like Gumurjina (Komotini), were inhabited by Turks;

86 *Ibid.*, p. 460.
87 *Ibid.*
88 Driault, *Histoire Diplomatique*, p. 133.
89 *Ibid.*, p. 134.

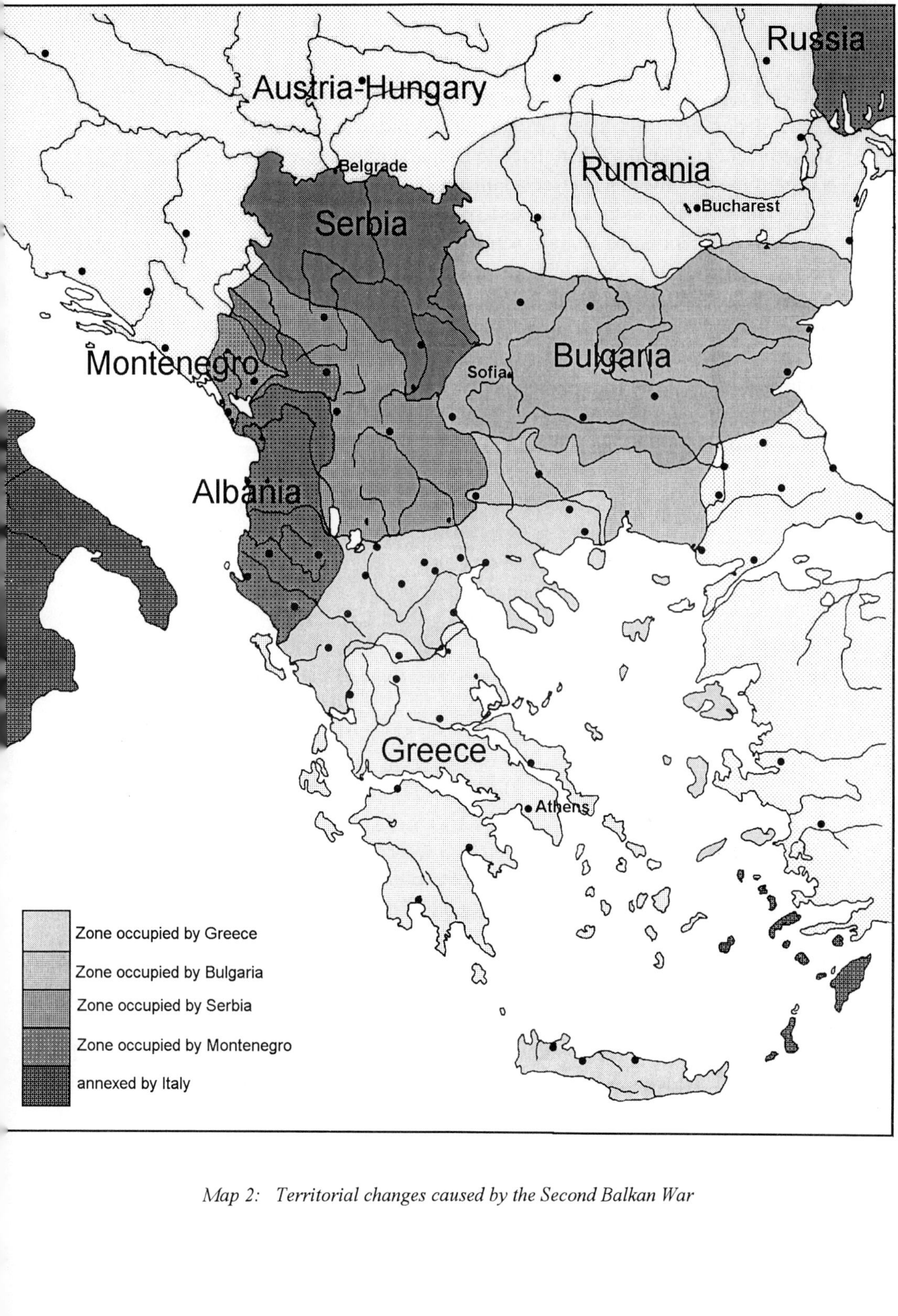

Map 2: Territorial changes caused by the Second Balkan War

but other regions, like the prosperous city of Xanthi and its environs, had an exclusively Greek population, and these Greeks felt the bitterest resentment against the Greek Government for handling them back to Bulgaria only a few days after they had given a rapturous welcome to King Constantine as their liberator from Bulgarian occupation.

The Greek frontier to the north was to run from a point just north of Korytsa, between Monastir and Florina to Doiran, south of Strumnitza (which the Greek Army were obliged to evacuate), south of Petrich, south of Nevrokop, eastwards to the crest of Mount Belasica Planina. From the crest of the mountain the boundary line ran down to the delta of the River Nestor on the Aegean, twenty miles east of Kavalla. Western and Southern Macedonia went to Greece, including Salonica, Kavalla, Serres, and Drama. The Treaty of Bucharest also recognized the union of Crete with Greece. The following table gives a picture of the area and the population of the several Balkan States before and after the Balkan Wars.[90]

	Area in sq. miles		Estimated Population	
	Before	After	Before	After
Albania	.....	11,317	.....	850,000
Bulgaria	33,647	43,310	4,337,516	4,467,006
Greece	25,014	41,933	2,666,000	4,363,000
Montenegro	3,474	5,603	250,000	500,000
Romania	50,720	53,489	7,230,418	7,516,418
Serbia	18,650	33,891	2,911,701	4,527,992
Turkey in Europe	65,350	10,882	6,130,200	1,891,000

Thus, while the population of Greece increased by two-thirds, the population of Turkey-in-Europe decreased inversely by two-thirds -- a decrease of one-sixth in the total population of Turkey. The population of Serbia increased by one-half and that of Montenegro doubled. Not only Greece, but Serbia and Montenegro as well, almost doubled their territories. As a result of the Balkan Wars, a near-perfect balance of power was achieved between Greece, Bulgaria and Serbia in terms both of territory and population.

Western observers have traditionally deplored the Balkan Wars of 1912-1913 because, in their view, the Wars settled nothing but, on the contrary, only succeeded in fragmenting the Balkan Peninsula into small, antagonistic States -- a process which

90 Carnegie, *Report*, p. 418.

they labelled "Balkanization." Those who disapproved of Balkanization had at the back of their minds a cosy picture of a contented peasantry dwelling in tranquillity under the benevolent eye of their Turkish rulers. Nothing could have been further from the truth. The various races of the Balkan Peninsula, frustrated in their long struggles for national independence, were often at each other's throats, usually incited by their Turkish overlords. The Young Turk Revolution of 1908 sounded the death-knoll of the national aspirations of the Christian subjects of the Ottoman Empire. Had these unfortunate people not taken their destiny into their own hands and had waited in the patient hope that the European Powers would one day persuade the Turks to undertake reforms, the Christians of the Balkan Peninsula would have met the same fate as befell the hapless Armenians. Europe's traditional romantic and indulgent attitude towards Turkey blinded the Western Powers to the rising nationalism of the ethnic groups of the Balkan Peninsula. The Balkan Wars came as the climax of the liberation movements by the Christian subjects of the Sultan and they brought freedom, dignity and pride to millions who, until then, had been forced to live as the despised *rayahs* of the Ottoman Empire. This new-found sense of national identity and strength among the Balkan peoples, far from being divisive, provided in the long run a more solid foundation for understanding and cooperation.

The sense of national consciousness and purpose felt by the Balkan States was much strengthened by the extensive migrations which resulted from the Wars. Always a painful and often a tragic event for the uprooted and homeless victims, the enforced movement of populations nevertheless mitigated the causes of friction and resulted in a closer unity among the citizens of each independent State. The inhabitants of whole towns and villages fled before the advancing armies or were expelled after an enemy occupation, so the new Balkan States attained a great measure of homogeneity. The Turkish peasants of Epirus and Macedonia were transferred to Eastern Thrace and Anatolia. The Greeks were driven out of Thrace and sought refuge in Greek Macedonia. The Bulgarians were driven out of Central Macedonia and fell back to Old Bulgaria and Eastern Rumelia from whence only a few years before they had driven out the Greeks. There was also a considerable shift of populations between the Serbs and the Bulgarians and to a lesser degree between the Serbs and the Greeks. As a consequence of the Balkan Wars there was to be in future a Greek Macedonia, a Serbian Macedonia, a Bulgarian Macedonia, and the world would soon forget from where that agreeable concoction, *salade macédoine*, derived its name.

Still in Salonica, Metaxas wrote to his wife on 12 August, a few days before the parade, telling her that he and the rest of the General Staff would shortly return with the King to Athens "with all pomp and circumstance." After disembarking at Phaleron, the Royal party would proceed to Athens for the official reception and then attend the *Te Deum* at the Cathedral.

"Well then, rent a window overlooking Stadium Street, or Constitution Square, or Hermes Street. We shall arrive at Omonoia Station. Whatever it costs, rent it, and telegraph me here immediately through the Ministry [of War] -- "I have rented a window at such a place" -- and describe the place to me exactly, so that, when I pass by, I shall be able to see you and greet you. You will also be waving to me, so I shall single you out at once. In this way you will also be able to see the parade, which will be a fine spectacle. After the Cathedral I shall come round to collect you.[91]

In Athens Venizelos remained.secluded in his house until two o'clock in the afternoon, the hour of Constantine's scheduled arrival at Phaleron. Then he drove down to the quay and, as head of the Government, proffered an official welcome to the victorious King. At 5:30 p.m. Constantine made his entry into Athens. After the *Te Deum* had been celebrated in the Cathedral, Venizelos once more discreetly withdrew to his house, leaving the King and his Staff Officers to ride in triumph through the streets of the city and enjoy the apotheosis of a delirious populace.

Even before the celebrations were over, a sombre assessment of the price that had been paid for glory and for a greater Greece had already begun. For the thousands of families throughout the land who had lost their loved ones and for the numerous refugees who had lost all their earthly possessions, the joy of victory was tempered by the grief of bereavement and loss. In many a Greek town and village, next to the marble memorial commemorating those who gave their lives in the War of Independence of 1821-1828, a new memorial was now erected, inscribed with the names of those who fell no less gloriously in the Balkan Wars of 1912-1913. Greek losses in men did not compare unfavourably with the losses suffered by the other Balkan States, although the number of officers lost by the Greek Army, especially in the short but ferocious Second Balkan War, was disproportionably high. The official statistics for the Greek casualties are as follows:[92]

	Killed or Died		Wounded or Sick	
	Officers	Soldiers	Officers	Soldiers
First Balkan War (9 months)	138	5,031	189	23,313
Second Balkan War (1 month)	166	2,397	429	18,878
Total...	304	7,428	618	42,191

Greek revenues after the War had a net increase of about one-third (while those of Turkey decreased by about one-third). By the Spring of 1913 the price of basic

91 Metaxas, *Diary,* II, p. 225.

92 Diplomatist [Sir George Young], *Nationalism and War in the Near East* (Oxford, 1915), p. 308.

necessities had gone up sharply in the Balkan Peninsula. In Serbia and Bulgaria the price of bread rose 25 per cent and that of fuel 50 per cent; but in Greece the Government regulated prices with some success. In Greece the Balkan Wars activated a great flow of money. The shipping industry made high profits out of the building of army transports. The farmers and many local industrialists made large profits out of the Wars. (The surplus raisin crop was no longer burned because raisins made up part of the fighting men's rations.) A great deal of money poured into the country as contributions or investments from the Greeks of the Diaspora. Finally, the successful conclusion for Greece of the Balkan Wars inspired a new sense of confidence and generated a tremendous impetus to agriculture, trade and industry.

During the War there was a great shortage of labour all over the country and many services had to be run by skeleton staffs because of the general mobilization. Even these smaller numbers had to be reduced still further so that some of their personnel could be used in the introduction of services in the conquered territories. The central office of the National Bank of Athens, for instance, was short of 120 employees, one-third of its regular staff. Labour deficiencies were eventually met by the influx of refugees. By the end of the War Greece had 157,000 refugees on her hands, compared with Bulgaria's refugee count of 105,000. The refugee problem was far less severe in Serbia. It was not only those of Greek origin who sought refuge in Greece; many thousands of Turks, rather than live under Bulgarian rule in Western Thrace, chose to flee to Greek-occupied territory. Greek philanthropic societies distributed clothes and blankets and the Greek state voted a special budget for their needs and distributed food. Transport ships were made available to all Moslems wishing to emigrate to Turkey. As for the Greeks, they were settled in the new territories. Loans were made to them to enable them to start again in their new homes; but the Greek Government, which had grown cautious after its experience with the 30,000 Greek refugees from Bulgarian Rumelia in 1906, refused to finance these loans. A Government loan had proved to be a bad debt. Therefore the task of granting loans to these poor refugees was entrusted to the Agricultural Bank of Greece, which was set up for the purpose.

The new territories, which were easily accessible by sea and were inhabited (after the expulsion of the Turks and Bulgarians) mainly by Greeks, whose numbers were vastly increased by successive waves of refugees, provided Greece with what had been most lacking. Only one-fifth of pre-1912 Greece was arable, while a great part of the newly acquired territories were fertile, with great potential. Her cultivatable land increased from 2,150,000 acres in 1911 to 3,325,000 acres in 1914, and the value of the agricultural product rose from 262 million drachmas in 1912 to 413 million in 1914. Moreover, the nature of the agricultural economy changed. The flat, rich valleys in Macedonia and Thrace produced wheat and maize and relieved to a great extent the constant necessity of grain imports. (But it was not until 1957 that Greece managed to produce a surplus of wheat, and this was partly due to changes in the national dietary patterns.) The tobacco producing districts of the north made Greece a major tobacco exporter in the world market and tobacco replaced currants in earning foreign exchange for the country. Greece also now exported olives and olive-oil from the rich olive-groves of Crete, Lesbos, Lemnos, and the other islands. The forests of Macedonia provided much needed timber for the barren islands and for Old Greece. The new economic opportunities created by the new lands slowed down the exodus of young men from the country. The outward movement was partly reversed. A large number of Greek emigrants, many of whom had come home to fight in the Balkan Wars, now began to return and buy land in the new territories and to invest their money. These Greeks expatriates were still close to their roots and welcomed the opportunity to return to their native land. They brought with them not only their savings, but also the skills they had acquired abroad and often a new democratic spirit of political independence.

The social changes resulting from the Balkan Wars were of no small significance, either. Not only did the Wars bring together thousands of young men from all parts of the country and many from overseas, including 40,000 Greeks from the United States, who fought shoulder to shoulder for the same patriotic ideals; the liberation of such vast numbers of Greeks and their incorporation into the Greek Kingdom infused fresh, often progressive blood into the veins of the nation. The newly liberated Greeks were not all peasants; many of them came from important centers like Salonica, Ioannina, Kavalla, Serres, Veroia, Kozani, Mytilene, Chios, Herakleion, and Chania. More importantly, while the urban classes of Athens and Old Greece were concerned mostly with the professions and politics, the citizens of the urban centers of New Greece were interested mostly in trade and industry. Many of the new arrivals came from the commercial elite of the Ottoman Empire and brought with them a spirit of enterprise and valuable business connections around the world. The first step the Greek Government took to serve the interests of the new urban classes was to make plans for the linking up of the railway system of Old Greece with that of Macedonia and therefore of Europe. In the past this project had been frustrated by Turkey for military reasons, and until this time Greece could only be reached by sea. But the First World War intervened, and it was not until July 1920 that the Simplon Orient Express made its first journey from Paris to Athens.

The victory celebrations in Athens in which many representatives of the newly liberated provinces participated, made a great impression upon foreign observers in the Greek capital. For a brief moment Greece appeared strong and united under a far-seeing and dynamic Prime Minister and a heroic warrior King. Never before or after did modern Greece experience such national euphoria and such unbounded faith in the future. Little more than a minor principality in the Nineteenth Century, Greece emerged from the Balkan Wars as a minor Power, whose potential strength and influence in the Near East were to engage the attention of the Great Powers. Until this time Greece had been treated by the Powers either as a weak and insignificant country which must be "protected" or, because of her cultural heritage, accorded some kind of special treatment; no sooner were the Balkan Wars concluded than the Great Powers began courting Greece as an ally. Greece could now easily muster a fighting force of 250,000 men, and her control of the Aegean afforded her several excellent harbours and also many seafarers from the islands with whom to build up a strong navy.

The enhanced position of the country carried with it new dangers and new responsibilities. Greece now had a long northern border and an extended coastline, plus an increased number of islands, to defend. Having shared prior to 1911 a common border with Turkey only, Greece now had a border with Turkey, Bulgaria and Serbia, and a new border to be delineated with Albania. The Italian occupation of the Dodecanese brought Greece's western rival into Greek waters. Greece had made new friends, but also new enemies. She now realized that her irredentist aspirations clashed with those of her new neighbours in the north and her vital interests conflicted not only with those of Turkey, but also with those of Russia and Italy. The enhanced position of the country in the international community proved to be a mixed blessing. Greece now had to make some hard choices on her own behalf, the first being between the Triple Entente and the Triple Alliance. Sharp differences over the course Greece should pursue abroad heightened political antagonisms at home and brought to the fore questions concerning both the constitution and the dynasty.

The Balkan Wars of 1912-1913 were not only of great importance in the history of modern Greece; they were also important in the personal history of Ioannis Metaxas. During the Wars Metaxas not only exhibited some of his basic strengths; he also revealed some of his basic weaknesses: his inordinate ambition, his inflated self-esteem, his capacity for self-deception and hypocrisy. He hungered and thirsted for power and universal acclaim, while at the same time avowing to his wife, his only confidante, that he had no interest in wordly fame. On 6 December 1912 he wrote to her: "They say they intend to reward us, etc. I am sickened by all this. They can keep all their honour and promotions."[93] Lust for power was his life-long daemon, yet to his wife he wrote in the same letter: "I shall do my duty until the end, until we conclude the peace, and then my aim is to resign my commission and devote myself to our home."[94] To be under the command of others he could not brook and, until absolute power was his, his first impulse was to retire into private life.

The Balkan Wars also exposed Metaxas' lack of vision, a serious limitation which was to become all too apparent in his later political career. Blinded by his hatred for the Military League, which had prepared the ground for Greece to embark upon the Wars, blinded by his resentment of the French Military Mission, which had trained the Greek

93 Metaxas, *Diary,* II, p. 178.

94 *Ibid.*

Army for the enterprise, blinded by his antipathy for Venizelos, who was the mastermind behind the Balkan Alliance, Metaxas completely failed to perceive the unique opportunity which the Balkan Wars afforded Greece to double her territory and her population. He disapproved of the alliance between Greece and her Slav neighbours against Turkey, the protégé of his beloved Germany; sent to Sofia to negotiate a military convention with Bulgaria, he was still hopeful that war could be avoided. From Sofia he wrote to his wife: "The storm has dispersed in the Balkans so often that I hope this will prove to be the case again."[95] Even after Greece had captured a great part of Macedonia, including Salonica, Metaxas wrote from London, where as a member of the Greek delegation he was negotiating the peace with Turkey: "This war, which has brought us so much glory, was a great mistake politically."[96] And, later in the Spring of 1913, while negotiating a military convention with Serbia and planning the war against Bulgaria, Metaxas still earnestly hoped that war might be prevented. He was not a pacifist, but the Balkan Wars were the conception of others and his egoism did not allow him to see very far beyond the immediate political rivalries at home.

Notwithstanding his reservations about the Balkan Wars, when called upon by the State in the hour of national emergency, Metaxas, the most brilliant officer on the Greek General Staff, proved his military genius. The Balkan Wars were the most significant episode in his army career. The successful planning of the campaigns in Macedonia, Epirus and Thrace and the effective strategy of the various battles owed much to Metaxas' expertise. As a Staff Officer he kept the over-all picture of the war constantly in view; yet no detail was too small to escape his methodical mind and no task beneath his conscientious attention. He was a practical man, who genuinely cared about the welfare of the men in the field and he made certain that they were well-fed and well-equipped before they went under enemy fire. He negotiated the military convention with Bulgaria and the preliminary military convention with Serbia. With other officers he negotiated the surrender of Salonica and Ioannina. Never a modest man, Metaxas was fully aware of his talents and achievements, always possessing a sublime confidence in his own abilities and wisdom. He was a firm believer in the intrinsic worth of an individual, the competence and character of a man, his merit, and the respect due to individual value and rank - what in Greek is known as *axia.*[97] Metaxas had not the slightest doubt that he himself was such a man, one possessing

95 *Ibid.*, p. 144.

96 *Ibid.*, p. 180.

97 To be regarded as ἄξιος, a man of αξία, is, for a Greek, the highest expression of approbation. Venizelos, on his return from the Peace Conference of Versailles, was declared by the Greek Parliament to be ἄξιος της πατρίδος - a man worthy of the motherland. In a similar instance, the ordination of a Greek cleric, be he simple priest or Patriarch, cannot proceed without the unanimous acclamation of ἄξιος by the assembled congregation. The English words "axiom" and "axiomatic" are derived from the same root.

limitless αξία. The Balkan Wars increased his conceit and further inflated his formidable ego.

Despite his considerable services to the State, for Metaxas recognition was niggardly and slow in coming and, when it did come, he felt no gratitude. He had been only a Captain when he fought the war in Macedonia and Epirus. On 2 June 1913, just before the outbreak of the Second Balkan War, he was promoted Major and in September 1913 to the rank of Lieutenant-Colonel; a short while later the King decorated him with the Gold Cross of the Saviour. After the War Metaxas became Director of the General Staff - still, however, second-in-command to General Dousmanis. He was also appointed Principal of the Higher Military Academy [The Captains' School - *Σχολή Λοχαγών*], an academy for the advanced training of army officers. But nothing could appease his wounded ego. This sense of injured merit, this obsessive conviction that he was, at every turn, the victim of some kind of intolerable injustice inflicted upon him by a malicious and envious world, was to remain with Metaxas for the rest of his life.

In May 1914, when on a visit with the King and the General Staff to the old battle-grounds, he wrote to his wife:

"Dousmanis is attentive, but I remain cold and indifferent, not from calculation, but from real indifference. During the tours of inspection I draw back and examine what I want by myself. Today the King had all the officers of the General Staff for breakfast [in fact, a meal at lunchtime]. On the Queen's right was Dousmanis; I on her left. She was very gracious and I very polite, as much as I could, but I confess without much taste for it."[98] A few days later he wrote to Lela again: *"At Verroia I saw again the little room where I conceived the plan for the battle of Jannitsa. But I was as a stranger; because the world only recognizes high rank. The battleground did not move me at all ... Then, Florina. There the war against me began, because they thought that the war against the Turks had ended ... Then Kozani. Kozani! The first fruit of the victory at Sarantaporo.... But what is it to me now, the battle of Sarantaporo or Jannitsa, the years of 1912 and 1913? All these things have already passed away. Let him who desires these laurels take them."*[99]

The King "in the beginning did not even see me. But didn't he really? Neither did I make haste to go to him."[100] At Florina the King invited him to pose with him for a photograph. Metaxas assured Lela that he was plagued by worldly vanities no longer: "I assure you, I hate myself because in the past I was small enough to suffer in this way. Thank God, all that is over and done with."[101] But his wife should not think that the journey had disappointed him.

---

98 Metaxas, *Diary*, II, p. 267.

99 *Ibid.*, p. 268.

100 *Ibid.*

101 *Ibid.*, p. 269.

"In the beginning the journey amused me a little, later the memories brought in me bitterness, then a tranquil apathy came over me. But disappointment with myself, that is, discouragement, not a bit! On the contrary, I regained my appetite for work and struggle.

I know that they took away from me my fame, my recognition, my feathers, with which others have plumed themselves. I am like a plucked eagle; but an eagle always and the feathers will grow again. The sense of my power and of my innermost being nobody can take away."[102]

Having written this, he had sudden misgivings that he had been too outspoken. He had considered registering his letter, but on second thoughts he decided to carry it home and hand it to his wife himself.

102 *Ibid.*, p. 268.

The National Schism 1915

The Balkan Alliance, which had been put together by the efforts of Venizelos, was virtually dead. Serbia and Romania no longer shared common borders with Turkey, while Bulgaria had patched up her old differences with her former ruler and vowed to wrest Macedonia from Greece. The Italians showed no signs of evacuating the Dodecanese which they had occupied during the Tripolitan War of 1912, temporarily, as they claimed. Both Austria and Italy demanded Greek evacuation of Northern Epirus. Italy had aspirations of turning the Adriatic into an Italian sea. Therefore she wanted the Albanian frontier to be drawn as far south as possible in order to exclude any Greek presence from the Straits of Otranto. Austria always desired an open door for Austrian penetration in the Balkans. Germany supported her partners in the Central Alliance. The Entente Powers yielded to Italian pressure, in the vague hope of winning Italy to their side. On 13 February 1914 the six Great Powers sent a Note to Greece demanding the evacuation of the Greek forces from Southern Albania. If Greece concurred, she could keep the Aegean islands which she had captured during the First Balkan War. Greece chose the islands.

While Turkey had become reconciled to her losses in the Balkan Peninsula and had come to an understanding with her former Slavic foes, she refused to accept as final the Greek annexation of the former Turkish islands in the Aegean and singled out Greece as the sole target of her enmity. Three of the largest of these islands, Lesbos, Chios and Samos, were only separated by narrow channels from the coast of Asia Minor where thousands of Greeks were concentrated in cities like Kydoniae [Aivali] and Smyrna [Izmir]. Cultural ties and economic activity between the islanders and the Greeks of Aeolia and Ionia joined them in a geographic unit of common outlook and interest. Turkey felt that she could not allow the islands to go to Greece, who might use them in the future as stepping stones for an invasion of Asia Minor. And the Turks, who had suffered two naval defeats during the Balkan Wars, proceeded to purchase in England two dreadnoughts and a number of smaller naval vessels.

The Turkish threat to Greece was apparent. In Athens there was widespread anxiety. Recalling those days, Metaxas wrote in the Athens newspaper *Politeia* in 1924, "Within a few months Greece would have certainly lost her naval superiority over Turkey; not only her islands but Macedonia also would have been exposed to danger, as no railway connection existed between Old Greece and Macedonia and no troops could be transported to Macedonia except by sea. The capital of the State [Athens] would itself be exposed to danger from the sea. The Government of Mr. Venizelos did not quite understand in the beginning what was happening and it took persistent representations on my part to awaken it from its lethargy."[1]

---

1 In the newspaper *Politeia* of 1 July 1924. Quoted by Xenophon Strategos in his book *He Hellas en*

Metaxas often discussed the question of naval supremacy with the Prime Minister. Venizelos said that if Greece had to fight a naval war she would do so as an ally of the Great Powers. "I do not intend to engage in a naval competition with Turkey," he once remarked to Metaxas.[2] On 8 January 1914 Venizelos set off for Europe on the thankless mission of drumming up support for his country at a time when the European Powers, now that the Greek forces had agreed to pull out from Albania and the islands of Imbros and Tenedos, had no need of Greek friendship and little desire to antagonize Turkey. On 21 January 1914 Venizelos paid a visit to Sir Edward Grey and asked for a guarantee of the security of the Aegean Islands by the Powers.[3] The British Foreign Minister suggested that, as such a guarantee should come from all the Powers who had collectively decided to allow Greece to retain the Islands, Venizelos should go to Berlin and propose it to the Germans first. The German involvement in Turkey was well-known and Grey's suggestion to Venizelos was singularly tactless, if it were not actually intended to crush the Greek Prime Minister. In a secret report communicated only to King George V, Prime Minister Asquith, Lord Morley and Lord Crewe, Sir Edward Grey wrote: "M. Venizelos broached with me this morning the idea of an 'Entente' between England and Greece to preserve the '*status quo*' in the Mediterranean."[4] The British Foreign Minister "thought it premature to consider a separate arrangement of that kind between the two Powers."[5] Venizelos returned to Athens on 13 February 1914. When Metaxas saw him Venizelos recounted the British reservation to him. "It was a rejection," concluded Metaxas.[6]

In the meantime, the persecution of Greeks in Turkey continued unabated and the horror stories brought by the swarms of refugees who reached Greek shores incensed the Government and the people. In Asia Minor the Greeks predominated along the Sea of Marmora, the ports of the Aegean, the Cilician coast in Southern Turkey, and along the southern shores of the Black Sea, particularly in Pontus. Four hundred and sixty years after the Turks had captured Constantinople, almost half of the population of the Byzantine capital was still Greek. The security and prosperity of the Greek communities in Turkey had been under constant threat since the outbreak of the Balkan Wars. In 1913 Hellenism in Asia Minor was estimated at two and a half million souls. These Greeks maintained 2,177 schools, employing 4,596 teachers in which as many as 177,505 pupils studied. There were 2,232 churches served by 2,870 priests. In the

Mikra Asia (Athens, 1925), p. 17.

2 Metaxas, *Diary.*, p. 250.

3 As Sir Edward Grey wrote to Sir Francis Elliot. See *British Documents on the Origins of the War. 1914-1918* edited by G.B. Gooch and H. W. V. Temperley (London, 1926-30), Vol X, Part One, p. 95.

4 *Ibid.*, pp. 194-5.

5 *Ibid.*

6 Metaxas, *Diary*, II, p. 235.

Ottoman Empire most of the industry, commerce, shipping and banking were in Greek hands. In the *vilayet* of Constantinople, which comprised 1,173,000 people, only 449,000 were Turks. In the *vilayet* of Trebizond in Pontus there were 350,000 Greeks. At the approach of the Turkish Army in the Second Balkan War there was a stampede of Greeks fleeing from Eastern Thrace to liberated Macedonia. But many Turks, too, abandoned their homes in Macedonia and Thrace during the Balkan Wars and poured into Constantinople as destitute refugees. Among them were the mother and sister of Mustafa Kemal, who was later to be known as Ataturk. In 1912 more than 100,000 Moslems fled through Eastern Thrace before the advance of the Bulgarian Army. Another 10,000 Turks left Macedonia the same year. In 1913 almost 10,000 left Western (Bulgarian) Thrace under the terms of the Turco-Bulgarian Treaty. Subsequently more than 100,000 Moslems evacuated Macedonia. Many of these refugees were taken to Western Turkey and set down among the Greek communities with little assistance for their resettlement from the Turkish authorities. These Turks had lost everything they owned in the Balkans and their frustration and desire for revenge was turned against the Christian populations of Turkey. Bands of irregulars were formed, the notorius *chettés,* who, with the collusion of the Ottoman authorities, plundered and pillaged the Greek towns and villages of Asia Minor. There are many eyewitness accounts of these persecutions from independent sources. On 17 June 1914 the British Ambassador in Constantinople Sir Louis Mallet reported to Sir Edward Grey: "From every side comes the same story of Greeks driven from their homes by Moslems or fleeing from them in terror, of cattle or other property plundered or sold under compulsion at nominal prices, and of official slackness or connivance."[7] Large numbers of these Greeks were forcibly transferred from the fertile valleys of the coastal regions to the inhospitable lands of the Anatolia plateau. Arnold Toynbee wrote: "Entire Greek communities were driven from their homes by terrorism, their homes and land and often their movable property were seized, and individuals were killed in the process...."[8] Certainly the desire for revenge and the need for resettlement of the Turkish refugees were reasons enough for the persecutions. But the persecutions were also motivated by the Turkish wish for a unified and homogeneous Turkish state in Anatolia after the loss of the European provinces. Even before Kemal Atatürk, the cornerstone of Turkish policy was to transform Anatolia into an exclusive fatherland for the Turks. As the Ottoman Empire was multi-racial and multi-religious, the pursuit of this policy took heavy toll of the lives and property of the ethnic minorities, especially the most numerous among them, the Greeks and Armenians. It did not worry Turkey, a nation made up of admixtures of conquering Turkish tribes and subject

7 Quoted by Christos Theodoulou, *Greece and the Entente, August 1, 1914-September 25, 1916* (Thessaloniki, 1971), p.6.

8 Arnold J. Toynbee, *The Western Question in Greece and Turkey* (London, 1923, 1970), p. 140.

peoples, if the inhabitants of Asia Minor were not ethnic Turks, as long as they embraced Mohammedanism and adopted the Turkish language and culture. Some observers attributed the Turkish persecution of the Greeks to German inspiration emanating from the mission of General Liman von Sanders. Henry Morgenthau the American Ambassador at Constantinople was told by the German Admiral Usedom that the idea of deporting the Christian minorities en masse originated in Germany. The reasons for this advice from the German military advisers in Turkey were strategic, although the Turks did not need much encouragement. It was a precautionary measure: the Turks were only thinning out the solid block of Greeks, particularly from the Aegean coast, which could potentially join an invading Greek army. The Turkish Minister of the Interior Talaat Pasha whose record of genocide can only be rivalled by that of Hitler, wrote on 14 May 1914 to Rahmi Bey the *vali* of the Smyrna *vilayet,* that "urgent political necessity" made it imperative for the Greeks to be transferred away from the coast to the interior of Anatolia. "If they refuse to depart to the above mentioned places, be kind enough to give oral instructions to our Moslem brothers to force the Greeks to abandon their towns and homes of their own accord. To this end the Moslems may use all kinds of outrages."[9] Such persecutions continued and were intensified during the First World War. Very few of those unfortunate people survived the long forced marches across the arid Turkish plain.

War seemed inevitable. Turkey refused to accept anything less than sovereignty over the Islands, although she was willing to accept local autonomy under Turkish rule. It was a proposition unacceptable to Greece. In order to recapture the Islands the Turks needed Bulgarian cooperation to threaten Greece from the north; the Bulgarians needed Turkish cooperation to keep Greece tied up in the Aegean so that they could recapture Macedonia. Such considerations and the common desire of Turkey and Bulgaria for a *revanche* against Greece brought the two countries together. As soon as the peace treaty between Bulgaria and Turkey was concluded at Constantinople, the Turkish attitude toward Greece over the Islands hardened. Fear of a Turco-Bulgarian alliance paralysed the Greek Government.

Something very daring and novel was required; something to force Turkey to the conference table and to accept terms which would safeguard the lives and property of ethnic Greek Ottoman subjects and oblige Turkey to abandon her designs on the Aegean Islands. "I studied the matter and came to the conclusion that a blow of such a nature and of such limited objective could only be dealt with the occupation of the Dardanelles and therefore of Constantinople. I then worked out a very detailed plan for forcing the Dardanelles."[10] Metaxas' plans (which have been published with the *Diary)* are of the

---

9 Quoted by Ventiris, *Ελλάς,* I, p. 263. From the Paris newspaper *Le Temps*, 29 July 1916.
10 Metaxas, *Diary*., p. 308.

greatest interest, especially in view of the failure of the Allies to force the Dardanelles in 1915 despite their staggering losses. His plans provided for the sudden landing by seventy ships of an army of at least three divisions at the Gulf of Saros, to be followed by a second and third landing of munitions and supporting services. Its greatest merit was the meticulous study of every detail, from the moment the decision was taken to the moment of landing which, Metaxas calculated, would take thirty days, and the hour by hour planning of the invasion. Absolute secrecy would cover all preparations and an effort would be made on the part of Greece to show that relations with Turkey were normal and even improving. Naval forces were to cooperate closely with land forces. (This the Allies failed to do in 1915, as they completely neglected the factor of secrecy and surprise). Metaxas spent many months studying every aspect of the expedition. "And I came to the conclusion that it could not succeed unless carried out unexpectedly, while peace prevailed, without Turkey suspecting anything," Metaxas noted in his *Diary*.[11] And in his memorandum to the Chief-of-Staff Metaxas wrote: "This is the safest way to carry out the operation. By this method all international laws are violated, but victory is ensured, as far as possible. The outcry against us will subside in the face of our success and we shall justify ourselves because, being in a state of legitimate defense, we chose to save ourselves rather than be destroyed."[12]

On several occasions in the spring of 1914 Metaxas imparted the results of his studies and thoughts to the Prime Minister. "The idea of such a venture did not appeal to him. He was very doubtful of its success. Nevertheless he did not discourage me but advised me to continue."[13] Apart from the few trusted officers who worked under Metaxas to prepare the logistics of the operation, only two others knew his plans, the Chief-of-Staff and the King.

On 29 May 1914 Venizelos, carried away by the general outcry over the intensified persecutions of the Greeks in Asia Minor, delivered to Turkey a threat of war in the Greek Parliament. Simultaneously in a Note to Turkey the Greek Government demanded an end to the persecutions and assurances for the security of the lives and property of the Greeks in Asia Minor. The enemy was thus warned and the element of surprise, so vital in forcing the Dardanelles, ceased to exist.

Abandoned by her friends and allies, Greece was now ready to modify her position on the Islands and come to an understanding with Turkey. Venizelos, using the correspondent of the London *Daily Telegraph* as an intermediary, made the first overtures and a meeting between the Greek Prime Minister and the Turkish Grand Vizier was eventually arranged to take place in Brussels.

---

11 *Ibid.*, p. 241.
12 *Ibid.*, p. 308.
13 *Ibid.*, p. 241.

On 28 June 1914 the Archduke Francis Ferdinand, heir to the Habsburg throne, was assassinated at Sarajevo in Bosnia by Serbian nationalists. Ominous clouds began to gather over Europe. In Athens Venizelos, with a heavy heart, was preparing to bow to the inevitable and give in to Turkish threats. On 21 July 1914 he set off for Brussels to meet with the Grand Vizier, Mehmed Said Halim Pasha. Three days later at Trieste he learned of the Austrian ultimatum to Serbia which had been presented at Belgrade the previous day. Venizelos immediately grasped the gravity of the situation and the implications for his own country. An Austro-Serbian war was imminent, perhaps a general European conflagration. Venizelos had been saved by the bell. Four days later in Munich he sent word to the Grand Vizier through the Greek Minister at Constantinople that he would be unable to meet him as he was obliged to interrupt his journey and return to Athens, "because of Bulgarian mobilization." This, of course, was a trumped-up excuse, but Venizelos' intuition proved correct. No longer would Greece have to solve her differences with Turkey by herself.

The Greco-Serbian Treaty was a defensive alliance between the two countries; but the military convention which was signed on 1 June 1913 and attached to the Treaty provided that "in case of war between one of the allied states and a third Power," the contracting parties would "afford to each other assistance with all their armed forces." Venizelos realized that if Serbia were to become involved in a war, the question of the *casus foederis* of the Greco-Serbian Treaty would certainly arise for Greece, despite Serbia's earlier reluctance to promise her assistance if Greece were to go to war with Turkey. But the Greek Prime Minister was careful not to commit his country immediately to a war against the Great Powers of Europe. While still in Munich he cabled Streit, his Foreign Minister, that Greece could not tolerate an attack on Serbia by Bulgaria, which would put in question the Treaty of Bucharest; in the case of an Austrian attack on Serbia, Greece would observe a benevolent neutrality, allowing all freedom for military supplies to reach Serbia through the port of Salonica. At the same time, Venizelos sent a message to the Greek Minister in Berlin instructing him to inform the German Government that if Bulgaria attacked Serbia it would be impossible for Greece to remain neutral. He was still in Munich when he received a dispatch from Pasic inquiring what policy Greece would adopt in the present emergency. Venizelos at once replied that as he was away from Athens and the information available to him was incomplete, he could make no official pronouncement, but that on his return to his capital he would support the view that Greece should go to the help of Serbia straightaway if Serbia suffered an attack from Bulgaria. And Venizelos cabled Streit from Munich:

"If in a localized Austro-Serbian war we can stay neutral, we must not forget that our alliance binds us to mobilize 40,000 men immediately. It is, however, to the joint interest of Serbia and Greece not to take this step immediately as liable to provoke a Bulgarian general mobilization, which might have serious consequences .... Our

attitude corresponds exactly with that decided on in our joint interest by the Serbian Government at the moment of our crisis with Turkey ... Consideration must also be given to the possibility of a general war with a view to deciding our policy in advance. My considered opinion is that in such an event the Government must on no account let itself be induced to range itself in the opposite camp to Serbia and co-operate with her enemies. It would be contrary both to Greek vital interests, her good faith as an ally and the dignity of the State. On no pretext would I depart from this policy."[14]

On 1 August 1914 Venizelos returned to Athens from his interrupted European journey. The following day Greece sent her official reply to the Serbian Prime Minister after a meeting of the Greek Cabinet presided over by King Constantine. The Greek Government felt that Greece could best fulfill her duty as a friend and ally of Serbia by keeping herself ready to repulse any attack against Serbia on the part of Bulgaria. Greece could not send her troops to fight on the Danube and thus expose Macedonia and Thrace to Bulgaria and Turkey and, as a belligerent, endanger the port of Salonica, the only route open for supplying Serbia with food and munitions. At this point King Constantine apparently shared the opinions of his Prime Minister.

In those dark hours Serbia had, perforce, to declare herself satisfied with the Greek answer. But in later years Greece was accused by friends and enemies alike of having failed to honour her obligations to Serbia deriving from the Graeco-Serbian Treaty. The interpretation of the Graeco-Serbian Treaty became the touchstone in the ensuing feud between the Greek Liberals and the Greek Royalists. The Royalists argued that the terms of the Treaty were confined to an exclusively Balkan situation and that Greece was under no obligation to fulfil it if the third Power attacking one of the contracting parties came from outside the Balkans. Adopting this interpretation, the Royalists subsequently refused to accept that Greece had any obligation to Serbia as she was involved in a wider European war with Austria. The Liberals, on the other hand, accused the Royalists of having failed to honour the country's treaty obligations. In later years Metaxas, remembering Venizelos' equivocal and vacillating attitude toward Serbia at the outbreak of the European war, charged that it was Venizelos himself, and not the Royalists, who had violated the terms of the Graeco-Serbian Treaty.[15]

Metaxas and his family were spending the hot summer of 1914 on the island of Tenos at the home of his mother-in-law. On 28 July he received a telegram from his office at General Staff Headquarters informing him of the fast-approaching war between Austria and Serbia. Metaxas, "foreseeing complications arising from the Treaty between Greece and Serbia," as he wrote, took the first boat to Athens. The vessel put in at the Island

14 Quoted by Albertini, *Origins of the War*, p. 630.

15 Eleftherios Venizelos and Ioannis Metaxas, *Η Ιστορία του Εθνικού Διχασμού, 1915-1936* [The History of the National Schism, 1915-1936](Athens, 1953).

of Syros. Metaxas went ashore and filled in the time until its departure by taking a long walk as far as a vantage point where he could enjoy an uninterrupted view of the surrounding islands. To the left he could see part of Andros; to the right Mykonos, Delos, Naxos, Paros. The whole town of Tenos was clearly visible and so was the Church of *Evangelistria,* the famous shrine of Our Lady. Metaxas was thinking of his wife and two young daughters - "to me the most precious beings in the world."

On arrival in Athens Metaxas learned that Austria had already declared war on Serbia. "A European war is imminent," he wrote to his wife on the evening of 30 July 1914. "In this great catastrophe I hope our dear little Greece will be spared because, according to all indications, we shall not participate but remain vigilant guardians of our country and let the Great Powers devour each other."[16] Metaxas, like so many others that summer, hoped that the prospect of the dreadful disasters bound to accompany a European war would act as a deterrent and at the eleventh hour inspire sufficient sanity to prevent a general conflagration. In the afternoon of 1 August 1914 at the Eleutheroudakis Bookshop, then situated in the basement of the Grand Hotel, a block away from its present position, Metaxas expressed to the manager Mr. Bart his confidence that the Great Powers would find a way to avoid war. One hour after this conversation took place extra editions of the Athens newspapers announced mobilization in Russia, Germany and France and printed the telegrams which were exchanged between these countries on the occasion.[17] That night Metaxas wrote to his wife.

"This European war will be frightful. The losses in life and property will be unheard of. In the face of this fact, one can only bow one's head before God; because the sins of the mighty are great: massacres of the Armenians, persecutions of the Greeks, strangulation of the liberty of the Epirotes, of the [Greek] islanders, oppression of Tripolitania [Libya], Algeria, Tunisia, Morocco, oppression of all justice and morality. There has not been a sacrilege which the Great Powers have not committed for gain - so that an aristocracy of wealth which has elevated pleasure and luxury as the supreme good could live in idle splendor. This is European civilization!"[18]

In letter after letter Metaxas wrote to his wife, who remained on Tenos, concerning the calamities which would soon befall the world. Victors and vanquished would suffer equally; unfortunately war was necessary: preparations for war and the mutually hostile reactions among the Powers had created an intolerable situation in Europe; and then there were all those crimes and injustices perpetrated against the weaker nations. "In Europe the moral condition is wretched: luxury, godlessness, corruption."[19] War was

16 Metaxas, *Diary,* II, p. 314.
17 *Ibid.,* p. 313.
18 *Ibid.,* p. 315.
19 *Ibid.,* p. 317.

a great purifier. "As war elevated us morally, so it will elevate Europe ... It is unfortunate that only through disasters and sacrifices can humanity progress."[20] Metaxas had to spend long hours in his office at the General Staff waiting for news; so he bought Balzac's *Les Courtisanes* "to pass the time," but he found reading difficult in the great heat. One evening a friend of his, Bishop Troyanos of the Archdiocese of Athens, called at his office and invited him to dinner that night at Old Phaleron. At the seaside resort it was cool and pleasant, but the Bishop had forgotten to bring along his wallet so Metaxas had to foot the bill. He wrote to Lela: "But I was compensated because I made him lay before me the proofs of the truth of Christian doctrine. Therefore, if someone tells you that I was seen at the Prinopoulos Restaurant with a lady dressed all in black, do not allow evil thoughts to enter your mind, it was Troyanos."[21]

But it was the outbreak of the war in Europe which primarily engaged Metaxas' attention. "What can I tell you? I am saddened when I reflect that this proud European system, so strong and so majestic, is coming to an end."[22] On 3 August he wrote, "Three days have gone by since Austria declared war and still the Austrians have not managed to invade Serbia."[23] Italy, despite her former brave words, "because she did not expect war," had at the last moment "betrayed her allies" and sided against Austria -- "she is a timid and cowardly nation."[24] Metaxas, although he would quote Dante in the original, retained this low opinion of Italy all his life, and when in power had no difficulty in rejecting the Italian ultimatum to Greece in the fall of 1940 and declaring that the Greeks would defeat the Italians.

Events moved fast. On 2 August 1914 Turkey signed the secret defensive and offensive treaty with Germany against Russia which Turkey had proposed six days earlier at the height of the crisis. The possibility of war with Russia made Turkey a valuable ally to Germany because it was Turkey who controlled the Straits, Russia's main supply artery. The Turco-German alliance provided that if Greece intervened against the Central Powers, Turkey was to receive the Aegean Islands and Crete. On 3 August Germany declared war on France and invaded Belgium. The following day Britain declared war on Germany and Winston Churchill First Lord of the Admiralty, although ignorant of the secret Turco-German treaty, requisitioned for the Royal Navy the two dreadnoughts that were being built for Turkey in British shipyards. This last piece of news was received in Greece with a strong sense of relief. The Turkish menace, which had hung over the Aegean Islands for so long was as if by magic suddenly

---

20 *Ibid.*
21 *Ibid.*, p. 316.
22 *Ibid.*, p. 316.
23 *Ibid.*, p. 315.
24 *Ibid.*, p. 316.

removed. Metaxas recorded that the Greek ministers chaffed Venizelos about it, telling him he was a lucky man. But the Prime Minister, who had spent many a sleepless night because of the threat from Turkey, did not consider it a laughing matter. "Venizelos had the face of a man reprieved from some great danger," wrote Metaxas.[25]

Venizelos, who had received the news of the outbreak of hostilities in Serbia with caution, soon realized that the conflict was going to develop into a general European war which would involve questions far beyond the Balance of Power in the Balkan Peninsula. The entry of Turkey into the war on the side of Germany radically changed the policy of Britain and France in the Near East. During the Nineteenth Century European policy had aimed at the preservation of "the integrity of the Ottoman Empire." Greek national aspirations had conflicted with the interests of Britain and France, but now this was no longer so. When Turkey sided with Germany, Greek interests suddenly coincided with those of the Western Allies. Venizelos was the first to perceive this. Not only would Greece be able to solve her problems with Turkey who had been threatening her ever since the conclusion of the Balkan Wars; the present war, Venizelos considered, was a unique opportunity for Greece to fulfill her national aspirations, free the Greek communities of Asia Minor and Thrace and realize the *Megali Idea*, the manifest destiny of the nation. Venizelos also believed that Britain, who controlled the seas with her Navy, would finally emerge victorious from the war, despite Germany's military might. Greece, a maritime country, with all her main cities built along the coasts of the Aegean and the Ionian Sea and scattered over a thousand islands, could only find her rightful place by the side of Britain. Her future fortunes were bound up with those of Britain. The Great War was in Venizelos' estimation a godsent opportunity for Greece to associate herself with three Great Powers, Britain, France and Russia, who were, historically, Greece's Protecting Powers. Furthermore, Venizelos believed that the dissolution of the Ottoman Empire was at hand and that the Great War would encourage the subject races of the Turks -- the Arabs, the Greeks, the Armenians, the Kurds -- to revolt and proclaim their independence. Greece should fight on the side of the Allies on the battlefield so that she could sit by their side at the conference table when the peace settlement was drawn up. To his mind, the Great War was a never-to-be-repeated opportunity which Greece could not afford to miss.

Metaxas, unlike Venizelos, did not believe that the Germans could be stopped at the Marne, much less that they would be finally crushed. Germany possessed the most efficient war machine in the world and, unlike the Allies, had been steadily building up her armaments. Metaxas, who had studied the science of war in Germany, had a first-hand knowledge of the German Army which, in the person of the Kaiser, possessed a leader of singular will and purpose. In the Balkans especially, the Germans and

25 *Ibid.*, p. 321.

Austrians would defeat their enemies and impose their will. Turkey and Bulgaria were bound to join the Central Alliance. If Greece sided with the opposite camp, the Bulgarians would snatch Macedonia from her, the Italians Epirus, and the Turks would recapture the Greek islands and destroy the Greek communities of Asia Minor. In Metaxas' view, Greek interests coincided with German interests and, if Greece could not join the Central Alliance because her ports and cities were exposed to the cannons of the Allied fleets, she should at least remain neutral. While Venizelos argued that Greece could not afford to be isolated, Metaxas argued that isolation would be the salvation of the country. As a military man, Metaxas was very much aware of the Bulgarian threat to the north. Greece had defeated the Bulgarians in the Second Balkan War, but she had then been fighting with strong allies. As long as Romania did not pose a threat to Bulgaria on the Danube, Greece had to live in constant fear of Bulgarian threats of *revanche.* Neither did Metaxas share Venizelos' opinion that the end of the Ottoman Empire was fast approaching. He read the lessons of history differently from the Prime Minister. Metaxas did not believe that Britain and France had suddenly performed a *volte face* and abandoned their policy of preserving Turkey as a bulwark against Russian penetration in the Mediterranean. If they now spoke as if they had changed their policy, it was only a temporary change of attitude dictated by the exigencies of the moment; alas for Greece if she were to base her own actions upon such an ephemeral stance, forgetting the age-old policy of the West in the Eastern Mediterranean. If Turkey were actually to be divided, the Russians had already put forward claims to Constantinople and the Straits. Italy and France claimed Anatolia and Britain was casting covetous eyes upon the Ottoman Arab provinces. That was why the Entente Powers had turned down the Greek offer of an alliance and Metaxas did not see why Greece should fight for the benefit of other nations when it had been made clear to her that her alliance was not wanted; if the Kaiser's attitude toward Greece was clumsy, the Allies' treatment of Greece was cavalier and patronising. For these reasons Metaxas considered Venizelos' pro-Entente policy reckless and irresponsible, especially as all Venizelos' offers were made without any conditions for the satisfaction of Greek claims. In later years Metaxas declared that it was not he and the Royalists who had prevented Greece from joining the Allies at the outbreak of war, as he had been accused of doing; it was the Allies themselves who did not want Greece in their camp. The Royalists regarded Pan-Slavism as the worst threat to Greek interests and the German war effort as an attempt to contain Pan-Slavism; a favourable outcome of the German efforts would benefit Greece. Metaxas pointed to Russian support for Bulgaria and Russian designs on Constantinople, but he did not take into serious consideration the essential differences between Bulgaria and Serbia. Metaxas and the Royalists could not accept that the individual nationalist aspirations of each Slavic country were stronger by far than the abstraction of Pan-Slavism which was invoked by Russia in order to promote her own expansionist goals.

Furthermore, there was an ideological cleavage between the King's advisers and Venizelos. Streit, the King's political adviser, of German descent and a well-known Germanophile, was a devoted Royalist and an anti-Venizelist. Colonel Metaxas, the King's influential military adviser, believed in German victory and hoped for a resolution of the war which would not disturb the European Balance of Power. Metaxas was imbued with German ideas and thought that the superior German civilization, German discipline and German seriousness of purpose would win the day over the fickle and decadent Western democracies. The Great War brought to the surface the dichotomy between the traditional conservative Royalist concepts and the bourgeois ideas of Venizelos and his Liberals. The Greek oligarchy which, through clientelism, had retained an almost feudal relationship with the peasants, was replaced after the Revolution of Ghoudi and the constitutional reforms of Venizelos by a new regime, a middle-class liberal democracy, a bourgeois state with free parliamentarian institutions. The forces of established and privileged interests which had been suppressed by the Revolution of 1909 found in the present war the opportunity to re-emerge and reclaim their old pre-eminence. This was a political and social confrontation in which Metaxas played a crucial role.

On 23 August 1914 the two German warships *Goeben* and *Breslau,* having given the British fleet the slip in the Mediterranean, entered the Dardanelles. These battleships had been refuelled surreptitiously on the Island of Syros on the evening of 5 August with the permission of the Greek Government; Venizelos claimed later that Quadt the German Minister in Athens misleadingly requested permission for the refuelling of two merchant ships and that he had no idea at the time that the two vessels were, in fact, *Goeben* and *Breslau,* on their way to Constantinople. In his journalistic duel with Venizelos in 1934 Metaxas charged that Venizelos had been aware of the identity of the two warships and he further implied that the Greek Prime Minister had acted in collusion with the British Government.[26] Admiral Koundouriotis sighted the two German cruisers off the island of Lemnos at the entrance to the Dardanelles on 22 August and offered to place his fleet under the command of the British Admiral who was pursuing them. But the British Admiral replied that he had no orders to press on with the chase into the Straits. It should be noted that this gesture of Koundouriotis was made without prior consultation with his Government. On 30 August Metaxas wrote to his wife: "Koundouriotis resigned; cause unknown."[27] Possibly the Admiral's resignation was connected with the offer he made on his own initiative to the Admiral of the British fleet. Churchill made no reference to this incident in his long account of the flight of the two German battle-cruisers through the Mediterranean. The German

---

26 Ιστορία Εθνικού, pp. 7-8.

27 Metaxas, *Diary,* II, p. 343.

historian William W. Gottlieb put forward the theory that the two German ships were intentionally allowed by the British and French to enter the Dardanelles in order to keep Russia in the war. William W. Medlicott the British historian in his book, *Contemporary England, 1914-1964*, described Gottlieb's contention as "fanciful." Others have argued that Britain's objective in allowing the ships to proceed to Constantinople was to keep the city and the Straits out of Russian hands, that is, they continued to pursue their old policy of Russian containment, even after Russia had become their ally. The Greek "Royalist" historian E. I. Malainos declared that Venizelos, by allowing the refuelling of the German warships on the night of 5-6 August, was "a voluntary accomplice" of the British.[28] Britain protested to Turkey, who was still nominally a neutral, over the presence of the German warships in the port of Constantinople; whereupon Turkey "bought" the two ships to make up for the two Turkish dreadnoughts which had been requisitioned by Britain, although the two German warships continued to be manned by their German crews. *Goeben* was renamed Sultan Selim and Breslau was renamed Mintillu, that is, Mytiline, the modern name for the Island of Lesbos, one of the Aegean Islands coveted by Turkey.

Winston Churchill was the first to realize the implications of the arrival of the two German battleships at Constantinople. In his account of the war he wrote: "In the early days of September it seemed highly probable that Turkey ... would make war upon us and upon Greece whatever we did."[29] The British Admiralty had learned of Metaxas' audacious plan for an attack and occupation of Gallipoli without a declaration of war. According to the Dardanelles Commission, Churchill set out to "work out a plan for the seizure, by means of a Greak army ... of the Gallipoli Peninsula, with a view to admitting a British Fleet to the Sea of Marmora."[30] Early in September 1914 Churchill cabled Rear-Admiral Mark Kerr head of the British Naval Mission in Greece instructing him to discuss plans for a joint Greek-English operation in the Dardanelles with the Greek General and Naval Staff. After seeing Venizelos, Admiral Kerr had an audience with Constantine.[31] The King, true to his promises to the German Emperor, replied that he had no intention of waging war against Turkey and that he therefore saw no point in discussing any plans of forcing the Dardanelles; but he suggested that Admiral Kerr should see the Prime Minister again before sending an answer to London. Venizelos requested the Admiral not to send his telegram to the British Admiralty until

28 E.I. Malainos, *Ιστορία των ξενικών επεμβάσεων* [History of Foreign Intervention] (Athens, 1968), III, pp. 14-21.

29 Winston S. Churchill, *The World Crisis* (New York, 1931), p. 283.

30 Quoted by Theodoulou, *Greece and the Entente*, p. 38.

31 Rear-Admiral Mark Kerr greatly admired king Constantine and later edited some of the king's private letters which show that Constantine never intended to join Germany and that his choice of neutrality was based on sound military considerations. The book is: Constantine I, *A King's Private Letters. Letters of Constantine to Paola, Princess of Saxe-Weimar 1912-1923* (London, 1925).

he himself had been given new instructions by the King. Then on 7 September 1914 Venizelos wrote a long letter to Constantine which contained the essence of his own interventionist policy, explained his disagreement with the King's position, and offered his resignation.[32]

In his letter to the King Venizelos agreed that Greece could not undertake an offensive war against Turkey without somehow securing her flank against Bulgaria. "But to declare that under no circumstances, not even if this condition were fulfilled, are we disposed to wage war on Turkey before Turkey attacks us, is clearly against the well-understood interests of the nation. Let us not deceive ourselves, Turkey has been waging an undeclared war against us."[33] Venizelos reminded the King that Turkey refused to recognize the decision of the Powers in the case of the Aegean Islands and that she was continuing the persecution of the Greeks in Turkey, 500,000 of whom had already been expelled and their property, to the value of at least 500 million drachmas, confiscated. All the indications were that Turkey would continue the persecutions; if Greece now lost the opportunity to wage war against Turkey with strong allies, she would be obliged later on to wage war alone, without allies and without friends. "If we refuse on principle and unconditionally to join in a war against Turkey, we do not thereby escape such a war but merely postpone it, not even for long. It is obvious that Turkey will not demobilize before she settles accounts with us."[34] Turkish mobilization, the Prime Minister declared, was directed not only against Russia, but also against Greece. Germany had already warned Greece to expect a Turkish attack if Greece went to war against Bulgaria in the event of a Bulgarian attack on Serbia. The Prime Minister protested against excessive fears of offending Germany at a time when she "furthered the plans of the Turks by giving them ships, money, arms, ammunition and even officers."[35] The Prime Minister went on to point out that Germany not only supported Turkey, but Bulgaria as well, the two traditional enemies of Hellenism. German support of Turkey and Bulgaria made imperative the orientation of Greek foreign policy toward the Entente. Greece had no interest in declaring war against the Central Powers, but Venizelos believed that, as far as was humanly possible to predict, Britain and her friends would be victorious in the Near East, whatever might be the outcome of the war in Central Europe. Geopolitical considerations as well as economic interests made Greek friendship with Britain and France inevitable.

Constantine would have welcomed the opportunity to rid himself of Venizelos, but he was afraid to have Venizelos in opposition at a time when the Royalist Party was

---

32 Spyros Markezinis, *Πολιτική Ιστορία Νεωτέρας Ελλάδος* [Political History of Modern Greece] (Athens, 1966), IV, pp. 369-71.

33 *Ibid.*

34 *Ibid.*

35 *Ibid.*

weak. In his reply to the Prime Minister the same day, the King insisted that there was no disagreement between them, only a "nuance."[36] To Admiral Kerr, with whom he was well acquainted, Constantine spoke informally, as the Admiral knew the Kaiser well and understood his "character." Constantine further wrote that he would prefer to wait for Turkey to attack first, "so that I personally do not fall out with the Emperor now and for evermore."[37] As the King would not recognize any real disagreement with his Prime Minister, he refused to accept Venizelos' resignation.

On 28 September 1914 Weber Pasha, a German naval commander with the Liman von Sanders mission in Turkey, mined and closed the Straits to all shipping. Russia's main artery for the supply of arms and ammunition was thus blocked, severely limiting her effectiveness as an ally of the Entente. Nevertheless, the Turks were still giving solemn assurances of their neutrality to the Entente embassies in Constantinople. "The Sublime Porte played the comedy out without any hitch," wrote the historian R. B. Mowat.[38]

Metaxas made no attempt to see Venizelos when the Prime Minister returned from his interrupted journey -- "because they must get accustomed to ask for me themselves," as he wrote to his wife. On 3 August, three days after Venizelos' arrival, when news reached Greece that the first skirmishes had taken place on the French and Russian borders and that Turkey had ordered general mobilization, Venizelos telephoned Metaxas and kept him for an hour, consulting him on the ominous news. In the afternoon of the same day the Prime Minister went to General Staff Headquarters to hand an order to General Dousmanis, but not finding him in his office, he sat for half an hour with Metaxas, again talking with him about the War.

The following day the Prime Minister invited the Chief-of-Staff and Metaxas to his house. Metaxas made a note of this interview on 7 August 1918 while exiled in Corsica. In Europe the War had become general and Venizelos asked his military advisers for their "considered opinion" as to which Powers were likely to emerge victorious. General Dousmanis replied that it was impossible for him to guess the outcome of the War, or even the direction that military operations might take; but Germany had the advantage of superiority of arms. Metaxas said: "I cannot foresee the outcome of the War. I am of the opinion that Germany will not be defeated; what she will be able to accomplish beyond that, it is impossible for me to predict."[39]

The Prime Minister was not satisfied with this; he had expected more concrete answers. He now asked for the "personal opinion" of the two officers, not in their capacity as members of the General Staff: did they think that Germany and Austria

---

36 Markezinis, *Πολιτικῆς Ιστορία*, IV, p. 371.

37 *Ibid.*

38 R. B. Mowat, *A History of European Diplomacy, 1914-1925* (New York, 1931), p. 15.

39 Metaxas, *Diary.*, p. 318

would be able to wage a war on two fronts? And, if so, how? The Chief-of-Staff said that he could not give an opinion, but again insisted that Germany had military superiority.

Metaxas: *I believe that Germany will first attack with all her forces against one of her opponents, probably against France, and, after she has neutralised her, she will transfer most of her forces against Russia.*

Venizelos: *Will she be in time?*

Metaxas: *Certainly. Her railway communications are excellent.*

Venizelos: *Will the part of her army she will have to leave behind against the French Army hold out? Do not forget that Russian is a vast country and cannot be beaten by force of arms.*[40]

Metaxas expounded in some detail his ideas concerning the probable course of the War. He emphasised the importance of communications and how Germany, being in the center, would be able to move her armies fast enough to deliver decisive blows both on the Eastern and Western Fronts. That same afternoon Metaxas went to see the Prime Minister in his house on some urgent business and again reiterated his opinion about the War. He explained the progress the French Army had made since 1870 but how it was still, numerically at least, inferior to the German. The Germans, of course, would have to halt their advance against the French in order to transfer their armies to the Eastern Front. The Germans would probably not be able to capture Paris, but Metaxas still did not believe that they would suffer a total defeat.[41]

Metaxas thought that it was quite possible that as the War progressed, "Bulgaria might abandon her neutrality and attack either Serbia or Greece. In either case, this would mean war for Greece."[42] The Romanian and Turkish attitudes would influence such a decision and would determine the distribution of Bulgarian forces and the conduct of the war. With these considerations in mind, Metaxas prepared a plan of campaign and presented it to the Chief-of-Staff on 12 August 1914. Otherwise, his job was to read all the incoming news, "to study it, to relate one item to another, and to follow the general situation."[43] The Ministry of Foreign Affairs sent him the news from all the embassies; the Prime Minister sent him the news from his own special sources; and Dousmanis brought him all the news from the King -- "therefore I hold all the threads in my hands, that is, as far as news is concerned," Metaxas noted in another letter to his wife.[44] As the situation changed from hour to hour, any safe prediction was made impossible. By mid-August 1914 Metaxas' views were more clarified but

40 *Ibid.*

41 *Ibid.*

42 *Ibid.* p. 328.

43 *Ibid.* p. 336.

44 *Ibid.*

essentially had not changed: the Germans would beat the French, but would not be able to finish them off because they would have to turn east to fight the Russians; they would beat the Russians, but again, they would not be able to put them out of action because of the sheer vastness of Russia; the Germans would be victorious but exhausted, while their enemies would not be completely knocked out; if there were an engagement at sea the Germans would be defeated by the English, and then "the blockade would force them to come to terms."[45]

Venizelos listened attentively to Metaxas' calculations, but he at no time doubted the eventual victory of the Allies. The question was whether France could withstand the first attack; then Britain, ruler of the seas, would blockade Germany, while she herself would have access to the raw materials of the whole world and could bring to the battlefield an inexhaustible number of men from her colonies and from her Allies. In buoyant mood, Venizelos used to say that if Britain had no more nations from which she could draw forces, she would create new nations! Winston Churchill naturally admired Venizelos' absolute faith in Britain.

"In all the Balkans only one clairvoyant eye, only the genius of Venizelos, discerned the fundamental moral issues of the struggle, measured justly the relative powers of the mighty combatants, and appraised at their true value both the victories of the German Army, and the Sea Power under which were slowly gathering the latent but inexhaustible resources of the British Empire."[46]

Venizelos and Metaxas not only had different opinions as to the outcome of the War; they also differed in their estimation of its duration. While Venizelos (like Lloyd George) thought that the War would shortly be decisively concluded in favour of the Allies and was anxious to enlist Greece on their side and thus secure for his country a voice at the Peace Conference, Metaxas (like Lord Kitchener) believed that this would be a long and arduous war. "There is nothing so sad as this War", Metaxas wrote. "The belligerents are still in the first flush of enthusiasm, but when the mourning starts, the disasters, the famine, the suffering? And the calamities will fall on both vanquished and victors. May God help us to avoid this trial."[47]But, whatever their differences, so long as Greece remained neutral, the two men continued to cooperate. The Prime Minister consulted Metaxas almost daily and if he had occasion to see the Chief-of-Staff he insisted that Metaxas be present, too. On one occasion Venizelos came to search Metaxas out and begged him not to harbour any hard feelings because the Prime Minister had, in the past, had his differences with the General Staff: the two of them had been "for many years connected by friendship and love and mutual respect," and

45 *Ibid.*

46 Churchill, *World Crisis*, p. 286.

47 Metaxas, *Diary*, II, p. 325.

neither of them should give credit to any rumours that might destroy their friendship.[48] The Prime Minister hinted that he was aware that General Dousmanis did not like Metaxas and was intriguing against him; finally Venizelos assured Metaxas that he considered him his friend.

"It was all billing and cooing with Venizelos," Metaxas wrote to his wife.[49] Such a demonstration of feeling from the wily politician aroused his underlying suspicions. Venizelos needed him just then, thus the endearments. During the previous fall and winter everybody had given him the cold shoulder. "Because I was not made an aide-de-camp to the King or the Crown Prince, or because I was not given a decoration or because we were not invited by Mrs. Bosdari [the wife of the Italian Ambassador] or Sir Francis Elliot ... or Admiral Kerr; and because we were not successful in this respect, everything was forgotten, all the victories ..."[50] General Dousmanis, the Chief-of-Staff, had advanced his rivals and raised his inferiors to his level. "At the same time he killed us socially. The King was completely indifferent, almost contemptuous. The Princes had forgotten me."[51] As for Venizelos, "who knows what ulterior motives he had! Anyway, he allowed all this to happen at my expense."[52] Metaxas could never fathom the motives behind the present advances of the Prime Minister; but one thing he was certain about: "I no longer need his support; neither do I need the King's support, nor that of Dousmanis. I can stand on my own feet."[53] To his wife Metaxas described the stages he had passed through in this process of personal liberation, and how he now did not have to attach himself to anyone --" as I progress I free myself from every connection and every need."[54] The Prime Minister's recent declaration of love only had the effect of making Metaxas withdraw still further. "He must abandon the idea that I can be dependent on him."[55] He added: "Now I do not even need Venizelos .... Anyway, the direction of his policy is mistaken and I am not so sure that he will not harm Greece; recently he has been carried away beyond all bounds by his inherent enmity against Germany."[56] For this reason Metaxas, although "optimistic" for his own future, "feared for Greece."[57]

In the latter part of August 1914 the Germans made a spectacular advance on the Western Front -- in his Diary Metaxas mentioned the German victories at Charleroi,

48 *Ibid.*, p. 335.
49 *Ibid.*
50 *Ibid.*, p. 356.
51 *Ibid.*, p. 370.
52 *Ibid.*
53 *Ibid.* p. 337.
54 *Ibid.*, p. 338.
55 *Ibid.*, p. 339.
56 *Ibid.*, p. 338.
57 *Ibid.*, p. 339.

Luneville and Longwy; on the Eastern Front, Hindenburg and Ludendorff were ranging their forces for the Battle of Tannenberg. Metaxas, instead of the "disgusting French novels," began to read in German the *Erinnerungen* of the Prussian general Verdy du Vernois (1832-1910) which were published in 1895. The author "was an officer of the German Staff and played a role analogous to mine in many ways, but not the same as far as influence is concerned."[58] As Metaxas read the book -- "my mind was instantly so invigorated that it bore fruit in a brilliant idea."[59] When he returned to the office in the afternoon Metaxas put his brainwave in writing and submitted it to the Chief-of-Staff, then rushed to the Ministry of Foreign Affairs and handed a copy to George Streit. Streit mentioned Metaxas' "confidential memorandum" in his own Diary.[60] Two days later the Foreign Minister read this memorandum to the King. Metaxas noted that the Chief-of-Staff should have communicated his memo to the King the Commander-in-Chief of the Armed Forces at once, but what could one expect form the envious Dousmanis? "This is the world! It is not enough that some people have the positions, they also want to have the brains of others as their slaves; but all this is past now."[61]

What was Metaxas' "brilliant idea?" It was very simple. "The salvation of Greece is secured only if Germany wins the War."[62] The more Metaxas thought about it, the more certain a German victory appeared to be. "Austria and Austrian policy in the Balkans has been the evil demon of Germany."[63] Nevertheless, "Germany will come out victorious from the great struggle. Now, in these trials, the great virtues of the German race will shine: Entsagung and Ergebung, their perseverance and religions piety. All those imponderabilia which cannot be calculated by numbers will play their part. ... these things should triumph, otherwise humanity will decline."[64] Again he wrote: "Germany is bound to win, but only after great and terrible struggles."[65] Once Metaxas had decided on the inevitability of German victory his logic became fuzzy and "metaphysical" to explain his conviction. He wrote: "Germany will win the War because German civilization is the civilization of the future and the hope of all humanity. No civilization can exist without power. Great and dreadful struggles are for the good of the German people because thus they will discard their arrogance which is

---

58 *Ibid.*, p. 338; J. v. Verdy du Vernois, *Im Großen Hauptquartier 1870/71. Persönliche Erinnerungen* (Berlin, 1895).

59 *Ibid.*, p. 340.

60 Streit noted that Metaxas submitted to him "a confidential memorandum of his by which he wants to prove that a German victory is beneficial to Greece...." George Streit, Metaxas, *Diary*, I, p. 24.

61 Metaxas, *Diary,* II, p. 344.

62 *Ibid.*, p. 340.

63 *Ibid.*, p. 360.

64 *Ibid.*

65 *Ibid.*, p. 361.

so harmful."[66] In this war the Germans would need "great tranquillity of soul, faith and dedication to the leader and devotion to duty. No enthusiasms and no disappointment, no discouragement, but great firmness in their decisions, great religious faith which gives strength in critical moments, great perseverance and tenacity. But all these are precisely the virtues of the German race! They are the virtues of strong men. This is why I believe in the final victory of the Germans."[67] Discipline and order would always triumph over individualism and higher intelligence. "Discipline means common efforts toward one goal, faith in the oath, submission, sacrifice of oneself for others, and only those with strong characters and lofty ideals can possess these qualities."[68] Metaxas' ideas were crystal-clear. Individualism produces artistic nations but not nations of progress and civilization. Clever races are not great. Individualism is a destructive element. Cleverness, which is merely the result of self-adulation, focuses all attention on the individual and impedes the search for truth. "Clever men are never deep, nor deep men ever clever."[69] The ancient Athenians were a race of clever individualists; but the Romans, disciplined and methodical, were able to crush Greece. It was the Romans who preserved for us as a precious heritage the works of a few great Greek minds. "But do the French have any great minds nowadays? Which?"[70] It was true that the French were clever, but they were also undisciplined and egoistical, "their cleverness is only good for *bons mots* and *mondanités* and *comédies*."[71] The Germans would win the War "because they are deep and serious: that is why I love them."[72]

In Metaxas' letters to his wife in which he advised and comforted her, he also analyzed the reasons why the majority of Greeks did not share his pro-German feelings and explained his conclusions to her. First, those Greeks who had studied in France stupidly believed that if France were to lose the War, they also would lose some of their own prestige! But the real reason was that "the serious German spirit which takes all things in life seriously, *ernst*, with a sense of duty and submission to God, does not appeal to the Greeks, who in respect of spiritual growth are but children."[73] The Greeks did not like the Germans "as children who do not like the strict teacher who wants to have order in his class; they prefer the other teacher with whom they can play and be bad."[74] When the news reached Greece that the Entente Allies had scored some successes at the Front, there were celebrations in Athens. Metaxas told his wife not to

66 *Ibid.*
67 *Ibid.*, p. 362.
68 *Ibid.*, p. 366.
69 *Ibid.*
70 *Ibid.*, p. 367.
71 *Ibid.*
72 *Ibid.*, p. 356.
73 *Ibid.*, p. 348.
74 *Ibid.*

be disturbed. "That is how they are here. Flippant. They do not go deep. They cannot understand where real strength lies and what real success is. They are overawed by self-display."[75]

The more Metaxas disagreed with his compatriots and the more he disliked their ways, the more isolated he felt. Venizelos, carrying the King with him, had offered on 14 August and again on 19 August to place Greece in the camp of the Entente Powers. If he succeeded he would destroy Greece and Colonel Metaxas would be compelled to fight on the side of those shallow, undisciplined and egoistical Allies against his beloved Germany. Metaxas, who all his life never had a close friend, felt very lonely. It was he alone, with his wife, against the whole world. He suddenly felt that he did not fit in anywhere and began withdrawing into himself. As the Great War developed he realized more and more how differently he thought from all those around him; he realized how right he was, how wrong they were. There was only one course left open to him: to "unfurl his standard"; to be a "leader" in his own right. To become his own man. On 28 August he wrote to his wife:

"I am a little tired of the monotony of the life I lead, but I detest going to the playhouses or to places of entertainment, as they are called. I prefer reveries in our garden, and I think of you and our children: this is a comfort. Then I go to the office and read the memories of Verdy du Vernois about the wars of 1866 and 1870....

I no longer see Venizelos ... I have begun to withdraw little by little from Dousmanis, too ... My purpose is, without any rupture or friction, to break away, to become independent of all and raise a standard of my own ... Finally I resolved to fly with my own wings -- I mean as a leader and not as a follower. I have indications that the time is ripe."[76]

After Metaxas had finished the military memoirs of the Prussian general, he went back to French and read Marcel Prévost, *Lettres de Femmes, Nouvelles Lettres de Femmes. Dernières Lettres de Femmes.* Books like these only confirmed his unfavourable opinion of the French. In them "one understands the depth of the decadence of the French race."[77] With malicious humor Metaxas described to his wife the infidelities of French husbands and wives as he was reading about them, and concluded that "neither the men nor the women have any ideas -- that is why they are paying now, because the foundation of a nation is the loving family, the loving and united couple."[78]

It was decided that Madame Metaxas should continue her summer holiday on Tenos -- if war were declared in Greece, Metaxas would send her a telegram in code telling her to hurry back to Athens. He often advised her to avoid any kind of discussion

75 *Ibid.*, p. 355.
76 *Ibid.*, p. 342.
77 *Ibid.*, p. 353.
78 *Ibid.*

concerning the European war and to pay no attention to those who might try to annoy her because of his pro-German views. He quoted to her from Dante: *Non ti curae di loro. ma guarda e passa*. He reminded her that the world was extremely envious of them. "They are jealous because of my fame, because of your virtue, because of our pride, because of our prosperity, because of our health, because of our domestic happiness ..."[79] God had been generous to the Metaxas family: He had given them "honours, power, wealth, health, harmony, two charming children and, most important, deep love. What else is happiness? How may people possess it? It is natural for the world to be jealous of us."[80]

Even after the Germans had suffered several setbacks on the Western Front, Metaxas' belief in the final victory of the Central Alliance remained unshaken. "This so-called victory of the French is not really a victory," he wrote to his wife on 15 September 1914.[81] Two days later, he wrote: "The German Military Attaché showed me a telegram to the effect that they are winning this battle."[82] It must have been the Battle of the Aisne, where the Germans, after falling back at the Marne, stood their ground. The Greek press, Metaxas thought, did great harm with their pro-Entente articles. Although he advised his wife not to be drawn into any discussion on the War, he felt strongly that "public opinion should be informed."[83] In August 1914 a series of articles appeared in the Athens newspaper Αθήναι, arguing the case for Germany, describing her superior military strength, explaining her policy and tactics and forecasting her certain victory. The articles were published under the pseudonym Alpha-Omega, the first and last letters of the Greek alphabet and, according to Αθήναι, were written by a military expert.[84] Some readers thought that the articles were written by the enterprising Chief of the German Secret Services in Greece Baron von Schenk; others thought they were written by the German Military Attaché in Athens. Metaxas wrote to Lela: "But all those who say this do not really believe it; deep down they always suspect me."[85] The articles were, in fact, written by the editor of Αθήναι, George Pop, who would secretly visit Metaxas and receive long expositions on the strategy of the war. Sometimes Pop did not get his facts straight, but Metaxas, tongue in cheek, hoped that the briefed journalist would "return somehow to the strait and narrow path. ... I

---

79 *Ibid.*, p. 538-9.

80 *Ibid.*, p. 359.

81 *Ibid.*, p. 361.

82 *Ibid.*, p. 363.

83 *Ibid.*, p. 350.

84 These articles appeared in 1914 on July 29, August 4, 8, 14,15, 17, 18, 19, 23, 24, 26, 28, 29, 31. On September 1, 2, 3, 4, 6, 8, 12, 16, 18, 19, 20, 25, 27, 30. On October 1, 4, 13, 16, 21, 22, 24, 25, 29. On November 23, 24. And also on January 16, 17, 19 and 21 of 1915. All dates are according to the Old Style.

85 Metaxas, *Diary.*, II, p. 350.

have the feeling that he was not well primed recently."[86] The articles made a tremendous impression in the country. Metaxas denied their authorship, but nobody believed him. The resentful Colonel had discovered a new source of power. As a result of these articles, people would go to see him and express their admiration for him. "My strength rests on the trust of public opinion," he wrote and insisted that he disliked being obliged to resort to such undercover tactics. "But in the world of intrigants, plagiarists, pompous hypocrites in which I live. ... I have no other means to defend myself. *Mit den Wölfen muss man heulen* -- when one is with wolves one must howl with the wolves."[87]

The general acclaim accorded to these articles at the time when Greece felt threatened by the Turkish mobilization reminded Metaxas' countrymen, especially his fellow officers, of the brilliant Staff Officer of the Balkan Wars. Metaxas was gratified. "I have surfaced again through the favour of the Army. This favour is genuine because the Army has confidence in me, because the Army pins its hopes on me for future victory."[88] Later in this letter Metaxas asked rhetorically: "Why does the Army show me this favour?" His answer was ready: "Because of my ability and my work and my character."[89] Metaxas reminded his wife of what they "had suffered together"[90] when, after the Balkan Wars, he was elbowed aside, when he was ignored by all. But the Army, which knew "who was leading and who was following, saw the injustice," and the Army's recognition rose up "like a tide" and won over public opinion.[91] Again the Chief-of-Staff was attentive. Again Venizelos was most friendly and there were friendly overtures from Crown Prince George. "Well, a shower of love from all directions," Metaxas wrote to his wife. "May the Lord have mercy on both of us!"[92]

To crown it all, on 6 September 1914 Metaxas was decorated by the King for his services in the Balkan Wars. Metaxas had arranged to go to the ceremony with Xenophon Strategos, who was to collect him in a taxi; but Strategos did not show up at the appointed time and the fuming Metaxas, unable to get a cab at the last moment, was compelled to set off on foot to catch the tram. Earlier while he was dressing -- "the idea came into my head to put on all my German medals because I wanted to provoke every adversary."[93] Then, decked out in full military regalia, he was waiting at the tram stop when he suddenly saw the Royal convertible with Constantine, Sophia and the young Princes inside coming from the direction of the Tatoi Palace. But let Metaxas tell

86 *Ibid.*, p. 361.
87 *Ibid.*, p. 363.
88 *Ibid.*, p. 370.
89 *Ibid.*
90 *Ibid.*
91 *Ibid.*
92 *Ibid.*, p. 348
93 *Ibid.*, p. 351.

us what happened. "I salute in the Prussian manner. The King, with great charm and a smile, salutes back and, in the middle of all this mutual sweetness, the wheel of the automobile drives through a puddle of water and splashes me miserably all over."[94] Poor Metaxas had to hurry back home and change, but he had his reward later; at the ceremony, as the King pinned on his breast the Gold Cross, he said to him, smiling, "Good luck! And a third one in the next war!"[95]

Metaxas always gave full credit to his wife, who stood by him through difficult times, sharing his unhappiness and giving him moral support when his spirits were low. Lela's pride in her husband and family prevented him from humiliating himself; she had faith in him and she had faith in God and created a warm home background where Metaxas could rest and recover his strength. Above all, she bore his name proudly and won the respect of everyone. "Virtue has an awful power," he wrote to her and reminded her of Caesar's wife who was above suspicion.[96] This was her role in the history of Greece. History, he told her, has never forgotten the wives or even the mistresses of great men who shared their men's triumphs and disasters.

"And if one day I become so great that History will deal with me, next to my name History will record yours, my Lela. This very letter I am writing now, who knows, in the future, how many will read it and how many women will mentally bow their heads before you after we are long dead."[97]

He then spoke to his wife about the common double endeavour that lay ahead for them. First, "to lead Greece forward in power and glory: in this I lead and you assist." Second, "to create a model Greek home and in this you lead and I assist."[98]

The best policy for Ioannis and Lela Metaxas was to disregard everybody and become "really independent"; then they could show their contempt for all small-minded people because they would have no further need of them. ["The Venizelists(?) -- the word is deleted] are the beginning of the evil. But where can one turn? Their opponents are even worse."[99] When George Streit the Germanophile Foreign Minister was dismissed by Venizelos the moral did not escape Metaxas. "That is how he treats people -- I would have been facing the same danger had I attached myself to him."[100] When Venizelos offered him the position of Governor-General of Macedonia at the conclusion

94 *Ibid.*
95 *Ibid.*
96 *Ibid.*, p. 371.
97 *Ibid.*
98 *Ibid.*
99 *Ibid.*, p. 370
100 *Ibid.*, p. 359.

of the Balkan Wars, Metaxas declined. "Had I accepted I should have been a lost man."[101]

Venizelos had also succeeded in subduing the Chief-of-Staff Victor Dousmanis, the dour general from the island of Corfu. Dousmanis had kept back some Royal Decrees signed by the King and the Prime Minister felt that the Chief-of-Staff had Constantine under his thumb. According to Metaxas, Venizelos was enraged at this incident and fairly bombarded Dousmanis with messengers demanding an apology. Metaxas wrote to his wife: "Dousmanis went into hiding. The messengers were informed that he was not at the office. He was in a miserable state: I had him with me all the evening and took him for a walk in a secluded place."[102] In the end, Dousmanis went to the Prime Minister and apologized. Metaxas noted in his Diary: "Dousmanis was most humble and Venizelos forgave him."[103] Metaxas harboured serious suspicions that Venizelos wanted to separate him from Constantine and use his military authority to scare the King into compliance with his own policies, "and then one fine day to cast me off when I was of no further use to him. But he had a Cephalonian to deal with, not a Corfiote."[104] Metaxas hailed from the island of Cephallonia -- its inhabitants were known as a truculent lot; Dousmanis came from the island of Corfu; the Corfiotes were a more gentle race.

Metaxas' estimation of Venizelos' motives was damning indeed. "Venizelos wants to humiliate others and will not promote men of merit (αξία)."[105] And again: "Venizelos wants subordinate men; but if I come to power, then he will learn how many beans make five." [In Greek, "how many pears go into a sack".[106]]

On 29 October 1914 the Turkish fleet, headed by Goeben and Breslau, unexpectedly bombarded Odessa, Sevastopol and Theodosia on the Russian Black Sea coast. This was a rude awakening for the gullible Allies who at the onset of the War had offered the Ottoman Empire handsome guarantees for its continued territorial integrity and had expected, despite every indication to the contrary, that Turkey would at least remain neutral; as Spyros Markezinis, the historian of Greece, wittily remarked, "the Allies, like deceived husbands, were the last to find out what everybody else had known all along." Four days after the bombardment, on 2 November, Russia declared war on Turkey and on 5 November Britain and France followed her example. On the same day Britain annexed Cyprus, which she had been governing since 1878; and on 18

101 *Ibid.*
102 *Ibid.*, p. 357.
103 *Ibid.* p. 355.
104 *Ibid.*, p. 358.
105 *Ibid.*, pp. 357-8
106 *Ibid.*, p. 357.

December she proclaimed a protectorate over Egypt, which she had been occupying since 1882. Until this time both Cyprus and Egypt were nominally Turkish possessions.

Notwithstanding the Turkish lesson, the Allies continued to court Bulgaria, offering her the "uncontested zone" of Macedonia, which was Serbian; the port of Kavalla, which was Greek; and the district of Dobrudja, which was Romanian. This high-handed policy - mainly on the part of Great Britain - of giving away the territories of its allies like Serbia, or friends like Greece, or potential friends like Romania, in flagrant violation of the Treaty of Bucharest, contributed a great deal to the discrediting of the Allied cause in the Balkans. In spite of these blandishments, Bulgaria remained neutral, building up her army and awaiting the opportune moment to attack Serbia. As King Ferdinand would say in his artless manifesto a year later on 3 October 1915, "our hitherto loyal neutrality has been the cleverest policy during the present War and has brought our land sufficient advantages."[107] By the end of the War, when all had been said and done, the unfortunate Bulgarians considered their King anything but clever. But in the fall of 1914 Sofia was flooded with alluring propositions from both Germany and the Entente Powers, enough to turn the heads of wiser men than King Ferdinand. By the winter of 1914 it was becoming obvious that this was going to be a long war. On the Western Front the combatants, entrenched in their dugouts, suffered great loss of life, but there was little territorial gain for either side. On the Eastern Front the Germans had successes at Tannenberg (26-30 August) and the Masurian Lakes (6-15 September) but the Russians obstinately held a long line of defense, despite their inferior military organization and a severe shortage of munitions. The Serbs, under a renewed attack by the Austrians, were losing ground and Belgrade fell on 2 December 1914.

Two days after the fall of Belgrade the Allies called upon Greece to honour her treaty obligations toward Serbia. Venizelos immediately sent to enquire what Romania's attitude would be and called in the General Staff to inform him what military aid Greece could afford Serbia. As the Staff's spokesman, Metaxas submitted his report the same day, 5 December 1914.[108] It was an elaborate memorandum opposing Greek intervention in the War. In this document Metaxas assessed the distances from the Greek bases in Macedonia to the Serbian Front and concluded that in the circumstances Greek assistance to Serbia would be of little value and the dangers involved very real, while "the road will be opened for Bulgaria to invade the Greek kingdom."[109] The intervention of Romania would have no effect on the situation because Bulgaria could easily stop the Romanians in the north and still invade Greece while the Greek armies

107 Mowat, *European Diplomacy*, p. 56. The whole manifesto can be found in Müller-Meiningen, *Diplomatie und Weltkrieg* (1917), II, p. 778 ff.

108 This memorandum is printed in the Metaxas, *Diary,* II, pp. 379-82.

109 *Ibid.,* p. 380.

were fighting in Serbia. Interestingly enough, Metaxas made no mention of any Turkish danger to Bulgaria, while the Allies had until recently been duped by Turkey into thinking that Turkish mobilization was solely for the purpose of waging war against Bulgaria. Metaxas further pointed out that a combined attack by Romania and Greece against Bulgaria would still mean a difficult war for Greece. "Because we should not imagine that the Bulgarians will show but faint resistance when fighting the struggle for survival."[110] A war fought by Greece alone with her fifteen divisions pitted against the twenty divisions of Bulgaria, Metaxas thought disastrous. In the meantime, the Austrians would have completely crushed the Serbs and most probably joined the Bulgarians against Greece. Finally Metaxas stressed that although he had excluded the Turkish factor from his calculations, the Turkish Army could intervene against Greece at a moment when the Greek forces would be engaged by other enemies.

By early 1915, Serbia's predicament was desperate. Neither Britain, France or Russia could spare any forces for their gallant Balkan ally. Greece and Romania, Serbia's partners in the Balkan Alliance, fearful to offend the powerful Central Alliance, seemed loth to honour their treaty obligations to her. On 21 January 1915 Lloyd George, with the approval of Prime Minister Asquith and Lord Kitchener, the Minister of War, informed the Greek and Romanian Governments that the British Government had learned that Austria and Germany were preparing a new attack on Serbia. Serbia could not withstand the attack without help and her destruction would encourage Bulgaria to cooperate actively with Germany, Austria and Turkey; so Lloyd George requested Greece and Romania to specify what kind of assistance they required from his Government in order to act at once in favour of Serbia. In the case of Greece, Lloyd George suggested joint Greek-English naval operations. Britain called for an answer by the evening of the following day.

This communication was contained in a telegram from the Greek Minister in London Ioannis Gennadius.[111] Venizelos went to the Palace and read the telegram to King Constantine. The King suggested that the General Staff be consulted. Metaxas was sent for. "It is impossible to take a decision without first knowing whether Romania is willing to fight for Serbia," he replied.[112] A Romanian intervention would lessen the Bulgarian danger. Accordingly, Venizelos' reply to the British Government was that Greece could not act until the threat from Bulgaria to Greek Macedonia was removed. The only way the Allies could remove this danger was to renew their propositions to Bulgaria of territorial expansion. And what a stroke of luck -- the Allies suddenly had such a large and tempting pie to hand around! Turkey had just joined the enemy camp

110 *Ibid.*, p. 381.

111 Ioannis Gennadius was Minister of Greece in London for many years and a great bibliophile. His books became the nucleus of the Gennadius Library in Athens.

112 Spyros Melas,"Ιωάννης Μεταξάς", in the newspaper *Καιροί* (Athens, 2 Dec. 1949).

and the Turkish lands could be divided up and offered with a good heart to please old friends and win new ones. Constantinople and the Straits had been promised to Russia in November 1914 to satisfy her age-old aspirations, an offer which was a complete turn-about of traditional British foreign policy. Italy was offered a large chunk of Anatolia extending from Attalia to Smyrna, although hardly any Italians lived there. And on 9 November 1914, Bulgaria was offered Eastern Thrace as far as the Enos-Midia line. However, Bulgaria was not satisfied. Apart from her other claims on Serbia and Romania, Bulgaria insisted she should be given the Kavalla-Drama-Serres district which she had lost to Greece in the Second Balkan War.

It was now the turn of Greece to be offered some compensation for the concessions she was called upon to make to Bulgaria. Greece could not be offered compensation in Macedonia because of conflicting Bulgarian and Serbian claims. She could not be offered Eastern Thrace because at the time the Entente was offering the region to Bulgaria. Greece could not be offered Constantinople and the Straits because of Russian objections. She could not be offered the Dodecanese because the Italians who had "temporarily" occupied the islands in 1912, had now decided to stay there. Nor could Greece be offered Northern Epirus, again because of Italian objections. The British historian Michael Llewelyn-Smith continues the story. "Lastly there was Cyprus, where the Greeks were some 80 per cent of the population. But Cyprus was British. It was easier to offer what belonged to others. Cyprus was a card which the British Government was prepared to play only in the last resort."[113] Such difficulties presented no problem to Sir Edward Grey the master of ceremonies at this pie-cutting party. On 23 January 1915 the British Foreign Minister sent a telegram to Sir Francis Elliot in Athens which Elliot handed on to Venizelos. The British offer provided that "if Greece will side with Serbia, as an ally, and participate in the war, I know that France and Russia will both willingly make to Greece very important territorial concessions on the coast of Asia Minor ..."[114] Venizelos, who had been informed as early as mid-December by Koromelas the Greek Minister in Rome about the secret treaty which gave part of Asia Minor to Italy, was anxious to join the party and claim for his country what he considered to be her rightful share of the pie. With Bulgaria hopefully placated and the Bulgarian danger removed, Greece could afford to assist Serbia and come out openly on the side of the Entente Powers. The offer of the coastal regions of Asia Minor would signal the realization of the Megali Idea, the ultimate national dream of a Greater Greece. Prince Demidov, the Russian Minister at Athens, wired Petrograd that on hearing of this offer, Venizelos was "electrified."

---

113 Michael Llewelyn-Smith, *The Ionian Vision* (London, 1974), p. 36.

114 Leon, *Greece and the Great Powers*, p. 107.

The day after Venizelos received Grey's offer he submitted a long memorandum to King Constantine urging the advantages of Greek participation in the war on the side of the Entente Powers. This memorandum was the first of three that Venizelos submitted to the King on this matter. He took it to the Palace himself and read it to Constantine. Greece, he argued, would be in grave danger if Austria and Bulgaria succeeded in annihilating Serbia. Greece should rally to the defense of Serbia, not only because of her treaty obligations, but also because her own interest demanded that she should fight on the Allied side.

"We are now called upon to participate in the war no longer in order to fulfil simply moral obligations, but for compensations, which if realized will create a great and powerful Greece such as not even the boldest optimist could have imagined only a few years back.[115]

In order to secure Bulgaria's participation, Venizelos would -- not hesitate, however painful the severance, to recommend the sacrifice of Kavalla in order to save Hellenism in Turkey and ... to create a real Magna Graecia which would include nearly all the provinces where Hellenism flourished through the long centuries of her history."[116]

The joint efforts of all the Christian nations of the Balkans might be decisive for the outcome of the present War. The sacrifice of Western Thrace was necessary if the greater part of Hellenism which lay within the borders of Turkey was to be saved. Otherwise, the massive expulsions which were bound to follow would not only destroy the Greek communities in Turkey but would also ruin Greece, while failure to honour the treaty obligations to Serbia would leave the country without friends and without credibility, endangering the future of the nation. Venizelos was willing to make painful concessions in pursuit of the Megali Idea. Greece, he wrote to the King, "finds herself confronted once more with one of the most critical events in her national history."[117] The Great War provided Greece with a unique opportunity to realize her national aspirations and Venizelos was quick to adapt his policy to the prevailing circumstances.

Such a glorious vision of national aggrandisement moved the impressionable King. Later that evening Venizelos told Elliot that he had persuaded Constantine to accept his policy. Next day, 26 January, Queen Sophia told Quadt the German Minister at Athens (who transmitted the conversation to Berlin the same day), that Constantine had said to her, "The present moment is serious. My country could consider me a traitor if, as the Kaiser's brother-in-law, I did not accept the Entente's offers through which my State

---

115 E. Venizelos, *Greece in Her True Light: Her Position in the World-wide War* (New York, 1916), pp. 20-28.

116 *Ibid.*

117 *Ibid.*

would be quintupled."[118] From Berlin Zimmerman the German Foreign Minister the same day instructed Quadt to tell Constantine that Germany did not intend to annihilate Serbia; Germany's major military objective was Russia.

If Venizelos thought that he had won over Constantine, he was underestimating the influence of the King's entourage and that of Colonel Metaxas in particular. Venizelos' proposals were anathema to the General Staff, which believed that the equilibrium established in the Balkans by the Treaty of Bucharest should not be disturbed; to make concessions to Bulgaria would only encourage her expansionist appetites. The Kavalla region was one of the richest in Greece, acquired at the cost of much bloodshed in the Second Balkan War, and national honour would never countenance the loss of the city, which Venizelos was offering so airily to Bulgaria. The Prime Minister's plan would also block any Greek expansion toward Western and Eastern Thrace; indeed, it would block the road to Constantinople. The Prime Minister's claim that he was creating a Greater Greece which would include all the territories historically associated with Hellenism was in fact not true. Venizelos was proposing to give away Greek territories and he was also giving up hopes of Greek expansion in Thrace for the sake of the uncertain prospects of a risky expansion in Asia Minor.

After he had, as he thought, persuaded the King, Venizelos recognized that the chief obstacle to his policy would be Metaxas. On the morning of 26 January 1915, the day after he had read his memorandum to Constantine, the Prime Minister summoned Metaxas to the Ministry of Foreign Affairs. Venizelos was now wearing his Foreign Minister's hat, which he had donned after dismissing Streit for actively opposing his pro-entente foreign policy. Romania, Venizelos told Metaxas, had just announced that she was not willing to make concessions to Bulgaria in order to secure her flank and join Greece in support of Serbia. Therefore the Greek offer of Kavalla was no longer relevant and would be withdrawn. Metaxas, "as a soldier," was pleased with this turn of events because the loss of the Kavalla region would have meant the loss of the existing strategically strong frontiers.[119] Then the conversation between the two men turned to the question of Asia Minor and the following exchange took place as reported by Metaxas in his Diary. The "stage directions" are included in Metaxas' account.

Metaxas: *What is going to happen to Turkey, Mr. Prime Minister?*
Venizelos: *[somewhat hesitant] Well, they will ... annihilate Turkey.*
Metaxas: *Who?*
Venizelos: *The Allies. Who else?*
Metaxas: *I consider that very difficult. Anyway, I think that the English and French have no desire to destroy Turkey.*

---

118 Leon, *Greece and the Great Powers*, p. 111.
119 Metaxas, *Diary*, II, p. 385.

Venizelos: *Oh no! I think they have now.*
Metaxas: *All right. How is this destruction going to be carried out? The only thing the Allies can do is to force the Dardanelles and the Bosphorus. But then the military power of Turkey will defend Asia Minor. Who will go and attack it there and destroy it?*
Venizelos: *[the Prime Minister was silent for some time, then he said] Then we, too, shall join in the struggle.*
Metaxas: *Shall we launch an expedition in Asia Minor?*
Venizelos: *Yes.*
Metaxas: *Who is going to protect our European borders?*
Venizelos: *Against whom?*
Metaxas: *The Bulgarians.*
Venizelos: *All this presupposes that the Bulgarians will be our allies ...*[120]

So, inevitably, the argument returned to the question of the Bulgarian attitude. The following evening Metaxas had another conversation with the Prime Minister. Again he insisted that Greece could not afford to aspire to any territorial expansion in Asia Minor without having first secured her position in Europe. "And I expounded to him the analogous policy of Philip of Macedon," Metaxas noted in his Diary."[121]

Metaxas recorded his views on the issue of Asia Minor in a long memorandum addressed to the Prime Minister.[122] Although he made several suggestions concerning the parcelling-out of Asia Minor, he emphasized the difficulties inherent in such a process. Asia Minor was one geographical entity and any division of the country along political lines was bound to create serious problems. In ancient times the state of Lydia aimed to reach the Aegean while the Persians, occupying present-day Armenia, clashed unavoidably with the Lydians. The Greeks of Ionia and Aeolia and the other coastal areas of Asia Minor were constantly at war with the inhabitants of the interior and could never be confident of their safety as they could not extend their domination over the whole of Anatolia. Byzantium kept all the sub-continent under its control and thus managed to rule it for centuries. The Turkish state derived its strength from Asia Minor, the home of the Turkish people, and so survived despite the losses it had suffered in the Ottoman territories outside the limits of Asia Minor. Greece would be required to keep a force of 100.000 men in Asia Minor in order to hold on to her new acquisitions; but such an undertaking would weaken her defenses against Bulgaria.

120 *Ibid.*, pp. 385-6.

121 *Ibid.*, p. 392.

122 Metaxas submitted this memorandum on 27 January 1915. An accomplished cartographer, he demonstrated his intimate knowledge of the physical and human geography of Asia Minor; but, as the narrative shows, Metaxas did not shy from bringing up old history to exemplify a new reality. This memorandum is published in the Metaxas, *Diary,* II, pp. 386-390.

Metaxas again expressed doubts as to whether the Allies, because of their conflicting interests in the Near East, would ever consent to the partition of Anatolia.

On 28 January 1915 the King gave an audience to Count Quadt. By now Constantine had accepted all Metaxas' arguments; in fact, all the arguments the King used in his conversation with the German Minister (which Quadt transmitted to Berlin) were taken almost word for word from Metaxas' memorandum! Quadt reported to Berlin that he had found Constantine "calm and logical." The next day, 29 January, the Kaiser sent a personal appeal to Constantine, exhorting him not to trust the Entente offers. "I think that history provides sufficient proof as to how England treats the interests of those who help her once she attains the aim for which she used them."[123] The Kaiser's telegram "made an excellent impression on the King," as Sophia told Quadt, who reported it to Berlin, adding that "Her Majesty the Queen has been freed of her profound anxiety."[124]

But Venizelos was not the man to give up easily. On 30 January he continued his barrage of pro-Entente arguments in a second memorandum to the King. In this document he returned to the question of Kavalla, comparing its population of 30,000 Greeks with that of the area in Asia Minor which Greece would claim following Sir Edward Grey's offer. This area, Venizelos speculated, would exceed 125,000 square kilometers, containing at that time a Greek population of over 800.000. Venizelos anticipated that Bulgaria would compensate the Kavalla Greeks, who could then be transferred and settled in Greece proper, while a Greek-controlled Western Asia Minor would also provide a home for the thousands of Greeks from the Turkish hinterland.

"I firmly believe that we ought to lay aside any hesitation. It is unlikely that such an opportunity as that offered to Hellenism today will ever arise again. If we do not participate in the War, whatever its outcome, according to every human calculation, the Hellenism of Asia Minor will be lost to us for good. If the Powers of the Triple Entente are victorious the Allies will divide either among themselves or with Italy, both Asia Minor and the rest of Turkey. If Germany and Turkey win the War, not only will the 200,000 Greeks who have already been driven out lose all hope of returning to their homes, but the number of future refugees from Turkey may assume alarming proportions."[125]

Venizelos then spoke of the opportunity to create a Greece which included almost all the lands where Hellenism had predominated throughout its long history; a new Greece with fertile lands and complete mastery in the Aegean. But, added the Prime Minister,

---

123 Leon, *Greece and the Great Powers*, p. 113.

124 *Ibid.*, pp. 113-4.

125 Venizelos' first and second memoranda to Constantine are printed in an English translation in Venizelos, *Greece in Her True Light*, pp. 12-14. All three memoranda are printed in the original in Ventiris, *Ελλάς*, at the end of volume I. They are also reprinted in S. Markezines, *Πολιτική Ιστορία*, IV, pp. 372-378.

"the General Staff, strangely enough, does not seem to be attracted too strongly by such considerations."[126]

Neither did Venizelos confine himself to geopolitical and economic arguments. He knew that Constantine had grown up with the dream of the Megali Idea and he therefore made a direct emotional appeal to the King.

"To Your Majesty, happily still in the prime of life, it may be given not only to create by your sword the Greater Greece, but also to consolidate your military achievement by a complete organization of the new State, and to hand on to your heir when the fullness of time demands, a work of such magnitude as has been given to few monarchs to accomplish."[127]

Again Constantine's attitude was ambivalent. Again Metaxas came to his rescue. If Venizelos was determined to bring Greece into the War on the side of the Allies, Metaxas was equally determined that this should not happen. On 2 February Metaxas submitted a new memorandum of his own to the Prime Minister on the question of Greece going to war to assist Serbia, this time with the knowledge that Romania would not be her ally but with the hope of Bulgarian neutrality or even a Bulgarian alliance.[128] In the preamble to this document Metaxas wrote that his conclusions were concerned only with the military aspect, "since it is only on this aspect that I have an expertise and an official duty to offer an opinion."[129] He added that he would deal with political questions only when they affected military considerations. In a document of nineteen closely hand-written pages, Metaxas examined all possible strategic combinations, always concluding that Greece would face fatal danger if she came out on the side of Serbia. On the question of Turkish persecutions of Greeks in Asia Minor Metaxas wrote that if Germany, and therefore Turkey, were defeated, no such persecutions could take place. A German victory on such a scale as would allow Germany to impose her will fully on the Entente Powers was very unlikely. The best Germany could expect was to reach a compromise with the Allies.

"But even if we concede this possibility for Germany, a strong and ethnologically homogeneous state, such a result for states like Austria, and especially Turkey, which is already crumbling, is absolutely impossible. Turkey will come out of the war always a state certainly, but completely crushed by the struggle. These states, and perhaps other secondary states, will pay the price of the compromise agreed upon between the Great Powers. This is what has always happened after great historic wars. In such circumstances there is no way of knowing whether Turkey will continue the persecutions of her ethnic Greek element. Weighed against this uncertainty, there

---

126 *Ibid.*
127 *Ibid.*
128 Metaxas, *Diary,* II, pp. 392-406.
129 *Ibid.* p. 392.

is the absolute certainty that as soon as Greece abandons her neutrality toward Turkey's allies, the final and permanent extermination of the Greeks in Asia Minor and Thrace will begin. The massacres and looting will start at once and on a wide scale and at once we will have on our soil the remnants of the disaster."[130]

In conclusion Metaxas reminded the Prime Minister that once a country in conducting her foreign policy had exhausted all channels of diplomacy and was then pursuing that policy through military action, such factors as time, distance and the relative strengths of the opposing armies would exert a critical influence. "A Staff Officer who, carried away by aspirations and sentiments, were to ignore this influence would be a very bad adviser and injurious to his country."[131]

Venizelos firmly believed that the making of decisions on such important questions of national policy was the exclusive domain of the politicians, particularly of the people's elected representatives, while the duty of the military was to obey and carry out the instructions of the responsible government. The Prime Minister was growing impatient with the stubborn resistance to his interventionist policies put up by Metaxas and the other Royalists. He had already got rid of George Streit, the pro-German Foreign Minister, who had now turned into a full-time privy-councillor to the King. Soon the restive Prime Minister was given the chance to hit back at the obstinate, recalcitrant General Staff. On 10 February 1915 the Athens newspaper Αθῆναι published a private letter from the Chief-of-Staff General Victor Dousmanis to a certain Lieutenant Basdekis in response to some criticisms of his concerning the Greek Army. In his letter Dousmanis reminded Basdekis that because of the Revolution of Ghoudi staged by the men of the Military League, the present-day Army had inherited a difficult situation. Constantine, "who, more than anyone else, has the welfare of the Army at heart, gave the correct opinion [on this matter] some time ago." Then the Chief-of-Staff explained to the aggrieved Lieutenant that "the way to govern an army is not by a majority vote but by absolutism. This absolutism is only now being established in the Army and this absolutism represents justice and impartiality."[132] How did this private letter find its way into the columns of an Athenian newspaper? According to some evidence, General Dousmanis, in a testimony to Pericles Mazarakis, asserted that his letter to Basdekis was not intended for publication, "but Metaxas, seeking to remove me and to occupy the position of Chief-of-Staff himself, persuaded Basdekis to give him the letter, which he then arranged to be published."[133] Whatever the truth of the matter, Venizelos' reaction was swift. On reading the letter in the newspaper he sat down and as Minister of War prepared a Royal Decree for the

---

130 *Ibid.*, p. 403.

131 *Ibid.*, p. 406.

132 Greek newspaper Αθῆναι (Athens, 28 February, O.S., 1915). Also in Ventiris, *Ελλάς*, I, p. 200.

133 Veremis, *Οι επεμβάσεις* (Athens, 1977), pp. 119-120.

dismissal of Dousmanis from the Army. The King thought the penalty too severe, upon which Venizelos submitted his resignation. The King, taken aback, wavered, and in the end the Prime Minister got his way. Venizelos brought the Chief-of-Staff to trial on a charge of high treason, had him condemned and cashiered from the Army. Lieutenant-Colonel Ioannis Metaxas, as second-in-command, became Acting Chief-of-Staff.

When the dust lifted after the latest round in the battle for the King's mind between Venizelos and Metaxas, it was clear that Metaxas, now Chief-of-Staff, had won the day. It was then learned in Athens that Bulgaria had just received from Germany and Austria a loan of 150 million gold francs and that a Turco-Bulgarian agreement had been signed, permitting Turkey to transport arms and ammunition through Bulgarian territory. Bulgaria and Turkey were ranging themselves on the side of the Germans and the position of Greece had to be reassessed. No longer could Greece count upon Bulgarian neutrality. Grey and the other Entente leaders had been deceiving themselves, and Venizelos, in his turn, had allowed the siren voices of the Entente to deceive him, despite the warnings of the Greek General Staff concerning Bulgarian intentions. Metaxas' forebodings had proved to be justified. On 6 February Venizelos hurriedly sent a Note to the Ministers of the Entente, withdrawing his former offers of participation in the War. A lull ensued in the contest of words between the two protagonists. Two weeks later, on 18 and 19 February, the startling news reached Athens that the British and French fleets had shelled the outer forts of the Dardanelles. The prospect of the Allies taking Constantinople from the Turks caused a great sensation in Greece and fired Venizelos' imagination. The Dardanelles Expedition provided the Greek Prime Minister with a new avenue through which to pursue his interventionist policy.

The story of the Dardanelles Expedition is inextricably related to the subsequent course of events in Greece and the conflict between Venizelos and Metaxas. Metaxas' earlier plan for forcing the Dardanelles was based on the premise of a surprise attack. In the view of the Greek Staff Officer, if once the Turks were warned, they could defend the Straits indefinitely. The element of surprise had been lost when Venizelos threatened Turkey with war in the Spring of 1914. At the outbreak of the European War the Turks, with German assistance, built up the defenses of the Straits and mined the Narrows. This did not deter the Western strategists, who had visions of a campaign in the Eastern Mediterranean which would, as Kitchener wrote later, "end, once and for all, the German *Drang nach dem Osten.*"[134] Chief among the champions of this plan was Winston Churchill First Lord of the British Admiralty.

In August 1914 Churchill was eager to storm the Dardanelles with the assistance of Greek forces. The subsequent stalemate on the Western Front and the plight of the

134 Quoted by Leon, *Greece and the Great Powers*, p. 101.

Russian armies at the end of the year made such an enterprise even more desirable. Early in January 1915 Grand Prince Nicholas requested the British "for a demonstration of some kind against the Turks elsewhere, either naval or military, which would cause the Turks to withdraw some of the forces now acting against the Russians in the Caucausus."[135] On 3-4 February the Turks attacked the Suez Canal. Although they were repulsed, this obliged the British thereafter to keep large numbers of troops in Egypt. The Turkish entry into the war had extended the theater of hostilities to a vast degree. For a moment the eyes of the Western Allies turned away from the deadlock on the Western Front and surveyed, with a glint of new hope, the coastline of the Near East. Churchill's plan for forcing the Dardanelles was now looked upon with more favour. The British leaders especially, who were familiar with the Eastern Mediterranean, welcomed the opportunity to extend and consolidate British interests in the area, that part of the world so vital for their larger interests in India and Africa. The Ottoman Empire was by far the most exposed and weakest partner of the Central Alliance and Winston Churchill, Lloyd George and Lord Kitchener wanted to open a new front in the Near East and dispatch there the newly-raised British armies. The exponents of this policy were called "Easterners" and included among the French Aristide Briand and Generals Galliéni, d'Esperey, and Castelnau. Opposed to them were the British General Sir John French and the French Marshall Joseph Joffre, who both believed that the war would be decided on the Western Front, where the enemy had concentrated his main striking force. The "Easterners," on the other hand, argued that a front in the Eastern Mediterranean would resolve the statemate in Western Europe. They further urged that a successful campaign in the Near East would severely damage the prestige of the Central Alliance and open communications through which Allied assistance could reach Russia at a time when the Arctic Ocean was frozen and the Baltic Sea was blockaded by the German fleet. Such a campaign would remove all danger from Egypt and the "route to India"; it would assure support to the rebellious Arabs; and it would put an end to all hesitation on the part of Greece, Bulgaria and Romania to cast their lot with the Allied cause.

Three separate prospective fronts in the Near East were considered. Lord Kitchener the British Minister of War advocated landing a strong force in the Gulf of Alexandretta [Iskanderum] to cut the railway communications between Anatolia and Syria, which would prevent any transportation of Turkish troops to Egypt and Mesopotamia and would encourage the Arabs to revolt against the Turks. Lloyd George and the French High Command favoured opening a front in Salonica, landing troops there and advancing up the Vardar Valley to relieve the Serbs; Salonica could also be used as a starting point for a march against Constantinople. It was hoped that the presence of

135 Howard, *The Partition of Turkey*, p. 122.

Allied troops in Salonica would draw Greece and Bulgaria on to the side of the Allies. The fact that landing troops in Salonica would inevitably violate Greek neutrality did not perturb any of the Entente Powers, least of all the French.

Churchill was at last able to grasp the opportunity to promote his own pet project. He now wrote to the British War Council that a successful operation in the Dardanelles would frustrate Germany's intention "to break through Serbia, seduce Bulgaria, establish a through route to Constantinople, gain full control of the Turkish Empire.... and open to herself avenues to Persia and India."[136] Churchill's scheme was at once the most ambitious and the most dangerous of the three. It was then thought that the opening of the Straits would somehow hasten the end of the War. Venizelos still believed this in 1934.[137]

The Dardanelles campaign ran into difficulties from the outset. The British and French fleets succeeded in silencing the outer forts on either side of the Dardanelles, but made no serious attempt to land troops or to sail up the Straits. The Turks, with German assistance, had effectively mined the Narrows, which made it impossible for the heavy Allied warships to force their way into the Sea of Marmora. Venizelos at once remembered how the British had previously suggested, through Admiral Kerr, a concerted Greek-English operation for forcing the Dardanelles; he took off the shelf Metaxas' earlier plans and without a second thought offered the Allies Greek participation in the campaign. He was ready, he assured them, to dispatch that which they sorely needed -- light naval craft which could sail unscathed over the minefields, plus an army unit of 40,000 men which would occupy the Gallipoli Peninsula. Sir Edward Grey replied that Britain would gladly accept Greek aid and, according to Churchill, added that "the Admiralty was very anxious that the Greeks should assist with ships as well as troops in the Dardanelles."[138] On 3 March 1915 the British Military Attaché in Athens cabled London that "the view of the Greek General Staff is universally that the naval attack should be assisted by land operations." And he gave a summary of what was essentially Metaxas' plan.[139]

---

136 Quoted by Leon, *Greece and the Great Powers*, p. 101.

137 Lord Kitchener dispatched Sir Ian Hamilton, the general to whom he entrusted the Dardanelles Expedition, with these words : "If the Fleet gets through Constantinople will fall of its own accord, and you will have won not a battle, but the war". A.J.P. Taylor, who quotes this, comments : "It is a mystery why most people, then and since, assumed that the fall of Constantinople would lead to the defeat of Germany. The only immediate gain would be to open a line of supply to Russia, and this gain was purely theoretical since neither Great Britain nor France had, at this time, supplies to send. Turkey might have been knocked out of the war but this would have lessened the burden on Germany. An army would have had no light task to march from Constantinople to Central Europe and, in any case, there was no army to spare". A. J. P. Taylor, *English History 1914-19145* (New York and Oxford, 1970), pp. 24-25.

138 Churchill, *The World Crisis*, p. 384.

139 *Ibid.*, p. 385. The rest of the telegram reads: "Their plan was to disembark four or five Greek

But when Venizelos called in his Chief-of-Staff and announced his intention to participate in the campaign, Metaxas completely disagreed. He was adamant; he wanted to have nothing to do with it; and he asked to be relieved of his duties. Metaxas followed up his oral observations with a memorandum listing his objections.[140] Two factors influenced his opinion, he wrote. "One political: the attitude of Bulgaria and Romania. And one military: the strength of the British and French forces which were going to participate in the campaign."[141] On the first question Metaxas noted that it was quite possible that Bulgaria, encouraged by Austria and Germany, would attack not Serbia, but Greece. On the other hand, a joint operation with the Greeks for the capture of Constantinople "is not, of course, agreeable to the Russian soul."[142] The pro-Russian sentiments of a great part of the Bulgarian people would this time be in harmony with the official policy of the Bulgarian Government. It would have been different if Russia had undertaken to hold back the Bulgarians in time by landing a strong army in Varna or Burgas, but no such possibility was conceivable. On the other hand, the Romanian attitude had remained extremely doubtful. Then Metaxas considered the strength and the plans, or rather the absence of plans, of the Allies. The Turks had been fortifying the Dardanelles since the previous summer and it was to be expected that preparations for their defense had been hastened since the entry of Turkey into the war and her decision to close the Straits. His information was that Turkey presently had at least fifteen divisions ready to defend the Dardanelles, well-equipped and amply alerted by the Allied shelling of the forts. Against them the proposed Allied force, even with Greek participation, was quite inadequate. But forcing the Dardanelles would not bring the campaign to an end and secure free navigation through the Straits. Turkish troops in Thrace and Asia Minor would continue the fight. For Greek troops to abandon the defense of the Greek frontiers in Macedonia and participate in such an adventure would be courting military disaster "which will knock out Greece, not only for the present but also in the future, from all political considerations, even by her friends, and most probably destroy for ever the integrity of the country."[143] Metaxas concluded his memorandum by observing that the whole conception of the Dardanelles campaign was amateurish. "I may add that, judging from the Allied measures against the Dardanelles

---

divisions at the Southern extremity of the Peninsula and to advance against the heights East of Maidos. Three successive defended positions would have to be carried, but Turks could not develop large forces owing to lack of space for deployment. If simultaneously an attack by a separate and sufficient force was made against lines of Bulair, either by disembarking troops North of [the] lines or at head of Gulf of Xeros, the Turks would have to abandon the Maidos region or run risk of being cut off".

140 The memorandum is printed in Metaxas, *Diary,* II, pp. 407-413.

141 *Ibid.,* p. 407

142 *Ibid.,* p. 408.

143 *Ibid.,* p. 409 .

so far, it looks as if the operation has not been studied at all, and that the enemy has been very much under-estimated."[144]

The Prime Minister, although he later admitted that Metaxas' memorandum caused "some doubts" in his mind,[145] was not deterred from his policy. Soon after seeing Metaxas, Venizelos prepared a new memorandum for the King, the third one he submitted to Constantine advocating Greek intervention in the European War. On 2 March, not content to send his memorandum by courier, he took it to the Palace himself.

Venizelos: *Your Majesty, with your permission, I shall read you my paper myself. It was for this reason that I requested an audience.*[146]

Venizelos first reminded Constantine that until then he himself had been in agreement with the General Staff. The Powers of the Triple Entente had twice requested Greece to come to the assistance of Serbia, but on both occasions he had shared the view of the Staff that such a move would expose Greece to a Bulgarian attack. He had also agreed with the Staff that if Bulgaria attacked the Serbs, Greece would attack Bulgaria, honouring her treaty obligations to Serbia. But now more important issues were at stake, which Greece could not afford to ignore.

"There is no need for me to emphasize the gains that will accrue to us through our participation in the Allied campaign against the Dardanelles and Constantinople. On the one hand, we, too, shall take part in the resolution of the question of Constantinople and the Straits ... on the other hand, we shall have a right to expect, in the case of the victory of the Triple Entente, the territorial concessions in Asia Minor already offered to us, much enhanced. Your Majesty is aware that since the outbreak of the war I have always been of the strong opinion that whatever may be the outcome of the war on the battlefields of Russia or France, England, even if standing alone, will finally be able to impose the terms of the peace."[147]

Venizelos believed that "for the present time" Greek national interests would be best served if Constantinople and the Straits were internationalized. The territorial acquisitions in Asia Minor would make possible the return of the Greek refugees to their homes and ensure their safety and prosperity in the future. Perhaps even Cyprus would be allowed by Britain to unite with Greece, as had been promised earlier. If Greece participated in a victorious war she could repudiate her portion of the burden of the Ottoman Debt, which she had been compelled to shoulder by the treaty of

---

144 *Ibid.*, p. 412.

145 At one of the Crown Councils which met later in the course of this crisis. Quoted by Metaxas in a newspaper article on 25 October 1934. Reprinted in Venizelos and Metaxas, *Ιστορία Εθνικού Διχασμού*, p. 31.

146 Ventiris, *Ιστορία*, I, p. 279.

147 Kordatos, *Historia*, V, p. 422

Bucharest. Venizelos reminded the King that the present policy of benevolent neutrality could not be continued without hazard to the country. "As long as the war lasts, our involvement in it is possible any day -- even against our own will."[148] This time, the Prime Minister disagreed with the General Staff. Greece, he said, by participating in the Dardanelles with one army of 40,000 men, would not weaken her defenses against Bulgaria because the four other Greek armies would be reserved intact to defend Macedonia. If the campaign were successful the army fighting at the Dardanelles could turn west and attack the Bulgarians through Eastern Thrace. If the campaign were not successful, this army could be shipped back to Macedonia, in which case the Allied armies would most probably join Greece in fighting Bulgaria in aid of Serbia.

Venizelos himself later recounted how he went to the Palace and read his memorandum to Constantine "in a voice vibrating with enthusiasm."

"Such was the earnestness with which I spoke, so strong were the arguments that were set forth in the memorandum, that the King, who, quite evidently (as is clearly proved by subsequent events) had from the very beginning promised the German Emperor that he would never be found in the Entente camp unless one of the Balkan States attacked him -- the King said to me with great emotion (I remember the very words) -- "Very well then, in God's name." That is to say, he consented."[149]

Elated, Venizelos left the King's study. Rather to his surprise he found Metaxas waiting for him in the antechamber. The Prime Minister at once announced the Royal consent for Greek participation in the Dardanelles Expedition to the Chief-of-Staff and asked him to accompany him to the Ministry of War where they would prepare the order of mobilization. But, according to Venizelos, Metaxas, "instead of any other answer, pulls out from his pocket his letter of resignation," and handed it to him.[150] "Mr. Prime Minister, this is my resignation. I cannot remain Chief-of-Staff if a policy of which I do not personally approve is decided on."[151] Metaxas' letter ran as follows.

"I respectfully submit to you the request that you study my memorandum to you, considering it not as a protest or a shirking of responsibility but as the expression of my beliefs and my love for Greece. I have reached a radical disagreement with you, not on a political but a military matter, and one that is closely associated with my duties. In essence it is about the war strategy of Greece and the deployment of her military forces in the case that she enters the war. Consequently under such circumstances I believe it is not permissible for me to continue as Chief-of-Staff.

---

148 *Ibid.*

149 Venizelos gave an account of this incident in his speech in Parliament on 26 August 1917. He said then: "The King read the memorandum and was visibly disturbed". E. Venizelos, *The Vindication of Greek National Policy, 1912-1917* (London, 1918), p. 83.

150 Venizelos and Metaxas, *Ιστορία Εθνικού Διχασμού*, p. 22.

151 Venizelos, *Vindication*, p. 84.

I previously submitted to you the request that I might be relieved of these duties [as Chief-of-Staff] and you asked me to refer the matter to His Majesty the King, who would make the decision. I did so. But His Majesty the King intends to refer the matter back to you, in order to resolve it as far as I personally am concerned.

Desirous of extricating you both from this difficulty, I submit the enclosed petition for my retirement from the Army. Retirement is a right granted by law and therefore this petition of mine cannot reflect in the least upon discipline. Sacrificing my career, I follow the dictates of my conscience, which for me is the highest law.

This notwithstanding, I do not intend to cease serving my Native Land. In time of war, if I were to be recalled from retirement, I should again serve Greece as I have done until now. I am submitting my petition directly to you in order to avoid normal service channels, which would not have maintained the necessary secrecy. When you yourself decide that the time is right, you may give my petition to your office so that the serial number may be officially affixed.

Be assured that I more than anyone else feel the deepest grief at finding myself under the necessity of taking such a step.[152]

Venizelos was taken aback. As he was to say in Parliament on 26 August 1917, he had "the highest opinion of the military talents of Colonel Metaxas" and "was afraid the insubordinate impulse of the Chief-of-Staff, who, for all his long studies in Germany, had not learned that the first duty of a soldier is discipline, might shake public opinion, and prejudice the future administration of public affairs."[153] Holding Metaxas' letter in his hand, Venizelos returned to the King's study. "Metaxas is engaging in politics," he announced to Constantine.[154] It may be wondered why the Prime Minister did not appoint someone else of his own choice Chief-of-Staff. "I believe," Venizelos replied to this years later in a letter to the historian George Ventiris *that even if I had requested the immediate replacement of Metaxas, the King would have asked [for time] to think about Metaxas' successor and, again coming in touch with those circles which influenced him, would have changed his mind. His former approval was the result of the strong influence I exercised upon him when we were alone ... But, as soon as I went outside, the feeling of excitement dissolved and Constantine again found himself under the influence of his evil environment."*

The Prime Minister suggested to the King that a Crown Council be convened immediately to give its views. Soon after Venizelos left the Palace he discovered that

---

152 Metaxas, *Diary,* II. pp. 406-7.

153 Venizelos Vindication.... p. 84. In his speech to Parliament on this occasion, Venizelos added : "The General Staff is not responsible for the political views of the Government. It is the responsible head of the military executive; war is decided by the politicians, not by the General Staff". *Ibid.*

154 Ventiris, *Ελλάς,* I, p. 280.

special editions of the leading newspapers were carrying the news of Metaxas' resignation in banner headlines.

The Crown Council met the next day, 3 March 1915, presided over by Constantine. As well as Venizelos, Rallis, Theotokis, Zaimis, Dragounis and Mavromichalis were present, all former premiers of Greece. It was at once apparent that the King was no longer willing to listen to his Prime Minister. Under the impact of Metaxas' dramatic resignation, all Constantine's former doubts and hesitations came to the fore. Metaxas' stand and Metaxas' memorandum on the Dardanelles afforded new support and new ammunition to the King's pro-German courtiers and to his consort Queen Sophia, who had now forgotten and forgiven her differences with her brother and praised "the excellent personal feelings of the Emperor today."[155] All the former premiers urged the King to accept Venizelos' policy. Rallis is known to have exhorted the King, "Be daring, Your Majesty." Even the Germanophile George Theotokis advised Constantine to follow the policy of his Prime Minister, who enjoyed the support of the majority of the Greek people. But the King had lost his nerve. He had given his word to the German Emperor that he would not fight against Germany's allies unless Greece were attacked first. Constantine was honest, upright, and a brilliant soldier, but he had neither the constitutional sensitivity nor the intellectual acuteness of his father George I. Metaxas' arguments crystallized the King's own ideas and Metaxas' defiance inspired him to come out into the open himself as a man with his own will and convictions. The King now insisted that the Crown Council should be convened again to listen to Metaxas explaining his position. Venizelos was obliged to agree -- "however unpleasant the presence of Mr. Metaxas will be to me, although Your Majesty knows how much I respect his military talents."[156] Still, the Prime Minister made it clear that he was not willing to listen to Metaxas discussing the political aspect of the matter, which was the sole concern of the Government, but only to hear his views on the military considerations involved in any Greek participation in the Dardanelles.

The following day, 4 March 1915, on the occasion of the celebrations for the anniversary of the liberation of Ioannina, Venizelos reinstated General Dousmanis as Chief-of-Staff. So when the second Crown Council met one day later the General Staff was represented not by Metaxas but Dousmanis. At this meeting Venizelos reduced his original request for an army corps for the Dardanelles Expedition to only one division, so that no argument could be put forward that Macedonia would be left undefended

155 Quoted by Foivos N. Gregoriadis, *Διχασμός, Μικρά Ασία, 1909-1930* [Schism, Asia Minor, 1909-1930] (Athens, 1971), p. 187.

156 Streit, Diary, II, Part One, p. 34. One of the "differences" between the Kaiser and his sister arose when Sophia chose of her own accord to adopt the Greek Orthodox rite when she married Constantine. The Kaiser, protector of the Protestant faith, then forbade his sister to set foot on German soil for three years; but, as Prince Nicholas wrote, "gradually the term of banishment was lessened when the Emperor's wrath abated". Fifty Years, p. 94.

against a Bulgarian attack. The Prime Minister was anxious to commit his country to the Allied cause, no doubt expecting that full involvement would follow. According to all accounts, Venizelos spoke with great eloquence, and all the former premiers urged the King to throw off all hesitation and go along with his Prime Minister. Then Metaxas went over the objections against such an enterprise, pointing out that what was possible a few months before when he had prepared his plan for forcing the Dardanelles, was possible no longer; the Allies had neither proper campaign plans, nor were they able or willing to employ the necessary forces for such an operation; their success was extremely doubtful; but even if the Allied fleet reached Constantinople, that would not bring an end to Turkish resistance. A new war would be necessary in Thrace and, worse, in the hinterland of Asia Minor, in order to crush the Turks. As Metaxas always believed that neither Britain nor France had any genuine desire to destroy Turkey, but only wanted to replace German influence and patronage over the country, he considered that any commitment of Greek troops in a venture like the Dardanelles would be a military and political error of the first magnitude. General Dousmanis, the reinstated Chief-of-Staff, agreed with Metaxas. Not only, added Dousmanis, had the Allies selected the least favourable place to attack, but they had also chosen to carry out the operation in the depths of winter when the frequent storms in the Straits would delay them, giving the Turks time to recuperate.

King Constantine asked for twenty-hours in which to reflect before giving his opinion. One of the factors which weighed heaviest on Constantine's mind came from Russia. The Russians, who had been converted to Orthodox Christianity and civilized by Byzantium, considered themselves the natural heirs to the Eastern Roman Empire and expected Constantinople to go to them as their rightful prize for their part in the European War. Economic and strategic reasons underlay the Russian desire to occupy the Straits, the only waterway to the sunny Mediterranean -- and to Europe, as the Arctic Sea is frozen half the year and the Baltic is practically a closed sea, fenced in by Germany and several other nations. When Sir Edward Grey declined earlier offers of Greek participation in the War, he did so mainly in order not to offend and alienate the Russians. He wrote in his memoirs:

"King Constantine was to head the Greek Army; and, if the operations were successful, he would have entered Constantinople in triumph at the head of Greek troops. The effect on Russia would have been disastrous; there is no limit to the disaster that would have ensued. Even the authority of the Czar and Sazonov and their loyalty to the Allies might not have sufficed to keep Russia in the war."[157]

Now that the Dardanelles campaign had been decided upon, troops and ships had to be found to carry it out. Russia, hard pressed on the Eastern Front, could not provide

157 Alastos, *Venizelos,* p. 174.

any military assistance; Greece, on the other hand, until then untouched by the War, could send both troops and light naval craft which could sail over the minefields. For this reason, Britain had a change of heart and now actively sought Greek participation in the campaign. But Russia saw in this a threat to her claims on Constantinople. On 3 March 1915, the day the first Crown Council was meeting in Athens, far away in St. Petersburgh, Sazonov the Russian Minister of Foreign Affairs, informed Sir George Buchanan the British Ambassador, that "the Russian government could not consent to Greece participating in operations in the Dardanelles, as it would be sure to lead to complications ..." Sazonov added that the Czar, when he had received him in audience the previous day, had declared that he could not in any circumstances consent to Greek cooperation in the Dardanelles.[158] The Russian Minister in Athens Prince E.P. Demidov, under instructions from his Government, indicated to all concerned that Greek intervention in the Dardanelles was unwelcome and made it abundantly clear that the Greek King would never be allowed to enter Constantinople with his troops. Churchill wrote: "Can one wonder that, with his German consort and German leanings, with every appeal on the one hand and this violent rebuff upon the other, King Constantine was thrown back, and relapsed into his previous attitude of hostile reserve?"[159] George Streit the King's privy councillor reported later that he had heard the King murmur several times, "What can I say? Constantinople lures me on. If only Russia were not involved..."[160]

On 6 March 1915 Venizelos made a brief announcement in the Greek Parliament of the resignation of his Government owing to a disagreement with the Crown. Constantine Zavitsianos the Speaker of the House announced that the session was adjourned until the formation of a new government. There was uproar in the Chamber.

Government deputies: *Long live Venizelos!*
Opposition deputies: *Long live the King!*
Government deputies: *Long live the Nation!*
Opposition deputies: *Long live the King!*
Government deputies: *Long live the Nation!*

Venizelos, speaking in Parliament on 26 August 1917, claimed that if the King had followed his advice and if "Colonel Metaxas had not become a tool of German policy by resigning and engendering those momentary hesitations,"[161] the Allies, with Greek

---

158 Grey, *Twenty-five years*, II, p. 186.

159 Churchill, *World Crisis*, p. 385. Churchill comments in his inimitable way : "This was a hard saying. Was there no finger to write upon the wall, was there no ancestral spirit to conjure up before this unfortunate Prince, the downfall of his House, the ruin of his people -- the bloody cellar of Ekaterinburg?" And, for good measure, he adds "the time-honoured quotation one learned as a schoolboy -- Quos deus vult perdere, prius dementant". *Ibid.*, pp. 385-7.

160 *Ibid.*, p. 386.

161 Ventiris, *Ελλάς*, I, p. 299.

assistance, would have broken through the Dardanelles, which according to reports the Prime Minister had in his hands were then unguarded. "Imagine," he exclaimed, "the prestige and authority Greece would have acquired if she had succeeded by her own efforts in tremendously influencing the history of the world by shortening even by one whole year this war."[162]

In his journalistic duel with Metaxas in 1934, Venizelos repeated his claim that, had Greece participated in the Dardanelles Expedition, the duration of the War would have been shortened; and he reiterated the charge that the responsibility for the failure of Greece to send troops to the Dardanelles, which had resulted in such calamities for Greece and the whole world, lay at Metaxas' door. By submitting and simultaneously announcing to the Press his resignation as Chief-of-Staff on 2 March 1915, Metaxas *"attempted to influence illegally the foreign policy of the country which according to our Constitution was conducted by the responsible Government as long as the Government enjoyed the confidence of the King on the one hand and of the Parliament on the other. Without Mr. Metaxas' illegal action ... the mobilisation order would have been issued that same evening, in less than a week the Gallipoli Peninsula would have been captured, the King would have entered Constantinople at the head of the Greek Army and the Anglo-French contingents; the Dardanelles and the Bosphorus would have been opened, the Russian Armies that were then at Przemysl would have been supplied with the war materiel which they lacked; Bulgaria and Romania would most probably have sided from that time with the Allies; and after the final failure at Verdun in the summer of 1916, Germany, unable to display to the German people a map of victories, would at that time have given up her claims to Alsace-Lorraine and sued for peace.*

The War would have been shortened by half, the number of the war dead and maimed would have been halved, the destruction of wealth would have been two thirds or at least three fifths less ... Therefore the shock from the War would not have been so severe for the whole world and the post-war problems we are now facing would have been much smaller and their solution much easier.

Such is the world disaster for which Mr. Metaxas is responsible. Anyone can judge how heavy his responsibility is toward Greece and toward King Constantine. Without his illegal action on that fateful day of February 1915, the National Schism would have been averted and Constantine would have been one of the main factors of the Allied victory and, instead of dying in exile in a foreign land, he would have reigned happy over a united nation while Greece, with relatively few sacrifices, would have accomplished all her national dreams."[163]

---

162 Gibbons, *Venizelos,* p. 232.
163 *Ibid.,* p. 233.

Venizelos' article appeared on 20 October 1934. In his reply five days later Metaxas made great fun of Venizelos' flights of fancy. They reminded him, Metaxas said, of a novel by Jules Verne which he had read in his carefree childhood. The hero of this book planned to give a new tilt to the axis of the earth and radically change the world climate because he wanted to exploit the coal-mines which were hidden under the ice at the North Pole. To achieve this end, he built an enormous cannon in the center of Mount Kilimanjaro and loaded it with dynamite; the hero expected that the recoil would do the trick and tilt the axis. But, when he fired his cannon, the surrounding countryside was devastated and thousands of his workers were killed, and the earth continued revolving on its axis as before. A far larger cannon was needed for such a feat. Apparently Verne's hero had made a few miscalculations! If Greece had participated in the Dardanelles campaign, Metaxas concluded, what happened in the case of the cannon would also have happened to Greece. Metaxas claimed that it was he who prevented this disaster. "And I am glad that after so many years this historical justice is done to me by Mr. Venizelos himself."[164] The English alone lost at the Dardanelles 5,241 officers and 210,791 men and also their best ships in the Mediterranean. In this article Metaxas wrote that "there is no worse curse for a country than when its politicians who are completely untrained in the art of war demand to plan the military operations."[165] He mentioned the official British Report on the Dardanelles which blamed several British politicians, among them Lloyd George, Churchill and Asquith, for their part in the campaign. "The ancient Greeks and Romans expected their politicians to be generals as well, that is, real generals. And they were right."[166] And here Metaxas quoted Clausewitz to the effect that war is only the continuation of foreign policy by other means. If a Prime Minister is not a general, he should listen to his Chief-of-Staff. If they disagreed and the Prime Minister would not resign, then the Chief-of-Staff should do so, in order that a new one might be appointed who agreed with the Prime Minister. The British Admiral Lord Fisher resigned in 1915 after the failure at the Dardanelles because he held different views from the British Government concerning the way the Fleet had been used. Similarly the German General von Falkenhayn resigned in 1916 because he disagreed with the policy of his superiors. Finally Metaxas questioned the details in Venizelos' description of his resignation as Chief-of-Staff and he accused Venizelos of turning against Constantine personally and of allowing the Press to carry on a campaign against the King and to discredit him in the eyes of the Allies. Metaxas ended his article by demanding rhetorically: "Who caused the internal

164 Venizelos and Metaxas, *Historia Ethnikou Dichasmou*, p. 22.
165 *Ibid.*, p. 31
166 *Ibid.*

schism? I or Venizelos? I, who after resigning, retired to my home? Or Venizelos, who, after resigning, stirred up his followers against the King?"[167]

Thus the heart of the nation was rent asunder. The irrevocable Schism between the Royalists and the Liberals was perpetrated. For the next twenty years there were to be no Greeks, only Venizelists and Antivenizelists. Men broke off old friendships and families broke up. Shops, theaters and coffee-houses were known and patronised according to their political affiliation. In the Church, the Army, the Navy, in schools and universities, the professions and all classes of society, the Greeks belonged to either one group or the other. "The Great War," Toynbee observed, "split the Greek nation, like an earthquake, from top to bottom."[168] Metaxas' dramatic resignation signalled the first rupture between the pro-Entente Liberals and the pro-German Royalists. But the National Schism, as the split came to be called, had deeper roots in Greek history and society: it was the expression of two opposing views of life, two different philosophies, best exemplified by the personalities of the two protagonists.

On one side of the scales stood Venizelos, the consumate politician from Crete. He was a liberal, a democrat, often a demagogue; a born revolutionary, often reckless, he was a gambler who played for high stakes. A magnetic personality, he was admired around the globe. A visionary, he could often inspire the people. Impulsive, he followed his own intuition: he had faith in his own star, as he said, and often flirted with disaster. In 1915 Venizelos believed that a unique opportunity was presented to Greece to realize all her national aspirations. At least half of the Greek people did not think so, but Venizelos did not hesitate to divide the country and drag Greece, willy nilly, on the course he had decided upon. The National Schism brought disaster upon Greece and brought about the eventual undoing of Venizelos himself.

On the other side was poised Metaxas, the brilliant soldier from Cephalonia. He was an authoritarian and a convinced monarchist. Dogged and calculating, he believed above all in his own intrinsic worth and superior wisdom and nursed a bitter grudge against an ungrateful State for failing to recognize his outstanding abilities. While Venizelos believed that England, even if she were to be cut off from her allies, would finally win, Metaxas thought otherwise. According to Zavitsianos, the Speaker of the House, "Metaxas, more than any other Greek, believed that Germany would prevail. It was he who persuaded Theotokis and Gounaris to share his convictions."[169] Metaxas considered Venizelos' interventionist policy sheer madness and spared no effort to wreck the designs of the Prime Minister. Metaxas' tactics were very much responsible not only for the initial polarization of Greece but also for the chronic disarray of the

167 *Ibid.*

168 Arnold Toynbee, "Party Politics in Athens and Angora", *The Weekly Westminster* (London, 19 January 1924).

169 Constantine Zavitsianos, Αναμνήσεις, p. 40.

political life of the country which subsequently veered away from its hard-won parliamentary traditions and became prone to internal strife and easy prey to authoritarian regimes. Today Metaxas is remembered not primarily as the masterly strategist of the Balkan Wars and the Albanian Campaign of 1941, but chiefly as the feared and hated dictator of the Thirties.

Strong socio-economic factors played their part in the National Schism. Behind the two protagonists were two disparate ideologies. Behind Venizelos was a background of the revolutionary Greece of the klephtic tradition and the Wars of Liberation. Behind Metaxas was a background of notables and landlords, the descendants of the old phanariots and the former village kojabashis who gathered round the monarchy to preserve their vested interests and ancient privileges. These two different worlds first recognized each other under the impact of the 1897 disaster, and first confronted each other during the Revolution of Ghoudi in 1909. Metaxas' resignation in 1915 sparked off the flames that have been smouldering ever since. From that turning point the two worlds were ranged uncompromisingly against each other, for better or worse.

At that crucial moment Venizelos and Metaxas reached the parting of the ways and Metaxas at last "unfurled his own standard." Although he denied it in his letter of resignation to Venizelos, Metaxas' momentous gesture was a political move and was recognized as such by Liberals and Royalists alike. Metaxas did not seek any responsible political position for some time afterwards, but he was immediately identified for what he was -- ; the staunchest friend of the King and all things monarchical and the most dangerous foe of Venizelos and all things liberal. The Greek tragedy was destined to pass through many vicissitudes; the dictatorship which Metaxas established on 4 August 1936 was the final act.

Between the Devil and the Deep Blue Sea

After the resignation of Venizelos, the King invited Demetrios Gounaris (1867 - 1922), the Royalist Deputy from Patras, to form a new government. At the time Gounaris had only three followers in the Chamber. In an effort to give his government the appearance of impartiality, Gounaris selected the Liberal George Zographos, who was known for his pro-Entente sympathies, as his Foreign minister.

As soon as the new Government was put together Gounaris announced (on 22 March, 1915) that Greece would continue her policy of "benevolent neutrality" towards Serbia. But soon afterwards, the Prime Minister stated that his Government "was laboring to avert the Bulgarian peril without making concessions that others would perhaps not have judged incompatible with the interests of the country".[1] Gounaris was, of course, alluding to the confidential memoranda which Venizelos had submitted to the King suggesting that Kavalla should be sacrificed if necessary in order to secure Bulgarian neutrality so that Greece could pursue her irredentist policies in Asia Minor. Venizelos, offended at the insinuation, wrote to Zographos, (on 30 March 1915) explaining the conditions under which he had suggested to the King that concessions could be made to Bulgaria. Zographos referred the matter to his Prime Minister, who chose to answer Venizelos himself. Demetrios Gounaris pointed out that a real difference existed between Venizelos and the present Government on the question of concessions to Bulgaria and his statement was intended to clarify this difference. In answer to this, Venizelos published the first of the two confidential memoranda on the subject he had sent to the King and claimed that Constantine had accepted his suggestions and authorised him to do what was necessary. A new Government statement expressly denied that the King had ever consented to any territorial concessions to Bulgaria. Venizelos then appealed directly to the King, reminded him of his services for four and a half years to the Nation and the Throne and asked him to exonerate him; if the King refused, he wrote in his letter, the only course left open to him was to withdraw from politics. This was not the last time Venizelos was to make this threat. King Constantine did not even bother to answer. He was by now completely under the influence of the Palace clique, even more so than his puppet Government. The Greek historian and politician, Spyros Markezinis, wrote that "Demetrios Gounaris was not really in power, or rather, he was sharing the power with George Streit and Ioannis Metaxas under an irregular regime because the two latter had no responsible office, at least at that time."[2]

The hand of the Royalists in their determination to keep Greece out of the Allied camp was much strengthened by the British and French recognition of Russian claims over Constantinople and the Straits, which was made public about this time.

---

1 Cosmetatos, *op. cit.*, p. 21.
2 Markezinis, *op. cit.*, IV, p. 23.

Sir Edward Grey, the British Foreign Minister, as early as 14 November 1914 had (according to Churchill) instructed Sir George Buchanan, British Ambassador in Russia, to inform M. Sazonov that the British Government recognised that "the question of the Straits and of Constantinople should be settled in conformity with Russian desires".[3] At the time this promise was kept secret; but on 4 March 1915 Russia officially demanded Constantinople and the Straits. Britain and France, vainly hoping that a Russian fleet would attack the north entry of the Bosphorus and open a second theater of operations in the Straits, "apprised the Russian Government that they would agree to the annexation of Constantinople by Russia as a part of a victorious peace;" and, Churchill concludes, "this momentous fact was accordingly made public on the 12th."[4] That was in March 1915. The celebrated agreement also accorded Russia a piece of the hinterland on both sides of the Straits - from the Enos-Midye line on the European side and an equivalent stretch of land on the Asiatic side. Britain and France, who had fought the Crimean War to keep Russia out of the Straits, were now handing them over. The Czar announced to his people that this war was opening the way to the solution of a historic problem which had occupied Russia for generations. It was quite ridiculous: the Russians demanded that their troops should control the Hagia Sophia district, while the Pope was demanding from France that the great Byzantine cathedral of the Orthodox faith should be given to the Catholics! Poincaré wrote in his diary on 31 March 1915: "One would think that our flags were flying on the Golden Horn and the three faiths were contesting Hagia Sophia."[5]

On 18 March 1915 Admiral John de Robeck tried to force the Dardanelles with eighteen warships, but when four of his ships struck mines he withdrew. It was evident that lighter craft were needed which could sail over the mines and which were manned by crews that knew the area well. Immediately the Allies once more asked Greece to participate in the Dardanelles campaign, repeating earlier promises of territorial concessions in Asia Minor. The Greek Foreign Minister was expected to respond to this new overture on 21 March, 1915. On the eve of this day, Sunday, he was visited at the Ministry by Metaxas. The same evening Metaxas went to the Palace to brief the King and advise him against war with Turkey: Greece could not intervene with her fleet alone without involving all her land forces. The slightest Greek intervention would trigger Turkish reprisals against the Greeks of the Ottoman Empire; the popular outcry would force Greece to use all her forces in an all-out war. Nor should Greece be tempted by "the bait of easy occupation, as it is thought, of the coastal Turkish cities for the salvation of their populations,"[6] because again this would mean a total war.

---

3 Churchill, *World Crisis* p.382.

4 Ibid. p.383.

5 Raymond Poincaré, *Dairy*.

6 Metaxas, *Dairy*, II, p. 421.

Bulgaria would then intervene for the certain destruction of Greece. But even if Greece were not at war with Turkey, she should avoid a confrontation with Bulgaria because Greek forces were at that time inferior and there were serious shortages in Greek war preparations. Greece should not expect any substantial help from the English and the French. If Greece were to be forced to intervene in the present conflict she should at least wait for Bulgaria to come out on the side of the Allies first, but the Bulgarian danger would continue to exist, even if both Greece and Bulgaria were in the Entente camp.

When, therefore, the Greek Government offered on the following day, (21 March 1915) to assist in the Dardanelles, the offer was made conditional on a Bulgarian attack on Turkey first, and an Allied guarantee to Greece against the Bulgarian danger. Prince George, the King's brother, who was married to a Bonaparte, was sent to Paris to convince the Allies that the Greek offer was genuine and to ask that Constantinople, after it was taken, be internationalised. But the Allies, hot from courting Bulgaria, not only refused the Greek demand for guarantees, but also warned Greece not to provoke Bulgaria and drive her into the enemy camp. The Allies were offering to Bulgaria Kavalla and Eastern Macedonia (which were Greek), Dobrudja (which was Rumanian), and Northwestern Macedonia, both the contested and the uncontested area (which was Serbian). These concessions would have created a Greater Bulgaria almost as large as that envisaged by the Treaty of San Stefano in 1878, which had enraged the English and had been wiped out within a few months at the Congress of Berlin.

On 12 April the Entente Ministers in Athens repeated Sir Edward Grey's earlier offer of the Smyrna region to Greece in a final effort to win Greek help in the Dardanelles. The following day the Greek Foreign Minister, without consulting Metaxas, sent an official answer submitting his own proposals for Greek intervention in the war against Turkey. After drawing attention to Bulgarian hostility toward Greece, Zographos said that *"Greece would cooperate in the war against Turkey if the Powers would be willing to enter into a formal engagement to assure her the advantage of their complete solidarity with her, that is to say, if they would guarantee during the War and for a certain period after the War, the integrity of her continental and insular territories including Northern Epirus"*.[7] He further asked that *"the Act recording the terms of the Agreement should specify also the territorial concessions to be made to Greece in Asia Minor ... and also the facilities of a financial nature and for a military replenishment that the Entente Powers would allow her in order to place her in a position to fulfil the engagements entered into."*[8] The Greek Foreign Minister also

---

7 Cosmetatos, *op. cit.*, p. 23f.

8 *Ibid.*.

asked that the Act should state that the aim of the War was the destruction of the Ottoman Empire.

This statement greatly worried Metaxas, who went to see the King the same evening. Previously Greece had demanded Bulgarian participation as a condition for her intervention; now Greece only demanded guarantees of her integrity. The Allies would never be in a position to provide this guarantee, Metaxas explained to the King. The assurance Britain had just given to the King's emissary, Prince George, that she would use half a million men in the campaign against Turkey, Metaxas advised the King not to take seriously because, "if such an army was available it could be put into better use in France."[9] It was all a bluff, Metaxas insisted, in order to trick Greece into the War against the Central Powers. To state in a treaty, as the Foreign Minister asked, that the purpose of the war was the destruction of the Ottoman Empire did not necessarily create obligations for its realization. Many reasons would be invented, real or imaginary, to prevent this. "Didn't this happen in 1859 between Napoleon and Cavour?" Metaxas commented. He concluded. *"I do not believe that England and France really intend any more to force the Dardanelles and the Bosphorus - now that Russia has prepared a force to send to Constantinople as soon as it is captured - because in this way they are obliged to give away this area to Russia before the conclusion of the peace. If they do it Russia could conclude a separate peace with Germany and Austria and then the consequences would be disastrous both for England and France and for us. If they do it then we have only worked to put on our backs a colossal enemy. The idea that we would be useful to England and France as an instrument by which they could fight Russian aims is a fallacy."*[10]

Metaxas had the best of reasons for wanting to keep his country out of the war. Germany, he thought, because of her superior military organisation and central geographical position, and especially because of her superior civilization, would finally prevail against her enemies; already the Germans had pinned down the Russians on the Eastern Front and could now redirect some of their armies south towards the Balkans. The Allied campaign in the Dardanelles was doomed from its inception while Bulgaria was certain to come out on the side of the Central Powers, in spite of all predictions to the contrary by the "Balkan experts" of the Entente. If the Greek coasts were too vulnerable to the Allied fleets for Greece to join the Central Powers, then the wise course was to temporise. The Greek Government could declare its good intentions towards the Allies in order to avert any threat to her marine trade, but she should resist any pressure to intervene in the present War. Greece should be especially careful not to be tricked by

9 Metaxas, *Dairy*, II, p. 427

10 *Ibid.*, p. 428.

Allied promises of concessions in Asia Minor, which were both insincere and unrealistic.

Six days after Metaxas spoke to the King the Government attached a new condition to its offer of Greek intervention in the War: Greece demanded that the Entente Powers should provide 500,000 men to assist the Greek Army in its operations against Turkey. It was common knowledge that no such army was available at the time when the Allies were hard pressed on the Western Front and the Eastern Front and desperately needed men for their campaign in the Dardanelles. However, Douglas Dakin, the English historian of Greece, wrote that "the Greek offer was genuine."[11]

The Greek offer of 22 March 1915 to the Entente, if genuine, was only half-hearted; but the Greek fear of Bulgaria was real and strong; so was Greek belief that Bulgaria, because of her geographical position, because of her grandiose aspirations against Serbia and her other Balkan neighbours, because of King Ferdinand (a millionaire who kept his money in Austrian banks), sooner or later would join the Central Powers. On 1 April it was learned that Bulgaria had secured a loan of 200 million francs from Austria and Germany. The following day a Turko-Bulgarian agreement made provisions for the transportation of war material through Bulgaria for Turkey. Still the Allies believed that Bulgaria would soon come out on their side and refused to give guarantees for the territorial integrity of Greece as was demanded in the Greek offer of intervention, so as not to offend Bulgaria.

That summer of 1915 King Constantine fell seriously ill with pleurisy. The King's sickness became a subject of political intrigue and exploitation both by the Royalists and the Liberals. The monarchists suggested that the King's sickness was caused by the harassment and ill-treatment he had suffered at the hands of the warmongering Venizelists. The miraculous ikon of Our Lady of Tenos was brought over to Athens. With great pomp and ceremony, in Constitution Square, while the crowd wept and knelt in prayer for the ailing King, the ikon was delivered by the prelates of the Church to the Queen, who placed it in the sickroom of the King. The King continued to be ill and the Royalists carried on in government, alleging that that was no time to trouble the King with affairs of state. When elections were finally held the Liberals returned 184 deputies out of 310.

The National Opinion Party of Demetrios Gounaris gained only 90 deputies, but his Government refused to step down, claiming that the King was in no position to perform the duties involved in a change of government. Both George Streit, the King's privy councillor, and Gounaris the Prime Minister, were against such tactics; but Metaxas advised the King to make use of the exceptional right given to him by the Constitution, and postpone calling the new Government for one month. The Liberals accused the

---

11 Dakin, *Unification*, p. 207.

Royalists of using the illness of the King as a pretext to prolong their rule; if the King was too ill to perform his duties, then a Regent should replace him as provided by the Constitution. Metaxas, who advised the King, had weightier reasons. Streit noted in his Diary on 10 August, 1915: *"In the afternoon I was visited by Ioannis Metaxas, who expounded on the military aspect of the war which is definitely inclining in favor of Germany..."*[12] If the Royalists held out a little longer, perhaps the European War would be resolved before they handed over the destinies of the country to the Liberals.

The new Parliament met on 16 August. Constantinos Zavitsianos, a Liberal deputy, was chosen Speaker of the House. The following day the King asked Venizelos to form a government, which was sworn in on 23 August 1915. While Metaxas was suggesting to the King that he should convince Venizelos to turn Greek foreign policy toward Germany, Venizelos considered his re-election (although his majority fell from 75 per cent to 60 per cent) as a renewal of the people's approval of his interventionist policy on the side of the Allies. When Venizelos was called by the King to receive the mandate, he had agreed to pursue a policy of neutrality "if the present conditions remain unchanged;"[13] but as soon as he was in power he renewed his pledges to Serbia against a Bulgarian attack.

On 6 September 1915 King Ferdinand signed a treaty of alliance and a military convention with Germany. Bulgaria was promised most of Macedonia, plus the Dobrudja district if Rumania joined the Allies, and the Kavalla region if Greece joined the Allies. In a last-minute bid, the Allies persuaded Venizelos, the Greek Prime Minister, and Pasic, the Serbian Prime Minister, to agree (on 14 September) to Macedonian concessions to Bulgaria. But to no avail; on 21 September 1915, two days after the Germans launched their attack on Serbia, Bulgaria abandoned her opportunist policy and ordered a general mobilisation. After preparing and waiting for almost a year, King Ferdinand was anxious to annex Macedonia, even Salonica, before the Austrians took it for themselves. The Bulgarian mobilization caused great alarm to all parties in Athens. The Liberals wanted to rush to the help of Serbia, but the Royalists, convinced that the German armies could not be halted, were firmly against intervention.

The day after the Bulgarian mobilisation was ordered, Venizelos requested the King to authorise a general mobilisation of Greek troops as a deterrent to any Bulgarian intentions against Serbia. King Constantine agreed that the Greek forces should be mobilised, but only "as a precautionary measure" for the security of Greece and not in any way in connection with the Bulgarian threat to Serbia. Venizelos once more reminded the King of the Greco-Serbian Treaty of Alliance. A Bulgarian attack on Serbia would unquestionably provide the *causus foederis* for Greek intervention. Why

12 George Streit, *Dairy*, II, p. 59.

13 Markezinis, *op. cit.*, IV, p. 139.

allow the Bulgarians to crush the Serbs and then turn south and attack Greece? Was there any doubt about their intentions? The King remained unconvinced. He argued that Serbia, engaged on the Danube by the Austrians and Germans, could never put in the field 150,000 men against Bulgaria as the Greco-Serbian Treaty of Alliance specified. "What about the Allies?" suggested the Prime Minister. "Will they not be prepared to place that number of men at our disposal?" The King did not believe so. His military advisers had assured him that Germany was winning the War and, as he had observed in a private conversation with Zavitsianos six days earlier, he "would rather abdicate than allow Greece to be found in the camp of the defeated."[14] The prospect of fighting the Germans alarmed him. He said to the Prime Minister: "How would I ever be able to face the Emperor if I took part in a war against Germany?"[15]

Venizelos: *Your Majesty, having failed to persuade you, I am very sorry, but it is my duty, as representing at the present moment the sovereignty of the people, to tell you that this time you have no right to differ from me. By the elections of 13 June 1915 the people have approved my policy and given me their confidence; and the electorate knew that the foundation of my policy was that we should not allow Bulgaria to crush Serbia and expand overmuch so as to crush us tomorrow. At this point, therefore, you cannot depart from this policy: unless of course you are determined to set aside the Constitution, in which case you must say so clearly, abrogating the Constitution and assuming full responsibility by a Royal Decree.*

Constantine: *You know, I recognise that I am bound to obey the popular verdict when it is a question of the internal affairs of the country; but when it is a question of foreign affairs, great international questions, I think that so long as I believe a thing is right or not right, I must insist upon its being done or not being done, because I am responsible before God.*

Venizelos: *Alas, this is the theory of monarchy by the Grace of God, unhappy Greece!*[16]

The Prime Minister offered his resignation but the King asked him to stay on and first sign the order of mobilisation on which they had agreed. As Venizelos was ready to depart he suggested that Constantine should find out through the German Minister in Athens what guarantees and advantages Germany would be prepared to offer Greece in return for her continued neutrality. As soon as Venizelos reached Athens he sent a message to the King asking him not to proceed with his overtures to the German Minister. The King had gone to bed with a high fever. Bewildered by Venizelos' change of mind, he telephoned Count Mercati, the Court Marshal, instructing him to tell

14 C. Zavitsianos, *Αναμνήσεις* [Memoirs], I, p. 81.

15 *Ethnikos Dichasmos*, p.38.

16 *Vindication*, p. 105 this dialogue is given as reported by Venizelos himself to the Chamber on 26 August, 1917.

Venizelos that he on his part should also refrain from sounding the Allies about sending troops until they met again. When Count Mercati called to see Venizelos he found him in conference with the Allied Ministers. The Prime Minister, as soon as he had greeted the King's emissary, announced that he had just sounded the British, French and Russian Ministers and was assured that the Allies were ready to despatch 150,000 men to Salonica.

The order for Greek mobilisation was issued on 23 September 1915. King Constantine, on his own initiative, assured Sofia and Berlin that the mobilisation was purely a defensive measure and that he had no plans to fight anybody unless his country was attacked first. Three days later, on 23 September, England and France officially informed the Greek Government that the Allies had begun landing troops in Salonica. Three days after General Hamilton and his staff arrived in Salonica. On 2 October Venizelos yielded to pressure from the King and issued a *pro forma* protest against the Allied landings.

The Royalist press in Athens compared the Allied landings in Salonica to the German violation of Belgian neutrality. Metaxas was indignant. In his articles, years later, he accused Venizelos of violating the Constitution which, by Article 99, clearly stated that "Without a law no foreign army can be used in the Greek service, neither can it be stationed in the country nor pass through it". Metaxas called Venizelos a statesman of the Entente, not of Greece. On the other hand, the Allies contended that according to the Protocol of London of 3 February 1830, which was the first official recognition of Greek independence, any one of the three Protecting Powers, Britain, France or Russia, could send troops to Greece if the other two signatories had no objection. The consent of Greece was not necessary.[17] The Greek Parliament debated the issues in a stormy atmosphere. On 4 October Venizelos delivered a bellicose speech, asserting the determination of the Government to abandon its "benevolent neutrality" toward Serbia and actively assist her in her struggle for survival. This was one of the most tempestuous meetings in the history of the Greek Parliament and it lasted till five o'clock the next morning.

The Opposition accused Venizelos of agreeing to cede Eastern Macedonia to Bulgaria while Bulgaria never intended to come out on the side of the Allies, which would have allowed Greece to save Hellenism in Asia Minor. The Prime Minister answered that from the moment Bulgaria mobilized all offers to her were *null and void.* At one point George Theotokis, the deputy from Corfu, asked Venizelos what he would do if, while marching by the side of the Serbs, he came face to face with German and Austrian bayonets. "My duty", replied the Prime Minister. When a vote of confidence was taken at the end of the session, one hundred and forty-two approved the Government's policy

17 By Article 8 of the 1830 Protocol. See Cosmetatos, *op. cit.*, p. 102 ff

(plus the 10 Venizelists Ministers who did not vote on questions of confidence) while 102 voted against.

The King read the Minutes of the all-right session in Parliament the next morning and summoned Venizelos to go to see him at three o'clock that afternoon. As soon as the Prime Minister arrived at the Palace the King made it clear that he disagreed with his foreign policy, especially his remarks that Greece would fight, if necessary, against Germany. The Bulgarian threat against Serbia was not a purely Balkan affair for which the Greco-Serbian Treaty had provided. It was part of a general European conflict in which Serbia had been involved for some time. The King did not accept Venizelos' explanations in Parliament that the Allied troops came to Salonica on their way to assist Serbia. The actions of the Prime Minister "already today definitely place us by the side of the Entente." Venizelos remarked that the only solution of the question of neutrality was its abandonment. The King reminded him that, according to the General Staff, abandonment of neutrality was absolute madness. Then Constantine pointed out that the Allies had landed only 13,000 men in Salonica, not 150,000 - it was merely a trick to involve Greece without risking anything themselves. Venizelos then reminded the King that the recent elections showed that the Greek people approved his interventionist policy. A long discussion of the constitutional question followed this remark. Then the two men fell silent.

At last Venizelos suggested that the King should cable the Kaiser and explain to him the reasons for his disagreement. "It is not a question of the Kaiser, it is a question of disagreement between us,"[18] snapped the King testily. As the Prime Minister seemed determined to drag the country into war, the King dismissed him from office: this according to Article 31 of the Greek Constitution, which states that "The King appoints and dismisses his ministers."

The next day, 6 October, Prince Demidov, the Russian Minister in Athens, cabled Petrograd. *"The premature declarations of Venizelos in the Chamber provoked a rupture between him and the King. Unfortunately Venizelos allowed himself to be carried away; he declared his interventionist policy, contrary to our advice, without awaiting the completion of this mobilisation and the development of the grave events that were taking place... His haste is indeed a piece of folly, especially as he knows the endeavors of the King to keep out of the war."*[19] As Venizelos moved out, Metaxas moved in. Under general mobilisation Metaxas was called back to his old post as second-in-command on the General Staff.

The King asked a moderate politician, Alexandros Zaimis, to form a new government. This included Admiral Paul Koundouriotis, General Yiannakitsas and the former

18 Markezenis, *op. cit.*, IV, p. 52.

19 Cosmetatos, *op. cit.*, p. 55.

Premiers George Theodokis, Stephanos Dragoumis and Demetrios Gounaris. The Liberals, who commanded the majority in the Chamber, promised to give the new Ministry their provisional "tolerance." Zaimis cabled to all Greek Legations that the policy of his Government would "rest on the same essential basis as that followed by Greece since the beginning of the European War."[20]

On 9 October the German General August von Mackensen captured Belgrade. Two days later the Bulgarian Armies crossed the border north-east of Nish and attacked Serbia. The news created a fluster in the Allies capitals where the various "Balkan experts" were confidently predicting that King Ferdinand would certainly come out on their side because he drank his tea in the English way and was "almost" an English gentleman. The Turkish comedy of the previous fall was replayed by the Bulgarians to the end. On 15 October Britain declared war on Bulgaria and the next day France followed suit. The French General Maurice Sarrail was sent to Salonica to take over the command of the Allied Armée de l'Orient. The French, despite Clemenceau's warning, sent more troops to Salonica. On 9 October there were only 15,000 French and 5,000 British troops on the Macedonian Front. By the end of October there were over 30,000 men, including the Tenth British Division from Gallipoli.

The Royalists stuck to their original position of neutrality and the Greek General Staff rejected a request from the Serbian Staff for the preparation of combined military plans. On 11 October, the day Premier Zaimis gave his negative answer to Serbia, Venizelos, speaking in Parliament, said: *"Let us suppose that the Treaty with Serbia has never been concluded ... Can the Greek State allow one of the Balkan States ... to destroy another State which is part of the [Balkan] balance, while Bulgaria will expand to such an extent?"*[21] To allow such an upset in the Balance of Power in the Balkans was to endanger the integrity of Greece. Venizelos thought that the question was not whether Greece should join the War but when she should join. "Whatever the outcome of the War on the other fronts," he said, "it would be better for Greece if she took her seat at the Peace Conference occupying Bulgarian lands, or at least with her territorial integrity untouched, by the side of four still great Powers already her Allies."[22] Venizelos said that "none could with certainty forsee the outcome of the European War. Still, certain military men who had studied in Germany and were under the influence of German propaganda were certain of German victory and proclaimed so."[23] He himself believed that as the initial German attack was checked, time was working on the side of the Allies. He admired German organisational efficiency, but he thought that as time passed the Allies would be able to master their inexhaustible

20 E. S. Forster, *A Short History of Modern Greece, 1822-1956* ^{3}(London, 1958), p. 92.

21 *Ethnikos Dichasmos*, p. 26.

22 *Ibid.*.

23 *Ibid.*.

resources in men and materials, and this advantage would finally decide the fate of the War.

It was a long and bitter speech. "We are outside our free parliamentary system," the Liberal leader harangued the Chamber. In matters of foreign policy the opinion of the national representatives was ignored. "This body", he said, "has ceased in essence to be representative of the national sovereignty and is transformed into a simple assembly, a club, I could say, of the notables of the Greek people."[24] Two years later, on 13 August 1917, speaking in Parliament about Zaimis' responsibility in repudiating the Treaty with Serbia, Venizelos said: "The greatest dishonesty which a State can commit is to repudiate a promise to help another State after using that promise to obtain a corresponding pledge of mutual assistance."[25]

Now that the Bulgarian cat was out of the bag, all lands formerly promised to her could be promised to Greece and Sir Edward Grey was back at his old game again. On 16 October, writing to Sir Francis Elliot, the British Foreign Minister offered to Greece Western Thrace (with Dedeagatch) and the Island of Cyprus. The Germans had already offered Cyprus to Greece and so the Greek Royalists, who believed that the Germans would win the War, declined the British offer. The following day, 21 October 1915, Sir Edward withdrew the offer hurriedly. The Germans and the Bulgarians were sweeping through the Balkans and the Greek Government decided that the best course was to sit still, hoping that the raging storm would pass them by.

On 21 October 1915 Metaxas submitted a detailed memorandum to Premier Zaimis in which he reviewed the military situation in the Balkans and described the predicament of the Serbian Army. The Germans, he said, had managed to divert large armies to the Balkan peninsula because of their successes on the Eastern Front and because they held on to their defences on the Western Front. The Allies, hard pressed in Europe, could only send limited numbers of men to Macedonia. "Thus," Metaxas concluded, "the fate of the Balkan peninsula does not only indirectly depend on the outcome of the War in Europe in a political sense - because the terms of the Peace would be influenced by the outcome of the War - but it also depends directly in its military aspect on the course of the War on the European fronts."[26] For Greece to hope for any measure of success substantial Allied reinforcements would be required. The despatch of such reinforcements could only be possible if the Allies had the upper hand on the European fronts. At that time they did not.

---

24 *Ibid.* This speech, plus many others, and other useful material, is printed in English (slightly different from my translation) in *Greece in her True Light: Her Position in the World-Wide War as Expounded by El. K. Venizelos, Her Greatest Statesman in a Series of Official Documents* (New York, 1916).

25 Quoted by Forster, *op. cit.*, p. 93.

26 Metaxas, *Dairy*, II, p. 439. The memorandum is included in the *Dairy*, pp. 433-439.

On 25 October the Serbs, desperate, informed the Greek Government that they had no objection if Greece occupied Gevgelija, Doiran and Monastir (Bitola) an area with Greek populations which Greece had had to give up during the Second Balkan War in order to win the Serbian alliance against Bulgaria. This would have secured the rear of the Serbian Army and prevented the Bulgarians from cutting off communications with Salonica, from where Serbia, using the free zone of the port, provisioned her armies. But again the answer from Athens was no. General Sarrail then made an effort to advance from Salonica up the Vardar Valley to Demir Kapu and occupy these places himself. This was the first enterprise of the Allied Armée de l'Orient and it ended in defeat at the battle of Krivolak on 27 October 1915. General Sarrail returned to Salonica, saved by King Constantine, who personally intervened with the Kaiser to halt the advancing Germans from crossing the Greek border. With the Vardar Valley lost to the Germans and Bulgarians, the retreating Serbian Army turned west toward Prilep (the civilian population fleeing too), in bitter winter, harassed by hostile Albanian bands, and reached the Adriatic.

In Athens the epic struggle of the Serbs and their tragic misfortunes had a disturbing effect. The shabby treatment by the Greek Government of these "ancient allies" angered the people, who thought that their old traditions of friendship and honor were betrayed. The Liberal deputies were waiting for an excuse to withdraw their vote of sufferance and topple the Government. On 4 November 1915 General Yiannakitsas (1853 - 1923), the Minister of War, insulted the Chamber in some remarks he made and when asked to apologise, he refused: a heated debate followed and Venizelos indicted the Government for unconstitutionality and challenged a vote of confidence. 147 deputies voted against the Government, 114 in favor and 3 abstained. Zaimis resigned. The King (after appointing General Yiannakitsas as his aide-de-camp), instead of asking the leader of the parliamentary majority to take over, called upon another Royalist, Stephanos Skouloudis, a seventy-eight year old banker millionaire (who, incidentally, had made his money in Turkey) and asked him to form a government. At the same time the King dissolved the Chamber and called for new elections.

The dissolution of Parliament on 11 November 1915 and the proclamation of new elections brought to a head the constitutional question in Greece. By disregarding the majority party and bestowing the mandate on a favorite leader, King Constantine set a fatal precedent for Greek democracy. (The pattern was repeated twenty years later by his son, George II, which led to the Metaxas dictatorship of August 4; and by his grandson, Constantine II, in 1965, which led to the recent dictatorship of the the Colonels.) The constitutional crisis of 1915 was a major landmark upon the road to the totalitarian regime of the Thirties and therefore it deserves some attention in this study.

The right to dissolve Parliament was first adopted in Greece by the Constitution of 27 March 1832. According to Article 243, the Prince could dissolve the Lower House if it was violating the constitutional laws or attempting to assail the rights of the Nation or the Prince. At the same time as he dissolved Parliament the Prince, that is the King, had to proclaim new elections, to be held within two months and summon the new Parliament within three months of the dissolution. This provision was incorporated in the Constitution of 1844. But it is noteworthy that the 1844 Constitution, although based on the Belgian Constitution of 1831 (which in its turn was based on the French Constitution of 1830), did not copy Article 25 of the Belgian prototype, which stipulated that all power derived from popular sovereignty.[27]

The liberal Constitution of 1864 established a "Crowned Democracy," *vasilevomene demokratia*, not a "Constitutional Monarchy," which emphasised the democratic character of the Government rather than the idea of a contract between the King and his people - more in accordance with French ideas than English. The 1864 Constitution provided that the Royal Decree for the dissolution of Parliament had to be signed by the whole Cabinet (Article 37), while the previous Constitution of 1844 required only the signature of the competent Minister (Article 30). This was a step in the right direction. The 1864 Constitution also stated that the deputies represented the Nation, not their constituencies.

The first serious clash between the Crown and the Government occurred in the aftermath of the Cretan revolts of 1841 and 1856. In 1866 the Cretans unilaterally proclaimed their union with Greece, the Turks resorted to massacres and the Greek Government adopted a bellicose attitude toward Turkey. International opinion was against infringing on "the integrity of the Ottoman Empire" and King George I, returning from one of his frequent tours in Europe, adopted a policy of moderation, as advised by the Powers, contrary to that of his Government. Premier Koummoundouros resigned in 1867, despite the fact that he had a good majority in Parliament: 120 deputies to 80 of the Opposition. Twenty-five years later, in 1892, the Crown was again at variance with the Chamber, but this time the Prime Minister, Deliyiannis, refused to resign, so the King formally dismissed him. The Royal Decree for the dissolution of Parliament was countersigned by the new Prime Minister, who was appointed by the King.[28] It should be noted that Deliyiannis did not question the King's right to ask

---

27 The question of sovereignty was hotly debated in 1974 when, after the collapse of the last dictatorship, the National Assembly deliberated on the introduction of a new Constitution. Finally the Assembly decided in favour of the principle that sovereignty derives from the Nation (*Ethnos*), not from the People (*Laos*). This is important: the Nation is an unfathomable, mystic entity which various individuals or groups might claim to represent while the people means vote counting and such prosaic democratic practices. Semantics had something to do with the choice also. The Right Wing called themselves *Ethnikophrones* -- the National-Opinion Persons, a name first used to describe the Royalist Party in 1915. The word *laos, the people*, has been more and more associated with the Left Wing and often the Communist Party.

28 Deliyiannes lost in the elections which followed. Addressing Constantopoulos, his successor, 11 March 1903, he said: "You must thank God that the 1892 elections were not favourable to any party because had I been in the majority I would have taught you what ministerial responsibility

anyone to form a government if the new government sought the confidence of the House soon after its formation.[29] This, of course, left plenty of room for Crown interference, but it also served the interests of the politicians, who could bargain and manoeuvre for advantage and privilege: it became customary for deputies, most of them independent local politicians, to wait and see which way the wind was blowing before giving their vote of confidence; as their political career depended mainly on their ability to distribute "privilege" (the infamous *rousfeti*) to their voters, it was important for them to be on the winning side. A deputy without influence in government or prospects was as good as a dead deputy and the Greek electorate would turn a blind eye - - if not actually an admiring eye - - to any kind of deals which would transfer a politician to the winning side. Under this system the King's privilege to nominate a new Prime Minister could easily be abused and the King came to feel that he could form any government he wanted. The Prime Minister, of course, acquired great powers as a distributor of patronage.

Charilaos Tricoupis was the first to challenge this practice. In a famous article entitled "Who is to Blame?" published in Kairoi (The Times) of Athens on 29 June (O.S.) 1874, Tricoupis attacked the Crown as the source of all evils in the misgovernment of the country, especially after 1867, and for the minority governments which had ever since ruled Greece; the King's habit of giving the mandate to a minority group was "an abuse of the constitutional privilege of choosing and dismissing Ministers, leading to the multiplication of parties and the disruption of the system of government."[30]

King George I, a sensitive monarch who knew a clever man when he saw one, instead of becoming antagonistic toward Tricoupis, invited him to form a government himself. In the Speech from the Throne on 11 August 1875, written by Tricoupis, the King said that an indispensable condition of those called upon to govern the country was to possess the majority of the representatives of the people. This came to be known as the principle of *dedilomeni* i.e. the declared, or manifested majority. The idea was that if this majority was not evident from the elections it could be determined when the new House voted for its Speaker; the King would be expected to ask the leader of the party from which the Speaker was elected to form a government. Tricoupis' pure doctrine of declared majority was not always followed. It was Deliyiannis' version that was eventually adopted - a minority government could be appointed by the King if it secured the confidence of the Chamber or dissolved if it did not. If Tricoupis' doctrine had been

---

means when you countersign a decree dismissing a Minister in office." Parliamentary Debates, I T, a, 390 and 403. Quoted by B. S. Markezinis (the son of S. Markezines, the historian) in *The Theory and Practice of Dissolution of Parliament* (Cambridge, 1972), p. 153.

29 When Parliamentary rules were adopted in 1927, this was the principle which was accepted -- a mandate could be given to a minority party on the condition that it appeared immediately before the Chamber to seek vote of confidence.

30 Charilaos Tricoupis, *Kairoi*, (29 June (O.S.), 1874).

followed, dissolution would hardly ever have been used because only a majority party would have been able to advise it. (In Great Britain, for example, dissolution is usually advised by the majority party). Parliamentary stability would have been guaranteed and, unless there was a sudden desertion of Government deputies, Parliament would enjoy and exercise power for its four-year term. Unfortunately, not only the Crown but the politicians themselves did not want such stability as it would undercut their ability to distribute patronage and undermine their position.[31]

After the 1909 Revolution of the Military League King George I gave the mandate (on 19 September 1910) to Eleftherios Venizelos, who was the choice of the Revolution although very few deputies supported him. When Venizelos sought a vote of confidence there was no quorum in the Chamber because the old parties stayed away to protest the Revolution and the yielding of the King to its demands. Venizelos interpreted the no quorum as a no vote of confidence and King George I obligingly dissolved Parliament (25 October 1910) and proclaimed new elections to be held on 11 December 1910. The old political parties abstained from these elections - the first abstention in the parliamentary history of Greece - arguing that the dissolution was unconstitutional. Thus Venizelos was returned with an overwhelming majority!

The Constitution of 1911 accorded the King the right, by Article 31, to appoint and dismiss his Ministers. Article 37 stated that the King could dissolve the Chamber and call for new elections. According to Article 32, the King declares war and concludes peace. When King Constantine, after Venizelos' first resignation in March 1915, dissolved the Parliament and gave the mandate to Gounaris, one of the Opposition leaders, the King was acting according to custom and the Constitution. He was taking the issue of going or not going to war, on which he differed from his Prime Minister, directly to the people. The elections of 13 June 1915 were won by the Liberal Party, but the King, under the pretext that he was too sick to perform the constitutional duties involved in a change of government, did not recall Venizelos to the premiership until 23 August, only to dismiss him again on 5 October immediately after the Prime Minister had received a vote of confidence following a major debate on foreign policy. Zaimis, who succeeded him, stayed in power as long as he was "tolerated" by the Liberals, the majority party. When Zaimis fell the King appointed the extra-parliamentary government of Skouloudis and dissolved Parliament for the second time within less than seven months over the same issue.

Venizelos did not question the King's right to dissolve Parliament and give the mandate to a minority leader. He had never accepted, as he stated on several occasions,

31 Tricoupis also introduced another most important constitutional measure - the establishment of large electoral constituencies. This eliminated the small local bosses, the successors of the earlier kotza basis of Ottoman times, and encouraged the two-party system. The number of deputies were reduced from 245 to 150. The work in Parliament was also made easier.

Tricoupis' principle of declared majority-*dedilomeni*.[32] Neither did he question the Crown's right to disagree with the responsible government, although he did question the ability of Zaimis' minority government to conduct the foreign policy of the country. Venizelos considered the first dissolution of Parliament a Royal prerogative: the Crown differed with the Government on a major issue of foreign policy and the people were entitled to make their own decision through general elections. The second dissolution of Parliament was a different matter. The people had decided and Venizelos believed that the King had no right to differ with the representatives of the people and so, according to him, the second dissolution of Parliament was unconstitutional. The right of the King to dissolve Parliament, as a constitutional student recently wrote, "though in theory an institution intended to preserve a balance of power between the Executive and the Legislative, resulted in practice in the suppression of the vote of Parliament and, ultimately, of the electorate."[33]

It should be noted that even Tricoupis (and later Admiral Paul Koundouriotis) accepted that Parliament could be dissolved if it was no longer "in harmony" with the will of the people. But how could anyone, without elections, divine the will of the people? King Constantine had no doubts in his mind what "his people" desired and what was best for them; moreover, he considered himself accountable to God for the present and future happiness of his people. Especially in questions of foreign affairs he believed that his opinion should be followed. The Greek Crown had a tradition of considering itself the final arbiter of the international relations of the country. A change in foreign policy usually meant a dissolution of Parliament and a new government. No doubt the dynastic ties of the monarchy were an asset for a weak country like Greece; but they were also often a liability, especially at home. "It was, therefore, inevitable", as the Greek historian Kaltchas, wrote, "that the divergence of opinion on the question of the entry of Greece into the War should resolve itself into a conflict between the King, who claimed to be the authentic voice of that mystic entity, the nation, and the Prime Minister, who was the leader of the ephemeral parliamentary majority in a constitutional state."[34]

The constitutional conflict and the internal political strife centered so much on the person of King Constantine that a short description of the King's character and the circumstances surrounding his private life may be appropriate here. The first Greek

32 Speaking in Parliament on October 21, 1915, Venizelos said: "I accept the right of the Crown to disagree - in accordance with the Constitution - with the responsible Government." In a newspaper article on November 22, 1934, Venizelos wrote: "The right to dissolve Parliament (on the first occasion in February, 1915) belonged to the King and I never recognized the principle of *dedilomeni* of the late Tricoupis. " *Ethnikos Dichasmos*, p. 139.

33 B. S. Markezinis, *op. cit.*, p. 130.

34 Nicholas Kaltchas, *Introduction to the Constitutional History of Modern Greece*, (New York, 1940). p. 140.

Prince to be born on Greek soil, Constantine bore the illustrious name of the last Palaeologue Emperor of Byzantium and was brought up as a symbol of the nation's expectations to recover Constantinople one day and revive the Byzantine Empire. Even after he became *Vasileus* - - King - he was still known as *Diadochos* - - the Crown Prince or the Heir, as a reminder of the inheritance he would one day enter into. As a young man Constantine studied at the University of Heidelberg and at the Berlin War Academy. In Germany Constantine met his future wife, Princess Sophia, the daughter of the German Emperor. The first military experience he had was in the disastrous War of 1897 when he was made a scapegoat for the defeat of the Greek Army. It was then that he first met Metaxas. The two men fought side by side in the Balkan Wars, which brought great honors to Constantine. After the 1913 assassination of his father, George I, an urbane and cosmopolitan gentleman, Constantine came under the influence of two strong-minded women: the first, the Romanov Queen Olga, the Queen Mother, now spent most of her summers with her relations at the Czarist court. The loss of her husband turned her to religion and she had little patience with worldly affairs. The second, Constantine's wife, the Hohenzollern Queen Sophia, was known for her Germanic strictness. The Queen disliked all Greek politicians and was antagonistic to Venizelos from the time of his arrival from Crete; but she was very fond of Metaxas whom she called affectionately *Yiannaki* - Johnny. The Court of Constantine was a Royal one and his visitors were rarely the Greek politicians, as was the case with the Court of his father, but princes and dukes from the Royal houses of Europe. Although the Greek court had not the means to put on a show like the Romanovs in Russia or the Hohenzollerns in Germany, it certainly had something of the spirit of these two courts where the King's mother and the King's wife had originally lived. Constantine was in touch with his brother-in-law the Kaiser and he had had, since his childhood, a close friendship with his cousin, the illfated Czar Nicholas. As his chief political adviser Constantine chose George Streit, a Germanophile professor of German descent; but the King felt most comfortable with his military colleagues, most of them trained at the Berlin War Academy. The Greek General Staff was sometimes referred to as the "Grand Staff" in imitation of its German counterpart and Ioannis Metaxas was sometimes called "the Prussian."

Constantine loved his country - he was certainly "Greek" and not Russian or German or even Danish and he was honest (as his friend, Admiral Mark Kerr, testifies) in his desire to keep Greece out of the European War. He wanted to please the Allies because of a sense of historical gratitude to them as the old guarantors of Greek independence and because he realised how vulnerable his country was to the Allied fleets; yet Constantine did not want to offend the Kaiser because of the Queen, the Kaiser's sister, and because he felt a genuine admiration for German military organization and German might. Although a great leader of men on the battlefield, Constantine had little imagination and found the international diplomatic intricacies bewildering, the Kaiser's demands brutal, the Allied policies perfidious and Venizelos' tactics reckless; although brave and authoritative, the King was really a weak man, suspicious and obstinate as only a weak man can be. Although he wanted to observe the Constitution, he could never quite accept the fact that all final decisions and all final responsibility rested with the elected Government. Constantine did not see his role as the moderator in the political arena and interpreter of the Constitution but as a father to his people and their protector against the unscrupulous politicians.

This paternalistic image of the soldier-king fitted perfectly into the philosophy of Ioannis Metaxas, who saw in the dynasty the continuity of the national idea and had pledged his sword to serve his King, right or wrong. But Venizelos, although he believed that a Crowned Democracy was the best system of government for Greece, wanted the King to be a mere figurehead and resented his meddling with politics. "In a Parliamentary form of government the Crown never has a personal policy," he said in Parliament on 21 October 1915. Zavitsianos, then Liberal Speaker of the House (and Deputy Prime Minister in the Metaxas government in 1936) wrote in his diary that the problems of Greece during the Great War derived from the fact that Constantine wanted to play the Prime Minister and Venizelos wanted to play the King.

The Royalist government of Stephanos Skouloudis, which was appointed by the King after he dismissed Venizelos, set itself two main tasks: first, to resist all Allied pressures and keep Greece out of the War; second, to prepare the country for elections which would keep the Liberals out of office. The Allies, aware of the Government's intentions, used in turn promises, bribes, threats, arrests, open violence and flagrant violations of Greek territory and Greek sovereignty. The Liberals, rather than lose in the coming arranged elections, chose to abstain and transform their opposition to open rebellion.

Two days after Skouloudis formed his caretaker government, on 8 November 1915, he was asked first by the Serbian Minister and then by the French Minister in Athens what he would do if the retreating Serbs crossed the Greek border. Greece, he answered, as a neutral country, would have to disarm and intern them according to The *Hague Convention*. Switzerland and Holland did exactly that in similar circumstances, but the Allies were incensed by Skouloudis' answer. The following day Skouloudis tried to explain away his remarks and gave fresh promises of the determination of Greece to maintain her neutrality "in the form of the most sincere benevolence toward the Powers of the Entente."

This uncertain attitude of the Greek Government greatly worried the Entente Powers. In Salonica the Allied troops lived in an uneasy peace with the Greek authorities. General Sarrail, defeated in his first engagement on the Macedonian Front, with 60 per cent of his soldiers sick and dispersed in various camps around the city, was constantly afraid that one day or night he would be suddenly attacked from the rear by the Greek Royalist troops acting in concert with the German and Bulgarian troops from across the border. Reinforcements were slow to arrive. French Headquarters came to dislike the whole venture as much as English Headquarters came to dislike the Dardanelles. Clemenceau used to refer to Sarrail and his idle armies as "the gardeners of Salonica". The Germans called Salonica the largest Anglo-French internment camp. Sarrail himself was an irascible soldier who often clashed with General McMahon, his English colleague. In his memoirs, *Mon Commandement en Orient*, Sarrail complained that he was sent to Greece "without official instructions, knowing nothing of the country, or the people, or the events that had taken place since the beginning of the War ... I took as my directives my frankly republican views."[35] Sarrail treated all Royalists as traitors and harassed priests and raided monasteries. He used to say that he had never met a Greek who could not be bought with a little gold. Forced to stay inactive, frustrated, receiving little material or moral support from his country, General Sarrail lived constantly in fear like a trapped animal and no assurances from the Greek Government could relieve his mind.

Lord Kitchener, in his tour of inspection of British forces in the Near East, visited the Macedonian Front on 17 November 1915. General Sarrail tried to persuade Kitchener that strong measures should be taken with the Greeks. Kitchener reported to London that Sarrail thought that "a naval demonstration at Athens should be proceeded with at once," and that "the Greeks ought to be asked either to join us or to demobilise," and the "Germanophile Greek Staff Officers dismissed."[36]

After Salonica Lord Kitchener decided to go to Athens and find out how real Sarrail's fears were. He arrived in Piraeus on 20 November where he was received by two officers of the Greek General Staff, "both ardent Germanophiles"[37] (Dousmanis and Metaxas.) At noon he met the King. Their conversation culminated in a repartee, reported by Kitchener's biographer.

Constantine: *What am I to do when Germany threatens me with a million men?*
Kitchener: ... *Remember the four million England will have in the field next year.*[38]

In the afternoon Kitchener, accompanied by Sir Francis Elliot, the British Minister in Athens, visited the Prime Minister. The Entente Powers, Kitchener told Skouloudis, had no intention of forcing Greece to abandon her neutrality; but they demanded guarantees for the security of their troops in Salonica because certain recent declarations had aroused anxiety. Skouloudis assured Kitchener that the Allied forces in Greece had nothing to fear and objected to the campaign against Greece in the British press. "We have no complaint against Greece", said Kitchener - and went on: But I cannot conceal from you the painful impression created in England by Greece's failure

35 Quoted by Sir Basil Thompson, *The Allied Secret Service in Greece* (London, 1931), p. 81.
36 Sir George Arthur, *Life of Lord Kitchener* (London, 1920), III, p. 199.
37 *Ibid.*, p. 201.
38 *Ibid.*.

to take part in the expedition sent to the relief of Serbia. From the moment when you invited us to Salonica for that purpose, we all believed that you would be at our side. I was myself, at first, hostile to this expedition; but when your invitation, which France had made haste to accept, was read to me in the Cabinet, I did not wish to leave the French alone, and I believed that Greece had agreed to everything that was going on; so I joined in.[39]

The Prime Minister said that he found no such invitation in the Greek Ministry of Foreign Affairs and mentioned that Venizelos had officially declared in the Greek Chamber that he had never invited the Allies to Salonica. "Consequently it is not true that Greece has invited the Allies."[40]

Kitchener: *Is it possible that two great Powers should throw themselves into such an enterprise without being certain that they had been invited to it? How could they know that the word of the Greek Prime Minister carried no authority? If Mr. Asquith, for instance, were to make a statement of policy, no one would think of doubting that England would carry it out.*

Skouloudis: *Yes, because when Mr. Asquith makes a statement everyone knows that he is speaking after consultation with all the elements concerned under the Constitution. That is why his statement binds the nation. But if M. Venizelos invited you, as you say and as I believe he did, despite his vehement denials since, he did so without consulting any of the constitutional elements of the country. Neither Crown nor Chamber nor Cabinet had any knowledge of his step. Consequently, allow me to repeat that Greece never invited you.*[41]

Writing to the British Prime Minister about his conversations in Athens, Kitchener said that Constantine was determined to observe his neutrality, "though later they would fight the Bulgarians when they could do so without risk of being compromised with Germany".[42] The Greek King "was very angry with Venizelos, and said that the latter had not given the Allied troops an invitation to come, in which I (Kitchener) assured him that he was wrong".[43] Lord Kitchener then writes about his talks with the Greek General Staff.

I had some talk with the Greek Chief of the Staff and Colonel Metaxas, of whom the King had spoken to me very highly; they were evidently well primed with German ideas about the war, but were not able to argue that the strain of a prolongation of

39 Quote by Cosmetatos, *op. cit.*, pp. 109 - 110. This quotation and the one on the next page have been retranslated from the Greek; from the Archives of the Greek Ministry of Foreign Affairs; as quoted by Cosmetatos.

40 *Ibid.*.

41 *Ibid.*.

42 Arthur, *Life of Kitchener*, III, p. 203.

43 *Ibid.*

the war could be sustained by Germany. They were evidently much concerned about the Germano-Turkish attack on Egypt and the East, which they looked upon as very serious and for which preparations in heavy guns and munitions were, they said, being made at Constantinople. They curiously enough pressed upon me a concentration of our troops in the Eastern theatre almost exactly the same as detailed in my telegrams (with reference to Ayas Bay) and based their conclusions on the same argument almost word for word. They emphatically stated that there was no other way of preventing the accomplishment of the German project. I, of course, pretended to have never thought of such a scheme and to doubt its possibility; they seemed to be repeating a German phrase when stating "the war would end in Egypt".... Colonel Metaxas spoke a good deal about a possible peace, and appeared to think that Germany's demands would be very moderate.[44]

We also have Metaxas' impression of Lord Kitchener as reported by a Greek journalist and author in an Athenian paper:

He is a great soldier and we understood each other very easily. He was returning from an inspection tour of the English forces. I did not find him very enthusiastic about the Salonica campaign so I tried to reinforce this impression. I pointed out to him how futile it was, especially as Greece was determined to stay neutral. He accepted my opinions completely. The only thing he asked the King - as I have heard - was his word of honor that the Allied troops would suffer nothing from us. I also spoke to Lord Kitchener on the general subject of peace. And I stressed that Germany would be willing to sign without great demands.[45]

If anything, the visit of Kitchener strengthened the hand of King Constantine, who claimed that the British War Minister showed perfect understanding of his position. This came in the heat of the campaign for new elections which were set for 19 December 1915. The Royalists campaigned as the peace party which wanted to preserve Greek neutrality and spare the country the unprecedented slaughter and destruction of the European War. They labelled the Liberals war-mongering adventurers and Venizelos an intriguer and opportunist serving the interests of the Entente. The Gallipoli Expedition was doomed, Serbia was annihilated and the Germans, the Bulgarians and the Turks were kept back from invading Greek soil only by the dynastic connections of King Constantine and the sagacity and courage of his advisers. The Allies violated Greek sovereignty by landing troops in Salonica and Venizelos was accused of plotting with them to destroy the independence of his country. The hardships of mobilisation were placed squarely on his shoulders and an intensive propaganda program was carried out in the Army to discredit the Liberals and the

44 *Ibid.*, pp. 203-204.

45 Spyros Melas, "Ioannis Metaxas" *Kairoi*, (Athens, December 20, 1949).

Allied cause. The Royalists controlled the Army and the Government and, because of mobilization, the whole country. Venizelos was mostly followed by the younger generation and these had been called up and were serving under Royalist officers. It would have taken a reckless man to vote against the Royalists if he had a relative working in the Civil Service or had a son in the Army. Under the circumstances the Liberals were in retreat, so they chose to abstain from the elections. On 22 November 1915 (the day after Kitchener left Athens), they explained their reasons in a proclamation to the Greek people:

We are confronted with an open violation of our form of Government which is daily infringed. Repeated dissolutions and attempts to impose personal policies inaugurate a system of government that can be found only in absolute monarchies such as Prussia ... Holding elections at a time when a great number of Liberal M.P.'s of the last Parliament are serving in the Forces and hence unable to campaign actively ... when the combatant section of the population is in the army ... and when the government is prepared to allow its friends to vote but retains its enemies under strict military discipline ... is only part of the scenery of a political farce unworthy of free nations.[46]

Only 230,000 people went to the polls compared with the 730,000 who voted six months earlier in the elections of June 13. Skouloudis continued to lead a Royalist Government and only Royalists sat in Parliament. The Army leadership had always been in the hands of the Royalists; now any officers with Liberal leanings were dismissed and a systematic indoctrination program was undertaken to teach the rank and file blind obedience to the King. The Liberals were also expelled from all positions in the Civil Service and Public Education. It was an unhealthy state of affairs. Deprived of all legitimate means to criticise the Government and participate in the function of the Constitution, the Liberals were bound, sooner or later, to resort to extra-Parliamentary political action which culminated in open revolution nine months later.

Kitchener did not simply talk to the Greeks; there was a certain measure of arm-twisting, too. On 11 November 1915, Kitchener cabled London: "McMahon tells me 7,500 tons of wheat are being allowed to go from Egypt to Greece. I think all such shipments should be stopped at present. McMahon has still time to stop this wheat. Shall he do so?"[47] Evidently the answer was yes, because a week later, the day before Kitchener arrived in Athens, Sir Francis Elliot, the British Minister at Athens, announced the blockade of Greece. All importation and distribution of cereals, and also of petrol, was controlled by the British Legation, a fact which gave Sir Francis great power to exercise pressure on Greek Governments. On November 23 1915, two days after Lord

46 Quoted by B.S. Markezinis, *op. cit.*, p. 177. The whole text in Greek of Venizelos' Proclamation is printed in Spyros Markezinis, *op. cit.*, IV, Supplement.

47 Arthur, *op. cit.*, III, p. 197.

Kitchener left Athens, the Allies handed Greece an ultimatum demanding the withdrawal of Greek troops from Salonica, the use of roads and railways and the right to search for and destroy foreign submarines in Greek waters. The blockage lasted until 12 December when the Greek Government agreed to withdraw all troops from Salonica, except one division which was allowed to remain in order to ensure public order. On 27 November 1915, the Greek General Staff telegraphed instructions to the Greek Legations abroad to inform the Governments where they were accredited that the position of the Entente forces in Macedonia was precarious, that they had better leave and that the Greek Army was willing to cover their retreat and disembarkation. This attitude infuriated the Allies. At a meeting in Paris on 6 December the decision was taken to hold the Macedonian Front at any cost.

The year 1916 was one of the bloodiest years in the history of Modern Europe. For four months, from 21 February to 23 June, the Germans hurled their armies at the defences of Verdun without being able to break through. Here alone the French lost 350,000 men, the Germans only somewhat less. Then for the next four months, from 1 July to 25 October, the English and the French waged the Battle of the Somme - also unable in their turn to dislodge their adversaries. On the Somme the British losses reached over 400,000 men, the French 200,000 and the Germans between 400,000 and 500,000. In the Caucasus the spring campaign of the Russians brought them to Erzerum on 16 February, Bitlis on 2 March and finally, on 17 April, to Trepizond where the Greek inhabitants of Pontus welcomed them as liberators.[48] But the great Brusilov Offensive, which began on 4 June 1916, was finally halted after two and a half months with the loss of a million Russians.

This unprecedented slaughter in Europe had a direct impact on the situation in Greece. The Allies, because of their ignominious withdrawal from the Dardanelles (which was effected between 19 December 1915 and 9 January 1916) and because of their constant fear and uncertainty about the Macedonian Front, paid less attention to the niceties of diplomatic protocol and adopted increasingly hostile measures toward Greece designed to coerce her into their camp, or force the Royalists out of office. Metaxas, who believed that the fate of the War would be finally decided in Europe and

---

48 The Turks, before abandoning Trepizond, transferred all administrative authority to the Greek Metropolitan Chrysanthos and entrusted to his care the safety of the Moslem civilian population left behind. Chrysanthos received the Russian Commander-in-Chief Grand Duke Nicholas at the Greek cathedral where a *Te Deum* was sung. Prince Nicholas, aware of the shortcomings of the Russian Armies and perhaps foreseeing the coming political events in Russia, asked the Metropolitan to mediate with the Turks for an understanding between them and Russia. The Turks declined. The Greeks of Pontus paid dearly for their welcome to the Russians. Metropolitan Chrysanthos went to Paris to plead the cause for a Greek Republic of Pontus at the Conference of Versailles. Later he became Archbishop of Athens. In his book, *The Church of Trepizond,* he gives a vivid account of the persecution of the Armenians in Pontus of which he was an eye-witness.

not in the Balkans, desperately tried to preserve Greek neutrality and save Greece from the holocaust; rebelling against the flagrant violations of Greek independence by the Entente Powers, Metaxas often advised actions which exposed him to accusations of compromising the honor of his country. Unfortunately no papers are preserved in his Archives of this period, but the events of 1916 were vehemently debated by Metaxas and Venizelos in the Thirties.

All through 1916 the relations between the Royalist Government and the Allies steadily deteriorated. The Allies were especially exasperated when the Greek Government refused permission on 5 April 1916 for the transportation of the Serbian troops through Greece from Corfu to the Macedonian Front. The Allies said that the sea journey round Cape Matapan would have exposed the Serbian forces to the certain danger of German submarines. Their first request was for the use of the Patras-Salonica Railway; then, when this was denied, for the use of the Itea-Bralou Road. The Greek Government said that they did not want to expose the Greek population to the infectious diseases from which the Serbs suffered. In fact, the Government was afraid that the Serbian troops would join the Venizelists and attempt to overthrow the Royalists. In the end the Government consented to the sailing of the transport ships through the Corinth Canal. The Serbian Army made the journey to Salonica safely; but the Venizelist press in Athens, led by Keryx (The Herald) was loud in its protests against the Government over this incident.

By 29 May 1916, about 10,000 Serbian troops had been transferred to Salonica and joined the Entente forces on the Macedonian Front. The Allied lines of defence were greatly extended. General Sarrail could now think of resuming operations. An English cavalry regiment crossed the Struma River into Eastern Macedonia and a division of colonial troops advanced north along the river. In Western Macedonia Sarrail occupied Florina without opposition from Greece. The Germans and Bulgarians over the border believed that the Allies were preparing to occupy Eastern Macedonia as a first step before launching an attack against them. Between the two sides stood the frontier fortress of Rupel, commanding the exit of the Struma River defile, the only natural passage through the mountains between Bulgaria and Eastern Macedonia. (Fort Rupel was to be one of the major links in the famous "Metaxas Line" in the Second World War). On 10 May 1916, Metaxas in Athens personally issued orders to the Greek troops to defend Fort Rupel against any attack. On 23 May 1916 the German General Headquarters informed the Greek Government that in view of the movements of the Entente forces in Macedonia, the Germans and Bulgarians had to occupy Fort Rupel "for defensive reasons". Skouloudis, the Greek Prime Minister, tried to dissuade the Germans, but to no avail. The only thing Germany and Bulgaria promised was to respect Greek sovereignty over the area and to accord fair treatment to the Greek inhabitants. On 26 May 1916 German and Bulgarian troops appeared in the Struma Pass and demanded the surrender of Fort Rupel. The Greek defenders of the Fort, acting on standing orders, answered with fire. The Greek Commander of Eastern Macedonia then discovered that his communications with Athens, which went via Salonica, had been cut. Metaxas in later years argued that General Sarrail ordered the disruption of communications because he knew about the standing orders for the defence of Fort Rupel and did not want the Greek military authorities in Eastern Macedonia to be in touch with Athens, who might issue fresh orders. It was a trap, Metaxas claimed, aimed at forcing a clash between the Greek troops and the Germans. When the news of the German demands reached the Greek General Staff (over an untapped telegraph line from Kavalla *via* the island of Euboia), Colonel Metaxas immediately went to see the Prime Minister, convinced him that on no account should Greek troops clash with Germans and, on the spot, wrote the order for the surrender of Fort Rupel. The Minister of War was called in to initial the order, which was also later initialled by the Chief of Staff. "Thus", the historian William Miller writes, "the Government of Constantine 'the Bulgar-slayer' gave up to the Bulgars the historic fortress, which the Nicene Emperor, Theodore II Laskaris, had captured from their ancestors."[49]

The surrender of Fort Rupel - and Eastern Macedonia, which followed soon after - made a most unfavorable impression, both at home and abroad. Even among the Greek Royalists the effect was disturbing. Ion Dragoumis (the brilliant political writer who was arrested and brutally killed by Cretan gendarmes in Athens in August 1920) speaking in Parliament after the invasion of Eastern Macedonia by the Germans and Bulgarians, reminded the deputies that Fort Rupel was only a short distance from Demi-Hissar where three years earlier, in 1913, "the Bulgarians buried alive Metropolitan Melenikou and one hundred other Greek notables ..."[50] The Liberals accused King Constantine and the Greek Royalists of connivance with the Germans and Bulgarians. Premier Skouloudis denied any such slanders on 6 June 1916. Nevertheless, when Venizelos returned to power in 1917, he brought to trial the octogenarian ex-Premier for failing to resist by force the German-Bulgarian invasion of Eastern Macedonia. Metaxas was in exile in Corsica during the trial. Venizelos, writing on 15 November 1934, said that the efforts of the Skouloudis Government to prevent the invasion of the country were undoubtedly sincere, "but the proposed arguments were undignified and only the mentally retarded could believe that they would be successful."[51] Taking issue with this insult, three days later Metaxas answered *"on the part of the vilified and silent dead, whose arguments would have also been*

---

49 William Miller, *The Ottoman Empire and its Successors, 1801-1927* (Chambridge, 1936), p. 531. King Constantine was sometimes referred to as such after the Second Balkan War against Bulgaria in imitation of the Byzantine Emperor Basil II *Bulgaroktonos*, "the Bulgar-slayer" (936-1025).

50 Quoted by Spyros Markezinis, *op. cit.*, IV. pp. 133,. 246.

51 *Ethnikos Dichasmos*, p. 106.

superfluous if their vilifier had not, through a snare, brought to our country foreign armies and fleets and had not incited foreign Powers to oppress, to tyrannize and starve the Greek people merely to satiate his passion against the King and in order to subjugate by foreign bayonets the Greek people who were in revolt against him."[52]

Metaxas was singled out as the chief archvillain of this "treachery". Throughout the rest of his life Metaxas had to suffer the poisoned barbs of his enemies who always mentioned Fort Rupel when they wanted to call him a coward and a traitor. But for Metaxas, who took full responsibility for the surrender of Fort Rupel, the matter was crystal-clear: The Allied troops in Macedonia provoked the German decision to cross the Greek border. If the weak, isolated Greek forces had offered any resistance, the Allied forces of General Sarrail, close behind, would have come to their assistance, and this would have brought about the armed intervention of Greece on the Allied side and an irrevocable state of war against the Germans and Bulgarians. But this was not what the Greek Government and the Entente Ministers had agreed upon on 10 December 1915: according to Article 4 of that Agreement, if the War was transferred to Greek soil because of Allied troop movements, the Greek forces would withdraw in such a way as to allow the two warring parties to fight it out.[53]

The Allies, who had repeatedly violated Greek neutrality, and who had demanded and occupied the fortresses of Greek Central Macedonia, were outraged at the surrender of Fort Rupel (which was compared in the western press to Verdun in importance, although it was nothing of the sort). Anxious about the safety of their troops on the Balkan Front, the Allies were now determined to settle the Greek question and once and for all remove any threat from the Royalists of Athens. A partial blockade of Greece was immediately imposed and all ships carrying coal were seized and their cargo confiscated. General Sarrail, on 21 May [O.S.], King Constantine's Name Day according to the Old Calendar observed then in Greece, in order to prevent a demonstration in Salonica where a Te Deum in honor of the King was to be sung at the Cathedral, proclaimed martial law in the city and all districts occupied by Allied troops in Macedonia and took over control of police, postal and telegraphic services. Five days later, the Greek Government, in an attempt to show that they had no intention of attacking Sarrail, demobilised twelve "classes". But this did not appease the Allies. The following day, 9 June 1916, the English occupied the island of Thasos off the coast of Eastern Macedonia where they established a naval base. The Italians, in the meantime, claiming that Greece was not to be trusted not to surrender Southern Albania (Northern Epirus) to the Germans, asked permission, and were allowed by the Entente Powers to extend their occupation from Valona to all Epirus, including the city of Jannina.

---

52 *Ibid.*, p. 112.
53 *Ibid.*, p. 111.

On 14 June 1916 Sir Edward Grey sent for the Greek Minister in London and complained that the Greek police had failed to disperse a hostile demonstration against the British Legation in Athens; the British Foreign Minister claimed that the Greek police was under German direction and that highly-placed persons in Greece were acting on German instigation and had allowed Germany and Bulgaria to occupy Greek forts. A week later, on 21 June 1916, the British, French and Russian Ministers in Athens handed an ultimatum (euphemistically called a Note) to the Greek Government in which, after calling attention to the anti-Entente policies of the Greek Government, they demanded the complete demobilisation of the Greek Army, the immediate dismissal of the Skouloudis Ministry and its replacement by a non-political government, the dissolution of Parliament and the proclamation of new elections (to be held on 17 September 1916), and, finally, the discharge of certain Police officials suspected of anti-Entente activities. The ultimatum ended by saying that "the Protecting Powers leave to the Hellenic Government the entire responsibility for the events which would supervene if their just demands were not immediately accepted."[54]

"The whole nation felt deeply the injustice and the outrage of which it was a victim, but, to avoid worse things, yielded all along the line, as becomes the small and the weak",[55] wrote a Greek historian. Stephanos Skouloudis resigned on 19 June and the King sent for Alexandros Zaimis, the only non-Venizelist acceptable to the Allies, who was sworn in on 23 June. On 8 July 1916 the Allies made an effort to explain the reasons for their intervention; their interests had nothing to do with it, they protested, and the blame was squarely placed on the internal situation in Greece: "The Greek Constitution had been ignored, the free exercise of the right to vote restricted. Parliament had been dissolved twice within less than a year ... and elections held amidst general mobilisation in a manner proving that the present Parliament did not reflect public opinion." Venizelos, unfortunately, made no protest against this patronizing attitude of Britain, France and Russia toward Greece.

Zaimis, the new Premier, wrote to the Entente Ministers in Athens and accepted the Note-Ultimatum. The Chiefs of the Police were dismissed and, on 27 June the Decree of general demobilisation was published. John Metaxas was removed from the Army leadership. He wrote in 1934: "After the Zaimis Government took over, Mr. Dousmanis and I were privately informed that higher State interests connected with the good relations of Greece and the Entente made necessary our departure from the General Staff."[56] On his departure Captain Metaxas was promoted to Colonel. He was pleased to leave the Army, he wrote, and he discouraged any attempt for his reinstatement,

54 The Allied Note is reprinted almost in its entirety by Cosmetatos, p. 189. For the French text, see A.F. Frangulis (Frangoules), *La Greece et la Crise Mondiale* (Paris, 1926), I. p. 380 ff.

55 Cosmetatos, *op. cit.*, p. 189.

56 *Ethnikos Dichasmos*, p. 124.

"because I decided irrevocably to get out of the Army completely so that I could enter politics in the coming elections."[57]

The demobilisation was a direct threat to the authority of the King and the General Staff. "It will make Greece unable to defend herself, to protect her honor,"[58] commented Metaxas. The demobilized men felt deeply that a great injustice was done to Greece; their fierce sense of honor was outraged by the humiliations that they and their King were subjected to. Many of these men had spent the last four years under the colors since the First Balkan War; their officers had served much longer. Forced into civilian life at a time when, because of the Allied blockade, inflation and unemployment were rampant, the 360,000 demobilised men found it difficult to readjust. A great number of them came to Athens and other urban centers, seeking work that could not be found. The more frustrated they became the more they hated the Allies and blamed Venizelos - "the cause of so many evils",[59] as Metaxas wrote. "Wasn't it he who brought the Anglo-French to Macedonia by a crafty stratagem? Wasn't it he who, by his Note of 21 June - because the Allied Note was actually his - imposed on Greece the end of what he calls the "criminal" mobilisation and thus deprived his fatherland of every means to defend Eastern Macedonia?"[60]

The demobilized men organised themselves into Leagues of the Reservists, an association of officers and men, in order to avow their devotion to Constantine, their ill-treated, long-suffering King, a victim of the perfidious Allies and the traitor Venizelos. An announcement of the establishment of the "Association of Officers" which soon became part of the Leagues of the Reservists stated that "the purpose of the new organisation is to strengthen the Royal factor and restrain the political parties from excesses".[61] Colonel Metaxas, whose removal from the General Staff was demanded by the foreign representatives of the Entente, the consummate strategist who had led these veterans to victory in the Balkan Wars, who had kept them out of the disastrous campaign in the Dardanelles, Metaxas, who, even when the King wavered, alone stood firm, was the natural and inevitable leader of the movement. But what began as an expression of reasserted dignity and independence soon deteriorated into politics and violence - a movement not unlike the later German *Freikorps*. Under the leadership of Ioannis Metaxas, the Reservists (*Epistratoi* in Greek) dominated all civil life, beat up,

57 *Ibid.*. The next time Metaxas was promoted (from Colonel to Lieutenant-General) was on his return from exile, On that occasion the Royal Decrees for his reinstatement in the Army, his promotion and retirement were published simultaneously on 7 January 1921. In both cases his promotion was granted on the understanding that he would immediately leave the army. It was, as it were, a case of being „kicked upwards."

58 *Ibid.*.

59 *Ibid.*, p. 130.

60 *Ibid.*.

61 *Ibid.*, p. 108.

kidnapped and killed opponents, sacked homes and terrorised both the cities and the countryside. Now that the official State was destroyed by the Allied Note, the private armies of the Reservists became the real State which exercised authority. From June 1916 to June 1917, when the Allies finally deposed the King, packed Metaxas off to Corsica and restored the Liberals to office, the arbitrary power of the Reservists reigned supreme. And, although the Allies demanded in June 1917 the dismantling of the Reservists, their sinister influence continued until 1920, when the Royalists returned to power and absorbed them into the State structure.

Venizelos had often charged that the general mobilization which was kept for nine months at great expense when the Royalists had no intention of entering the War, had only one purpose: the Royalist indoctrination of the men and the increase of the political power of the General Staff. The demobilization provided Metaxas with a rare opportunity. Venizelos wrote: "By utilizing the results of the systematic teaching through which the mobilized Reservists had been poisoned for nine months, Mr. Metaxas had organised the Leagues of the Reservists which had exercised such great and such disastrous influence on the Nation during the years of 1916-1920. These Leagues openly aimed at strengthening Royal absolutism."[62] And as an example Venizelos quotes a telegram sent to the King by the Reservists of Roumeli: "Your Majesty, we trust in you alone, our fate and the fate of the Fatherland, as the true successor of the Paleologues, entrusted by Divine Providence to realise and guard the ideals of our race."[63] Venizelos, in this newspaper article which he wrote in 1934, added a prophetic note: "The activities of the Leagues of the Reservists in those days provide us with a picture of what Greece would have to suffer if she had the misfortune to be subjected one day to the dictatorship of Mr. Metaxas."[64]

Three weeks later John Metaxas eloquently defended the Reservists and his association with them. On 11 December 1934, he wrote in a newspaper article:

The demobilization had another, unexpected consequence. The demobilized Reservist officers and men organised by their own initiative the Leagues of the Reservists. Who were these Reservists? They were the youth of Greece ... they were the soldiers of 1912 and 1913 who carried the Greek flag over the battlefields of Macedonia, Epirus and the Aegean Islands. They were scientists, merchants, industrialists, professionals and artisans, workers, farmers, bourgeois, peasants, the whole youth of Greece! They were not enemies of the Entente ... But they were all of them, to a man, enemies of Mr Venizelos. Not because they remained mobilized for nine months, as he would like to represent it, but because they saw at first hand, with their own eyes, the humiliations of their Fatherland by the foreigners, the humilia-

62 *Ethnikos Dichasmos*, p. 118

63 *Ibid.*.

64 *Ibid.*.

tions which Mr. Venizelos himself provoked, directed, encouraged. They all knew that it was he who brought foreign armies to Greece and did everything to make them stay and enslave her ... For these men the King was the symbol of the traditions of the Greek race. He was the victorious leader with whom they themselves had corrected on the battlefields of 1912-1913 the errors of Mr. Venizelos' policy in those days.

With the demobilization, as they were being transferred from Macedonia to the interior of Greece, in the trains, in the ships, they, by themselves, alone, organised the Leagues of the Reservists. They themselves adopted this name. It was a primitive movement, irresistible, elemental. It was the protest of the Greek soul against the destruction of the independence of the Fatherland ... Mr. Venizelos has accused me in the past and he is accusing me today, that I was the organiser of this movement. But I consider this an honor. Yes! The whole Greek youth of that day alone created the movement. And I placed myself in its service and I struggled with a multitude of other unforgettable comrades so that the movement acquired a definite organisation ... I wish today also the youth of Greece, the former combatants, inspired by those pure ideals, would raise itself in revolt once more against the internal enemies and dangers, and once more I should be happy to offer it my small services.[65]

When Metaxas did become the dictator of Greece two years after these lines were written, some people at home and abroad expressed their surprise: Metaxas reminded them that he had spoken and written about his intentions all his life. The above is as clear a warning as could be. But, as in other historical instances, people were not listening. The Liberals, too, attempted to organise their own reservists; but with the Royalist Leagues of the Reservists in complete control of the country, the Liberal officers had no chance and the coming revolutionary movement of the Venizelists in Salonica absorbed the more hot-blooded amongst them. Still, someone - probably the enterprising agents of the French Secret Service - almost succeeded in burning to death King Constantine when the estate of the summer Palace at Tatoi was set on fire. The Palace was in the middle of a thick forest in the foothills of Mount Parnes and the fire started on 13 July 1916 at three distinct points and spread rapidly to the center. The King, driving to investigate, was surrounded by the flames and had to abandon the car and manage to escape at considerable risk through a deep ravine in the mountains. The Palace was burned, three officers and seven men of the Royal Guard lost their lives. It was "a very singular fire," wrote the Italian Minister in Athens, Count Bosdari.

The invading Germans and Bulgarians did not halt at Fort Rupel but pressed their advance into Macedonia. In Western Macedonia the Bulgarians occupied the city of Florina (on 17 August 1916) and in Eastern Macedonia the cities of Drama and Serres. The road to Kavalla was open. The Royalist Government of Athens appealed to

65 *Ibid.*, p. 168.

Germany in a hopeless attempt to stop them. On 27 August Rumania, stirred by the Russian offensive in Galicia and Bukovina, finally declared war against the Central Alliance. In Athens the news sparked off a mammoth demonstration of the Liberals protesting the policy of the Royalist Government and the violation of the Constitution. Venizelos addressed the seething crowds from the balcony of his house on Panepistemiou Street. In his speech the Liberal leader admonished the King to free himself from those persons who exploited the affection the Greek people had for him and who were dragging the Royal House and the country to certain national disaster.

You are the victim of your military advisers, who, with a soldier's narrow outlook and with the hope of setting up an absolutist regime which shall make them masters of the situation, have persuaded you that Germany will emerge victorious from the European War ... The telegrams from the Leagues of the Reservists in which they claim that they are again ready to shed their blood at your first gesture do not correspond to reality because these men were instructed that you had no intention of abandoning neutrality ...[66] *What was the use, demanded Venizelos, of having elections and the Liberal Party returning to power, perhaps then to be called upon to intervene in the War, "when the criminal policy of the General Staff has dissolved the Army and made Greece defenseless?"*[67] *Venizelos exhorted the King to send away those persons who exploited his name and give his attention to rebuilding the national morale of the Army which a long mobilization and foreign indoctrination in the barracks had weakened. The Liberal Party, he said, was not an enemy of the Crown but "a devout observer of the free Constitution" - and the observance of the Constitution was in the best interests of the Crown.*

Metaxas had often argued that if Rumania were to enter the war on the side of the Allies, the Greek position *vis-à-vis* Bulgaria would change radically and many Greeks expected the present development to be the opportune moment for Greek intervention. But the Greek Government, assured by the General Staff that Rumania had no chance in the world and would soon be crushed, kept silent. King Constantine for his part refused to receive the deputation which was chosen by the Liberal mass meeting. Nikolaos Stratos, a Royalist politician who had supported neutrality until then, submitted a memorandum to the King and published a declaration urging participation in the War. It was all to no avail. Two days after the Liberal demonstration, on 29 August 1916, the Royalists organised their own rally in Athens to reaffirm their determination to keep Greece neutral and to express their devotion to the King. The former Premiers, Stephanos Dragoumis, Demetrios Gounaris and Demetrios Rallis,

---

66 See the whole speech in Spyros Markezinis, *op. cit.*, IV., Supplement, pp. 30-32. The speech is reprinted from *Orations of the Greek Parliament* (in Greek), published by *Ethnikos Keryx*, Second Period, IV, pp. 344-345.

67 *Ibid.*.

addressed the crowds from the balcony of Rallis' house, again on Panepistemiou Street. The next day, 30 August, the Allied Fleets under Admiral Dartige du Fournet, lest the Greeks in their excitement had forgotten their presence, staged a naval demonstration at the island of Melos. Thirty-two ships and warships were mustered for the occasion.

In Salonica the Eleventh Greek Division and several other Army units mutinied, while a number of Cretan policemen and Venizelist officers, under the leadership of P. Argyropoulos and Lieutenant-Colonel Zymbrakakis, met on this same day, 30 August 1916 (by a curious coincidence, in the same building which nine years earlier the Young Turks had used as their headquarters) and established a Committee of National Defense. The troops who remained faithful to their oath departed for Athens where the King received them in a solemn ceremony: "With such an Army", he said, "and at the head of men like you, possessing your morale, your sentiments and your faith, I am ready to face no matter what enemy".[68]

On 1 September 1916, the Anglo-French Fleets sailed to Salamis. First they seized the thirteen German and Austrian ships interned there since the outbreak of the War. Then they landed marines at Piraeus, occupied the postal and telegraph offices in Athens and arrested and deported Baron von Schenck, the notorious Chief of the German Secret Service, and some of his agents. But they did not attempt to remove the civil authorities of the country as they were incited to do by the French Secret Service. Some days later, at 7.45 p.m. on 9 September 1916, while the Allied Ministers were holding a meeting at the French Legation in Athens, pro-Entente *agents provocateurs* organised by Commandant de Roquefeuil, the Chief of the French Secret Service, attacked the Embassy building, firing their pistols and shouting "Down with France!", "Down with England!", "Long live King Constantine!" But the British Minister, Sir Francis Elliot, despite the provocation, would not agree to the immediate occupation of Athens. The French sent Marines to guard their Legation and the French Minister at Athens, M. Guillemin, demanded from the Greek Prime Minister the indefinite postponement of the coming General Elections.

The French Minister clearly acted after an understanding with Venizelos, who had realised that, with the Reservists running amok, no free elections could be held at that time. Venizelos, according to the testimony of Zaimis at Premier Skouloudis' trial, proposed that the question of neutrality should not be part of the platform of any political party in the coming elections. The Royalists rejected Venizelos' suggestion. "Precisely then," Zaimis said, "the Minister of France, M. Guillemin, demanded that I should postpone the elections indefinitely".[69] John Metaxas discussed these events in his newspaper articles in 1934. "Was Mr. Venizelos afraid of the elections?" he wrote.

---

68 Forster, *op. cit.*, p. 111.

69 *Ethnikos Dichasmos*, p. 130.

"Then, what about his Note of 21 June by which he imposed the elections? What about his claim that the King violated the Greek Constitution? What about the liberties of the Greek people? What about his assurance to the Allies that he was followed by 80 per cent of the Greeks?"[70]

Premier Zaimis, forbidden on the one hand by the Allies to carry out the elections for which he had expressly assumed office, and controlled on the other hand by the Palace in such a way that he could not cooperate with the Allies, regarded his position untenable and resigned on 11 September 1916. Six days later the King asked Kalogeropoulos to form a new Government. The new Prime Minister began his term of office by initiating legal proceedings against the rebel soldiers and police officers of Salonica. The Ministers of the Entente at Athens refused to have anything to do with him and he resigned hurriedly. The King then asked Spyridon Lambros, a university professor in the field of Medieval History, to try his luck.

Lambros filled his cabinet mostly with fellow professors. Compiling anthologies must have always been a professor's pastime, because the Paris press promptly dubbed them "the Cabinet of Anthologians."

On 11 September 1916 General Hadjopoulos and the Fourth Greek Army in Eastern Macedonia surrendered without a shot to the invading German armies. The British fleet, under Admiral Thursby, which had established a naval base at the nearby island of Thasos, kept a close watch on the coast of Eastern Macedonia and forbade the approach of any Greek supply or transport ships. Kavalla was on the brink of starvation. Metaxas argued later that the aim of the Allies was to force a confrontation between the Greek forces and the Germans and Bulgarians. When Hadjopoulos asked for his troops to be transferred to Old Greece, the British refused; instead they offered to transfer them to Salonica. General Hadjopoulos and most of his men, rather than go to Salonica and join the rebels of the National Defense, chose to give themselves up to the Germans. The General and 8,000 men were sent to Goerlitz [Lower Silesia] where they were interned as "guests" and not as prisoners of war until the conclusion of peace. The day after the surrender of the Greek Army in Eastern Macedonia, the Bulgarians entered Kavalla. The country was shocked; many feared worse disasters ahead. On 26 September 1916 Venizelos slipped out of Athens with his friends - in an escapade staged by Commandant de Roquefeuil which was described as a carnival masquerade. Captain Chamonard, who was an eyewitness, said in his testimony to the Naval Commission of the French Chamber: "Doubles of M. Venizelos paraded themselves while Venizelos himself and his companions, disguised with false beards, made for a

70 *Ibid.*.

restaurant at Phaleron; officers of the (French) Intelligence Service, accompanied by women, created an uproar in order to distract attention..."[71]

When the report of Commandant de Roquefeuil was read to the French Cabinet it was greeted with laughter. Admiral Dartige du Fournet, who was at the time anchored at Salamis, wrote in his Memoirs: *"Le Service des Renseignements organisa ce départ comme un scénario de carnaval dont il eut mieux fait de taire les détails pénibles que de les raconter avec complaisance."*[72] Metaxas, quoting the above, said that he, too, would ignore the details of this episode because he was ashamed of the Greeks involved, whoever they were. And he added: "But how dearly and with how much blood we, the Greeks, paid for these roisterings and escapades of Mr. Venizelos' associates!"[73]

Venizelos and his entourage boarded the Greek ship Hesperia, made available by his friend the shipowner Empeirikos and, escorted by two Allied warships, the British *Fearless* and the French *Magon*, sailed for Crete. There he was joined by Admiral Paul Koundouriotis, the hero of the Balkan Wars. At Chania, the main city of the island, a proclamation was issued announcing the formation of a Provisional Government under a triumvirate made up of Venizelos, Koundouriotis and a third yet undisclosed member. This was General Danglis, who joined the revolutionaries later but who was still in Athens, arranging his secret departure. After the proclamation was read, Venizelos said to the crowds: "Allow me to express the wish that the Crown, even at this last moment, getting rid of its evil advisers and placing itself at the head of the national forces, will turn resolutely toward the road which the national interests demand."[74]

In Crete Venizelos received declarations from the islands of Samos, Chios, Lesbos, Lemnos, and Ikaria that they were joining his movement. After Crete Venizelos' party sailed up the Aegean, stopping at several islands, and reached Salonica on 9 October 1916, where the Committee of the National Defense placed itself under the orders of the Provisional Government. The National Schism was thus translated into reality. Old Greece (the Peloponnese, Continental Greece, the Ionian Islands) remained Royalist and neutral. New Greece (Crete, the Aegean Islands, Northern Greece) joined the Pro-Entente movement of Venizelos. There followed a mass exodus of Liberals from Athens to Salonica. From Chania Venizelos telegraphed Guillemin, the French Minister at Athens. "If on arrival in Crete I was obliged to declare that my movement was not against Constantine, I did it solely not to expose the Allied Powers. Otherwise I am convinced that the King would have delivered himself to Germany irrevocably."[75] He

71 Quoted by Cosmetatos, *op. cit.*, p. 222.

72 Dartige du Fournet, *op. cit.*, p. 131.

73 *Ethnikos Dichasmos,* p. 171.

74 Markezinis, *op. cit.*, IV, Supplement, p. 3.

75 Ethnikos Dichasmos, p. 145. Guillemin sent this telegram to the French Foreign Ministry for their information; there it was communicated to Isvolsky, the Russian Ambassador in Paris; Isvolsky in

also telegraphed Briand, the French Premier, congratulating him on the recent successes of the French troops on the Somme, expressing his faith and warm wishes for the final victory of the Allies. As soon as he arrived in Salonica Venizelos requested the Entente Powers to recognise his Government. Italy, which did not want to have a rival for the spoils of victory at the future peace conference, was strongly against it. Britain was wary before giving her support to a rebellion against the lawful King of the country. On 21 October Prince Demidof, the Russian Minister at Athens, telegraphed Petrograd that Sir Francis Elliot had warned Venizelos that Britain would not support his movement if it was anti-dynastic. Venizelos cabled Elliot: "The Provisional Government never had and has not now an anti-dynastic program." But "The Greek Army shall henceforth be inspired by strictly democratic principles, and ... the country shall no longer be governed by Prussian methods."[76] Finally, at the Conference of Boulogne on 30 October 1916, the Allies decided not to recognise the Provisional Government in Salonica because they were afraid that it might lead to civil war in Greece at a time when they had enough difficulties on their hands on the Macedonian Front; so they continued to retain their Ministers at Athens, while Britain and France agreed to grant a loan to Venizelos to assist him to raise an army which could take its place under the Allies High Command on the Macedonian Front. On 8 November Asquith, the British Prime Minister, speaking at the Lord Mayor's Banquet, said: "M. Venizelos has assured us, and we do not doubt it, that his efforts and his organisation are in no sense directed against the throne of Greece. His sole object is to ensure that Greece takes a worthy part in a world-wide struggle for liberty."[77] The Provisional Government at Salonica was a government *de facto*, if not *de jure*, and although in revolt against Athens it published all laws under the Royal coat-of-arms and the title "Kingdom of Greece."

One of the first acts of the Provisional Government was to declare war against Germany and Bulgaria; but it was not as easy to recruit soldiers and only on 22 October was a first battalion able to leave for the front. Even in Crete mobilization was only partly successful. "Send deputies to stir up the zeal of the population and allow them 500 drachmas for travelling expenses,"[78] instructed Venizelos. When in some islands the Reservists protested that they would only respond to an appeal from the King, Venizelos cabled: "Send some Cretan gendarmes."[79] In Chalcidique Captain Kondylis, (who was later made general by Venizelos), imprisoned men and executed

---

his turn cabled it to Petrograd on October, 15, 1916. The telegram was included in the Russian diplomatic documents which the Bolsheviks published in 1922.

76 Quoted by Cosmetatos, *op. cit.*, p. 235-6.

77 *Ibid.*, p. 250.

78 General Sarrail in *Revue de Paris* (December 15, 1919), pp. 694-700. Quoted by Cosmetatos, *op.cit.*, p. 224.

79 *Ibid.*.

deserters in his efforts to build a pro-Entente army. The Allied Secret Services came to the help of Venizelos and several stubborn islands were invaded by Allied agents and Greek irregulars in their pay. The usual pattern was to storm these defenceless islands in the middle of the night, kidnap the local Royalist authorities and wake up the local Venizelists, who would then gather the next morning at the central square and "spontaneously" proclaim the deliverance of their islands from the tyranny of the King and send jubilant telegrams of devotion to Venizelos.[80] The English Secret Service also participated in these stunts. Author Compton Mackenzie, the chief of the English Secret Services in Greece, describes in his *Athenian Memories* how he kidnapped the Royalist chieftains of Skiathos in their sleep, while J.C. Lawson, a Cambridge don with a temporary commission as Naval Intelligence Officer in Crete, in his book *Tales of Aegean Intrigue* boasts of his part in what he calls "The Conquest of Cerigo" on behalf of the Greek Liberals.

80 One day the news reached Athens that the island of Cythera (Cerigo) was occupied by the Allies. Neither the British nor the French Minister at Athens could explain it. They cabled London and Paris. Nobody had ever heard of Cythera or if they had it was in connection with the old legend about the birth of Aphrodite, the goddess of Love. What had happened? A British Naval Intelligence officer, J.C. Lawson, in private life a Tutor and Fellow of Pembroke College, Cambridge, led an expedition against Cythera, rounded up all Royalist officers and notables and transported them for internment in Crete. Venizelists were installed in their places. When instructed from London to quit, the enterprising don promptly organized the islanders into the Republic of Cythera which proclaimed its alliance with the Entente and claimed the protection of the Allied Fleet. J.C. Lawson recounted some of his more successful exploits, including the above, in *Tales of Aegean Intrigue,* London, 1920). Sir Compton Mackenzie, the Chief of the British Intelligence, gives vivid accounts of some of his own "stunts" in Athens and the islands in his books. The first two volumes of Memoirs by Sir Compton Mackenzie were entitled *Athenian Memories* and *First Athenian Memories* and were published in 1931. The third volume was entitled *Greek Memories* and was suppressed under the Official Secrets Act in 1933 and reissued six years later in 1939. (In 1943 Sir Compton Mackenzie published an account of the Italian attack on Greece under the title *Wind of Freedom.*) And then again, in 1960, he published a new book, *Greece in my Life,* in which he describes a journey to Greece and his experiences as secret agent in Greece during the Great War. His publishers were Chatto & Windus of London.

National Humiliation

On 5 November 1916 forces of the Provisional Government, attacked the Royalist troops in Ekaterini, a town guarding the entrance to Thessaly, the bread basket of Greece. The attack was made by 200 Cretan *Amynites*, troops of the *Ethnike Amyna*, the National Defence, under the command of Nikolaos Plastiras, who was to figure prominently in the later history of Modern Greece. Another unit of Liberal troops marched from the city of Verroia toward the river Aliakmon. The King, who had been assured by the Allies that the Venizelists would not invade his territory if his troops were sent to the Peloponnese, considered the attack sheer treachery and immediately stopped the surrender of his batteries and munitions. The King believed that a trap had been prepared to disarm him so that the rebel troops of the Provisional Government could attack him from the north and march, unopposed, to Athens. The reaction of the Royalists was particularly strong. The Athens Government rounded up the remnants of the Venizelists in the Army, the Navy and the Civil Service. The officers who had deserted to Venizelos were cashiered; magistrates, civil servants and mayors were arrested and imprisoned. Metaxas' Reservists were especially active in these operations. "In the towns and villages the Reservist Leagues made themselves accusers and judges of all who disagreed with them,"[1] wrote Sir Basil Thompson. Venizelist houses were marked and looted and many Venizelists were molested. A wave of terror swept over the country.

As a result of the Ekaterini incident, a neutral zone was established between the territories controlled by Royalist Athens and Venizelist Salonica. But the King refused to give up any more of his arms and ammunition. The patience of the Allies was running out. Admiral du Fournet, who was anchored in the Bay of Saronikos, the Bay of Athens, was given the task of disarming Royalist Greece so that at no time would she be a threat to the Allies in Macedonia. Fournet was a straightforward honest man, but easily taken in by the French Secret Service. Often he was bewildered by the maze of Greek politics, but he believed in carrying out orders, in doing his duty for France.

On 16 November 1916 Admiral du Fournet sent a Note to the Greek Government in Athens demanding the Allied control of the Greek Post and Telegraph Services because there was evidence that they were being used to transmit military information to the Germans. He also asked in the name of France for the surrender to him of the Greek war *matériel* as a counter-balance for the artillery and supplies which were surrendered to the Germans and Bulgarians in Eastern Macedonia.

Three days went by before the Crown Council was convened to consider the demands of the French Admiral. The Crown Council had also to consider a new Note, just received, demanding the expulsion from Royalist Greece of all the diplomatic

1 Thompson, *op. cit.*, p. 175.

representatives (and therefore all kinds of secret agents) of Germany, Austria and Bulgaria. Former Premier Skouloudis warned the Council that the officers, even if the order were given, would refuse to give up their arms.

After the meeting the King invited Admiral du Fournet to the Palace to hear his complaints. The French Admiral explained that the Allies did not trust the Royalists to refrain from attacking *l'Armée d'Orient* of General Sarrail. For this reason he demanded that the King should surrender all his arms. The King retorted that to surrender his arms at a time when his troops were under attack was to invite rebellion. "The matter is now closed", said the King. "The people and the Army will not allow me to surrender the rifles and guns which, indeed, are theirs .... You are giving M. Venizelos hardly disguised protection. You want me to give up arms which he will use against me. You are supporting this man, who is nothing but a rebel and a traitor."[2]

The following day Fournet notified the Legations of the Central Alliance in Athens of the decision of the Entente to expel their personnel within 48 hours. The day after, 21 November 1916, the Royalist Government rejected the Allied demands and at the same time protested to the Neutrals about the treatment Greece was receiving from the Entente.

In the next day or two Fournet was kept busy rounding up the diplomats of the Central Powers. Then, on 24 November, he sent a threatening ultimatum to the Greek Government demanding that by 1 December they surrender 18 field and 16 mountain batteries with a thousand rounds of ammunition, 140 machine guns, 4,000 Mannlicher rifles with 2,000 cartridges per rifle and 50 automatic trucks. The rest of the war *matériel* Fournet wanted by 16 December. If his demands were not met, Fournet said that he would be obliged to take "all the measures which the situation may demand."[3]

For the next few days, "the situation in Athens took a threatening turn," wrote Metaxas. "The popular anger reached its peak. The people rushed to arms."[4] The troops of the Athens garrison were under the command of Lieutenant-General Kallaris, a disciplined officer who was not easily swayed by the crowd. But Metaxas had arranged the transfer from Epirus of Major-General Papoulas, an ambitious and fanatical Reservist.[5] Papoulas was made Chief of the troops of the Active Defence, who were

---

2 Quoted by Cosmetatos, *op. cit.* p. 245. From a telegram to Paris of the French Minister in Athens, M. Guillemin.
The same day the King received yet another Frenchman, Denis Cochin (1851-1922), a new envoy from Premier Briand. Cochin advised Constantine to read chapter Twenty-One of Machiavelli's *The Prince*, where the advice is given to a ruler to take sides when a war is being waged on his borders, otherwise he runs the risk of being attacked by both his neighbors.

3 *Ibid.*.

4 *Ethnikos Dichasmos*, p. 174.

5 General Anastasios Papoulas (1859-1935) had an eventful career. Commander-in-chief of the Greek Army in Anatolia until May, 1922, he was the chief prosecution witness at the Trial of the Six in 1923 when the Prime Minister Gounaris, four of his Ministers and the new Commander- in

mostly drawn from the ranks of the Reservists, and Inspector-General of all Greek troops in the Athens region. According to the historian Ventiris, the decision to resist the Allies was taken at the Officers' Club, "as Metaxas had suggested to Papoulas several days earlier."[6] When the idea was put forward that the Reservists should be used because the regular Army available was too small, General Papoulas suggested that the Reservists should be regularly called up to increase the regiments. At that point John Sayias, the General President of the Reservists, was called and had a meeting with Papavasiliou, an officer on the Staff of General Kallaris. They decided that the Reservists should not be called up but that volunteers should be allowed to join the regular Army. The Reservists, of course, were more than willing to volunteer.

After this meeting General Papoulas went to the Palace and reported to the King. Constantine said:

An action such as you describe might hurt the State because, by adopting such an attitude, we shall find ourselves face to face with the Allies. Nevertheless, even in Germany, where the Army is completely disciplined, when it is a question of national dignity, when it is a matter that threatens the integrity of the State, the forms of discipline retreat and everyone is brushed aside and all cooperate and try to harmonise their actions to the demands and interests of the people and the nation."[7]

According to other reports, King Constantine admonished other officers who went to see him to restrain themselves and avoid any clash with the Allies. General Papoulas, who was put in command of both the Reservists and the regular Army, received his instructions from Metaxas. Papoulas wrote: "In those years I knew that Metaxas' activities and involvement in many matters allowed him to know better than anybody else the real situation."[8] Ventiris comments: "Naturally Metaxas knew the situation, but he would not communicate it to his fellow officers."[9] Metaxas had his own ambitions and kept his own counsel. "The capital of the State", wrote Ventiris, "became the seat of a wide conspiracy in which most of the officers participated. The guiding mind was the former Staff Officer, Ioannis Metaxas. Because of his position near Constantine he inspired confidence in the officers and his instructions were carried out because he was considered the real representative of the King."[10]

---

chief in Anatolia were sentenced to the firing squad for the Greek disaster. Papoulas himself was finally condemned and executed on April 24, 1935 for his part in the Venizelist abortive Revolution of March 1, 1935.

6 George Ventiris, *Η Ελλάς των Ετών 1910-1920* [Greece in the Years 1901 - 1920], vol. II (Athens,), p. 246.

7 *Ibid.*, p. 256.

8 *Ibid.*, p. 245.

9 *Ibid.*.

10 *Ibid.*.

On 26 November, 200 French marines came to reinforce the French contingent stationed at the Zappeion. The next day Zalocostas, the Greek Foreign Minister, sent a letter to the representatives of the Neutral Powers in Athens protesting the Allied control and blockade, the Allied demand for the surrender of Greek war *matériel* and the expulsion by the Allies of the German, Austrian and Bulgarian diplomats. On 27 November, Fournet saw the King again. He writes in his *Memoirs*: "He protested his good faith ... But the affair of the war *matériel* had so excited public opinion and the Army that he felt powerless ...."[11] The next day the Crown Council was convened once more to consider the last ultimatum of the Admiral of the Allied Fleet in the Mediterranean.

The following day, 29 November, Fournet saw the King for the last time. He complained about the way the Reservists were treating the Venizelists and asked for the war *matériel* as was set out in his earlier Note. Constantine held to his earlier position, but the Admiral left with the impression that the King would yield to *force majeure*, which would save his face. The day before, the Reservists had announced that they would oppose by force the surrender of weapons to the Entente. Now a Government decree was issued allowing voluntary enlistment in the Army. More than 10,000 Reservists volunteered the first day and were incorporated into the garrison of Athens. Armed Reservists paraded the streets of Athens, cheered by the excited crowds. Greek marines occupied public buildings. The Greek troops were given orders not to hinder the disembarkation of Allied troops but to follow them in equal numbers and prevent them from carrying out the demands of the Allied ultimatum.

On 30 November 1916 French ships moved into the port of Piraeus. General Kallaris went to the Palace with his Staff Officer Papavasileiou and persuaded the King that the Greeks should not resist. Thus the French occupied the Raouf Barracks. When Metaxas heard of this, "he went to the Palace and put things back in their right place," as a Royalist deputy wrote.[12] "It was Metaxas who forced the King to resistance and it was Papoulas who generated enthusiasm among the multitude in order to resist by force those who demanded the arms of the Greek Army."[13]

At 6:30 p.m. on 30 November 1916 the Greek Government sent its answer to the French Admiral's Note of 24 November. The "measures" which Fournet threatened, Premier Lambros said, would be considered hostile acts ordered by the Government of the French Republic. The King, unable all along to decide which way to go and unwilling to leave the civil authorities to make the decisions and take the responsibility, found himself in a dreadful dilemma. Metaxas had convinced him that armed resistance was necessary and all the King's followers rushed to comply. Now the King began

11 Fournet, *op. cit.*

12 Quoted by Ventiris, *op. cit.*, II, p. 262.

13 *Ibid.*, p. 265.

doubting and worrying about the consequences. He dispatched two of his brothers to the Military Club to persuade the officers to show restraint. The officers would not hear of it. The King then asked the French Military Attaché to tell Fournet that the Army would not give up its guns and that public opinion was behind the Army. Late in the evening, while the French Admiral was in conference with the Ministers of the Entente, the King's Chamberlain, Count Mercati, brought a message from the King asking if the surrender of ten batteries would satisfy them. Fournet could not promise. Count Mercati then handed him a letter assuring him that the legal authorities would maintain public order and that the security of the Venizelists was guaranteed. The letter further read: "These assurances are given, needless to say, on the express condition that neither the Secret Police in the service of the Entente Powers, nor the landing detachments, will indulge in arrests, disappearances, or the deportation of Greek subjects and that the Venizelists will abstain from any act of violence or abuse that may provoke reprisals."[14] The King's messenger then tried to explain that the officers were hostile, that no politician would accept responsibility for the surrender of the war *matériel*, and pleaded for time. Fournet said that he had no choice in the matter, that the instructions of his Government were definite; he reminded the King's envoy that the Note expired at midnight and asked for the King to order his troops not to fire. Metaxas, discussing these events, wrote:

"On the evening of 30 November the people of Athens and the surrounding districts seethed with agitation. Greek military units occupied the exits of Athens. All efforts of the Greek Government to reach a conciliatory solution proved fruitless. The Admiral had certain orders and insisted upon them. Roquefeuil, [the Chief of the French Intelligence Services] who had just returned from France, was egging him on."[15] Again there was an appeal to the U.S. Embassy and the other Neutrals.

Early next day, between 3:00 and 5:00 a.m., on 1 December 1916, about 3,000 Allied troops, mostly French but also some English and Italian, landed in Piraeus and advanced from different directions toward Athens. An infantry battalion remained on the outskirts while the rest of the troops marched in columns into the city. At 11:00 a.m. Allied detachments clashed with the Reservists near the ancient temple of Theseion. Soon afterwards the French Marines encamped at the Zappeion were also involved in the fighting. At midday Prince Demidof, the Russian Minister at Athens, arranged for a ceasefire and tried to negotiate a truce. The King offered to surrender six batteries, but no agreement could be reached. At 4:30 p.m. the battle was resumed. The Reservists attacked the Headquarters of the Allied Police in Athens and the Zappeion where Admiral du Fournet had his headquarters. The beseiged Admiral ordered by

14 Thompson, *op.cit.*, p. 176.
15 *Ethnikos Dichasmos*, p. 175.

wireless the warships of the Allied Fleet in Phaleron Bay to bombard Athens. Most of the shells fell in the gardens and the courtyard of the Royal Palace (the present-day Parliament building). Queen Sophia and the young princes and princesses took shelter in the cellars. The Allied Ministers hurried to the Palace through the deafening bombardment to see the King. Constantine was waiting for them in his study.

Constantine: *Are these your arguments, gentlemen? For two years you have tried by every means to force us out of our neutrality ... do you now want, by waging an undeclared war on us, to force us into the ranks of your enemies?*

Sir Francis Elliot: I protest.[16]

As if on cue, a shell hit the lower part of the wall of the King's study. The Ministers were shaken. The King, a seasoned soldier, remained calm. At 6:30 p.m. agreement was reached and the French, English and Russian Ministers (Count Bosdari, the Italian Minister, dissenting), accompanied by a Colonel from the Greek General Staff, took the five minute walk to the Zappeion to show Admiral du Fournet the document, which had been ratified in the meantime by the Greek Government. The Agreement provided that only six batteries were to be handed over to the Allies and the exasperated Admiral had a good mind to bombard Athens until all the demands of his Note were met. He was eventually dissuaded by the Allied Ministers and at 7.00 p.m. he ordered a ceasefire. Prisoners were exchanged. The wounded from both sides were treated in Greek hospitals. Most of the Allied troops retreated to their ships during the night. The detachment from the Zappeion was withdrawn the next day escorted by Greek cavalry and Greek military trucks carried their equipment.

Casualties of the "Battle of Athens" were heavy, considering that it had all begun as a "pacific demonstration" by the Commander-in-Chief of the Entente Mediterranean Fleet. 57 French were killed and 154 wounded. The British, who had orders not to take part in the fighting, lost 5 men and had several others wounded. The Italians turned back as soon as the firing began and had no losses. (Count Bosdari wrote in his *Memoirs* with naïve simplicity: "We were not fired upon because we did not fire."[17] Of the Greek Army and the Reservists, 30 were killed and 52 wounded by the French and 11 killed and 12 wounded by the Venizelists who joined in the affray. The Reservists also killed 3 Venizelists and wounded 2. Two years later, on the anniversary of the *Noemvriana* (the events of November 1916, Old Style, which Greece observed at that time - in fact early December) Ioannis Metaxas noted in his *Diary*: "A holy day, when the Greek people fought the Anglo-French despotism."[18] He was charged then, while a fugitive in Italy, with high treason for his part in the November disturbances and was sentenced to death *in absentia*.

---

16 Prince Nicholas of Greece, *Political Memoirs, 1914-1917* (London, 1928), p. 244.

17 Quoted by Thompson, *op. cit.* p. 151.

18 Metaxas, *Diary*, II, p. 563.

At last the Reservists had revenged themselves for the humiliations they and their King had been subjected to since the outbreak of the War. The day after the confrontation, on 2 December 1916, the Greek Minister of War congratulated the Athens garrison and "the other combatants." "Your loyalty, self-sacrifice and courage," he said, "have saved the Fatherland which was in danger from enemies who hoped to disturb public order and overthrow the dynasty."[19] After the "victory" over the Entente, the Reservists decided to punish the Liberals for aiding and abetting the hateful foreigners. An orgy of violence followed, unprecedented in the annals of Modern Greek history. The Reservists ran amok. The Venizelist homes, marked beforehand with red crosses, were systematically looted and set on fire while ordinary citizens were dragged through the streets, beaten up, ill-treated, shot at, wounded, imprisoned, killed. 250 Greeks were arrested by the Royalist Police: they were military men like Major-General Aristotle Korakas (1858-1947) who did not approve of the tactics of the Reservists; they were friends and relatives of Venizelist officers who had fled to Salonica, like Pericles Mazarakis, the brother of General Alexander Mazarakis, a high official in the Ministry of the Interior. The journalists who worked on the Liberal papers, such as the Cypriot Achillefs Kyrou, Spyros Nikolopoulos, Demetrios Lambrakis and A. Pournaras, were arrested and the newspaper offices sacked and the printing machines presses destroyed. The former Mayor of Athens, (1914-1916) Emmanuel Benakis, was also arrested, subjected to indignities and thrown into prison. The persecution of the Liberals went on for several days. Finally, their task accomplished, the Reservists were discharged. The Central Bureau of the *Leagues of the Reservists* sent out a circular to the members:

On the occasion of the temporary discharge for a time of the members of the Pan-Hellenic Association of Reservists, accept the fraternal embrace of the Central Bureau for the glorious events that have occurred; announce to all our friends with whom you are in contact that we shall remain here obedient to the word of command and that as for them, they have now only to return to their families, full of pride in the great work accomplished. Let them wait, though, with bayonets fixed, ready to return, when the need arises, and place themselves under the colors in order to fulfil their supreme and sacred duty toward King and Country.[20]

Replete with revenge, the Reservists and the Royalist multitude flocked to the Cathedral of Athens where a Thanksgiving Service took place and a *Te Deum* was sung in honor of King Constantine.

A few days later (on 6 November 1916) Queen Sophia described the *Noemvriana* in a secret radiotelegram to her brother, the Kaiser.

19 Mazarakis, *op. cit.*, p. 219.

20 Auguste Gauvain, *The Greek Question* (New York, 1918), p. 84.

By a miracle we are safe after a three-hours' bombardment of the Palace by the French fleet, which fired without warning. The shells exploded very near us. We took refuge in the cellars. Serious engagements also took place next day in the streets; the revolutionaries fired from the houses. The Army and the people fought in a magnificent manner [on the previous day] and behaved loyally. The page has been turned. It was a great victory against four Great Powers, whose troops fled before the Greeks and who later retreated under the escort of Greek troops. The Mayor has been imprisoned. Many arrests have been made. The panic has subsided. The garrison has been reinforced to ten regiments. Great excitement! What will the demands of the Entente be?[21]

While the Royalists were praying in the Cathedral for King Constantine, the Athens newspapers published a proclamation calling on the people to gather at the parade ground of the Field of Mars on 25 December at 3:00 p.m. in order "to anathematize the thrice-cursed traitor Venizelos."[22] The proclamation admonished: "All without any exception, young, old, men, women and children, throw a stone of anathema against the heinous traitor and assassin of the Fatherland and our King."[23] At the appointed time the people of Athens, headed by the clergy, went to the Field of Mars to perform the ancient ritual of anathema. The Archbishop of Greece, Theocletos, surrounded by eight bishops, threw the first stone, intoning the malediction: "Cursed be Eleftherios Venizelos who imprisons bishops and plots against the King and the Fatherland!"[24] "Cursed be he!" cried the crowd and each then cast a stone upon the cairn. The historian Stavrianos writes: "Sixty thousand Athenians took part in this ceremony, each bringing his stone and his curse."[25] Zalocostas, the Greek Foreign Minister, cabled the Greek Legations abroad the following day: "Multitudes of people, reaching tens of thousands, went to the Field of Mars and threw a stone of anathema against the traitor. At the request of the Trade Unions the Archbishop of Athens took part. ..."[26]

The shock-waves from the *Noemvriana* reached not only Salonica but also Paris, London and Berlin. The history of Greece took a new turn after the *Noemvriana*. Ioannis Metaxas, the "sinister" leader of the Reservists and the "evil" mind behind the

---

21 *White Book*, p. 74.

22 Spyros Markezinis, *op. cit.*, IV, p. 183.

23 *Ibid.*.

24 *Ibid.*.

25 Stavrianos, *The Balkans Since 1453*, p. 568.

26 Telegram No. 9963 of the Greek Foreign Office. Quoted by Ventiris. The historian William Miller in his book *The Ottoman Empire and its Successors 1801-1927*, p. 535, fn, mentions three other instances when the medieval ritual of anathema took place earlier in Greece -- *"in the cases of the traitors at Patras and Nauplia in 1715, of the Athenian primates who favoured the tyrant Haji Ali in 1785, and of Zographos, author of the unpopular Turkish commercial treaty in 1840"*. The custom may have its origin in the Bible story when Shimei stoned and cursed David.

Noemvriana was discreetly asked to withdraw from the General Staff - "Dousmanis and I were asked privately to depart from the Staff for reasons concerning State interests of the highest importance and the good relations of Greece with the Entente," he wrote much later in an article on 21 November 1934.

The Provisional Government at Salonica in a Proclamation issued on 7 December declared that the disturbances in Athens created "an unbridgable chasm between the King and the Nation. The King did not hesitate to sacrifice the highest interests of Hellenism in order to impose his despotism ... in order to assist Germany to win the War ... From this moment King Constantine is deposed from his throne."[27]

The French took these incidents, in which 57 French sailors lost their lives, very seriously. From Premier Aristide Briand downward, the French spoke with rancour of the "ambush" or "trap" of Athens. Clemenceau was disillusioned with the Greeks. "Greece has betrayed her history and her spirit," he declared.[28] In Paris the newspapers were writing that "the brother-in-law of the Kaiser" had trapped and massacred French sailors. Commandant de Roquefeuil, with a flair for propagandist exaggeration, talked about the "Athenian Vespers" -- after the Sicilian Vespers when the French were massacred in Sicily on Easter Monday, 30 March 1282 on the stroke of the Vesper bell. Admiral du Fournet, who had the odious task of carrying out unwise orders based on misleading information from the French Secret Service, had a different opinion of these sad events. "We took part," he wrote in his *Memoirs*, "in an explosion of civil war; in striking our sailors, the Royalists struck the protectors of their political enemies."[29]

Aristide Briand, on hearing the news from Athens, protested to the French representatives there for accepting a few guns to compensate for the humiliating treatment France had suffered at the hands of the Greek Royalists. The French Premier suggested to the Allied Governments the immediate dethronement of King Constantine. But the British had reservations for dynastic reasons, while the Russians and the Italians did not want to see Venizelos returned to power and competing with the first over Constantinople and with the second over Anatolia. The Czar, particularly, objected outright to the removal of Constantine, who was a first cousin of his and a friend. The Greek King also found support in the press of neutral America -- the only international press where his opinions were reported. But the French had a mind to show Royalist Greece their displeasure. Admiral du Fournet was ordered to hand a new Note to the Greek Government on 8 December 1916. Three days later he was recalled and relieved of his duties.

The Entente Note of 14 December demanded reparations for the "outrages" of 1 and 2 December 1916 and the immediate transfer of the Greek Royalist troops to the

---

27 Mazarakis, *op. cit.*, p. 220.

28 Doros Alastos, *Venizelos* (London, 1942), p. 261.

29 Quoted by Prince Nicholas, *Political Memoirs*, p. 245. From Fournet, *op. cit.*, p. 251.

Peloponnese. It also demanded an official apology. The Greek Government promised to satisfy these demands but asked for the lifting of the blockade. As no progress was made, the Entente delivered a new Note on 31 December 1916 which demanded: 1. complete demobilization in Continental Greece, leaving only the bare minimum of troops for the maintenance of public order, and the transfer to the Peloponnese of all war *matériel*; 2. the banning of all meetings by the Reservists north of the Corinth Canal; 3. the prohibition of civilians to carry arms; 4. the release of the Venizelists and all political prisoners who had been arrested during the recent disturbances and compensation to the victims; 5. the official expression of apologies by the Greek Government to the Allied Ministers; 6. a public ceremony of contrition by the Greek Army in the presence of the Entente Forces; 7. re-establishment of Allied controls over Greek telegraph, telephone and mail communications; 8. free use by the Allies of the port-town of Itea on the Gulf of Corinth and the road and railway route from Itea to Larissa to Salonica.

The Note affirmed that the blockade was to be maintained "until satisfaction has been afforded on all the points above indicated." In a Supplementary Note a week later the Allies assured the Greek Government that they would not allow the troops of the Provisional Government at Salonica to take advantage of the withdrawal of Royalist troops and cross the Neutral Zone and occupy Thessaly and Epirus.

Again the Note was accepted but again the Allies suspected that the King was temporizing. So when the Allies met at a conference in Rome on 8 January (the Prime Ministers of Italy, France and Britain and a representative of Russia) they discussed the Greek Question and instructed their Ministers in Athens to hand over a new Note-Ultimatum to Greece. The Ultimatum was issued from the warship *Ambassia* which was anchored at Salamis and was dated 8 January 1917. The Ultimatum demanded the departure of all Greek troops to the Peloponnese within 15 days under Allied supervision. If the Allies were satisfied, they would lift the blockade - otherwise they would occupy Greece "in order to ensure by their own means both on land and on the sea the security of their Army."[30] By this they meant the Allied *Armée d'Orient* on the Macedonian Front. But the Ultimatum also promised that the Allies would respect the desire of Greece to keep out of the European War and promised not to allow the withdrawal of the Greek troops to the Peloponnese to be taken advantage of by the partisans of the Provisional Government in Salonica.

The Crown Council advised the acceptance of the Allied Ultimatum. On 25 January 1917 Greece addressed formal apologies to the four Ministers of the Entente at Athens "for the regrettable incidents of 1 December 1916." Three days later, in Zappeion Square, at the same spot where a French unit had surrendered to the Greeks, Greek

---

30 This Note - Ultimatum is printed in Spyros Markezinis, *op. cit.*, IV, Supplement, p. 84.

Army units, in a humiliating ceremony, marched solemnly by with lowered flags and saluted the Allied colors in the presence of the Allied Ministers and before detachments of the land and sea forces of the four Allied Powers. It was an unprecedented way for a nation to expiate its sins and it wounded everyone to the quick. To emphasise the humiliation, members of the Greek Cabinet were obliged to be present; present was also the Commander of the 1st Greek Army. The command of the Greek units at the parade was under General Prince Andrew, the King's brother. (Father of Prince Philip, Duke of Edinburgh). King Constantine wrote to his friend Paola, Princess of Saxe-Weimar: "And those are the Powers who are supposed to be fighting for Justice and the rights of small nations."[31]

The next day, 26 January 1917, the Greek King and Queen, their spirits sufficiently revived, congratulated Kaiser Wilhelm II on his birthday.

We send you from the bottom of our heart our cordial wishes for Your birthday. We follow with admiration the great events by land and sea. May God soon give you a glorious victory over all Your infamous enemies! They have honored us by the landing of forty Senagalese soldiers, in order to guard the Legation of France. A charming picture of civilization! Affectionate greetings.[32]

The blockade, which was imposed on Greece on 8 December, 1916 by the Allies after the *Noemvriana*, continued to be in force. All imports and exports were strictly controlled. No war *matériel*, foodstuffs, coal and oil were permitted to come in. The Greek Fleet had already been taken over by the Allies; now the Greek merchant ships were requisitioned and many of them were sunk in the following months by German submarines. All mail and telegraph communications were under the censorship of the Allies. Letters were read and destroyed or merely returned to the sender stamped *"Retour pour cause du blocus."* Greece was cut off completely from the entire world. No foreign publications were allowed into the country. The only news came from the *French Radio Agency* which provided sententious communiques.[33]

For seven months Greece suffered severe privations. The blockade started in the middle of a harsh winter and soon there was no fuel for heating; local lignite, an inferior type of coal, and wood from the Tatoi forest (what was left of it after the fire in the previous July) was used to generate electricity and run the railways. But the worst

---

31 Quoted by Dakin, *op. cit.*, p. 215.

32 *Greek White Book*, p. 96

33 The French Radio Agency was financed by Sir Basil Zaharoff, a Greek millionaire born in Mersin, Asia Minor. Zaharoff made some of his money from the building of the Baghdad railway. During the Great War he was also a munitions merchant. He was a friend of royalty and politicians on every continent. After the Great War he established a Foch Chair at Oxford and a Haig Chair at the Sorbonne. Zaharoff staunchly supported Venizelos' policy for the expansion of Greece to his native Asia Minor and, it was rumored, contributed vast sums of money toward the Anatolian expedition of Greece in 1920.

hardship was the shortage of food. Greece had been dependent on imported wheat since antiquity. Wheat was mainly imported from Egypt; but the Allied fleets, the British fully cooperating with the French, saw to it that for 104 days no cargo of wheat passed through any port under King Constantine's jurisdiction. Before the end of February 1917 fifty deaths from starvation were reported. In the large towns public kitchens were operated and famished children in the streets were begging for "raisins" - the only thing left for the starving population to eat. Supplies of wheat purchased in America by the Greek Government were seized by the Allies on the high seas and sent to Salonica. The islanders, of course, suffered most. In Cephallonia, Metaxas' home island, French colonial troops commandeered all the meager stocks.

The hardships from the blockade were very real indeed. All strata of society were affected. The blockade provided an ideal opportunity for Royalist propaganda and a popular basis for the Royal oligarchy. In 1934 Metaxas, writing in the newspapers, reminded his public of those dark days.

Those of our readers who were children in those days will surely remember how sad your parents were in the winter of 1915, during 1916, during 1917, because they could not give you bread but only a dry, black, mildewed crust and this only in small quantities. You were hungry then. You had no light at night, you were cold because you had no fire .... You must have heard then that the cause of all these deprivations was the "blockade." You must have heard that foreign fleets prevented wheat and food from coming to Greece.[34]

And Metaxas charged Venizelos with inciting the Allies to starve his countrymen so that they would turn against the King.

Through these turbulent times the Athens Royal Court was in secret touch by cypher with Berlin. The Athens Royalists attempted to lure the Germans into attacking the Allied Forces on the Macedonian Front. The Royalists, partly disarmed and under great stress from the blockade, argued that they could not initiate an operation against the *Armée d'Orient*, but if the Germans threw Sarrail back, the Greek Royalist troops, fighting nearer to their base, could attack the Allies from the south. The Germans, for their part, wanted King Constantine to fire the first shot before they would open a full scale offensive in Macedonia.

Queen Sophia was at the center of these plans and it was in her name that most of these messages between Berlin and Athens were transmitted. King Constantine knew about these plans, but he was more cautious than the Queen. The former German Military Attache Falkenhausen, who had been expelled from Athens by Admiral Fournet and who was now in Berlin, was also part of the conspiracy and Queen Sophia often instructed that her telegrams be shown to him, too. The Kaiser, Zimmerman,

---

34 *Ethnikos Dichasmos.*

Hindenburg and Ludendorff, at one time or another, all considered the idea of Greek-German cooperation in the Balkans.

All reports tell that the Queen developed her plans with the help of Ioannis Metaxas. Metaxas was the Queen's most trusted friend, perhaps the only person she ever trusted in her adopted country. He spoke her language and shared her absolute admiration for Germany. Metaxas also had been a close acquaintance of Falkenhausen since the outbreak of the War.

Berlin was naturally interested in people like Metaxas and when a rumour reached them that he and Dousmanis were reinstated in their old positions on the General Staff, they asked Athens for confirmation. On 6 December the Master of Ceremonies at the Court of Queen Sophia cabled the Greek Minister at Berlin that "as for Dousmanis and Metaxas, the news is inexact. If the situation demands it, they will be restored."[35]

Finally, on 8 January 1917, the Greek Minister in Berlin received from Zimmerman Hindenburg's answer and transmitted it to Athens. Hindenburg explained that a German attack in Macedonia could not be undertaken with any prospect of success unless Greece advanced with strong forces toward Monastir. In other words, while the Greek Royalists were asking the help of the Germans, the Germans were asking the help of the Greek Royalists. In his memoirs Marshall von Hindenburg noted:

In the winter of 1916-1917 we had information in the guise of tempting invitations on the development of the political situation in Greece and on the question of an attack on Macedonia. To these siren voices I remained unmoved. I doubted that the Greek people were enthusiastic about the War, especially as they would have to fight it as allies of the Bulgarians ... We could not endanger our Western or our Russian Front so that we could collect cheap laurels on the Vardar.[36]

When all attempts to convince the Germans to launch a major attack in Macedonia failed, Metaxas organised out of the *Leagues of the Reservists* Greek guerilla bands which operated in the mountains of Epirus and Western Macedonia. The first objectives of these bands was to re-establish the communications between Royalist Greece and Germany which seem to have been disrupted during the troubles of the *Noemvriana*.

However sporadic, the activity of the Royalist bands did irritate the Allies and contributed greatly to General Sarrail's paranoia that his rear was threatened by the Royalists of Athens. But as Athens was at the mercy of the Allied Fleet, once it became evident that the Germans had no intention of opening up a major offensive in Greece, King Constantine and the Royalists were virtual prisoners of the Entente and there were limits to the extent they could give trouble with impunity. Constantine, afraid that his throne was in danger, tried to appease the Allies and establish a *modus vivendi* with

35 *Greek White Book*, p. 75.

36 Quoted by Ventiris, *op. cit.*, II, p.

them. His Minister of War Constantine Demertzis [who was to be the last Prime Minister of Greece before Metaxas took over in 1936], once went to see the King and explained the harm these bands were doing, especially as they were connected with military people like Metaxas.

On 24 April 1917 Isvolsky, the Russian Ambassador in Paris, sent a new cable to Petrograd to reassure his country that the removal of Constantine would not hurt Russian interests. Ribot, he said, had asked him to give formal assurances to the Russian Foreign Minister that "France will assume no engagement towards Venizelos in regard to the vast nationalist ambitions of the Greeks."[37] In this telegram Isvolsky also quoted another French politician, Jules Cambon, as saying to him: "Nothing serves us better than to accumulate grounds of ill-feeling and friction with Greece, in order to disembarrass ourselves of all moral obligations towards that country."[38]

By the spring of 1917 it became apparent that the Allies were not going to tolerate for much longer the Greek Royalists of Athens. General Sarrail, the Commander-in-Chief of the Allied Forces in Salonica, sounded almost hysterical in his protestations against the threat to his troops from the directions of Athens.

The Greek Royalists, after failing to incite a German offensive in Macedonia in which they might have joined, now hoped to weather the storm of the European War and at all costs preserve the King, the symbol of their endeavors and the promise of their future. The Allies, especially the French, had a strong desire to get even with Constantine, whose suspect policy made the whole project of the Macedonian Front ineffective. The *Noemvriana* incidents so much exacerbated political passions in divided Greece that, short of civil war or a full scale invasion by either of the European rivals, there was no visible solution to the "Greek Question."

As so often in the history of Greece, distant international events played a decisive part in her internal political problems. On 15 March 1917 the Czar abdicated. Nicholas II, a first cousin and a friend of King Constantine, often disapproved of Allied coercive measures against Royalist Greece; and although the Kerensky Government continued to condemn the Allied intervention in Greece, King Constantine lost in the Czar one of his staunchest supporters.

Two days after the deposition of the Czar the Briand Cabinet fell in France - ostensibly over the replacement of the Minister of War; a French journalist wrote, however, that it was certain that "its authority had been weakened by its way of handling the Greek Question."[39] Aristide Briand had generally supported King

---

37 Cosmetatos, *op. cit.*, p. 272.

38 The full implications of Russian and French attitudes became apparent soon after the conclusion of the Great War when Bolshevik Russia and France hastened to assist Kemal Atatürk with arms and munitions in his struggle against the Greeks in Asia Minor.

39 Gauvain, *op.cit.*, p. 98.

Constantine because of his friendship with Marie Buonaparte, the student of Freud, wife of Prince George, Constantine's brother. Alexandre Ribot, who took over, was determined right from the beginning to work for the dethronement of the Greek King. This was in accord with the prevailing mood in France. On 11 April 1917 the Paris newspaper *Temps* published its most vicious attack to date on Constantine in an article entitled "Le Dossier du Roi Constantine," reputedly written by Clemenceau.[40]

Finally, on 6 April 1917 the United States of America entered the War. In their pursuit of neutrality the Greek Royalists were, at least indirectly, supported by America. Prince Christophoros, the King's youngest brother, was married to a rich American widow, and this may have helped somewhat. Whenever the Royalists could escape the notice of the Allied Fleet, they could always buy war *matériel* and wheat from America. The Royalist views were freely printed in the American press, unlike the Allied press where the Royalists were often labelled as Germanophiles and traitors. Once America entered the War, she could not speak for the Neutrals. The Allies, who until then had refrained because of their concern for American public opinion, now felt free to depose Constantine.

The third obstacle to the dethronement of Constantine was the attitude of Italy, which was soon to change. On 19 April 1917 at the Conference of Saint Jean-de-Maurienne, Ribot, Lloyd George, Boselli and Sonnino discussed the situation in Greece. Italy was given liberty of action on the Adriatic coast and lavish promises in Anatolia - thus Italy was less afraid of the return of Venizelos to power whose nationalistic ambitions conflicted with Italy's expansionist pretensions. Italy, therefore, modified her attitude toward Greece and was now willing to go along with her Allies in settling the Greek Question. According to a cable (dated 21 April 1917) from Isvolky to Petrograd, at the Conference of Saint Jean-de-Maurienne Ribot succeeded in obtaining from Lloyd George and Sonnino "a liberty of action for France in Greece, which did not exclude the possibility of the dethronement of King Constantine."[41] Ribot, the French Premier, had argued that General Sarrail could not take the offensive on the Macedonian Front because he had to keep two divisions to guard his rear from the Royalist troops of King Constantine.

Ribot thought that the only solution was the dethronement of Constantine and the establishment of a Greek Republic. But the English were not so enthusiastic about removing Kings -- with the Russian news so fresh, it was almost like cooperating in setting a sinister trend. They invited, therefore, the French to London for a conference to be held on 28-29 May 1917 in order to talk over the matter. Lord Robert Cecil, substituting for Arthur Balfour, the Minister of Foreign Affairs, who was then in the

40 Thompson, *op. cit.*, p. 212.

41 Quoted by Cosmetatos, *op. cit.*, p. 271.

U.S.A., sent the invitations. Along with the French Premier went his Minister of Foreign Affairs, Léon Bourgeois; his Minister of War, Painlevé; Admiral Lacaze; General Foche, the Chief of Staff, and Senator Charles Jonnart. The French wanted the military occupation of the Corinth Canal and Athens as a certain guarantee that the rear of General Sarrail would not be threatened. Lloyd George, citing also the views of Lord Curzon, did not agree. Lord Robert Cecil was averse to the idea of dethroning a King by force and "he was hesitant and vacillating in his opinions when it came to drastic action," Lloyd George writes. Finally the British Prime Minister invited Painlevé, Lord Milner and General Ian Smuts to his country cottage so they could come to a decision. The way Lloyd George tells it, it was not all that difficult.

We sat out under a tree in the garden for hours on a beautiful summer night to thrash out the whole problem, and we came to the unanimous conclusion that as the French had troops on the spot they should land them at the Piraeus, occupy Athens, dethrone the King and set up either the heir - Prince George - or his second son, Prince Alexander.[42]

As soon as the French returned to Paris, Senator Charles Jonnart, a former Governor-General of Algeria, (and later Minister of Foreign Affairs) was dispatched to Greece with orders to secure the removal of King Constantine. The Senator first went to Corfu, which had been occupied by the French since 1 January 1916. There he was joined by the Mediterranean Allied Fleet which accompanied him for the rest of his journey to Salamis where the French had requisitioned the Greek Navy. The Allied Fleet anchored off Keratsini while the Senator himself sailed to Salonica to confer with General Sarrail and Venizelos.

On June 10 Jonnart sailed to Salamis and established himself on the French cruiser *Justice*. From Salonica he brought along General Regnault and his troops. The same evening the French Senator invited the Greek Prime Minister for a first meeting on the *Justice*. Zaimis, knowing perfectly well the situation, did not even bother to ask to see the credentials of the "High Commissioner of the Protecting Powers."

While Zaimis was on his way to meet Senator Jonnart, Metaxas went to the Palace, where many politicians and higher ranking officers had gathered. Since the previous July when the Allies had demanded his dismissal from the Army, Metaxas had kept a low profile, choosing to work surreptitiously from the back room. Even during the *Noemvriana* in which the Leagues of the Reservists played the leading role, Metaxas kept in the background, letting other less important men take the risks, physical and political. His opportunism was often commented upon, but he himself wrote that during this crucial period he kept away from politics so as not to embarrass the King. He writes (on 28 December 1934): "The second Zaimis Government and the Kalogeropou-

42 Lloyd George, *Memoirs*, p. 790.

los Government and the Lambros Government and the third Zaimis Government assiduously avoided having any contact with me so that they would not be misunderstood by the different agents and spies in Athens and accused that they were in any way influenced by me ... and to many persons of the King's environment even my accidental appearance, I felt, caused no pleasant feeling. I was, in a word, undesirable."[43] Metaxas broke the rule then because, as he writes, he had a strong intuition that Jonnart's mission to Greece was the dethronement of the King. "I did not communicate my thought to anyone, I knew they considered me an extremist. But I could see passivity everywhere and no action whatsoever was contemplated."[44] When the King came out of his study and spoke to those present, Metaxas moved over to him and asked for a few minutes' private audience. The King took him aside and listened to him attentively. Metaxas told Constantine what he thought of Jonnart's mission and suggested to him that he leave Athens immediately. The King could not go north towards Thebes, not only because he could not defend his position from there but because his enemies would again accuse him of threatening the security of the Allied Armies in Macedonia. The King should go immediately to Tripolis, the central mountain city of the Peloponnese, Metaxas urged, "amongst his Army and his people, absolutely loyal."[45] By staying in Athens, which was exposed to the cannons of the Allied Fleet, the King was "a virtual prisoner and every time he would have to negotiate as such,"[46] while from the Peloponnese he would deal with the Allies free of threats or pressures. It would have taken the Allies quite an Army to conquer the Peloponnese, which Army they could not spare at the moment from anywhere. The Allies could blockade the Peloponnese but the summer crop from there would have lasted the population for many months to come. Metaxas suggested that the King should take with him only two or three faithful persons, leaving his family behind and telling no one about his plans. According to reliable information Metaxas had acquired, the Allied ships could not reach the Canal before midnight and the landing of troops there should not be expected before the next morning. (That is exactly what happened.) Metaxas made this suggestion at seven o'clock in the evening. By midnight the King could easily have crossed over to the Peloponnese. The King had discussed this idea with Metaxas for some time when Premier Zaimis returned and the King took him to his study to hear the latest news. It was nothing like as drastic as Metaxas had warned. Senator Jonnart was very pleasant and spoke only about the distribution of the Thessalian crop and hinted that the Allies might occupy the Isthmus of Corinth to make certain that no Royalist troops would cross north and threaten the rear of General Sarrail. But Jonnart added that he was

43 *Ethnikos Dichasmos,* p. 193.

44 *Ibid.*, pp. 193-194.

45 *Ibid.*, p. 194.

46 *Ibid.*.

waiting new instructions from Paris and he asked the Greek Prime Minister to call on him again the next morning. The news was reassuring. The King, coming out of his private interview with Zaimis, bade farewell to the bystanders and retired. Metaxas writes: "He did not give me any answer and I realised my proposition was not accepted. Then I felt clearly that the fate of the King was sealed."[47]

The next morning, at 9 a.m. on 11 June 1917, Zaimis returned to the *Justice*, as arranged. Senator Jonnart, without any preliminaries, handed the Greek Prime Minister a *démarche* in which, after accusing King Constantine of having violated the Constitution of which France, Great Britain and Russia were the guarantors, "the King had lost the confidence of the Protecting Powers";[48] therefore it was Jonnart's mission to demand the abdication of the King in order to reestablish the integrity of the Constitution ("en vue de rétablir la vérité constitutionelle.").[49]

In this Note it was stated that the King "would himself choose, with the agreement of the Protecting Powers, a successor among his heirs."[50] But in an *aide-memoire* attached to the above document Jonnart excluded from the succession the Crown Prince George of whose pro-German and absolutist views the Allies were well aware. The Prince Royal did not have "the guarantees which France, Great Britain and Russia were bound to demand from the constitutional sovereign of the Hellenes."[51] Prince George (1890-1947) was to become George II in 1922, be exiled in 1923 and restored in 1935 when, a short while after, with his blessing, Ioannis Metaxas established the fascist dictatorship. Jonnart suggested that the throne should go to Prince Alexander (1893-1920) the second son of King Constantine. The *aide-memoire* also promised that no reprisals would be condoned and that King Constantine would be given half a million francs after his departure. The ultimatum expired in twenty-four hours. When Zaimis

---

47 *Ibid.*.

48 Raymond M. Recouly, *M. Jonnart en Grèce et l'abdication de Constantin* (Paris, 1918), pp. 109-110. The whole document reads:
"Monsieur le Président,
"Les Puissances protectrices de la Grèce ont décidé de reconstituer l'unité du royaume sans porter atteinte aux institutions monarchiques constitutionnelles qu'elles ont garanties à la Grèce.
S. M. le roi Constantin, ayant manifestement violé, de sa propre initiative, la Constitution dont la France, la Grande-Bretagne and la Russie sont les garantes, j'ai l' honneur de déclarer à Votre Excellence que le Roi a perdu la confiance des Puissances protectrices et que celles-ci se considèrent comme dégagées à son égard des obligations résultant de leurs droits de protection.
J'ai, en conséquence, pour mission, en vue de rétablir la vérité constitutionnelle, de réclamer l'abdication de S.M. le roi Constantin, qui désignera lui-même, d'accord avec les Puissances protectrices, un successeur parmi ses héritiers.
Je suis dans l'obligation de vous demander une réponse dans un délai de vingt-quatre heures.
Veuillez agréer, monsieur le Président, l'assurance de ma haute considération.
Jonnart

49 *Ibid.*.

50 *Ibid.*.

51 Cosmetatos, *op.cit.*, p. 283.

hesitated, Senator Jonnart pointed out that the French troops now in the Ports of Piraeus and Phaleron were ready at the first signal to disembark and march against Athens. Senator Jonnart reminded Zaimis of the fate of Arras, a city in his constituency, le Pas-de-Calais, which had been devastated by the Germans. If the Greek people resisted him he would not hesitate to do to Athens what the Germans had done to Arras.[52] Metaxas wrote that Premier Zaimis, listening to these threats, was reportedly moved to tears. Even as Jonnart delivered his ultimatum, Allied forces were taking Elassona at the entry to Thessaly and the Isthmus of Corinth.

Premier Zaimis returned to the Palace. The King, after reading the Allied *ultimatum*, asked Metaxas if they would really have been able to cross over the Corinth Isthmus had they left the previous night. Yes, they would, Metaxas answered, but now it was too late. That very morning Allied troops had occupied the Canal. Metaxas writes: "If my proposition had been known, perhaps a great many wise men would have said that I was mad. But in the light of hindsight, in exceedingly critical situations what appears as madness is the best way out."[53] Metaxas believed that if the King had gone to the Peloponnese, the Allies, because of their differences, would have finally offered to negotiate with him and he would never have had to leave the country.

As it was, King Constantine, with a heavy heart, asked Zaimis to convene the Crown Council at the Palace. According to tradition, ex-Premiers and Party leaders made up the Crown Council. Metaxas did not attend; he had nothing further to say, anyway. Former Premiers Rallis, Dragoumis, Skouloudis, Gounaris, Lambros and Kalogeropoulos were there. Also present were the Party leaders Demetrakopoulos and Stratos. They

---

52 It is interesting to compare how different writers report the French Senator's words. According to the Greek historian Cosmetatos, Jonnart said (p. 284): "I come from the invaded territories. I have seen Arras, where not one stone rests on another. If Athens has become German, we shall treat her as the Germans have treated Arras". According to Sir Basil Thompson, Jonnart's words were (p. 221): "If the people attempt to resist us, we shall no longer allow ourselves to be restrained by compassion. I have seen Arras, my native town, where not one stone rests on another. If it becomes necessary I shall treat Athens as the Germans have treated Arras."
Raymond Recouly reported Jonnart as saying (pp. 112-113): "Dans cette guerre, où l'Allemagne a accumulé les férocités et les crimes, où elle a dévasté nos provinces, réduit les populations en esclavage, violé les lois divines et humaines, nous nous défendons; nous défendrons, sans jamais nous laisser abattre, les intérêtes essentiels et l'existence de *notre patrie*. Mon département d'origine, le Pas-de-Calais, est en partie dévasté par le barbares. Arras, où je me trouvais il y a quelques jours, est en ruines. S'il faut que demain je fasse subir à Athènes le même sort, la mort dans l'âme, je le ferai, je vous l'affirme. Les troupes que j'ai amenées de Salonique doivent retourner au plus tôt sur le front macédonien. Je suis pressé."
Robert David, writing in *Revue hebdomadaire*, (Paris, 1er déc. 1917) under the title "M. Jonnart en Grèce. Pourquoi et comment on dépose un roi", had Senator Jonnart saying to Premier Zaimes: "Arras, ma ville natale, a été rasée par les Allemands. Quelque affligeante que serait pour mon coeur de Français la pensée de faire tirer sur une ville historique comme Athènes, si votre résistance m'y obligeait, j'irais jusque' à faire d'Athènes une nouvelle Arras!"

53 *Ethnikos Dichasmos*, p. 194.

all knew that any resistance was useless. The few Army units which were not demobilized had been transferred to the Peloponnese, while the Allies had just occupied the Corinth Canal to prevent them from crossing over to Attica. The Allied Fleet had complete command of the Greek seas, Athens was exposed to the cannons of the French Navy and French marines threatened to land and take the city. General Sarrail from Salonica was ready to advance against Thessaly. Finally the King announced his decision to leave the country, taking with him the Queen and the Crown Prince. On the advice of Skouloudis, neither Constantine nor Prince George were to abdicate formally. King Constantine appointed his second son, Prince Alexander, to succeed him. In the evening of 11 June 1917 Premier Zaimis informed Senator Jonnart that "His Majesty the King, anxious as always for the welfare of Greece, has decided to leave the country, together with the Crown Prince and has designated as his successor Prince Alexander."[54]

"When these things became known in Athens," Metaxas wrote in 1934, "the people rose up as one man, the shops closed, the streets were filled with rebellious inhabitants and the Palace was besieged by the people, who were threatening to prevent by force the departure of the King. The situation was explosive. The wrath of the people of Athens reached a dangerous level."[55] All accounts indicate that the Reservists were foremost among the demonstrators. All through the night of 11 June and the following day, while the church bells tolled mournfully as though for a funeral, the crowds kept vigil and nobody was permitted to enter or leave the Palace. It was a passionate display of devotion to the "martyred King" who was being ill-treated by the foreigners. The Greek *philotimo*, the native sense of *amour-propre*, was hurt and the Athenians, even those who did not approve of the King's pro-German sympathies, came out into the streets and the squares to protest the Allied intervention. The crowds seethed outside the Palace, shouting "Vengeance!" and "He shall not go!" Constantine issued a Proclamation exhorting the people to submit without any disturbance.[56] Senator

54 Premier Zaimis' letter to Senator Jonnart reads as follows:

Athènes, le 11 juin 1917

Monsieur Le Haut Commissaire,

La France, la Grande-Bretagne et la Russie ayant réclamé par votre note d'aujour'hui l'abdication de S.M. le roi Constantin et la désignation de son successeur, le soussigné, président du Conseil des ministres, ministre des Affaires étrangères, a l'honneur de porter à la connaissance de Votre Excellence que S.M. le Roi, soucieux comme toujours du seul intrêt de la Grèce, a désidé de quitter avec le Prince royal le pays et désigné pour son successeur le prince Alexandre.
Veuillez agréer, monsieur le Haut Commissaire, les assurances de ma haute considération.

Zaimis

55 *Ethnikos Dichasmos*, p. 195.

56 The King's proclamation reads as follows:
Bowing to necessity, and accomplishing a duty towards Greece, concerned at all times only for her interests, I am leaving my beloved country with the Crown Prince, leaving my son Alexander on

Jonnart, alarmed at this popular outburst, landed troops in Piraeus and advanced strong detachments to strategic points toward Athens. At the same time he notified Premier Zaimis that if the Greek police could not disperse the crowds to allow the King to depart, he would dispatch French marines with machineguns to do the job.

Metaxas, as he related years later, was the only one to remain till the end with his King. The last thing he requested Constantine to do was to sign a paper for his release from the Army. The prospect of being under orders from the Venizelists did not appeal to him. "I did not want to stay in the Army anymore," he wrote.[57] The King, with tears in his eyes, said to Metaxas, "You will live and have a career in our land. One day you will govern Greece. I am certain of this and I beg you, when you ascend to power, to bring me back. It is the only thing I ask you. I want to return and rest at Tatoi and die in Greece."[58] As it happened, Constantine was restored to his throne three and a half years later in December 1920, only to go into exile again in 1922, where he died soon afterwards. When Metaxas did come to power in 1936, the first thing he did was to bring back from Italy the remains of Constantine and have them interred at the Royal family cemetery at Tatoi. On that occasion a bronze equestrian statue of Constantine was erected at the Field of Mars Gardens (*Pedion Areos*, which is adjacent to the National Archeological Museum). Metaxas, eulogizing the dead King at the ceremony, told of Constantine's last request to him. And Metaxas added: "I gave him my word. And I think I have kept it. As his early end did not allow me to bring him back alive, I bring back the corpse of the King, who was the greatest figure in modern Greek History."[59]

At 5:00 p.m. on 12 June 1917 King Constantine managed by a stratagem to escape the notice of the crowds and left the Palace for Tatoi by a back door. Three days later he embarked on the royal yacht *Sphacteria* at Oropos, a small port in Attica and departed. The peasants from the nearby villages gave him a touching farewell.[60] Sir Francis Elliot offered the King an English warship for his journey but he declined. "I am not King Otho," he remarked. Two French torpedo boats and the small Greek ship

---

the throne ...

In order that my sacrifice for the country may not be in vain I appeal to you all, if you love God, your country and myself, to submit without any disturbance. The smallest disorder, even if prompted by an elevated sentiment, may lead to-day to great evils.

At this moment the greatest consolation for the Queen and myself lies in the affection and devotion which you have always shown me in happy and unhappy days alike. May God protect Greece!

Constantine R.

From Thompson, *op.cit.*, p. 244.

57 Undersecretary of Press and Tourism, *King Constantine* (in Greek), (Athens, 1939), p. 88.

58 *Ibid.*, p. 89.

59 *Ibid.*.

60 The departure of the King at Oropos was described at length in the Paris *Journal* of January 4, 1918.

Spetsai, carrying his staff and his luggage, accompanied the royal yacht, which anchored at the Villa di San Giovanni opposite Messina, Sicily. From there a special train transported the King and Queen to Switzerland. With the royal party went the King's political adviser, George Streit and the Queen's Master of Ceremonies, John Theotokis. In Switzerland, Constantine was later joined by his brothers Nicholas, Andrew and Christoforos.

The French, with the connivance of the English and the tolerance of the other western democracies, had at last succeeded in deposing King Constantine. Metaxas had not a good word to say about the ethics of the western democracies. But his harshest criticism he saved for those Greeks who, to his mind, had collaborated with the foreigners to depose the Soldier-King and humiliate Greece. In 1934 Metaxas wrote:

The same day as the departure of the King M. Ribot and Mr. Venizelos exchanged congratulatory telegrams for the restoration of free institutions in Greece. Mr. Venizelos especially thanked M. Ribot in the name of "Hellenism, Civilization and Liberty."[61]

Senator Jonnart, on his return to Paris, writing to Premier Ribot on 22 July 1917 said that France had risked her prestige in Greece and that the Ministers of England, Italy and Russia at Athens had repeatedly telegraphed their Governments that French public opinion had been deceived by the activities of the French Secret Service in Greece. "This has been a far from glorious page in the history of France," wrote Jonnart. "I hasten to close it." (*une page peu glorieuse pour la France, je la ferme bien vite!*).[62]

On the day of the departure of the King, Senator Jonnart issued a proclamation to the Greek people in the name of France, Great Britain and Russia. The Proclamation announced that the Protecting Powers, wishing "to put an end to the repeated violations of the Constitution and of the treaties, and the deplorable intrigues which culminated in the massacre of soldiers of friendly countries," and in order "to reestablish the constitutional integrity and the unity of Greece," had demanded the abdication of King Constantine.[63] The Senator promised to lift the blockade and prevent any reprisals or

---

61 *Ethnikos Dichasmos*, p. 195.

62 A. F. Frangoulis, *La Grèce, son statut international, son histoire diplomatique* (Paris, 1934) 2 vols. This is the second edition of *La Grèce et la crise mondiale* (Paris, 1926).

63 Recouly, *op.cit.*, pp. 137-140. This most interesting document reads:

AU PEUPLE HELLÈNE

La France, la Grande-Bretagne et la Russie ont voulu l'indépendance, la grandeur et la prospérité de la Grèce.

Elles entendent défendre le noble pays qu'elles ont libéré contre les efforts réunis des Turcs, des Bulgares et des Allemands.

Elles sont ici pour déjouer les moneuvres des ennemis héréditaires du royaume.

Elles veulent mettre fin aux violations répétées de la Constitution et des traités, aux déplorables intrigues qui ont abouti au massacre des soldats des pays amis.

any disturbance of the public order whatsoever. *"Vos destinées sont étroitement associées a celles des Puissances garantes,"* Jonnart told the Greeks.[64] At the same time Allied troops from Salonica crossed the Neutral Zone and occupied Thessaly, thus securing the wheat harvest. The German wireless commented: "For the first time the Entente has carried through with complete success a joint military action. This success has been won at the expense of an army which had previously been disarmed, and a people who had been starved."[65]

As soon as the King had set sail, the self-styled High Commissioner of the Protecting Powers sent to Premier Zaimis a list of about thirty people he wanted delivered to him for exile -- "among them was the writer of these lines," Metaxas notes; and he added: "And the Greek Government complied for the honor and glory of Article 4 of the restored Greek Constitution."[66] Metaxas' name was entered thus: *Colonel Jean Metaxas, ex-sous-chef de l'état-major général.* The list also included ex-Premier Demetrios Gounaris; the former mayor of Athens Spyros Merkouris and his son, the deputy George Merkouris; K. Eslin; the deputy George Pesmazoglou; the President of the Reservists John Sayias; the ex-Chief of Staff Victor Dousmanis; General Bairas; Douphas and Ramos, *"chefs des bands;"* Giannaros; Regas and the political writer Ion Dragoumis. Dragoumis' name was added at the last moment: he had just published an article in the *Political Review* of Athens severely criticizing the Allies and Venizelos.

Berlin commandait hier à Athènes et conduisait graduellement le peuple sous le joug bulgare-allemand.
Nous avons résolu de rétablir la vérité constitutionnelle et l'unité de la Grèce.
Les Puissances garantes ont en conséquence demandé au roi Constantin d'abdiquer.
Elles ne prétendent pas toucher à la royauté constitutionnelle. Elles n'ont d'autre ambition que d'assurer le fonctionnement régulier de la Constitution à laquelle le roi Georges, de glorieuse mémoire, avait toujours été scrupuleusement fidèle et que le roi Constantin a cessé de respecter.

HELLÈNES!

L'heure de la réconciliation est venue. Vos destinées sont étroitement associées à celles des Puissances garantes. Votre idéal est le même, vos espérances sont les mêmes.
Nous faisons appel à votre sagesse et à votre patriotisme.
Aujourd'hui le blocus est levé. Toute représaille contre les Grecs, à quelque parti qu'ils appartiennent, sera impitoyablement réprimée.
Aucune atteinte a l'ordre public ne sera tolérée.
Les biens and la liberté de chacun seront sauvegardés.
C'est une ère nouvelle de paix et de travail qui va s'ouvrir devant vous.
Sachez que, respectueuses de la Souveraineté nationale, les Puissances protectrices n'ont nullement l'intention d'imposer au peuple grec la mobilisation générale.
Vive la Grèce unie grand et libre!.
Au nom de la France, de la Grande-Bretagne et de la Russie,
Le Haut Commissaire des Puissances protectrices,

JONNART

64 Ibid..

65 Forster, *op.cit.*, p. 129ff.

66 *Ethnikos Dichasmos*, pp. 195-196.

In his newspaper articles in 1934, Metaxas claimed that it was Venizelos himself who provided Jonnart with this list of his political opponents and who had in fact demanded their banishment from the Allies. However, it seems more likely that the lists were complied by Commandant de Roquefeuil, the Chief of the French Secret Service.[67] Two Germans named Blum and Hossling were also on the list. Later the King's brothers were also sent into exile.

A second, much longer list of 130 persons headed by ex-Premiers Stephanos Skouloudis and Spyridon Lambros and including half-a-dozen ex-Cabinet Ministers, one general and one admiral, were placed under surveillance. If anyone of those persons attempted to escape, he was declared an outlaw and his property confiscated. When Livieratos, the President of a Royalist "Federation" of professions and trades, *"un agitateur des plus dangereux,"* as he was described by the French, managed to escape to the Peloponnese, Jonnart ordered the French troops to occupy his property in Cephalonia and use it to house Greek refugees. Other monarchists were later arrested in Athens, put on a French warship and first taken to Salonica and then to the island of Lesbos, where they were put in a concentration camp. More Greek Royalists from all parts of the country were sent to this camp until the number of prisoners reached 600. Metaxas wrote with bitter irony in 1934: "These were not 'reprisals' because in his Proclamation Jonnart forbade any reprisals; it was described as 'weeding the ground,' that is, weeding the plants unfavorable to Venizelos so that Mr. Venizelos, that is, the Tree of Liberty, could be planted in their stead."[68]

On 20 June Ioannis Metaxas was put on the Greek SS *Vasilefs Constantinos* in Piraeus for the journey into exile. The same day Eleftherios Venizelos boarded a Greek destroyer at Salonica for the journey to Athens and to power. The next day, as the ship with the exiles was leaving Greek waters on its way to Corsica, Venizelos transferred to the French cruiser *Justice* where Jonnart was waiting for him. Under Jonnart's direction representatives of the Athens Government and representatives of the Provisional Government of Salonica were carrying out acrimonious negotiations for the unification of the country. A personal confidential letter which came to light later, was sent by Rentis, a diplomatic clerk of the Provisional Government, to Professor Nicholas Politis, Minister of Foreign Affairs in the Provisional Government. Rentis was attached to Repoulis, Venizelos' representative to Senator Jonnart. In many ways the letter, (dated 17 June 1917) is revealing and damaging to the Venizelist cause. The letter shows that the French had apparently promised to help the Provisional Government occupy Thessaly. Rentis, the letter-writer, observed to Senator Jonnart that without the presence of the Allied Army the return of Venizelos to Athens might prove difficult.

67 Recouly, *op. cit.*, p. 143.

68 *Ethnikos Dichasmos*, p. 196.

Jonnart said that it seemed the Greek people did not like foreigners interfering in their internal affairs and that the Venizelists should stop asking for violent actions and pressures and be satisfied with what had been accomplished. Jonnart said to Rentis that he himself had not realised before his coming to Greece that "Constantine had power in the country and was loved by the people."[69] Had this been known in England the decision for the King's deposition would not have been taken. On the constitutional question Senator Jonnart is reported as saying that "In spite of all we know, the King, nevertheless, had the right of dissolution."[70] "Here! Here!!" cries Metaxas, who quoted this amazing letter in full in one of his articles in 1934. Venizelos must have been cursing Rentis, Metaxas notes, who had the inspiration to put everything down in writing instead of following the wise advice of Joseph Fouché, the Minister of Police during the French Revolution and in the times of Napoleon, who used to advise, "Never put anything in writing." In this letter Rentis explained to Jonnart that the removal of the King did not affect the state of terrorism in Greece which was created by the use of force, the bands and the *Leagues of the Reservists*: this was the reason why the people could not express their pro-Venizelist feelings. "Were not the Reservists people?" asks Metaxas.[71]

At these negotiations the Venizelists were demanding the abolition of life tenure for judges, the revision of the Constitution and the recall to life of the Chamber of 31 May, 1915 which, they claimed was unconstitutionally dissolved. A few days earlier Premier Ribot had telegraphed Jonnart that if the state of opinion in Greece was favorable to Venizelos, he might proceed to elections. Otherwise he should recall the Venizelist Chamber which was dissolved by the King two years before."[72] The Prime Minister, Zaimis, unable to accept these conditions, resigned. The same day, 24 June 1917, Jonnart asked King Alexander to recall Venizelos to power. The young King agreed. When the news spread that the French were bringing back Venizelos there was a demonstration in Athens. The Liberal leader himself, staying on the French cruiser at Salamis, had serious misgivings about the reception the Athenian people were preparing for him. On 25 June General Regnault, commanding a French division, ordered what he described as "the conquest of Athens."[73] French troops occupied all the hills surrounding the city: the Observatory, the Pnyx, the Stadium Hill, the Acropolis, Lycavitos. Still, Venizelos was hesitant. The French General went aboard the *Justice* to reassure him.

---

69 *Ibid.*, p. 196f.

70 *Ibid.*.

71 *Ibid.*.

72 Quoted by Cosmetatos, *op. cit.*, p. 288.

73 In his book, *La Conquête d'Athènes* (Paris: L. Fournier, 1920).

General Regnault: Well, Monsieur le President, here you are in power. The moment has come for you to assume responsibility. I have the necessary force for installing you in Athens ..."[74]

Venizelos (finally agreeing with the French General): After all, there is no doubt that they will always say anyhow that I returned to Athens with the support of the Allies.

The following day the French troops occupied the main squares of the city, the gardens of Zappeion, the Grande Bretagne Hotel where Venizelos was to take up residence, and the environs of the Palace. They also lined up along the route from Piraeus to Athens. The French troops were reinforced by 400 Cretan gendarmes. Venizelos, after having had breakfast with Jonnart on the *Justice*, drove up to Athens with his Cabinet of the Provisional Government and "under the protection of foreign bayonets ... they entered Athens triumphantly; they went to the Palace and took the oath and then, through double lines of foreign troops, went to the Grande Bretagne", wrote Metaxas.[75] Venizelos came out on the balcony and said a few words. But his main speech ("which whoever has the stomach to read can find in the newspapers of those times," Metaxas wrote)[76] Venizelos delivered in the afternoon, while his followers cheered him from the street below.

Metaxas, who described with great relish in his newspaper articles of 1934 the return of Venizelos, ended his account with these words:

You may ask me, my readers, why I have related in such detail those moments which are so painful for the national honor? So that your cheeks may blush with shame! Because there must be circumstances, after all, when the blood should go to our heads and when we, the Greeks, too, should learn to blush from shame![77]

The new Liberal Cabinet in Athens was essentially the same as that of the Provisional Government in Salonica. Moreover, Venizelos recalled the Chamber of 13 June 1915 which had been dissolved on 6 November 1915, unconstitutionally, as he argued. The resurrected Chamber was nicknamed "the Chamber of Lazaruses" by the anti-Venizelists. The life of this Chamber was prolonged for fifteen months after it was due to expire and it was at last dissolved in September 1920. The National Opinion Party of Demetrios Gounaris, who had been sent into exile with Metaxas, refused to attend the sessions, but the Royalist ex-Premier, Demetrios Rallis, attended and so did Nikolaos Stratos, who had formed a new party, the Conservatives. The Liberal Government in the next few months carried out a systematic purge of all Royalist

74 Quoted from the above book by Metaxas, *Ethnikos Dichasmos*, p. 199.

75 *Ibid.*.

76 *Ibid.*.

77 *Ibid.*.

elements from the Civil Service and the Armed Forces. Venizelist civil servants and Venizelist officers took over. For the last three years the Venizelists had been purged in Athens and the Peloponnese while the Royalists had been purged in Salonica, Crete and the other islands. For the next three years, from 1917 to 1920, the Royalists were removed from all positions of power in the whole of unified Greece.[78] (Between 1920 and 1922 it was the turn of the Venizelists to be purged. In 1922 it was the turn of the Royalists. In 1936 John Metaxas made a clean sweep of all Democrats, whether Venizelists or not.)

The purge of the Royalists did not spare the Church, whose head, the Archbishop of Athens, was among the first to be dismissed. But what made the most painful impression was the interference with the Bench. It was Venizelos himself who had championed reforms which placed the Judiciary outside party politics and secured the life tenure of judges and the inviolability of their office when he revised the Constitution in 1911. Now, by Royal Decree, he withdrew the life tenure of all judges and dismissed the President of the Areios Pagos, the Supreme Court of Greece, together with many judges, high and low. A French writer records an interesting conversation between the young King Alexander and Senator Jonnart on this subject. On 29 June 1917, two days after Venizelos and his Cabinet took the oath of office, King Alexander invited Senator Jonnart to the Palace and asked him the following question.

King Alexander: *I should very much like to know if on this subject you are in agreement with him [Venizelos]. They reproached my father that he had violated the Constitution. However, the first acts they are asking from me, notably the suspension of the immovability of the magistrates by a simple decree, seems to me contrary to the Constitution.*[79]

Senator Jonnart succeeded without difficulty in calming the apprehensions of the young King. He explained to him that the Constituent Assembly, which was to be convened soon, would sanction and legitimize all these measures. On the occasion the Senator gave the King a short friendly lesson on Constitutional Law (as R. Recouly writes disarmingly: *"Il lui fait à ce propos un petit exposé familier de droit constitutionnel."*)[80] Finally the Senator said, "Soon Your Majesty will know as much

78 According to some accounts, as many as 7,356 public officials were dismissed from the Civil Service. (Metaxas puts the figure at 6,500). Of these 3,149 were from the Ministry of Education. 19 professors were dismissed from the University of Athens and 9 from the Technical University (*Polytechneion*). A figure approaching 7,000 is mentioned for officers and other members of the Armed Forces and the Police who were cashiered, deported, imprisoned or demoted to a lower rank. Metaxas breaks down this figure into various categories in one of his articles. See E. Malainos, vol. V., p. 10 f.; A. Frangoulis, vol. I, p. 572 f.; and for Metaxas' figures, *Ethnikos Dichasmos*, p. 200.

79 Recouly, *op. cit.*, p. 194.

80 Ibid.. Metaxas comments: "We too should have liked to hear the little lesson on Constitutional Law by M. Jonnart, according to which a King and a Government can alter the Constitution by single

about these matters as any of your Ministers."[81] When the King complained that both the Venizelists and their opponents often criticised him, the High Commissioner of the Protecting Powers hastened to reassure him:

These things happen all the time. Your Majesty should remember the famous fable by La Fontaine, The Miller, His Son and the Donkey.

King Alexander: *I have La Fontaine in my library and I will read this fable again.*[82]

According to Metaxas, 570 judges were dismissed from their posts, which brought the number of persons acted against by Venizelos to well over 10,000. They were replaced by Venizelists in a chaotic reshuffle from which, Metaxas wrote in 1934, the civil and military organization of Greece was still suffering. Many anti-Venizelists were deported to various islands, to Thera (Santorini), Amorgos, Sikinos, Folegandros, Anaphe. (This last island, was Metaxas' favorite as a place of exile for his opponents in 1936-1941.) The historian and politician Spyros Markezinis wrote that Venizelos "between the years 1917-1920, governed more dictatorially than did John Metaxas in 1936-1940, despite the fact that in the later period the Parliament was not functioning."[83]

The political education of King Alexander during these few months is not without interest. On 12 June 1917 on his accession to the throne, Alexander issued a proclamation in which he spoke of his "august father" and his endeavor to carry out his "sacred mandate in harmony with the precedents of his brilliant reign." The Allies disapproved of the reference to ex-King Constantine and the proclamation was withdrawn. A week later (on 20 June) King Alexander wrote to Venizelos to express his interest in the efforts of the Government to reunite Greece and his desire to observe the Constitution. The King also expressed his faith in the Guaranteeing Powers and his desire to cooperate with them in the reconciliation of the country.[84]

Decrees with the hypothesis that the National Assembly which was to be convened on a future date would undoubtedly legitimize these actions" *Ethnikos Dichasmos*, p. 200.

81 *Ibid.*.

82 *Ibid.*.

83 Spyros Markezinis, *op. cit.*, V. p. 225.

84 Here is the King's letter in a French translation:

Athènes, 7/20 juin 1917.

Monsieur le Président,

Je suis avec un vif intérêt les efforts du gouvernement en vue de rétablir l'unité de la Grèce. En ce qui me concerne, demeurant le fidèle gardien de la Charte constitutionnelle et confiant dans les dispositions bienveillantes des Puissances garantes, je suis prêt à collaborer avec elles, pour l'apaisement des esprits et la réconciliation du pays.

Alexandre, Roi

From Recouly, *op. cit.*, p. 142.

On 17 August 1917 King Alexander took the oath before the Greek Chamber. A few days later the Chamber met to discuss its reply to the King's speech. Several important speeches were delivered in this session. On 26 August Venizelos defended the policy he had pursued since 1912 in an oration of Demosthenian proportions.[85] The Liberal Prime Minister was on the platform from 5:30 p.m. to 3:00 a.m. the following morning with only one hour's break. Venizelos never spoke so well and with such passion. His speech was an eloquent vindication of the pro-Allied Liberal Party and a fierce indictment against the pro-German Royalists.

Venizelos attacked King Constantine, Queen Sophia, the Palace clique, the Royalist Governments. He especially lashed out against Colonel Ioannis Metaxas and the military establishment - "the real government." The hanging of our General Staff would be a very lenient punishment,"[86] he commented acidly. The Royalists, he said, did not pursue a policy of neutrality but a pro-German policy. The Royalists never intended to use the Army to fight the Germans and the Bulgarians, and the crippling mobilisation which was retained for nine months had only one purpose, to teach the Greek people the ways of absolutism. "These unprincipled men, the Old Men in the Ministry and the General Staff, aspired further, by extending the general mobilisation, to crush the Greek people physically and morally, so as to make them incapable of ever rising up to call them to account."[87] The Liberal Leader spoke about "the military terrorism" which was established in Royalist Greece and the abolition of all civil liberties and he quoted from the Royalist press "a string of constitutional blasphemies,"[88] which extolled the King as the "only Lord and Master in our own house of Greece."[89]

Venizelos then spoke at great length about the surrender of Fort Rupel and the occupation of Eastern Macedonia by Bulgaria. "She will never go away unless we have the strength to drive her from our territory," he said.[90] The Royalists had an understanding with Bulgaria. King Constantine had assured Bulgaria that she had nothing to fear on the part of Greece. Venizelos said that "after Rumania's declaration of war ... above all after the Bulgarian invasion of Macedonia, after the capture of our troops (the Greek Army which was transferred and interned in Germany), after the disregard of

85 This speech was published, together with several other important speeches of this session of Parliament in an English translation under the title *The Vindication of Greek National Policy, 1912-1917* (London: Allen & Unwin, 1918). It is an interesting thought that students in Greece, while spending many years laboring to decipher a few of the orations from the classical age, hardly ever come across in their studies some of these speeches of more recent date which, in human passion and political argument, are not far behind the ancient models and are certainly more relevant to the present history of Greece.

86 *Ibid.*, p. 125.

87 *Ibid.*, p. 126

88 *Ibid.*, p. 139

89 *Ibid.*.

90 *Ibid.*, p. 137.

Germany's written promise that the Bulgarians would not enter Serres, Drama and Kavalla, I considered that the conditions were now removed which had hitherto kept me from undertaking the fight against autocracy."[91] Venizelos said that he warned Constantine, through Premier Zaimis, that if the policy of neutrality was not abandoned, he, Venizelos, would not hesitate to divide the country "so as to avert the dangers that the German policy had created."[92] Still the Royalists, while pretending they were negotiating to enter the War on the side of the Allies, proved that "in reality there was no intention of making any change in Greek policy. Then I decided to become a rebel."[93] Venizelos spoke about the National Defence in Salonica, the removal of the King and mentioned to the Chamber an engraved inscription in the Palace of Westminster which recalls the beheading of King Charles of England as a constant reminder to the English Kings. The Greeks should put up a similar plaque in the Greek Parliament so that future Greek Kings should read it whenever they come to proclaim its opening. The inscription should read:

King Constantine having dissolved for the second time the Chamber of 1915, in order to impose a personal policy, himself lost his throne, while the Chamber which had been dissolved was called together again and continued its work according to the Constitution.[94]

As soon as Venizelos was installed in Athens, the Allied blockade was lifted and foodstuffs and war *matériel* began to come in. On 2 July 1917 the new Liberal Government in Athens declared war against the Central Powers and Nicholaos Politis, the new Foreign Minister, through the Greek charge d'affaires in Berne, instructed the Greek representatives in Berlin, Vienna, Sofia and Constantinople to request their passports immediately. The Allies promised to grant a loan and although only a fraction of the original sum ever reached Greece, it did contribute to revitalising the economy and building a new Army.[95] But the *Reservists*, demoted and resentful, were not at all enthusiastic to fight under the Venizelist officers who had "betrayed" King Constantine. The mobilisation was variously resisted and there were several mutinies in the ranks which were ruthlessly suppressed and the ringleaders shot.

---

91 *Ibid.*, p. 147

92 *Ibid.*.

93 *Ibid.*, p. 148

94 *Ibid.*, p. 157

95 The final agreement was reached in October, 1917, when Venizelos went to Paris and London (and also visited the Western Front) and took part in the Allied Conference at which he offered to put in the field 300 thousand men. The Allies then agreed to lend Greece 750 million francs. In May, 1919 the French and English portion of this loan was decreased from 250 to 100 million francs each. By the end of October 1920 Greece had received only 6.5 million English pounds out of the original 12 promised by England and 15 million dollars out of the original 48 million promised by the U.S.A. The French did not send a sou. Ethnikos Dichasmos, p. 201. See also E. Tsouderos, *To συμμαχικόν δάνειον* [The Allied Loan] (Athens, 1924).

In Macedonia the situation was far from rosy. The spring offensive, in which three battalions of Venizelist troops took part, had 14,000 casualties but won the Allies only a few outposts. By the end of May the Macedonian Army was entrenched in a defensive line running from Lake Prespa in the west to the Struma River in the east. The Serbian contingent was politically divided. And when the Bolshevik agitators arrived, the Russian brigades became insubordinate and a year later, in March 1918, they mutinied. There were serious doubts among the Allied Cabinets about the Macedonian Front, with the exception of Lloyd George, who not only believed that the Macedonian Front could seriously threaten Germany from the south-east, but also liked the idea of keeping British troops within easy reach of Constantinople. The Italians, the Serbs, the Greeks, the British, even many French, did not like General Sarrail as Commander-in-Chief; nevertheless, in March 1917 Sarrail had the support of Painlevé, the War Minister, who became French Premier the following September. Thus Sarrail kept his post until November 1917 when Clemenceau came to power and promptly replaced him by General Guillaumat as Commander-in-Chief of the *Armée d'Orient*.

By the spring of 1918 a quarter of a million Greeks were on the Macedonian Front under the command of General Guillaumat. On 15 April the Greek troops, commanded by General Nider, crossed the Struma River. By the end of May the Greek troops, with some French support, attacked the Bulgarian stronghold of Skra di Legen on the River Vardar, completely eliminating a whole enemy regiment and capturing 1,800 prisoners, including 200 Germans. (In the Victory March in Paris in 1919, along with the names of the Marne, Somme, Verdun, etc., was the name of Skra di Legen -- and a unit of Greek *evzones*.) After this victory the task of Greek mobilisation became much easier and a flow of Greek volunteers joined the ranks.

Clemenceau, impressed by General Guillaumat, recalled him to Paris to have him near at hand in case Foche or Pétain were found deficient. In his place he sent General Franchet d'Espérey, who arrived in Salonica on 17 June 1918. In September 1918 the Allied Forces launched their major offensive. Their superiority in numbers was overwhelming. 248 regiments took part: 92 French, 63 Greek, 57 Serbian, 46 British, 24 Italian and 2 Albanian, a total of 650,000 men. Facing them were about 380,000 men: 356,000 Bulgarians and 24,000 Germans. Moreover, Albania was occupied by 40,000 Austrians and in Western Thrace there were 12,000 Bulgarians. The disadvantage of the Enemy was not only in numbers. It was noted that in many Bulgarian units half the men had no shoes. The Greek troops were the first to cross the Bulgarian frontier. On 16 September 1918 the Greeks, supported by the British, entered the town of Doiran and soon had the Bulgarians in rapid retreat. In Thrace the Greek troops advanced to the River Nestos [Mesta], ready for the march to Constantinople. Serbian and French troops soon broke through the enemy lines in Western Macedonia and pursued the Germans and Bulgarians out of Serbia. By 30 September 1918 the enemy asked for suspension of hostilities. It was the first complete Allied victory against the Central Powers. Already, two days earlier, Bulgarian delegates had arrived at Salonica to sue for peace. That same day, 28 September 1918, Hindenburg and Ludendorff, meeting at Spa, reached the decision that with the collapse of the Macedonian Front the War was lost and (as Ludendorff wrote in his memoirs), instructed Berlin to begin negotiations for Peace. On 4 October King Ferdinand of Bulgaria abdicated. After the collapse of Bulgaria, Greek and British forces under the British General Milner started the long march to Constantinople. The capitulation of Bulgaria severed communications between Germany and Turkey. The Turks in the meantime had been routed in Mesopotamia and Enver and Talaat had resigned. On 30 October 1918, while the Greek and British advance guard reached Dedeagatch [Alexandroupolis] the Turks signed the armistice at Mudros on the Greek island of Lemnos. On 3 November Austria signed the armistice. On 9 November the Kaiser abdicated and left Germany with the Crown Prince for Holland. (He settled quietly at Doorn where he lived until his death in 1941). And on 11 November 1918 the armistice with Germany was signed at Rhétondes, France.

The Allied victory in the Balkans was, in effect, the beginning of the end of the Great War which had been started in a small Balkan town four years earlier. Under Eleftherios Venizelos Greece participated in the final effort of the victorious Allies. But Metaxas never forgave him and the Liberals and the Allies for the "humiliations" to which they had subjected Greece in order to coerce her into the War. On 31 December 1934 Metaxas wrote in an Athens newspaper:

Perhaps they will tell us that the successes from the victory will cloak all these shames! Do you think so? Do you think there is a success big enough to cloak the national ruins into which Greece was transformed by such disgraces and such disasters?[96]

A few days earler, on 18 December 1934 he wrote:

Mr. Venizelos perhaps might ask us: what does all this matter if he managed to get out of the War a Greece double in territory and strength? This is "the big lie" and we shall prove it to him when we discuss the Treaty of Sèvres .... But even if Greece had come out of the War increased in territory, which did not actually happen, because of this policy of Mr. Venizelos, who used foreign troops to subjugate his fellow-citizens, Greece was crushed morally, and lost her national pride and her self-respect. Into her blood entered the habit of being mercenary, even against her own citizens and the absolute, exclusive sentiment toward the Fatherland was decreased. Such a moral decadence cannot really contribute even in the preservation of her territorial gains.

96 *Ethnikos Dichasmos*, p. 199.

Who knows how many years longer it will take for us, the Greeks, to come to ourselves![97]

Two years had not elapsed after Metaxas wrote these words when he staged a *coup d'etat*, perhaps in an attempt to bring the Greeks to themselves ... The roots of the Metaxas dictatorship are very much embedded in this soil of fraternal discord and national humiliation. Metaxas wrote that the example of Venizelos, who used foreign armies and foreign fleets in order to return to power, was unique in modern history. In his tortuous mind the future dictator of Greece could easily forget the series of usurpations of the liberties of the Greek people if the King was responsible. As he had written while a student in Berlin, it was immaterial whether the King was right or wrong ... What really mattered was that the will of the King should reign supreme and there were no limits to which Colonel Metaxas would not go to make certain that his King had his way. The high-handed actions of the Allies, their blunders and their self-righteousness and the insults and the insolence of the Greek Liberals provided Metaxas with plenty of fuel to feed his passion against the enemies of his King and against those institutions which favored the spirit of insubordination and defiance.

The Venizelists were, in Metaxas' view, the men who had stabbed the King and the country in the back, who had brought dire degradation and mortification to the King and the country. To Metaxas this was a very personal matter, a personal wound which stayed raw and festering and which allowed him no peace of mind until he evened scores with his enemies and the enemies of his King. When Metaxas debated the events of the Great War in 1934 he did so with such anger and acrimony that it seemed as if the Greek political conflicts during the Great War had only just occurred. He was writing then:

The French nation never forgave the return of the Bourbons by foreign bayonets and it paid them back for it. The Greek nation would do the same to Mr. Venizelos on 1 November 1920. [On this day the Liberals lost the Elections and Venizelos and his friends fled the country in their turn.] Peoples do not forget such things. The Greek people will never forget the June of 1917.[98]

How Venizelos, despite his diplomatic successes at the Peace Conference in Paris, lost the confidence of the Greek people we shall see in the following chapters. Metaxas spent this time first in enforced exile in Corsica and then as a fugitive in Italy - wavering between abject despair for the present and wild hopes for the future.

---

97 *Ibid.*, p. 180.

98 *Ibid.*, p. 176.

The Years of Exile

The journey from Piraeus to Corsica took nine days. The SS *Vasilefs Constantinos* lifted anchor at 2 p.m. on 20 June, 1917 and after a circuitous journey through the Mediterranean - to avoid enemy interception - arrived at Ajaccio on 29 June. About one hundred people had gathered at the port to watch the arrival of the Greek exiles, curious islanders asking each other, "Which one is the former Prime Minister?" "Which is the former Mayor of Athens?" "Which one is Colonel Metaxas?"[1] Some of the exiles had brought along their families and they must have looked like a party of tourists, well groomed and prosperous. Metaxas had with him his wife, Lela, and his two small daughters, both under the age of six.

Ajaccio, the capital of Corsica, is on the west coast of the island, but it is actually facing south and is some considerable distance from the coast of the French Riviera. The imposing buildings of the corniche and the caiques, reflected in the calm waters of the harbor, must have reminded Metaxas of Ithaca, where he was born; and the narrow streets of the old quarter of Ajaccio must have reminded him of Argostoli where he grew up.

The Greek exiles were divided between two large hotels. The Metaxas family and other important exiles were accommodated at the *Grand Hotel*, a period structure with beautiful gardens in front, palm trees and a great variety of rare flowers. At the back of the hotel there were pines and olive trees on a hill, a landscape not unlike many in Attica or the Ionian islands. At noon the Greek residents of the *Grand Hotel* would walk over to the *Hotel de France* to have lunch with the other exiles and talk politics. The emotional stress of most of the exiles did not contribute to a friendly atmosphere and relations among them were not always harmonious. With some of his fellow exiles Metaxas had very little in common and with two or three he was not on speaking terms. As was natural, Metaxas often discussed politics and military matters with his fellow exiles who were politicians and military men. Every day he perused the newspapers and followed closely the developments of the European War. He also read a great deal and took private lessons to improve his French. On Sundays he went to Mass with his family at the Serbian Orthodox Church.

Every evening Metaxas observed the ritual promenading walk of a Greek islander. Often leaving his wife and children behind in a cafe, he would go for long walks as far as what was then known as "the English forest," where from a beautiful chapel he could see the Gulf of Ajaccio. At other times he would walk along the coastal road which led to the *Chapelle des Grecs*, a small church built in the seventeenth century by Greek

1 Some of the pieces of information in this section come from D. Kallonas, *Ioannis Metaxas* (Athens, 1938).

immigrants from Mani in the Peloponnese. At other times he would climb to the top of Punta to the ancient castle of Duke Pozzo di Borgo, the rival of Buonaparte. From there he could see the white tops of Monte d'Oro and the little islands of Sangner. On his long walks he often took with him his sketchbook. Some of his pencil drawings of landscapes and churches and houses, of little artistic value, are still preserved among his papers in the National Archives in Athens.

One day, on 11 August 1917, from 10 a.m. to 3 p.m., he wrote twenty handwritten pages of the first draft of a comedy entitled *Twenty-four Hours Delay*, on the trite theme of domestic misunderstandings with servants and telephones. Although he wrote on the cover "Copyright by Mr. Ioannis Metaxas," he never composed a final draft.

Metaxas, in many ways an exemplary husband and father, devoted most of his time to his family. He taught Greek to his young daughters, himself composing a first Greek Reader for their use. This Reader he later had bound in Italy and it is preserved among his papers. On the inside cover he inscribed: "In 1917 in Ajaccio, Corsica, where we were held by the French by force, desiring to teach my children how to read and not having Greek teaching books, I composed this Primer (*Alphabetarion*) with which Lulu and Nana learned to read Greek. Then in October 1919 I had it bound in Siena, so it is preserved as a momento of the teaching of the first letters in family love and happiness amidst a savage and terrible age."[2]

Metaxas' chief preoccupation in Corsica was the Great War and its vicissitudes and the future world which would emerge from the terrible conflagration. With grave concern and mental anguish he followed the course of the War and often had long serious discussions about it with the other exiles who were either military men like the former Chief of Staff, Victor Dousmanis, or politicians like the former Prime Minister, Demetrios Gounaris. The intervention of the United States especially worried him. Would this tip the balance? Would this be the end? "There is no power in this world to change the fact that while the Allies of the Entente are fighting on the periphery, the Central Powers are fighting in the center,"[3] he wrote on 17 November 1917. But his concern went further than the immediate situation. What would the American involvement in Europe ultimately mean for the future of the world? Was this the beginning of a great confederation of all the English-speaking countries? Such a confederation, Metaxas decided, thinking of German unification in the Nineteenth Century, could only succeed if one of these countries was by far stronger than the others. Under the present circumstances any attempt at confederation would in time bring about open war between England and the United States over the question of hegemony. He writes:

---

2 General State Archives, Athens. Archive of Ioannis Metaxas.

3 Metaxas, *Diary*, II, p. 454.

Such struggles do not always end up in unification - example, the Peloponnesian War. The German struggle ended in unification (not a complete one) and because of the greater superiority of Prussian power, the tendency of the German States for union was very strong, not only because of their common interests but also because of the dangers of division. This is not the case in the Anglo-Saxon States. The separatist tendencies are by far the stronger.[4]

Some of Metaxas' prognostications are far-ranging and they apply better to the aftermath of the Second World War. On 5 August 1917 Metaxas wrote that if Germany and Austria were to be defeated a center of great instability would be created in the heart of Europe.

Because each of the victors will seek to exercise an influence on the tiny states which will be born of the collapse of these two great states the result will be quarrels and ruptures. Therefore the great European states of the present-day Entente will find it impossible to concentrate their attention on the pursuit of a colonial policy and international trade; neither would they have the forces to defend this policy against the strength of America and Asia. [The U.S.A. and Japan]. The African races, too, would be dangerous for their present masters when the African soldiers now fighting as underlings of France and England return at the end of the War to their countries.[5]

Metaxas thought that the Central Powers could not be crushed but Germany, surrounded by the other European states as she was, would need their friendship in order to keep open her communications with her colonies and the markets of other continents. For this reason Germany would be peaceful and conciliatory. "Such a European unity is essential for the existence of the European states, they will become subordinate to the United States and Japan after being crushed in a struggle with them."[6]

Things did not turn out to be quite as Metaxas predicted. The period when Germany was peaceful and conciliatory after the First World War did not last long. Metaxas, of course, believed that a "white peace" (as he used to refer to it), that is a peace without recriminations, spoils or reparations, would end the war. (He was later shocked by "the base system of Versailles.") Still, it is interesting to notice that Metaxas considered a strong Germany and European cooperation as the cornerstone for a peaceful world - which is only a step further from the old idea on which the Nineteenth Century Balance of Power was based. Metaxas, on the other hand, was correct about the polarization of the world between two superpowers with the European states in the middle subordinate or dependent upon them. At the time it would have been impossible to foresee the rise of the Russian colossus, since Russia was torn by revolution and civil war. It was the

4 *Ibid.* , p. 452.
5 *Ibid.*, pp. 452-453.
6 *Ibid.*, p. 453

Japanese sun that was then rising ominously in the East. Metaxas was more successful in prophesying the struggle for independence of the European colonies in Africa and Asia.

On the question of peace Metaxas wrote (on 6 October 1917) that the real victors of the present War would be those who "will not be afraid of future free competition."[7]

A victory based on the military destruction of the opponent or even on his national degradation through the Peace Treaty is not possible [is not a real victory]. The victor would be the one who had the courage to conclude peace upon equal terms, confident that his intrinsic value will give him the advantage in a free competitive world.[8]

A year later, on 5 November 1918, six days before the Armistice was signed, Metaxas wrote that no Entente nation believed in or could implement the principles President Wilson had announced for the end of the War and the conclusion of peace without undermining the base of its power - except, perhaps, Italy, "if her soul did not have all the faults of Romaism [imperialism?]"[9] The road the United States was following would lead, in one way or another, to the conquest of all America, perhaps of the whole world. "Under the standard of Wilson's principles, pretending faith in ideals foreign to them, the Allies mustered the world together in order to defeat Germany and now, on the pretext of a million sophistries, they are trying to get out of their promises."[10]

As the end was approaching, Metaxas' thoughts turned inward and he wrote about his ideals which "live with the soul an eternal life. They are undefeated. They are covered by the impenetrable breastplate of Faith."[11] Even unhappiness can be transformed into great happiness when one knows how to suffer it and appreciate it. "It is the divine fire inside us which consumes anything rotten or imperfect or perishable and loosens the chains of the soul."[12] Death itself is part of life and we shall always be ready to die at any time. "It is not enough to know that we shall die, we must feel it too."[13] Death is no great loss, because we are mainly the product of a group which will stay behind to carry on. "If, dying, we were to take with us what is actually ours, we would be taking very little, perhaps not worth the trouble of loading ourselves with."[14] There is a kind of victory even in death and a kind of death which is a source of life. "The heroes are

7 *Ibid.*, p. 454
8 *Ibid.*.
9 *Ibid.*, p. 463.
10 *Ibid.*.
11 *Ibid.*, p. 464
12 *Ibid.*.
13 *Ibid.*, p. 455.
14 *Ibid.*.

not defeated. They fight and die. But the earth, drinking their blood, gives birth to them again."[15]

A few days after Metaxas recorded these thoughts, on 9 November 1918, the news reached him that the German Emperor Wilhelm II had abdicated. That evening Metaxas wrote only two words in his notebook: *Sursum corda.*[16] Let us lift up our hearts. The words come from the Latin Mass before the Elevation of the Host.

What were Metaxas' ideals which, united "with the soul, lead an eternal life?" In Corsica Metaxas did not keep his *Diary*. But in a separate notebook he began jotting down his observations and meditations. (He continued to do so until a few days before his death in January 1941. All in all he recorded 117 passages, some of them only a few lines.) The basic ideas of his totalitarian philosophy (which Metaxas developed in hundreds of speeches when he came to power) were already formulated in his mind and he wrote them down in this *Notebook of Thoughts* during the eighteen months of his exile. These ideas centered around the failure of Nineteenth Century Liberalism, the rejection of equality and the elitist view of society, the concept of totality, the idea of struggle, the vision of a new civilization being born.

The Great War was the catalyst - and the starting point of his thoughts. For Metaxas the War was not only a clash between two camps of belligerent nations; it was above all a clash between two philosophies, two opposing views of life, whose truth and strength was being tested in the present "struggle." At the time of his arrival in Corsica, Metaxas had few doubts who was going to win the War and why. His reasons were not so much the product of factual calculations, military, economic, political or otherwise, as befitted a pragmatic staff officer; they were rather pseudo-historical and politico-philosophical considerations - very revealing of the future dictator of Greece. In July 1917 Metaxas explained why Germany was bound to win the war. He wrote in his *Notebook of Thoughts*:

The progress of civilization in the Nineteenth Century created the need for perfectly organised group activity. The unit of activity is today the group, i.e. the totality of different individuals, among which the unified activity of the total is diversified and subdivided into parts. The most perfect condition for the individual is to preserve his freedom and entity within the group. Only German society succeeded in interpreting the group in a more perfect way than any other society. Thus German victory is inevitable and necessary, because German civilization corresponds to the needs of society, as society was transformed through evolution in the Nineteenth Century and because the very natural adaptation of German civilization to present-day needs gives to German society a greater strength for predominance over other nations.[17]

---

15 *Ibid.*, p. 464.

16 *Ibid.*.

17 *Ibid.*, p. 452.

A year later Metaxas' belief in German victory was not so absolute. But his observations on the War were again veiled in historical and pseudo-metaphysical terms. They were also the passionate cries of a man whose ideals were being tested in the furnace of battle; and, in a more mundane way, of a man whose future happiness and political ambitions were inextricably connected with the progress and the outcome of the War. On 17 April 1918 Metaxas wrote in his *Notebook of Thoughts*:

I have often asked myself: why is this War fought with such fanaticism? And I have always reached the conclusion: because it is a religious War.[18] Metaxas compared the Great War with *"the struggle of the Reformation against Papism,"* although he admitted that *"many other elements - of a political and economic nature, personal ambitions and interests of princes, sentiments and passions -- had their influence on the origins of the War and its progress."*[19]

Metaxas says that any one of these factors might have sparked off the War; but in that case the War would have had a different character and a different development and certainly different results. The Seven Years War, he wrote, was similar to the present War from the military point of view, but it was not a religious war and therefore its character was different. (Further down the page Metaxas suddenly noted: "Isn't Greece perhaps the Magdeburg of the Thirty Years War?")[20]

Germany, according to Metaxas, was leading the revolutionary forces which were for change and progress while the Entente Powers stood for reaction and suppression. "In truth, Germany today is fighting for freedom, for the triumph of excellence - even if her goals were not the same when she entered the War,"[21] Metaxas wrote. Again, "Germany today is waging the same struggle as the one the Protestant nations fought against Papism. Her task is the Reformation of the modern Faith.[22]

What was this modern Faith in which excellence played no part and which was an obstacle to progress and civilization? It was the religion of Equality. What was the name of the God worshipped by the nations who professed this faith? It was Democracy.

For this reason these nations call themselves democracies. Their rulers are not considered to be superior and leaders of the rest, but servants of the sovereign masses. Consequently it is not superiority which brings them to power but their artful skill in flattering the masses. For this reason not only are the rulers not the best men

18 *Ibid.*, p. 459.
19 *Ibid.*, p. 461.
20 *Ibid.*.
21 *Ibid.*, p. 460.
22 *Ibid.*.

but men of inferior calibre seeking through power to serve their private interests. But in this way the faulty administration weakens the democracies.[23]

It is not good to be weak and alone. Thus the fanaticism against those nations whose superior achievements put the idea of equality in doubt. "For this reason they seek the triumph of Democracy, that is, the spread of the religion of Equality all over the whole world so that the disease becomes common among all the nations of the earth."[24]

This religion of Equality has its worship and its ritual. Faith alone is not enough, there are certain forms one has to observe. "It is not enough to submit to the power of the masses. One must talk about certain things in a certain manner, one must accept certain ideas expressed in a certain phraseology ... Otherwise one is not considered a co-religionist."[25] *As in other established religions, to observe the form is often enough to be admitted into the fold; what really matters is the ability to parade one's faith in Equality. To observe the ritual is to proclaim the faith. Hypocrisy is the main characteristic of the followers of the religion of Equality. "But hypocrisy gradually corrupts the character. And thus the level of personal worth (αξία) among the nations who believe in Equality sinks lower and lower".*[26]

This practice of hypocrisy and double talk among the democracies is amply illustrated from their policies in the European War. "I did not take the time to study in detail the social and moral conditions during earlier wars," Metaxas wrote. But in the present War, he thought that the Entente Powers had made greater use of calumny and deception than had ever been done before. And this was only natural because --

Germany, not considering violence immoral, but considering necessity the highest law, has no reason to cover her actions with the cloak of virtue. On the other hand, the men of the Entente, after declaring that they were fighting for Justice, Freedom, Truth and Morality, and obliged to use every kind of violence against their opponents, whether these were states or persons, were obliged to justify this violence as necessary for the victory of these moral principles; they were, therefore, obliged to fall back on lies and slanders against their opponents whenever the real facts did not agree with their claims.[27]

Metaxas examined the dogma of the religion of Equality. Is there really such a thing as equality in life? Are men really equal? Is equality good for them? What made them invent the religion of Equality? Ever since men decided to improve their material conditions, they have become "discontented" and blame all their sufferings on inequality. It is true that men, in their relations to God or Nature, are equal, but their

---

23 *Ibid.*, p. 456.
24 *Ibid.*.
25 *Ibid.*, p. 458.
26 *Ibid.*, p. 459.
27 *Ibid.*, p. 454.

rights begin to be less equal toward the world and even more unequal toward their nation, and even more so among the small society of their town or village. This inequality is partly the result of past history and partly the result of the different measure of virtue or worth (*αξία*) in each individual.

The various degrees of axia among men make some stronger and more able than others: consequently the second are governed by the first. And this is in the best interests of the governed. But this is anathema to the religion of Equality which teaches as divine dogma the election of the rulers by the multitude - that is, by the weak and less intelligent who subject the rulers to a jealous scrutiny, turning them into servants of the crowd. Thus, even if necessity would put men under submission to naturally superior men, equality strives to remove them from power by taking away from them first the glamor of their office, the dignity of Authority.[28]

According to Metaxas, "inequality among men is the natural condition of society. Any measure against this natural and elemental law will inevitably have harmful and perhaps disastrous consequences."[29] The individual *axia* of a person is the product of many factors: physical and mental qualities, qualities which are inherited and others which are acquired. The rights of the individual are, by the nature of things, proportionate to the absolute worth of the individual or to his relative worth in each circumstance. This is the law of Nature which nobody can change. The Democracies - "that is, what the present political dictators call democracies, whether monarchical or not" - through legislation, institutions, constitutional measures, and the unlimited power of the majority, aim at imposing a mandatory equality upon everybody.

Therefore they are in a constant inner struggle: the antagonism of one political religion against human nature. Civil war is therefore continuous, sometimes clandestine, sometimes open. One part of society, often the greater part, is under terrible oppression. And sometimes almost the whole of society is a slave to a small section which appears, on the strength of political-religious dogmas, to represent the will of the total.[30]

This is an unnatural and unhealthy situation which breeds doubts for the future among the citizens, impedes progress, makes men egoistical and destroys any sense of social solidarity. For these reasons, "the present-day democratic societies experience progress only externally - in volume and territory, and not internally, in depth and quality."[31]

Metaxas then gives us a very different picture of those countries where the people do not live by the "unnatural" law of equality.

---

28 *Ibid.*, p. 458.
29 *Ibid.*, p. 461.
30 *Ibid.*, p. 462.
31 *Ibid.*.

In countries where the aristocracy rules, where the state reflects the social hierarchy which corresponds to the natural inequality among men -- a permanent hierarchy developing in harmony with the progress of society and elastic enough to allow to those exceptional human beings their due influence on the whole according to their individual axia -- in these countries the prevailing sense of security liberates men for action, gives birth to self-confidence, to social solidarity, to self-respect and respect for others, and therefore to dignity, to that kind of superior patriotism which is so different from the fetishism toward the image of the fatherland. It is there (where one can find) the advance of true civilization, piety, morality, man's progress to perfection. And above all, only these [aristocratic] countries can secure to their citizens real freedom.[32]

As the Christians of an earlier age zealously fought the normal impulses of human nature, so do the present religious fanatics fight the natural law of inequality. Those who do not proclaim the established Faith of Equality are heretics to be converted or excommunicated and if necessary burned at the stake.

Germany was denounced by the Democracies, the nations which believe in Equality, as a heretic and an enemy of humanity exactly as the Protestants were denounced by the Pope as heretics and enemies of Christianity. Clemenceau, Lloyd George and above all Wilson, are not they the Popes of Equality? Are they not the representatives of Democracy on earth? Do not they, too, want to save the people from the threat of militarism, exactly as the Popes wanted to save the people from Satan?[33]

Militarism, according to Metaxas, means "a hierarchy in society, an inequality of rights, a proportion of rights according to one's *axia*."[34] The Democracies also have armies, but because they believe in the dogma of equality their citizens are free, while the rest of the world are children of the Devil. As the Popes of old tried to free the souls of the Christians from the virus of Lutheranism, so do the Popes of Democracy seek to free the world from the virus of "Germanism". "Germany is an Antidemocracy, as Luther was Antichrist. For this reason she must be crushed."[35]

Germany, Metaxas continues, is thought to spill over with every evil and impurity. She has given her soul to the devil of militarism and therefore her actions cannot be judged by the same standards as similar actions by other nations. Any gesture of goodwill on her part is only a devil's trick aimed at deceiving and destroying. For this reason she cannot expect any mercy from the devotees of Equality. Her annihilation is a task pleasing to God and it is necessary for the redemption of the world. There is only one way for the Germans to be saved: to banish their leaders and submit to the modern

32 *Ibid.*.

33 *Ibid.*.

34 *Ibid.*, p. 459.

35 *Ibid.*.

Popes, to confess their sins and do penance, to renounce Militarism and return to the bosom of the one and only holy catholic and apostolic Democratic State, the only source of divine grace. Against unrepentant heretics there is only one answer -- holy war.

"Thus Germany today is fighting the same struggle the Protestant nations fought against Papism. Her task is the Reformation of the modern Faith."[36] As Luther and his followers tried, at the beginning, to remain within the Catholic Church, so Germany at first, argued Metaxas, tried to placate the Democracies by adopting certain political reforms. Germany was then under the influence of egalitarian ideas.

But the longer the struggle goes on the more the separation of ideas is apparent and the more boldly the new Protestants declare their ideas and the clearer is their task ahead. Indeed Germany struggles today for freedom, for the triumph of excellence (axia) -- even if her goals were different when she entered the War. The Protestants, too, ended up being the carriers and protectors of freedom of conscience and freedom for the search for truth, although these were not their original goals.[37]

According to Metaxas, it was only natural for the cult of Equality to degenerate and corrupt -- it was not in accord with human nature, neither did it fulfil human expectations.

The reformation of the universal religion [of Equality] was inevitable. The people who could not live any longer under its aging dogmas broke away and earned the name of rebels. These people are formulating in the present struggle the new dogmas of a new religion.[38]

The chosen people who were then, in the Great War, waging the struggle for "freedom of conscience" and who were working out the political reformation of the world were, of course, the Germans. The War was not only inevitable but necessary. On 17 October 1918 Metaxas wrote:

The blows which Germany is suffering are the blows of the hammer by which the rust is removed and discarded so that the pure metal beneath can shine. In this way, welded together, the metal will become stronger and acquire its true value.[39]

Metaxas considered the separate armistice which Austria had signed on 3 November, 1918 "a great blessing for Germany."

Germany only now can raise, full of sincerity and faith, the standard of the great ideals of mankind, which correspond to the tendencies of the German soul in a much greater degree than any other race.[40]

---

36 *Ibid.*, p. 460.
37 *Ibid.*.
38 *Ibid.*, p. 460f.
39 *Ibid.*, p. 462.
40 *Ibid.*, p. 463.

These were the signs of the times and a portent for the future. On 17 April 1918 Metaxas wrote in his *Notebook of Thoughts*: "Mankind is entering upon a new stage, a new civilization is being born."[41]

The Armistice was signed on 11 November 1918. The Allied victory was complete. Venizelos' belief in the final triumph of the Allies was justified and his unwavering pro-Entente policies were vindicated. In Athens there were jubilant celebrations. The Greek Liberals exulted not only over the victories of the Greek Army in Macedonia; the Allied success also reaffirmed their victory over their domestic enemies, the Royalists.

In Corsica a cloud of gloom and despair descended over the Greek exiles. Germany, despite her central position, despite her "superior civilization", was totally crushed. Metaxas' predictions had turned out to be wrong. It was not even a "white peace." The collapse of the Central Powers was humiliating. There were reports that the Allies were to put on trial the leaders of their defeated enemies and demand their exemplary punishment. Metaxas, who had personally signed the surrender order of Fort Rupel to the Germans and Bulgarians, who had organised the Reservists and confronted the Allied troops in the streets of Athens, was apprehensive that he would be made the object of the victors' vengeance. He was especially apprehensive of "French vindictiveness." Soon after the Armistice, news reached Ajaccio that the Liberals of Athens had asked, and the French Government was considering, the extradition of the Greek Royalists. "Oh, no! This will never happen. We shall not surrender with tied hands to the Liberals,"[42] Metaxas said when he heard the news.

One day Metaxas, after visiting "Napoleon's Cave", was on his way to see the house where Buonaparte was born, when he suddenly conceived the idea of escape. His plan was to travel by car at night from Ajaccio to the Bay of Bonifacio and from there to sail to Sardinia. Then, travelling *incognito* through Italy, to cross over the border in the north to Switzerland, where King Constantine and many Royalists had found refuge. If he failed to reach Switzerland, he could ask for asylum from Italy, which had demonstrated in the recent Greek troubles her sympathy with the Greek Royalists. Once he had thought out his plan Metaxas tried to sound some of the other exiles, those closer to him, to see if they would like to join in the attempt. Two of them agreed. They were the former Prime Minister Demetrios Gounaris and the former deputy George Pesmazoglou. John Sayias, the President-General of the Reservists, would not go, despite Metaxas' grave concern for his safety if he stayed behind.

To put this plan of escape into action Metaxas needed local help. During his eighteen months sojourn in Corsica he had become acquainted with several people and there is a strong indication in his *Diary* that he employed and paid secret agents to keep him

41 *Ibid.*, p. 461.

42 Kallonas, *Metaxas*, p. 51.

informed on certain matters. Eventually he made contact with two bandits, fugitives from the law, who, for a price, agreed to help. The first part of the plan was to travel by night the difficult mountain road from Ajaccio to Bonifacio Bay. No one was then allowed to use a car on the island after dark except the Prefect of Corsica, a certain G. Allain. It was therefore decided to steal the Prefect's official car for the night drive to Bonifacio.

The escape was carried out on the night of 6 December 1918. Exactly one year later, while living in Siena, Metaxas wrote a brief account of his escape in his *Diary*.[43] The three men who were to make the attempt were anxiously awaiting word from their contacts all through the night of 5 December. Early next morning the message arrived: "Today is the day." Metaxas made a last minute effort to persuade Sayias to go with them. It was in vain. Then he went up to his hotel room with his wife, balanced his accounts and made his final preparations. After that he wrote a note to his teacher of French that they would not have a lesson that day. Then he went out for a walk with Gounaris in the *Cours Napoléon* and the corniche. From a distance one of their contacts, who had not heard of the latest developments, waved a distress signal that nothing new was happening. The two men sat at a café in the *Cours Napoleon*. After twelve o'clock Metaxas went to the *Hotel de France* and gave money to Sayias. He assured Sayias of his friendship but this time he did not tell him anything about his plans. After lunch at the *Grand Hotel* the three men met upstairs. Gounaris was a bachelor, but young Pesmazoglou had his wife and children with him. He and Metaxas repeated their detailed instructions to their wives whom they were leaving behind. Metaxas wrote about his wife: "Lela [was] daring, courageous."[44] The two married men then went to Gounaris' room and arranged their money in several envelopes. The weather was calm, the sky clouded. The hotel was quiet.

About five in the afternoon Metaxas and Gounaris went out and strolled up and down in *Cours Napoleon* so that the people could see them. From a *delicatessen* they bought various things for the journey. At six they returned to the *Grand Hotel*. Outside the hotel a small boy they had been using to carry secret messages informed them that their "stuff" could not go with them. This worried Metaxas and he wondered whether he could trust the bandits. But the time of departure was drawing near and he went up and started to dress. Gounaris got ready first and after saying goodbye to the ladies went out. They had arranged to meet at 6:30 p.m. by the statue of the Premier Consul.

Metaxas put on his new heavy suit and said goodbye to his children. "I did not kiss them very much so as not to arouse suspicion,"[45] he wrote. One of the little girls said

43 Metaxas, *Diary*, II, pp. 564-7.

44 *Ibid.*, p. 565.

45 *Ibid.*.

to him, "Why did you put on these clothes?"[46] The children went to their room to sleep. Metaxas filled his pockets with various articles for the journey. Then it was time to say goodbye to his wife. They were both moved. Lela said to him: "That's why I wanted you, that's why I married you, because I knew that you could be daring, brave."[47] Metaxas wrote: "She is brave, heroic. We say goodbye. I walk out of the room, she follows me up to the top of the staircase. I go down a few steps. She calls me back. A last warm kiss."[48] On the second floor Metaxas said goodbye to Madame Pesmazoglou, who was sick in bed, and then walked out through the deserted hall to the garden where he was joined by George Pesmazoglou.

It was approaching seven. The night was dark. No lantern was lighted. The sky was overcast. The two men walked to the *Rue Grand Val*, then to the square, then to the *Avenue Premier Consul*. A shadowy form was following them. It was Gounaris. The three men walked some distance. They reached the appointed place and waited anxiously for some time. Then a light flashed. It was their contact. The three men followed through the dark to where the Prefect's stolen car was waiting. They piled in and set off. It was past eight p.m. It was a long, difficult drive through the dense, dark night. They joked nervously among themselves. At several check points the police, recognising the Prefect's car, waved them on. Often they had to follow a circuitous route, but the bandits knew the terrain well. Metaxas writes: "Narrow passes. Uphill and down. Labyrinth."[49] At five the next morning they reached the Straits of Bonifacio. There again they had to wait for some time. Then they saw a little light from the sea below. Metaxas signalled back with his flashlight. It was important to make the channel crossing before daybreak.

The fishermen quietly rowed the boat with Metaxas and his friends in it through the Bonifacio Straits. In the east a line of lights appeared on the horizon. For a moment they thought it was a searchlight and the three fugitives ducked down. But it was only the dawn. There was a gust of wind and the boat rocked. Drops of rain fell. (Metaxas graphically describes the escape - in the telegraphic language he had adopted for his *Diary* since he took up writing it again on the day after his escape). In the distance there were small islands. With the early morning they saw the beams from the lighthouse of Sardinia. The fishermen then noticed in the far distance the small boat of the Italian coastguard and immediately turned west to avoid it. Then, when they were at a safe distance, they veered round, lifted the sail and headed toward the coast of Sardinia. At 9:00 a.m. the three runaways landed on a deserted rocky beach and the boat put out to

46 *Ibid.*.

47 *Ibid.*.

48 *Ibid.*, p. 565f.

49 *Ibid.*, p. 566.

sea at once. Soon after the Italian coastguard cruised by, but the three men hid among the rocks.

From there, after a difficult three hours walk, they reached Santa Teresa di Gallura. As they walked they could clearly see Bonifacio beyond the channel. The rest of Corsica was hidden in the mist. Metaxas was thinking of his wife. "My heart aches. In front of me the unknown",[50] he wrote later of that moment. As they had aroused the suspicions of the coastguard, Metaxas was against their entering Santa Teresa. He wanted them instead to hide until the evening and then find a carriage to take them to Tempio, the next town. But the other two men, although younger than him, were exhausted and disagreed. They needed sleep and they were hungry. At the hotel they avoided signing the register by breaking the pen. At eight in the evening the local police, probably alerted by the Corsican authorities by then, arrived. Metaxas wrote: "We had been recognised. So we disclosed our identities. It is finished! Prisoners again!"[51] A uniformed guard was placed outside the hotel. The next day the hotel manager, whom Metaxas suspected of having betrayed them, said to him plaintively: "If you had only warned me beforehand!"[52]

The Greek fugitives stayed for three days in Santa Teresa di Gallura. Here Metaxas decided to start his *Diary* again. The style he now adopted, perhaps because of his harassed life as a fugitive, is different from his earlier entries. The sentences are short, telegraphic, often cryptic, but still informative concerning his movements and his state of mind.

On 10 December 1918 the three men moved to the town of Tempio. The newspapers carried stories about them and their escape from Corsica. The French Government asked for their extradition, but the Italians, whose relations with the French had been hardening since the Armistice, were reluctant to comply. The Italians hoped to use Venizelos' political rivals in their conflict with the Greek Prime Minister. The Italian Foreign Minister in the Government of Signor Orlando was Baron Sonnino, with strong antipathies toward Greece and personally envious of Venizelos. Venizelos was just then on an official visit to Rome. If he asked the Italians to hand over Metaxas and his friends, he was disappointed. The Italian Government directed that the Greek fugitives should go to Cagliari, the main city of Sardinia, and remain there under police supervision. So after nine days in Tempio, accompanied by the deputy Prefect, they travelled to Sassari where the Prefect himself was waiting to question them. Three days later, on 21 December, they made the long journey to Cagliari on the south coast of Sardinia.

---

50 *Ibid.*, p. 567.
51 *Ibid.*.
52 *Ibid.*, p. 465.

The three Greek fugitives spent the next seven months in Cagliari, staying at the hotel *Scala di Ferro*. It was, perhaps, the worst period of Metaxas' life. His ideals had collapsed, he was separated from his family, he lived in constant fear that his enemies would catch up with him. At times he even doubted if he had done the right thing: "Was it a mistake to escape from Corsica?" he wrote in his *Diary*: "Not to stay behind and surrender and face trial? What was I afraid of? Right was on my side. Thus I sacrificed my family and launched myself into an adventure whose end is unknown." In Sardinia Metaxas made plans to escape by boat to Genoa and hence to Switzerland. Pesmazoglou was willing to go with him, but not Gounaris. In mid-January 1919 his plans were reported in the newspaper and a month later he heard that Switzerland would not have them. These plans were abandoned but the Italian Police, fearing that the three Greek fugitives would slip through their fingers, followed them everywhere, on their walks, to the library, to the cinema, in the corridors of their hotel. This constant surveillance was kept up throughout their stay in Sardinia. Metaxas was kept under special surveillance; this irritated him excessively and a few times he had words with the police. He wrote in his *Diary*: "The policemen are trailing us shamelessly. For five months we have had them after us. Liberal Italy! Liberal Orlando!"[53]

In Sardinia Metaxas made contact with the Italian Masons and through them applied to the Grand Master (a certain Nathan) of the Italian Freemasonry and asked for assistance. Metaxas ranked Thirtieth in the Mason hierarchy - there are only three higher degrees - while George Pesmazoglou ranked Eighteenth. The Masons of Sardinia extended the hand of friendship to "brother" Metaxas and his two companions. The Masonic Lodge at Cagliari was called Sigismondo Arquez. At a reception at the Lodge (on 14 June 1919) the speakers mentioned the Greek exiles and expressed the wish that the three men should soon return to their country in safety and be united with their families. The Italian Masons were bitter against France, which pleased Metaxas. A colonel sitting next to him remarked: "Within a few years the Italians will be allies of the Germans."[54]

It was a miserable rainy winter, the sky was usually overcast. Metaxas was bored and restless, bitter over his misfortunes. His confidence reached its lowest ebb and he was often in despair. He was very lonely and went for long walks by himself to the cemetery, to Malobra, to the corniche. He writes in his *Diary*: "Alone. Sadness. Bitter memories of life."[55] On the national day of Greece (25 March/7 April 1919 - observed according to the Old Style then) a time of celebration in Athens, of official parties, parades with V.I.Ps in the grandstand, Metaxas thought of how often he had been ignored and slighted. He wrote: "Today is 25 March! Memories from the past. Always

53 *Ibid.*, p. 502.
54 *Ibid.*, p. 516.
55 *Ibid.*.

bitter memories. I was always passed over...."[56] On 25 April 1919 he wrote: "My birthday. I have finished my 48th year and I enter my 49th. My God, what I have suffered!"[57] From time to time he wrote in his *Diary* the German word *Ergebung* - submission, resignation. He often took sedatives to calm himself and to be able to sleep.

He wrote: "I suffer terribly.[58] ... I have become neurotic. [59].... Sometimes my mind wavers."[60] One afternoon, after a short nap, he read *La parte del baritone* by Lucatelli. He noted in his *Diary*: "At the moment of triumph, I was so moved by the triumph of worth and remembering my misfortunes, I burst into sobs. I weep. I weep. I call upon God. Where are you? *Are you?* All my despair pours out of my soul. Wails of woe ...."[61] For a desperate moment, he even thought of committing suicide. "If I hadn't been thinking what would become of Lela and the children, I would have killed myself."[62] A devoted husband and father, Metaxas missed his family terribly. Their love had sustained him in Corsica. The separation was unbearable and the other men often had to comfort and encourage him. Gounaris and Pesmazoglou met two Greek sisters from Trieste who had been deported to Cagliari and became special friends. Not Metaxas: "I think of my Lela",[63] he wrote. A month after he had left his family behind in Ajaccio he wrote: "Shall I ever see them again?"[64] But any suggestion by Pesmazoglou that they should hire a boat and sail to Corsica to kidnap the wives Metaxas considered absurd. While in Sardinia Metaxas corresponded with his wife through a certain Castaldi, a French merchant of Marseilles, who was the brother-in-law of the Greek General Bairas. Bairas, who had married the sister of this Frenchman, was one of the Greek exiles in Corsica.[65] Metaxas spent agonised days and nights when he did not hear from his wife, but when a letter arrived he was in seventh heaven. The delays and the interference with his letters by the censor greatly irritated him. At one point he noted in his *Diary*: "Liberté - Egalité - Fraternité = Prefettura - Questura - Censura!"[66]

When Metaxas heard that the *internés* of the Allies were to be released he wrote: "Nothing about us ... Will they ever let our wives go? I boil inside."[67] He wrote a letter

56 *Ibid.*, p. 493.
57 *Ibid.*, p. 498.
58 *Ibid.*.
59 *Ibid.*, p. 482.
60 *Ibid.*, p. 478.
61 *Ibid.*, p. 493.
62 *Ibid.*, p. 509.
63 *Ibid.*.
64 *Ibid.*, p. 470.
65 General Bairas wrote a book in French about Fort Rupel and his experiences on the Macedonian Front.
66 Metaxas, *Diary*, II, p. 487.
67 *Ibid.*, p. 477.

to the Italian Government through the local Perfect asking that his family and the family of Pesmazoglou be allowed to join them. Through the intervention of the Masons, his request went as high as Sonnino, the Italian Foreign Minister. The Italians, who had refused to return the three refugees to France, declined to intervene. They had already had problems with France at the Peace Conference. It was hardly the time to ask favors of them. Metaxas then wrote to the *Ligue des Droits de l'Homme*. They answered that they would do their best. Metaxas wrote back to them immediately. He also wrote to Clemenceau, the French Premier, and to Signor Orlando in Paris, but there is no record that he ever received an answer.

Every day Metaxas would go to a café to read the newspapers. On 18 January 1919, the Peace Conference in Paris officially opened and Metaxas followed its deliberations with great interest. The cavalier treatment of Germany by the victorious Allies angered and distressed him; to watch once mighty Germany on her knees was especially painful to him. He wrote on 13 March 1919: "News: situation in Germany dreadful. It affects me because of the harshness of the French."[68] In Cagliari the young people staged a demonstration and, waving Italian flags, marched to the port "with shouts of enthusiasm in front of two surrendered German submarines which had their flags lowered ... The German flag!"[69] It broke his heart ... the collapse of Germany signified to him the end of an era. He wrote on 19 May 1919:

The defeat of Germany, which I never expected, overturned a great civilization of the highest value at its peak. Hatred, jealousy, injustice, violence, calumny, money, hypocrisy [appearances and not realities], prevailed. Is it possible for a situation like this to continue?[70]

When he read in the newspapers that the French, who had supported the Polish claims on Danzig, had agreed that it should be made a Free City, Metaxas was jubilant. "Hurrah! This signals the retreat of the chauvinist spirit."[71] The Germans were not invited to the drafting of the Versailles Treaty. The German delegation, which had arrived on 7 May 1919, was then asked to read the Allied draft and give their comments. The German reply ran to five hundred pages. Metaxas writes: "The Germans sent a whole delegation. And what a reply [they gave]! It was a slap in the face for the French. Joy, joy!"[72] The Germans protested that the terms were not in accord with the conditions on which Germany signed the Armistice; they also protested that many of the terms were impossible to fulfil. The Allies made insignificant changes

68 *Ibid.*, p. 486.
69 *Ibid.*, p. 499.
70 *Ibid.*, p. 507.
71 *Ibid.*, p. 493.
72 *Ibid.*, p. 498.

in the text and the Germans signed - there was nothing else they could do - on 28 June 1919 in the *Galerie des Glaces* of the Palace of Versailles, the same Hall of Mirrors where in January 1871 the German Empire had been proclaimed.

In Corsica Metaxas had studied French with a French tutor. In Sardinia he began reading Dante with an Italian tutor. He also read in Italian a book of philosophy, *Introduzione alla Filosofia* by Paulsen. On their walks about the city the intellectual Demetrios Gounaris, who spoke fluent Italian, had the habit of stopping at every bookstore, which annoyed Metaxas. The Greek exiles were frequent visitors at the local library. Once Metaxas borrowed and very carefully copied an inflammatory proclamation against the French written by the philosopher and historian Carlo Cattaneo (1801 - 1869). The proclamation called upon the Italians to boycott French goods after the French armies invaded Rome in 1849 to help restore Pope Pius, *"al perfide pontefice, capo degli oppressori d'ogni lingua e d'ogni religione."*[73] The Pope had fled to Gaeta, fearing the revolutionary agitation in Rome. After an armistice was negotiated by Ferdinand de Lesseps, the citizens of Rome opened the gates, but the French recalled de Lesseps and laid siege to the city. Guiseppe Garibaldi, after a valiant defence, retreated, and his 5,000 men were killed to a man. Garibaldi himself escaped after dramatic adventures. The French then sent some of their enemies to work in the mines of Corsica. Obviously Metaxas saw a parallel between the French expedition against Rome in 1849 and the French expedition against Athens in 1917. In both cases the French dispatched their enemies to Corsica. Cattaneo, the writer of this proclamation, was an implacable opponent of Cavour, as Metaxas was of Venizelos. At the bottom of his copy of the proclamation Metaxas made this note:

30 January/12 February 1919. In Cagliari, Sardinia, on a cold, rainy and windy day, in a modest room of the Hotel Scala di Ferro, alone, shivering, dejected, deprived of my wife and children who are held arbitrarily by the French in Corsica, deprived of my fatherland which was enslaved by the French [and was placed] under the tyranny of Venizelos.[74]

As if the proclamation had soothed him and given him fresh courage, he noted in his *Diary* the same day: "I live among the ruins of my ideals -- I shall rebuild a new ideal from the ruins!"[75] That evening he was calmer and, as he records, he slept well.

In Sardinia Metaxas lived with the constant fear that his powerful enemies would find a way to negotiate his extradition and carry him off to Athens for trial and certain sentence of death. He and Gounaris, who was a lawyer by training, spent long hours

---

73 Carlo Cataneo, "Circulare contro il commercio francese" Dal vol.II degli scritti politici (Firenze: Barbara, 1894). Taken from *Letture del Risorgimento italiano scelto e ordivate da Giosme Carducci* (Bologna ditta Nicola Zamichelli, 1897).

74 Metaxas, *Diary* , II, p. 478f.

75 *Ibid.*, p. 478.

at the local library studying the international law on extradition. In March the Greek government tried and sentenced to death *in absentia* Victor Dousmanis, who was one of the exiles in Corsica. Venizelos, not a vindictive man, commuted the sentence to life imprisonment. Metaxas noted in his *Diary*: "Therefore France refuses to grant extradition. But [in Athens] they grant pardons -- therefore, no amnesty?"[76] In May, the French did hand over to Greece the exiles from Corsica. Immediately Metaxas' mind went to the President-General of the *Leagues of the Reservists* whom he had tried unsuccessfully to induce to flee with him. "Poor John Sayias",[77] he wrote. Again, two days later: "Unfortunate comrades! Poor John Sayias!"[78] All that night he could not sleep. A few days later, on 18 May 1919, he wrote: "Since last night I am full of fears and anxieties. The delivery [by France to Greece] of the exiles from Corsica made a fearful impression on me. I must compose myself. It is shameful! I am neurotic ... I sense the enemy, vigilant, lying in wait all around me."[79] A Greek newspaper wrote that Metaxas, before his escape from Corsica, was reported to have said that he would rather commit suicide than fall into the hands of Venizelos. The report was false, but still Metaxas could find no rest. On 10 February 1919 he wrote that his return to Greece would be impossible and that he must find some kind of work abroad. "Need for courage," he wrote. Now, in May 1919, seeing his comrades being shipped to Athens to face charges of high treason for resisting "French despotism" and "the tyranny of Venizelos", as Metaxas put it, he blamed the Greek people and predicted that the future held disasters for his country. "We have been defeated because the Greek people, being corrupted, did not have the courage to fight for their freedom. Destiny will justify us. Everything that partakes of the evil will come to naught. The fate of Greece is heavy."[80] As Metaxas had foreseen, the President-General of the *Reservists*, as soon as he was brought back to Athens, was tried and sentenced to death. So were the exiles Merkouris, Constantine Eslin and George Pesmazoglou, the latter *in absentia*. Metaxas noted in his *Diary*: "Oh Sayias! What a weight I bear!"[81] And he worried about his own fortunes. The local French consul was reported to have said that Metaxas was to be sent to The Hague for trial. Were they saving him till last so they could make a world spectacle of him? On 5 June 1919 he wrote: "In the afternoon I slept badly, worrying about the International Court. It is absurd, but this suspicion will not leave me. Our enemies are so strong and so persistent."[82]

---

76 *Ibid.*, p. 491.
77 *Ibid.*, p. 504.
78 *Ibid.*, p. 505.
79 *Ibid.*, p. 506.
80 *Ibid.*, p. 517.
81 *Ibid.*, p. 522.
82 *Ibid.*, p. 517.

On 8 June 1919 the French authorities in Corsica returned their passports to Madame Lela Metaxas and to Madame Pesmazoglou. But the women and the children were not allowed to cross the channel to Italy and meet their husbands; instead they were directed to Marseilles and thence to Barcelona in Spain from where they were free to go anywhere they liked. It was a kind of bureaucratic revenge for the escape of the husbands. "How mean of the French," Metaxas noted in his *Diary*. *Unione Sarda* reported that Italy was releasing all persons detained because of the War: "And we continue to be *internati*," Metaxas noted in his *Diary*. "Deep disappointment! Wild anger! I have no taste for anything anymore. Gounaris accepts everything passively .... Fatalism. But I mean to win my freedom."[83]

On 19 June the Vittorio Orlando cabinet resigned and a new ministry was formed by Francesco Nitti. Tommaso Tittoni took over the Ministry of Foreign Affairs. Tittoni did not share the anti-Greek feelings of his predecessor Sonnino. Tittoni, who had already been approached by the Italian Masons, immediately gave instructions that the three Greek fugitives were free to leave Cagliari and sail over to mainland Italy. Metaxas and his two friends were given the choice of three Italian cities, Perugia, Lucca or Siena, where they could live with their families. After some reading about each city at the local library, they chose Siena.

Before leaving Cagliari, Metaxas bought a bracelet for his wife and gold buttons for his two daughters. He packed and dispatched his books and then travelled to Siena with the other two Greek exiles, where they arrived on 15 July 1919. Waiting for him there was his family. He noted in his *Diary* at the end of the day of his arrival: "Evening, 10 o'clock in Siena: Lela. Children. Happiness! Happiness! Happiness! At last reunited."[84] He and his wife occupied one room in a hotel and his two daughters an adjoining room. Then he rented a third room which he used as a study. He ordered shelves to be made and assembled his books and papers. Here in the mornings Metaxas busied himself with his correspondence and in the evenings he received his friends. When the cold days drew on he had a fire lit in the study. But life in a hotel was restrictive and after a while the Metaxas family moved to a rented house.

Metaxas stayed in Siena, under police supervision, for about a year. Siena then had a population of 30,000 people. Metaxas' first impressions of the medieval town were mixed. Four days after his arrival he wrote: "Sweet city, gentle lines, harmonious ... Nevertheless, I want to get out of the hibernation of the past and enter into a new life. I want a new city, modern, brimming with life."[85] In Siena, Metaxas often visited the *Duomo*. He thought the facade of the Renaissance cathedral was rich, "but without

83 *Ibid.*, p. 524.
84 *Ibid.*, p. 530.
85 *Ibid.*, p. 531.

unity."[86] Inside the dome was dark and ugly, but he found the floor mosaics with the biblical scenes (mainly by Domenico Beccafumi, 1486-1551) beautiful. The famous pulpit by Niccolo Pizano (died 1278) was "on the whole barbarous",[87] but he admired some of the reliefs. In his *Diary* Metaxas described quite vividly the *Palio delle Contrade*, the horseraces in which the seventeen neighbourhoods of Siena competed with each other twice a year in the *Piazza del' Campo*.[88] As he explored Siena he read books on the history of the city. But he was not in the mood to bury himself in the past. "Siena", he wrote, "with its narrow streets, the crowded houses, the churches, the palaces, its walls and all its medievalism oppresses me. The Middle Ages dishearten me. I am bored with all its poets and painters and sculptors and architects - I'm also bored with all the Renaissance."[89]

In the evenings Metaxas often went out with his wife to the theatre or the cinema. He had always liked to go to a play or a film or a concert and he never missed a chance to do so. In Cagliari he had seen a film called *Femina* which he liked, so in Siena he took his wife to see it. Gradually he settled down somewhat into the idle life of sleepy Siena. In September 1919 he had written that Siena was unbearable. Reading this again two months later he noted: "No, I have come to terms with Siena. The Middle Ages are not antipathetic."[90]

In Siena Metaxas had his Bible and some other valued books bound. One of these was the Greek primer he had written himself in Corsica. He himself now taught Greek and Italian to the girls and found tutors to teach them German and music. He translated *Pinocchio* for the children and read to them *The Wild Swans* by Hans Christian Andersen, which moved the little girls to tears. Madame Metaxas, who was a graduate of a French Catholic High School, taught the girls French. At the end of the fall quarter he conducted, "as formally as possible," examinations for his two daughters in the presence of his wife, his mother-in-law (who had come from Greece to visit them) and a lady-friend of the family. The subjects were Greek, French, Italian, Arithmetic, Geography and Anthropology. The girls "answered very well .... Then we drank chocolate. An unforgettable family occasion."[91]

The Greek exiles were not allowed to go to another city without a permit from the Prefect, but they were allowed to take trips to the surrounding countryside. Metaxas observed: "Beautiful resorts, the lines of the mountains gentle, harmony of colors. Here anything is calm and civilized. But where is that wild romanticism of Corsica! I cannot

86 *Ibid.*, p. 544.
87 *Ibid.*.
88 *Ibid.*, p. 540f.
89 *Ibid.*, p. 552.
90 *Ibid.*, p. 568.
91 *Ibid.*, p. 573.

forget the ravines and rocks on the coast of Ajaccio."[92] Like a true Greek, he missed the open horizons of the sea. "This restriction of liberty is something terrible. It is [a sign of] the age we live in. But I seek light, freedom. I want the sea: to gaze at open horizons, stretching to infinity. If we could only go to the sea!"[93] Again, "if I could only go to a little town on the Riviera to see the sea! To get away from the atmosphere and the environment of Siena which takes me five centuries back and suffocates me. To see a free horizon, a free sea!"[94] But he himself doubts whether the sea would be enough to comfort him. "Even there will I not be followed by the thoughts and bitterness of the past, the hopeless expectation for the future? .... The absence of an ideal ... all collapsed!"[95] But, remembering his family, which he loved dearly, he added: "I have Lela and the children. Forward! Courage!"[96]An entry in his *Diary* records that while in Siena Metaxas had finished the first chapter of his memoirs, but no such manuscript has been found among his papers. In Siena he carefully copied his *Diary* covering the period 23 November 1918 [O.S.] to 6 July 1920 [O.S.] from the small notebooks into 126 large pages. He also painted and, of course, he read voraciously, as was his habit. He read Greek newspapers, French novels, Italian poetry. In Siena (and later in Athens), he subscribed to the *Semaine de Suzette*. He read *Spartacus* by Giovagnioli, which he found "a beautiful book ... It very much interests me." Together with his wife he read *Innocente* by D'Annunzio and *Memorie di un ottuagenario*, a book Metaxas very much liked. From Siena he wrote to John Theotokis, the former Minister of Greece at Berlin and now in the entourage of the exiled King Constantine in Switzerland, and asked him for Ludendorff's *Memoirs of the Great War* - the German text, Metaxas specified. He also resumed reading Poulsen's *Introduzione alla Filosofia* which he had started in Sardinia, but - "I found it tiring: I want things which speak to my emotions, not to the intellect."[97]

And he started reading *The Renaissance* by Joseph Arthur Gobineau (1816-1882). Gobineau, who had been French Minister in Athens, was well known to the Greeks for his racialist theories. Gobineau believed in the superiority of the strong man and the strong race and had scandalized many Greeks when, in his writings, he expressed his regrets that the Persians, the mighty imperial conquerors from Asia, failed to crush the fickle, squabbling and undisciplined Greeks of Fifth Century Athens. Metaxas, although no racialist, had a spiritual affinity with the French writer. It was the virile,

---

92 *Ibid.*, p. 551.
93 *Ibid.*, p. 552.
94 *Ibid.*.
95 *Ibid.*, p. 551.
96 *Ibid.*.
97 *Ibid.*.

military states of Sparta, Macedonia and Rome, he believed, which had preserved and transmitted the highest products of civilization.

Gobineau was the first to propound the idea of the superior Aryan man and to speak of the universal racial corruption and degenerate condition of the modern world; history exemplified the great decline from the racial purity of the heroic past. Similarly Metaxas viewed the collapse of the German Empire as the end of a great civilization and the victory of the western democracies as the victory of everything shallow, hypocritical and corrupt. Metaxas spoke on similar lines about his own country. In Sardinia he had written in his *Diary*:

Greece, despite her enlargement, has been spiritually corrupted. The sentiment of freedom has been debased. Flattery, jealousy, obsession for material gain, obsession for social climbing by any means - these things have reached their zenith. The men in Greece are struggling today by means of insult, intrigue, calumny, violence and injustice. This is the influence of Ententeism. I saw this, I foresaw it. Let us revolt against this situation. Now? Time will show if I was right or wrong. The struggle [agon] is not over yet.[98]

In the meanwhile in Athens, in a series of show trials, the Liberal Government tried to discredit the Royalists, charging them with treason for the way they had run the country before their removal from power. Metaxas was not indicted in the first series of trials; nevertheless, he lived with the fear that sooner or later his enemies would catch up with him. On 23 July 1919 he wrote in his *Diary*: "All the time here I have troubled dreams, fraught with dangers from Venizelos."[99] The Court in Greece sentenced to death several Royalists who were brought back from Corsica, but the Liberal Government granted them pardons. In August Metaxas wrote: "I forgot to note that the lives of our four friends, Dousmanis, Eslin, Merkouris, Sayias, were spared by Venizelos through the intervention of the Pope!"[100] While Venizelos was in Paris, acting the great statesman, his Liberal Government in Athens could not afford the scandal of the execution of his opponents. The Italians, who wanted to pose as protectors of the Greek Royalists, used the Pope to make some appropriate gestures.

Finally it was Metaxas' turn. On 17 August he wrote: "News from Greece -- they are trying me on a charge of high treason together with Dousmanis, Strategos, Hexadactylos and others. No comment. Is it perhaps possible to confiscate our property for the loss of the treasury of the 4th Army Corps? I do not believe so. It belongs to Lela."[101] This trial of the "former General Staff", as it was called, opened on 7 November 1919 and lasted three months. On trial were the late Chief-of-Staff Victor Dousmanis (who

98 *Ibid.*, p. 507.
99 *Ibid.*, p. 534.
100 *Ibid.*, p. 540.
101 *Ibid.*, p. 542.

had just been pardoned for a previous conviction) Ioannis Metaxas, the late Deputy Chief-of-Staff, who was tried *in absentia*, and two Staff Officers, Xenophon Strategos (Metaxas' fellow student in Berlin) and Athanasios Hexadactylos. Metaxas, always fearing a trial of this kind, had in Corsica invited Dousmanis to escape with him, but his former Chief would not be persuaded. On 13 November 1919 Metaxas wrote:

I fear for Dousmanis, but I have my conscience clear. He himself separated his fate from mine when he was ascending to glory. Why does he complain now? ... How much bitterness his envy made me swallow. When I returned from the war in 1913 I was elbowed away by all and I shrank within myself as if I were a criminal because his envy would not let anyone raise me up. I do not wish him harm, I wish him to be saved. If I could I would have saved him ... But not by sacrificing or risking myself.[102]

The four men were charged before a Special Military Court with a number of crimes which led, among other things, to the surrender of Fort Rupel to the Germans and Bulgarians. Dousmanis and Metaxas were the perpetrators of the crimes, while the other two Staff Officers were their accomplices.

According to the Prosecuting Officer, a certain S. Kolokythas, the members of the former Greek General Staff - conceived and attempted to change our constitutional system into despotic absolutism. All their actions, all their interference in the political life of the country, the surrender of Fort Rupel and Eastern Macedonia, the Civil War which followed, the betrayal of State secrets and lastly the destruction of all incriminating documents which they carried out, all these measures were only the means by which they attempted to achieve their main goal [of establishing "despotic absolutism"]. Both Dousmanis and Metaxas, the former out of calculation, the latter out of sentiment, had been staunch Germanophiles and they desired the triumph of Germany as a precondition in the success of their plans against our constitutional system, by means of which they would have made the deposed King absolute monarch so that they could exploit, for personal gains, their position near him. It is, after all, well known how they manipulated the former king as they pleased.[103]

Further, the Prosecuting Officer said that "the four men had conspired against the fundamental Articles of the Constitution"[104] by concentrating all the power of the Ministry of War in their hands, by setting up illegal authorities such as the Security Battalions, the Secret Military Police and the Leagues of the Reservists. The accused actively and passively assisted the Central Alliance in the Balkans, "not even hesitating to deliver Greek lands to the hereditary enemy, the Bulgar."[105] These men "perverted the temper of the people by proseletyzing in the Army; they prevented Greece from

---

102 *Ibid.*, p. 559f.

103 Newspaper *Patris*, (Athens, October 25, 1919), p. 1.

104 *Ibid.*.

105 *Ibid.*.

fulfilling her obligations as an ally to Serbia; they fought Mr. Venizelos, who had sought Greek cooperation with the Entente while he was in or out of office; they expressed the wish for the expulsion from Greek soil of the Allied troops in Salonica, a wish which manifested itself in a total of 23 instances, the most serious being the clash of 18 November [O.S.], 1916 and the organisation of guerrilla bands to harass the rear of the Army of General Sarrail."[106] The Prosecuting Officer then mentioned several instances when the former Staff had cooperated with German agents and spoke at length about the surrender of Fort Rupel.

At the trial the attempt was made to show that the former Staff had persistently ignored the laws and institutions of the country and, instead, recognised and obeyed only the will of the King (and the Queen) as the final arbiter of all matters of State. One of the witnesses, an officer who had been sentenced to imprisonment by the former General Staff, testified that Metaxas, whom he knew personally, had explained to him that his punishment was demanded by the King, the German Minister in Athens and Queen Sophia. Metaxas promised him to appeal to the Queen for the repeal of his sentence, as indeed he did with immediate success.[107] Another witness testified that he had often observed Metaxas in the company of the Reservists.[108] The Chief of the Constabulary testified that the Reservists were set up to terrorize the Venizelists. Sayias and Livieratos told him that the Reservists were directed from the Palace. He himself had evidence that the leader of the Reservists was Ioannis Metaxas. The money for their organization came from Baron von Schenk, the Chief of the German Secret Services in Greece.[109] General Kallaris, who had commanded the Athens garrison during the *Noemvriana*, testified that a group of officers with whom Metaxas was associated made it clear to him that they were determined to oppose the Allied occupation of Athens in 1916; when he mentioned this to the King, Constantine censored the attitude of his officers, but said that he was not planning to do anything about it because he was afraid of a rebellion.[110]

Metaxas was the most valuable catch in this trial who, to the chagrin of his enemies, was not in the net. One of them burst out that Metaxas "should not see the sky of Greece again." Another voice said that Metaxas "had turned out to be a bad character, ungrateful to Venizelos." Metaxas, who notes these comments without identifying the speakers, writes: "For which benefaction?"[111] Madame Dousmanis was reported as saying that Metaxas had betrayed her husband. Metaxas writes: "They all wanted me

106 *Ibid.*.
107 *Ibid.*, (November 12, 1919), p. 3.
108 *Ibid.*, (November 29, 1919), p. 1.
109 *Ibid.* (November 30, 1919).
110 *Ibid.*, (December 3, 1919), p. 2.
111 Metaxas, Diary, II, p. 560.

to be a lamb whose wool is sheared every year and which on the first opportunity they kill and eat! Let it be ... I pity them."[112] Metaxas followed the proceedings of the trial from the Greek newspapers. The witnesses were "base liars,"[113] he wrote, the Public Prosecutor was "an evil man, cunning, of bad faith, but clever, knowing how to slander and scheme."[114] The judges were "six beasts."[115]

In December 1919 Venizelos, while on a visit to Rome, asked the Italian Government for the extradition of the three Greek exiles on the grounds that they were plotting against the Greek Government. But Nitti, the Italian Prime Minister, declined. On 14 1920 Metaxas heard that he had been sentenced to death *in absentia* by the Special Military Court of Athens.

Today the news arrived that I have been sentenced to death. Dousmanis was sentenced to life imprisonment. Strategos and Hexadactylos were found innocent. I am both proud and sad. Yes, I was their enemy. But I did not bow my head! Was not I, then, right, when I escaped from Corsica, not to listen to Dousmanis?[116]

The Special Military Court, in passing judgement, concluded that Metaxas "had armed Greek citizens against Greek citizens, causing murders to be committed."[117] Would he now, after his death sentence, be extradited? The day after he heard the news he noted in his *Diary*: "The Allies retreated from their position on the question of extradition of Germans; this surely must have a favorable influence on our position."[118]

The reunion with his family soothed and comforted Metaxas, but he was troubled by the court trials in Athens, saddened by his failure to escape to Switzerland and worried about the uncertainty of the future.

Lela is by my side, she is my comfort and I am surrounded by the joy of my children. But the future before me is dark. How oppressed I am by my detention in Italy - I want to go, to go! But where?[119]

Often he doubted and his faith in himself wavered. "My character has become timid, hesitant, indecisive," he wrote.[120] Then, the following day, he noted: "I could live my life all over again; but a certain bitterness will always stay inside me."[121] An Italian lady

112 *Ibid.*, p. 560f.
113 *Ibid.*, p. 564.
114 *Ibid.*.
115 *Ibid.*, p. 561.
116 *Ibid.*, p. 583.
117 Kallonas, *op. cit.*, p. 53.
118 Metaxas, *Diary*, II p. 584.
119 *Ibid.*, p. 551.
120 *Ibid.*, p. 555.
121 *Ibid.*.

told him his fortune and divined his character. "She was successful with my character: the cause of the failures in my life is a lack of self-confidence."[122]

A letter from Greece had an enclosure from his mentally disturbed brother who was confined in an insane asylum in Athens. Metaxas noted in his *Diary*: "It tore my heart. Memories .... My conscience rebuked me: but what can be done? My God, have mercy on me, and especially have mercy on him, the unfortunate one."[123] On the last evening of the year 1919 [according to the Old Style] he wrote: "This year also comes to a close. The world in turmoil. The future dark. We exiled and persecuted."[124] He thought of the happiness that existed in his home and called on God for help. He remembered his mother, his sister and her children and his brother in Athens. Then he remembered his dead father. "My father, poor father! Rest in peace."[125]

A week later, on 7 January [O.S.] was the feast of St. John the Baptist, according to the Greek Orthodox calendar. This was Metaxas' name day, which he had always celebrated. The Greek custom is to observe the nameday rather than the birthday. Metaxas noted in his *Diary* that for the third time he would spend his nameday in exile. Would he ever return to Greece? Early in 1920 he sent money to a bank in Switzerland. "Melancholy. I am thinking about a future in permanent exile."[126] Life as an expatriate seems to have depressed him out of all proportion. In spite of the news he had received that the Venizelist government was unpopular, one side of his nature could not believe that he would ever be able to return to his native land. In March he wrote: "Slowly, slowly, I am losing that which was left to me. After some time nobody will know me anymore".[127] In April 1920 he wrote: "Uneasy heaviness of the heart. The future dark. Exiled, persecuted, a prisoner here. How shall I be able to free myself from here?"[128] Again, the next day: "Tired. Remembrance of ancient days."[129] A few days later: "At night and in the morning heavy thoughts about the dark future."[130]

In Siena the three Greek exiles were visited by other Greek Royalists who came to consult with them and evaluate their chances of returning to Athens and to power. The *Diary* gives evidence of intrigues and plotting among the Royalists, but, because of Metaxas' secretive nature, we do not know exactly to what extent these plans were formulated. Metaxas makes suggestions, but he does not seem to believe that the Royalists will succeed in toppling Venizelos. When Protopapadakis (who was later one

122 *Ibid.*, p. 557.
123 *Ibid.*, p. 545.
124 *Ibid.*, p. 575.
125 *Ibid.*, p.
126 *Ibid.*, p. 587.
127 *Ibid.*, p. 589.
128 *Ibid.*, p. 592.
129 *Ibid.*.
130 *Ibid.*, p. 593.

of the Royalists to be put on trial and shot during the Revolution of 1922) visited the Greek exiles and sat talking with them till 1:00 a.m., Metaxas noted in his *Diary*: "Abundant news, but essentially the same as we already know: the Greek people are against the tyrannical Venizelist *regime*."[131]

From Siena Metaxas corresponded by trusted couriers with Queen Sophia in Switzerland. There was a long and close association between Metaxas and Sophia. Of all the men she met in her adopted country, the Kaiser's sister trusted and admired Metaxas most. His fluency in German, his love for Germany, his loyalty to the dynasty, his innate seriousness, his fight against Venizelos (whom Sophia intensely disliked), endeared "Prussian" Metaxas to the severe Prussian princess. The Queen followed closely the fortunes of Metaxas and she wrote to him from exile to express her sympathy, but also to extend promises for the future. On 26 October 1919 the Queen wrote: [132]

It is such a frightful feeling for one not to be able to help those who suffer such dreadful things and who remain faithful to a just cause. How joyfully one will reciprocate as soon as the opportunity arises and everything ends well, as we all believe.[133]

The Queen, the sister of the Kaiser, was quite talkative in her long letters to Metaxas. The shock of the German defeat which, like Metaxas, she had never expected, was still bewildering to her. "One still wonders", she wrote, "how Germany could collapse utterly in a few hours."[134] The Queen thought of several reasons, of the Kaiser being left in the dark, of too many enemies attacking Germany all at once, of America joining the enemy camp, of hunger, of the blockade; also of "the dreadful Russian-Jewish propaganda which undermined the exhausted heroic army."[135] Sophia observed that "Mankind is in a state of madness, contracted from the Bolsheviks."[136] She wrote to Metaxas:

We wait with patience for whatever fate will decide for us. I hope that soon the opportunity will arise so that one may speak with you and I shall be happy in that moment -- there are so many things one would be able to say then which are impossible to write.[137]

---

131 *Ibid.*, p. 558.

132 Some of this correspondence, unpublished to date, survived in handwritten translations in Greek and is to be found among the Metaxas Papers in the General State Archives in Athens.

133 *Ibid.*.

134 *Ibid.*.

135 *Ibid.*.

136 *Ibid.*.

137 *Ibid.*.

In his long answer Metaxas spoke of his gratitude for the Queen's interest in him and his family. He had suffered a great deal and other people were still suffering. "But the feeling that we struggle and suffer for justice", he wrote, "that we act according to our conscience as human beings and Greeks, fortifies us in difficult moments, and it will be our personal self-satisfaction in the better times of the future."[138] Metaxas then explains to his Queen the reasons for the German collapse.

The collapse of Germany within a few hours was the end of a development which had been taking place for some time in the soul of this nation and whose beginning should be sought in the very distant past.

In her general forward impetus Germany was so much further ahead of the others that she was, as a result, isolated. Unfortunately, in this maelstrom-like progress of Germany, the old ideals were lost among the mass of the people and a new ideal [to replace the old ones] was lacking, the faith in a higher universal ideal which would have been the lode star. In every branch of civilization, of the state and of private life, Germany extended her powers to the utmost limits. But there was no higher indivisible goal which could have joined and guided these isolated powers. Power for its own sake became Germany's goal and truly her power had become so great and terrible that, without the intervention of America, Germany, despite the hunger and the privations, would have become the master of the old world. But the intervention of America persuaded the Germans that their power had come to an end, and this feeling led the nation to collapse. Now chaos is spreading everywhere because the others, the victors, for egoistical reasons, discarded the standards of the ideal under which they had succeeded in amassing the whole world, so that the world is now without a spiritual [moral] leader. This fact opens up to a resurgent Germany a wide field of future activity which will not only revive Germany but will also raise her higher than before.[139]

Then Metaxas spoke about himself and the Greek Royalists and their "ideological struggle" against the "tyrant Venizelos."

As for us, [the Greek Royalists], our power is founded on the purely ideological character into which our struggle has evolved. We struggle for our freedom, for the freedom of Greece from foreign rule, for human rights, which tyranny has taken away from us. The King is the symbol of this higher goal: the faith in him, which was originally personal, has now become the national religion. A religion which has its martyrs whose sufferings simply strengthen the faith. We pray to God to preserve in health the King and his family and to arm them with patience and trust. Our cause is just. How it is going to end in victory we cannot determine in detail beforehand. If

138 *Ibid.*, Metaxas' answer is dated 26 November 1919.

139 *Ibid.*.

it is true - and it must be true - what is related to us from every source about the seething of the Greek people against the tyrant, I do not think that Venizelos will choose to face an election. Because elections would mean annihilation for him and his political system. Violence against the voters, court-martials, etc., will not help him in this case, because the elections will cause a great agitation throughout the land which, due to the general hatred against him, could easily be transformed into open rebellion. Acts of violence on the part of the Government would be the most suitable means of hastening the explosion of the general rebellion. Venizelos will, I think, postpone the elections and try to gain time and wait for more favorable circumstances. Only one thing is certain: the will of the people will prevail and no power can constantly oppose the realization of what the people want. (Certainly not the English.) We should base ourselves on and trust absolutely in the strong popular will; and we should avoid anything which will weaken this will and render it hesitant.[140]

Metaxas also corresponded with Prince Andrew, the brother of King Constantine, who was his personal friend. When the Prince communicated to Metaxas his plans for the return of the King, Metaxas answered that the restoration would be the result of the struggle; the objective was the liberation of the Greek people. He intimated that he, Metaxas, would follow "my own policy," and warned Prince Andrew against any interference [in the political life of the nation] from the members of the dynasty. Metaxas was also in contact with Prince Nicholas and Prince George.

With King Constantine Metaxas was not in direct communication, although he cabled the King from Sardinia to congratulate him on his nameday (21 May 1919) and the King responded. In August Metaxas read in *Corriere* that Constantine, in an interview, had expressed his good will toward England. Metaxas comments: "Was he, perhaps, given any promise? Anyway, it is shabby."[141] Six days later the King was interviewed by the *Telegraaf*. "Dignified," commented Metaxas in his *Diary*.[142] Early in May 1920, John Theodoky, the Queen's Master of Ceremonies, who had accompanied the Royal party into exile, came to see Metaxas in Siena and brought "important news," as Metaxas notes in his *Diary*.[143] (Metaxas had a new letter to Sophia ready for him to take.) On 6 June Metaxas received a letter from Levides, the King's Master of Ceremonies (who had also accompanied the Royal party to Switzerland) asking if Metaxas would like to meet the King. Obviously the answer was affirmative, because two days later an invitation arrived for Metaxas to meet Constantine in Milan. The meeting took place at eight o'clock in the evening at the Continental Hotel on 12 June

---

140 *Ibid.*.
141 Metaxas, *Diary*, II, p. 542.
142 *Ibid.*, p. 543.
143 *Ibid.*, p. 594.

1920. "I see him again after exactly three years," Metaxas wrote in his *Diary*.[144] The two men were moved. They dined together on the cold provisions the King had brought with him from Switzerland. (The Italian hotel employees had been on strike for weeks). They talked about Greece. "The King looks well," Metaxas noted in his *Diary*, "serious and kind, as always."[145] The next day he went to say goodbye to the King.

Then he visited the *Duomo* in Milan. "I imagined it more beautiful," he wrote.[146] On the train, travelling back to Siena, he was reading *The Idiot* by Dostoevsky. Four days after he arrived he received a letter from John Theotokis in which the old Royalist spoke about Napoleon and his departure from Elba, possibly suggesting that Metaxas should imitate the great Corsican. Metaxas comments in his *Diary*: "Mad plans. I get incensed ... May God have mercy on us! What does he take me for?"[147]

Metaxas in exile had time to think, to read, to reassess his life, to ponder about the future. His ideals had collapsed, as he wrote; in Greece his political opponents had won the day and mighty Germany, contrary to all his expectations, had been defeated by the Allied democracies. Everything he had believed in lay in ruins and Metaxas lived far from his country with "heavy thoughts about the dark future."

Strangely enough, there is very little in the *Diary* of this period about the deliberations at the Peace Conference in Paris, only an outcry here and there: "Ah, when will the base system of Versailles be crushed?" he wrote in August 1919.[148] He also noted down very little about Venizelos who represented Greece at the Peace Conference. But Metaxas was not impressed by the achievements of his great adversary. On 17 August 1919 he wrote in his Diary:

In the afternoon I read the Greek newspapers. The Greek people show indifference to the successes of Venizelos and the dangers which threaten Greek interests [because of these successes]. This is what the enslavement of a people means ....[149]

In December 1919 the Italian Government eased the restrictions on the three Greek exiles, who were then allowed to go anywhere in Italy as long as they informed the police first. Early in April 1920 Metaxas and his wife visited Florence and spent four crowded days there. The first evening they attended a performance of Wagner's *Die Walküre*, Metaxas' favorite opera. During the next few days they visited Ponte Vecchio, San Lorenzo, the Duomo, the Palazio Vecchio, Belle Arti, Santa Croce, the Buonarotti museum, the Uffizi Gallery, Palazzo Pitti and several other places. Recording his visit to St. Mark's, choked with emotion, Metaxas could only write one word in his *Diary*,

---

144 *Ibid.*, p. 600.
145 *Ibid.*.
146 *Ibid.*.
147 *Ibid.*, p. 601.
148 *Ibid.*, p. 544.
149 *Ibid.*, p. 542.

the name of the rebel prophet-martyr: "Savonarola!"[150] They took a long tour of the city in a horse-carriage -- "my mind full of Michelangelo," Metaxas wrote.[151]

11 Dimitrios Gounaris and Ioannis Metaxas in exile, outside an Italian railway station in 1920.

In May 1920 all restrictions on the movements of the three Greek exiles were lifted and the three men ceased to be *internés* of the Allies. As summer approached the Metaxas family found the heat and humidity of Siena oppressive (not to mention the swarms of flies which infested the city). They began thinking of moving somewhere near the sea. In early June they travelled to Livorno, but found life there was too expensive. Then they travelled by train along the coast of the Italian Riviera as far as Marina di Massa. In Pisa they went to the *Duomo* and the Leaning Tower. They liked

150 *Ibid.*, p. 591.
151 *Ibid.*.

best the sea-side resort of Quercianella where there was both forest and sea and which was cool, so a month later they returned and stayed there until the end of September. It was not a wrench to leave Siena. Metaxas wrote: "Everybody avoided us here. Perhaps because of inhospitality. Perhaps because of our politics. I depart without regrets."[152] Again, "In this city where we lived for twelve months, not a single person asked to be introduced to us."[153] In vivid language he described and bade farewell to Siena. He would take with him memories of long walks with his wife and children. "Another chapter of my life comes to an end".[154]

The only regrets Metaxas had in leaving Siena concerned were about the loss of the comradeship he had enjoyed with the other two Greek exiles. When, in Siena, the family of George Pesmazoglou moved to a house and Demetrios Gounaris to another hotel, Metaxas wrote: "I have a mild, vague sadness. Little by little the bonds which held the three of us together are being loosened. Each of us takes his own road."[155] Gounaris left Siena in May and the Pesmazoglou family were planning to move to Florence soon. "Our company is dispersed," Metaxas noted in his *Diary*.[156] Again, "All are dissolved around me and I am left free! Free from every bond and obligation! At last I shall follow my own road!"[157]

In Quercianella Metaxas could swim, sunbathe, take boat trips and go fishing. "We have regained our health here, we have found peace and tranquillity. From time to time letters from friends, or Greek newspapers, disturb my soul."[158] In Quercianella he received the news that Germany would accept him to live and work there, and though he liked the idea, he was doubtful about the climate and the "conditions of life." Quercianella, however lovely, was not the place to spend the winter and in the August of 1920 Metaxas went to Florence to find a house. Florence was a living museum, there were good schools for the children and Metaxas would have the company of other Greek Royalists who had already chosen Florence as their place of residence in exile. On 27 September the Metaxas family moved to the city of the Medicis.

152 *Ibid.*, p. 604.
153 *Ibid.*, p. 605.
154 *Ibid.*.
155 *Ibid.*, p. 546.
156 *Ibid.*, p. 596.
157 *Ibid.*.
158 *Ibid.*, p. 608.

The Wheel of Fortune

In 1919 the Allies in Paris drafted and imposed the Treaties on Germany, Austria and Bulgaria. The Treaty with Turkey, which more than any other affected Greece, had to wait.

The Treaty with Germany was signed at Versailles on 28 June 1919. Attached to it was also the Covenant of the League of Nations. Subsequently the Treaty was ratified by Germany, France, Great Britain and Italy. But the Senate of the U.S. Congress, to which President Wilson submitted the Treaty of Versailles, refused to ratify it. The American President then appealed directly to his country, but while speaking in Colorado, he suffered a stroke. Any hopes that the U.S. would assume responsibility for either Armenia or Constantinople (which would have had a direct effect on the fortunes of Greece) were dashed.

The Treaty with Austria, or the Treaty of Saint-Germain, as it was known, was signed on 10 September 1919. The Treaty confirmed the dissolution of the Habsburg Empire and the independence of Czechoslovakia, Yugoslavia, Poland and Hungary. By this Treaty Italy was given Southern Tyrol, Trieste and Istria. Yugoslavia was given Bosnia and Herzegovina. These two countries, neighbours to Greece, were much enlarged; especially Yugoslavia, which is contiguous to Greece, had, from tiny Serbia, become a major Power among the small Powers. In Greece there was a certain feeling of uneasiness, despite the friendly traditions between the two countries. Greece resigned herself to losing Monastir [Bitolia] and Venizelos, who had personally prevented King Constantine from capturing the city in the First Balkan War, felt a greater pressure to expand in the direction of Asia Minor.

The Treaty with Bulgaria - the Treaty of Neuilly - was signed on 27 November 1919. Bulgaria was made to pay for the follies of King Ferdinand and would no longer be able to pose as the Prussia of the Balkans. By the Treaty of Neuilly, Bulgaria could only keep an army of 20,000 men, "for the maintenance of order", who were to serve for "not less than twelve years". This provision ensured that the trained army was always to remain small. Bulgaria lost the Strumitza salient in the west to Yugoslavia, and in Dobrudja the Bulgarian frontier was pushed back in favour of Rumania. Bulgaria also lost her Aegean Littoral to Greece. Greece recovered Eastern Macedonia (which was invaded after Metaxas ordered the surrender of Fort Rupel) and gained Western Thrace with the small port and railway of Dedeagatch, which the Greeks promptly renamed Alexandroupolis. But the Treaty stipulated that Bulgaria was to be given an economic outlet to the Aegean. Bulgaria thus hoped to recover Dedeagatch, but the only outlet Greece would consent to was hundreds of miles from the Bulgarian border, west of Salonica. While Greece assumed responsibility for some portion of the Bulgarian Public Dept, Bulgaria agreed to pay reparations to the tune of 2,250,000,000 gold francs spread over 35 years. Greece was to receive most of this money. The Neuilly Treaty also provided for "the reciprocal and voluntary emigration of persons belonging to racial minorities". This provision helped to make the northern frontier of Greece a real demarcation line between the Greeks and Bulgarians.

On 4 June 1920 the Treaty of Trianon was signed. This was the peace settlement with Hungary by which Czechoslovakia gained Slovakia and Ruthenia; Rumania gained Transylvania and half of the Bánát; and Yugoslavia gained Croatia and the Voivodina. The Trianon Treaty caused great resentment in Hungary whose subsequent foreign policy was directed toward its revision. The Treaty of Trianon is of some importance to Greece because, in order to preserve the territorial arrangements of the Treaty, the Little Entente was set up by the beneficiary powers, Czechoslovakia, Yugoslavia and Rumania, with which Greece was later indirectly associated through the Balkan Alliance.

The Treaty with Turkey was another proposition altogether. The situation in the Near East at the conclusion of the Great War was very different from what it had been for generations. At the time, the new Russia had no ambitions over Constantinople and the Straits and the keen rivalry in the Balkans between the Habsburgs and the Romanovs evaporated into thin air. The territories through which the Baghdad Railway ran had acquired new masters and Germany could no longer hope to pursue the policy of *Drang nach Osten,* i.e. economic domination of the Middle East. Furthermore, the problems of the Turkish Empire were, in many ways, far more serious and complicated. It was not only the great variety of races and religions of the Empire that had no hope of combining into a union; it was also the jealousies of the Powers who vied with each other for some territorial gain or some financial advantage. In the dilapidated Empire, as Lloyd George wrote, "there was a wilderness of decay and ruin, the result of centuries of misrule prolonged to the last hours of Turkish dominion, which had to be dealt with. There were whole provinces devastated and depopulated by butchery inspired, decreed and directed by the State."[1] The Armenians, among all other minorities of Turkey, had the greatest number of victims. In his *Memoirs*, Lloyd George described how both the Old Turks and the Young Turks "had deliberately set themselves to the simplification of the Armenian difficulty by exterminating and deporting the whole race."[2] But the Armenians were not the only ones. Lloyd George writes:

The Greeks of Asia Minor had also suffered heavily from the brutalities of the Turks during the Great War. Hundreds of thousands were massacred in cold blood during the War and many more driven from their homes to find refuge in Greece and the Greek islands. The Turks worked incessantly and with a barbaric guile to improve their statistical position.[3]

---

1 David Llloyd George, *Memoirs of the Peace Conference* (Yale: Yale UP, 1939), p. 650.

2 *Ibid.*, p. 650.

3 *Ibid.*, p. 651.

12 *Greater Greece after the Treaty of Sèvres.*

In June 1919 the Grand Vizier, Damad Ferid Pasha, read to the Allied representatives in Paris a document admitting the Turkish massacres of the Christian populations of Asia Minor "which are such as to make the conscience of mankind shudder with horror forever. ...[4] Turkey deplores the murder of a great number of her Christian co-nationals,"[5] he said, but he pointed out that the Young Turks had also slaughtered many Moslems and therefore the Turkish massacres should not be attributed to religious fanaticism. It was not true that the Turks could not rule over other peoples, the Turkish Prime Minister argued, and he asked that the integrity of the Ottoman Empire be preserved on the basis of the *status quo ante bellum*. This amazing document maintained that the massacres were not in harmony with Turkish tradition and therefore Turkey should not be made to suffer because of them. Arthur Balfour, of the British delegation, was given the task of answering. He said that "the Council is anxious not to enter into unnecessary controversy, or to inflict needless pain on your Excellency and the delegates who accompany you."[6] Balfour pointed out that wherever Turkish rule was established a general material and cultural decay followed. The Turk "never has (he) shown himself able to develop in peace what he had won by war. Not in this direction do his talents lie."[7] It is strange to remember that Balfour had been Lord Salisbury's secretary at the Berlin Congress of 1878 when Disraeli insisted that the Armenians, liberated by Russian arms, should again be placed under Turkish rule.

But the greatest difficulty of all in writing and imposing a Treaty on Turkey was Kemal's Nationalist Movement. This difficulty, oddly enough, the peacemakers of Paris seemed to have ignored. On 10 July 1919 Venizelos submitted to Clemenceau, the French Premier, a memorandum in which he said that Kemal had an army of 60,000 at Konia alone and that the mobilization that was then in progress in Anatolia would soon produce a force of 300,000 which could be amply provided for from the war material that had not been delivered to the Allies according to the Armistice. In this memorandum Venizelos also referred in detail to Italian cooperation with the Turks. The military experts of the Allied Delegations had their apprehensions confirmed, but the politicians in Paris "went on merrily" discussing the terms that were to be imposed on Turkey.

The Treaty of Sèvres was signed by the representatives of the Sultan on 10 August 1920. The Nationalists of Mustafa Kemal declared immediately their determination to fight against the enforcement of the Treaty.

The Treaty of Sèvres gave Greece Eastern Thrace, including the Gallipoli Peninsula, but not Constantinople. The Straits were to remain open to all nations. Smyrna and its

4 *Ibid.*.
5 *Ibid.*.
6 *Ibid.*, p. 655.
7 *Ibid.*.

hinterland was left nominally under Turkish sovereignty but was placed under Greek administration. A plebiscite in five years time was to determine whether the area remained under Turkey or was to join the Hellenic Kingdom. Imbros and Tenedos, the two islands at the mouth of the Dardanelles, were to be left to Turkey, while the rest of the Aegean islands were recognised as part of Greece. The Dodecanese were left in the hands of Italy. Cyprus, which had been administered by Britain since 1878, was to become a British colony. Britain also received the mandate for Mesopotamia and Palestine, while France was given the mandate for Syria and Lebanon. The Kingdom of Hedjaz was proclaimed free, while Kurdistan was made autonomous.

In later years, Metaxas had the opportunity to discuss the controversial Treaty of Sèvres with Venizelos in their famous journalistic duel in 1934. The Great Powers, Metaxas wrote, protected their own interests, as was natural for any Great Power. By the armistice of Mudros, England secured for herself Palestine, Mesopotamia and Arabia and the freedom of navigation in the Straits. France secured Syria and Lebanon and Italy secured Libya (Tripolitania and Cyrenaica). Greece secured nothing.

The Treaty of Sèvres did not reflect the new realities in the Near East. Metaxas wrote: *The Treaty of Sèvres terminated the War of the Allies with the Turkey of Constantinople, and left Greece to fight alone against the Turkey of Kemal, in order to take by herself from Kemal what was theoretically recognised as hers by the Turks of Constantinople. Thus while Greece was at war with the Turkish nation represented by Kemal, the Allies were at peace with the same Turkish nation represented by the government at Constantinople, a city which they held in their hands as a pledge so that they could deliver it to the Turkish nation intact from any Greek operation.*[8] Greece would never have found herself in such a position, wrote Metaxas, if better counsels than those of Venizelos had prevailed. Then Metaxas compared the case of Greece with that of Rumania. Unlike Greece, Rumania, before she entered the War, had insisted on and received guarantees from the Great Powers that she would be helped to occupy the territories she sought.

„But then why had not Greece received beforehand, before she abandoned her neutrality and intervened for the Allies, the same guarantees that Rumania had received? This is the essential difference between the so-called Royalist policy and the policy of Mr. Venizelos."[9] Two days after the signing of the Treaty of Sèvres, as Venizelos was entering the Gare de Lyons to catch the Orient Express for the journey home, an attempt was made on his life by two disaffected former Greek officers. Ten shots were fired, but only two found their target. One bullet lodged in Venizelos' left shoulder and a second in his thigh. Venizelos was not seriously hurt and in fifteen days he was

---

8 *Ethnikos Dichasmos*, p. 15.

9 *Ibid.*.

able to reach Marseilles and board the Greek Flagship SS *Averov* bound for Greece. Metaxas noted in his *Diary*: "Assassination attempt against Venizelos in Paris has failed."[10] The next day he wrote: "I have the impression that the attempt will go against Venizelos."[11] Venizelos, writing in 1934, claimed that "the decision for the crime had been made by official representatives of the Royalist Party, under the chairmanship of a highly placed personage."[12] Metaxas, in answer to the above charge, wrote that Venizelos had no right to accuse anybody without proof except those who actually made the attempt. Metaxas declared that he himself was against any political murders, but he pointed out to Venizelos that one also commits political murder when one delivers up one's enemies to a Special Court constituted for the sole purpose of passing death sentences.[13] When the assassination attempt against Venizelos was made in Paris, Metaxas was living in Italy under the shadow of a death sentence passed on him by a Special Court in Athens. By 1934, when he was writing the above, he had two death sentences on his record, the second one after an abortive coup in 1923. Metaxas might have also had in mind the death sentences and executions, imposed by a Special Court, of the Royalist Ministry (*the Six* - Prime Minister Demetrios Gounaris, four of his Ministers and the Commander-in-Chief of the Army) in November 1922.

The news of the attempt on Venizelos provoked an outcry in Greece and in Athens wild scenes took place. (These events were known as *Iouliana*, the July incidents). Royalist clubs and newspapers were raided and the Cretan Guards intercepted the car in which Ion Dragoumis was travelling, dragged him out and killed him. Metaxas noted in his Diary:

According to the evening papers, in Athens they have burned and destroyed the offices and the presses of the Anti-Venizelist newspapers. They have imprisoned the leaders of the opposition, they have killed Dragoumis.[14]

The victim was a brilliant political writer and diplomat, the son of ex-Premier Stephanos Dragoumis. Metaxas wrote to the father from Italy to express his sympathy. George Pesmazoglou, Metaxas' companion in exile, who was a lawyer, wrote to a prominent Paris lawyer giving him instructions to defend the officers who had attempted to assassinate Venizelos.[15]

As soon as Venizelos returned to Athens he addressed the Chamber (on 7 September 1920) and presented the three treaties he had brought back - the Treaty with Italy, the

10 Metaxas, *Diary*, II, p. 613.

11 *Ibid.*.

12 *Ethnikos Dichasmos*, p. 10.

13 *Ibid.*, p. 14f.

14 Metaxas. Diary, II, p. 613.

15 The letter was dated October 16/23, 1920 and it was published in a small book entitled Pyros Giannopoulos Epirotes, *Constantinism and Ioannis Metaxas* (Athens, n.d.).

Treaty of Neuilly with Bulgaria and the Treaty of Sèvres with Turkey. The impossible vision of the *Megali Idea* suddenly seemed to take shape on the horizon. The Liberal Chamber expressed its gratitude and voted the Prime Minister "saviour of the fatherland" (*axios tis patridos*, literally, worthy of the fatherland). Venizelos, elated and flattered, announced that the Chamber would soon be dissolved and all restrictions on civil liberties would be removed so that the overdue elections could be held under normal constitutional conditions. Venizelos could have prolonged his tenure; he did not, not only because he was sensitive to accusations of authoritarian rule, but also because he believed, listening to the eulogies of his own deputies in the Chamber, that he would be returned with an overwhelming majority. The sad truth was that, with the Opposition absent from the Chamber and his political opponents banished in one way or another, Venizelos could not fathom the mood of the country from which he had been absent for so long. The resurrected Chamber of 31 May 1915, which was prolonged for fifteen months, was finally dissolved and the elections were scheduled for 25 October 1920.

While the Liberals were celebrating the return of Venizelos to Athens and preparing for the coming elections, in Italy Metaxas had transferred his family to Florence and was settling down for yet another winter in exile. After investigating the various schools in the city he decided to put his two daughters into an Anglo-Italian Institute. To have his daughters learn English was almost to admit the present victory and the future influence of the Anglo-Saxons. He noted in his *Diary*: "Thus they will learn English first. Even I gave in, what can be done! But we will hire a German teacher in the afternoon so they can study German as well."[16] In the evenings, while Madame Metaxas read *Robinson Crusoe* to the two girls, their father resumed his reading of Paulsen's *Introduction to Philosophy*. The Greek newspapers carried reports of the pre-election campaign and Metaxas felt frustrated that he could not be part of it. "Life in front of me is limited. [I have] drives of ambition, but I hold myself back: wife and children."[17]

Five days before Metaxas moved to Florence, on 22 September 1920 while he was in Quercianella, he received a letter from his friend Prince Andrew, who had gone to Rome to further his plans for the return of King Constantine to Athens. As soon as Metaxas had settled his family in Florence and cabled his whereabouts to Queen Sophia in Switzerland, he hastened to Rome to consult with the Royal Princes.

Gounaris was going back to Greece to take part in the elections, but Metaxas, who was under sentence of death, could not safely do so. "He goes to fight. And I am obliged to stay here with folded hands,"[18] he noted. The autumn weather in Florence was overcast and Metaxas often felt lonely and sad. Memories of his past life often disturbed him. On 8 October 1920 he wrote:

---

16 Metaxas, *Diary*, II, p. 629.

17 *Ibid.*, p. 628.

18 *Ibid.*.

Suddenly I remember! On a day like today, toward the evening father died! It has been fifteen years! I still remember the small, uncomfortable house, our poor furniture, the simple room in which he was in his last agony for two days. We were all gathered around him ... I was taking his pulse while he was giving up the ghost. He turned and looked at me vaguely: I still have before me his gaze. How much [that regard] had told me! And now little I have kept! My soul is heavy .... "[19]

From the newspapers Metaxas noticed that he was not even included on the Royalist ticket for Cephalonia, his native island. The Royalists, who resented his independent spirit and his past history which connected him with the Noemvriana, considered him a liability and did not want him as part of their campaign.

No one even speaks a word about me. So much the better! The separation, although painful to me, is to my benefit to become complete; however much it hurts me, it is my moral and material salvation and the salvation of my wife and children. I do not have the right myself to break away: if others do it for me, I accept."[20]

But he could not get used to the idea that the Royalists had abandoned him. Three days later he wrote: "Melancholy. They have all forgotten me. I have been erased from [the map of] Greece."[21] Eventually, in a letter from his mother, Metaxas learned that the law prohibited him and Pesmazoglou from taking part in the coming elections. "Better this way," Metaxas wrote in his *Diary*.[22] But it hurt to watch the other Royalists dissociate themselves from him.

Gounaris has departed. He did not even send me a farewell message. Not even Christodoulakis [later Prime Minister]. They have all turned their backs on me ... Why? Have I fallen so low?[23]

As the election campaign was getting into its stride fate played its part in this most Greek of all Greek tragedies. On 30 September 1920, while King Alexander was out for a walk with his wolfdog Fritz at Tatoi, the dog was attacked by a pet monkey. The King rushed to separate them, when a second monkey, the male partner of the first, attacked him with great ferocity. The German couple who supervised the estate and to whom the monkeys belonged, managed to free the King. But he was severely bitten on the hand and leg and was bleeding profusely. A medical examination showed streptococci in his blood and, despite all efforts, the King's condition deteriorated. On 10 October 1920 Metaxas wrote in his *Diary*: *A most important complication. But not to our detriment. Either he [Venizelos] will call a Constituent Assembly or he will postpone the elections and establish a new regime by coup d'etat. The Constitutional*

---

19 *Ibid.*, p. 630.
20 *Ibid.*, p. 631.
21 *Ibid.*.
22 *Ibid.*, p. 632.
23 *Ibid.*, p. 633.

solution is imperative.[24] Five days later he noted: "Alexander is dying. What will happen?"[25]The young King finally expired on 25 October 1920. Metaxas noted: "Alexander is dead. I grieved for him - what will happen?"[26]

The elections, which were to have taken place on 25 October 1920, the day the King died, were postponed to 14 November. Britain opposed any suggestion that Greece should become a Republic and Britain was the only ally left to Venizelos. Admiral Paul Koundouriotis was appointed Regent. The death of the King raised the question of the succession. King Constantine, who had been living in Switzerland for the past three years, had never abdicated from the Greek throne. After the death of Alexander the clamor for the restoration of Constantine became even louder. But the Venizelos Government did not send for Constantine to return; and it did not offer the throne to Crown Prince George (the future George II of the Metaxas dictatorship), because the Crown Prince was well known for his pro-German sympathies and his anti-liberal, autocratic views. Instead Venizelos offered the Crown to Prince Paul, the third son of King Constantine. Paul declined from Switzerland - as his father had never abdicated, he said, and his elder brother Prince George was first in line for the succession, it was inappropriate for him to accept the crown. It was now either Constantine or Venizelos. Metaxas wrote in his Diary: "The question of [the restoration of] King Constantine was made an issue by Venizelos in the elections".[27] The elections were held on 14 November 1920. The Royalists campaigned for "a small but honorable Greece" and promised peace and demobilisation. The Liberals campaigned for the new Greater Greece, the Greece of the *Megali Idea*, spanning two continents and five seas. (Black Sea, Marmora, Aegean, Libyan and Adriatic). It was not such a preposterous dream. At the time, the Greek Flagship *Averof* was anchored at the Golden Horn and Greek forces occupied Smyrna, Brussa, Ushak and Adrianople. Western and Eastern Thrace were Greek and the Greek forces were stationed only twenty miles from Constantinople and would have certainly taken the city if they had not been prevented by the Allies. The elections were held by the simple majority system, which favors the majority party and promotes a two party political system. (The "proportional representation," which is sometimes used in Greece, favors a fairer representation of all parties, but also contributes to a less stable government.) Venizelos retained some of his following among the city bourgeoisie, the Liberal middle classes and the city workers. But he lost heavily in the countryside where he was presented as a traitor to the King, a war-mongering anti-Christ in the service of the English imperialists. For eight years the Army had been on a war footing in one way or another and the prospects of the men

24 *Ibid.*, p. 630.
25 *Ibid.*, p. 632.
26 *Ibid.*, p. 633.
27 *Ibid.*, p. 637.

returning home to their neglected farms and unattended animals were dim indeed, if Venizelos were to win the elections. The simple peasantry were at a loss to understand why they should be fighting the Bolsheviks in the Ukraine, or, for that matter, the Turks in the heart of Anatolia, and they were weary of being told that Venizelos knew the answer. During the election campaign, there were serious clashes between the Liberals and the Royalists. News that some of their followers had been killed disturbed the exiled Royalist leaders. Metaxas, unperturbed, encouraged them: "This is a struggle," he wrote in his *Diary*.

The elections were a landslide. 240 Royalist deputies were elected against 140 Liberals and 4 Independents. (The Liberals, in fact, won 52% of the total vote - had the proportional system been in force, they would have secured 200 seats). Venizelos himself lost his seat. On 17 November 1920, three months after signing the Treaty of Sèvres, the Liberal leader boarded the British private yacht *Narcissus* and with many of his friends and ex-ministers went into exile on the French Riviera.

Demetrios Gounaris, Metaxas' comrade in Italy, became Minister of War. As Prime Minister, the Royalists chose the elderly Demetrios Rallis. Prince Nicholas described the first audience Rallis had at the Tatoi Palace with Olga, the Queen Mother, who was in Athens for the funeral of King Alexander:

When the aged statesman, who had also been one of the victims of the "Liberal Government," found himself in the presence of my mother, the widow of the King (King George I) whom he had faithfully served for so many years, he respectfully knelt before her and kissed her hand. My mother, who was deeply moved, begged the Prime Minister to rise; but he refused; so my mother also went down on her knees, assuring him that she would not get up unless he did.[28]

Presumably they both eventually arose and the Queen Mother agreed to act as Regent until the return of King Constantine.

Metaxas had his own explanation for the spectacular defeat of the Liberals. It was, of course, the "tyranny" of Venizelos during his term of office. But primarily Venizelos lost the elections because the Greek people never forgave him for inviting foreign armies to help restore him to power in 1917. Metaxas wrote: "That action was not only morally a crime, it was also a political error ... Peoples never submit, never forget, never forgive this method of interference of foreign troops in their internal affairs."[29] As the French people never forgave the return by foreign bayonets of the Bourbons in 1815, thus with the Greek people, "so long as they have as much self-respect as the French," will never forgive Venizelos.[30]

---

28 Prince Nicholas of Greece, *My Fifty Years* (London, 1926), p. 289.

29 Metaxas, *Dichasmos*, p. 205.

30 *Ibid.*, p. 176.

Surely, Metaxas argued, a man of Venizelos' acumen must have known the inevitable outcome. Why, then, did he call for elections? Especially if he were as certain, as he claimed later to be that only he, because of his close association with the victorious Allies, could turn into reality the Treaty of Sèvres, if he were so convinced that the return to power of his opponents would have brought to ruin his ambitious plans for Greece, then why did he call for the elections of November 1920, which he had postponed before? Furthermore, none of his opponents was then in Greece to prevent him from postponing them again. This was not the first time that this question had been put to Venizelos. In 1931 the Liberal Leader, writing at some length to George Venteris, a historian who wrote about those years, said that he held the elections simply because he was not made from the same stuff that dictators were made from. Venizelos wrote further:

As I have no blue blood in my veins, I cannot indulge in the fancy that I have God's decree to rule Greece. I would have despised myself if I had insisted on staying in power against the will of the people because I judged myself better than others. And also a dictatorship cannot tolerate freedom of the press. I would have then been obliged to abolish the free press and thus cease to know what was happening in the country while I was absorbed in such important foreign affairs. Having neither the psychology of a divinely appointed King, nor that of a modern dictator, I would have failed miserably, trying to play a role for which I was ill-suited.[31]

The Election of November 1920 had already been postponed while Venizelos was in Paris negotiating the Treaty of Sèvres. Once the Treaty had been signed, Venizelos felt that he should go to the people and ask for their confidence and a new mandate to carry out the terms of the Treaty.

Metaxas had a very different explanation to offer for the motivation behind Venizelos' call for elections in November 1920. Venizelos, Metaxas charged, knew that without Allied assistance Greece could not impose the Treaty of Sèvres on Turkey. Venizelos also was fully aware - indeed he had been repeatedly warned - that the victorious Allies had no inclination whatsoever to come to the assistance of Greece in a fresh war against Turkey - thus the Elections of November 1920. Metaxas wrote:

Whether it was Mr. Venizelos or his opponents who won the elections of 1920, Greece would have had to fight the war against Turkey alone if she had wanted to turn the Treaty of Sèvres into reality and, therefore, she would have been destined to failure, as in fact she was. The only problem the elections solved was who was to pay for the damage: Mr. Venizelos or his opponents? His opponents paid.[32]

---

31 George Ventiris, *Greece in the Years 1910-1920* (Athens, 1931), II, p. 419f. In Greek.

32 Metaxas, *Dichasmos*, p. 15.

If Venizelos had not fallen from power because of the Elections of November 1920, he would have had to face the same difficulties as his successors. "With the only difference, he caused the *impasse* in which Greece was entrapped; they suffered the consequences," concluded Metaxas.[33]

Immediately after the Elections the new Government proclaimed the Third Constituent National Assembly and sent a message to King Constantine inviting him to return to the throne. The King, to satisfy his pride and silence his adversaries, asked that a referendum first be held so that the people should have the opportunity to express their feelings about his return. In a note to the Greek Government three days before the referendum the Supreme Allied Council warned Greece that they were not prepared to recognise King Constantine and that they would withdraw all financial assistance from Greece if the King were restored.

Notwithstanding, the Royalists went ahead with their plans and the referendum was held on 5 December 1920. 1,010,788 votes were cast for the return of the King and only 10,883 against. Despite this overwhelming verdict, in a second Note to the Greek Government, the Allied Powers stressed that "though they had no wish to interfere in the internal affairs of Greece, they felt bound to declare publicly that the restoration of the throne to a King whose disloyal attitude and conduct towards the Allies during the war had caused them great embarrassment and loss could only be regarded by them as a ratification by Greece of his hostile acts."[34] A fortnight after the referendum, on 19 December 1920, King Constantine, his consort and his retainers came back to Greece.

In England and France public opinion was strongly prejudiced against Constantine -- his refusal to join the Allies in 1915 was presented by popular journalism as the cause of thousands, nay, millions of dead. England and France eagerly seized the opportunity to disengage themselves from any obligation toward Greece and to wash their hands of the dreadful consequences everybody expected to fall upon the Greek Army in Anatolia. The restoration of King Constantine marked the end of the Greek alliance with the Entente Powers. In the future, Britain, France, and Italy would revert to their traditional pro-Turkish policies. In his study of the Great War, Winston Churchill said as much:

Here was a potentate who, as we saw it, against the wishes and the interests of his people, had for personal and family reasons thrown his country, or tried to throw it, on the enemy side. The return of Constantine therefore dissolved all Allied loyalties to Greece and cancelled all but legal obligations. For the sake of Venizelos much had to be endured, but for Constantine less than nothing. After the first astonishment [at the defeat of Venizelos in the election of 14 November 1920] had worn off, an air of

33 *Ibid.*, p. 200.

34 Nicholas, *Fifty Years*, p. 289f.

relief became manifest in controlling circles. There was no need any more to pursue an anti-Turkish policy.[35]

Suddenly Greece, until the day before in the forefront of European affairs, was isolated. Her seat at the Council of the League of Nations was taken away from her and given to China. France and Italy were hostile, the U.S.A. indifferent and Great Britain weary of the Greeks. A Greek historian aptly wrote that "the Greece of Venizelos had been treated like a poor relation, whose importunities decency did not permit to be entirely ignored. The Greece of Constantine was treated as an impostor who had penetrated, under false pretences, into the family circle."[36] In Florence, two days after the Elections, Metaxas noted in his *Diary*:

All the newspaper reports and mine indicate that Venizelos has been defeated by a great majority. But I don't think that Gounaris can continue present day Greek foreign policy. Neither can Gounaris save the State internally: he has no strength, no initiative, no determination. As for me, they have all forgotten me ... So much the better! It is time for me to receive a moral baptism and thereafter to remain clean from the mire of vainglory."[37]

The same evening he wrote: "Wrangel has been ruined. The Bolsheviks were united with Kemal. How are Gounaris and the others going to come through the approaching storm?"[38] General Peter Wrangel had taken over the leadership of the Anti-Bolshevik forces from General Anthony Denikin. His defeat in November 1920 meant that Russian arms and money could flow freely to the Nationalists of Turkey. On 18 November 1920 Metaxas commented again: "Wrangel is ruined. Kemal and the Bolsheviks have been united. How are the new governors of Greece going to weather it? One day they will remember me, too."[39]

They did. Four days later Metaxas noted in his *Diary*: "Telegram from Gounaris to return at once! ... Hurriedly we [Metaxas and his wife, Lela] decided that I should return. And if everything is in accordance with our ideas, to stay ... if not, to come back to Florence." Metaxas saw that he would have to give up his quiet life in civilized Florence and interrupt the studies of his children. "Nevertheless, I have to do my duty. No ambition!"[40] By coincidence, the carriage which was carrying the Greek princes from Rome to Brindisi on their return journey to Greece was attached to the train in which Metaxas was travelling. At Brindisi there was a reception for the Greek Princes.

---

35 Churchill, *Aftermath*, p. 388.
36 Alexandre A. Pallis, Greece's *Anatolian Venture* (London, 1937), p. 73.
37 Metaxas, *Diary*, II, p. 640.
38 *Ibid.*.
39 *Ibid.*.
40 *Ibid.*, p. 641..

Metaxas hung back, "not wanting to be in their entourage."[41] From the offices of a Travel Agency, he wrote to his wife:

The more I think of it the more I am convinced that they will offer me a secondary position, e.g. as an Undersecretary [at a Ministry] with a million compliments and praise and promises about rapid promotion. It is unnecessary to repeat to you that I shall not accept .... I am constantly with you and the children. I am perfectly calm: nothing makes an impression on me any more.... I shall remain faithful to our resolutions. I have not the slightest ambition: my only ambition is to be an honest man making no compromise with my conscience.[42]

The underlining of the last line is Metaxas'. His real ambition, of course, was never again to place himself under anyone's authority. Thus he advises his wife to prepare her wardrobe for any eventuality, but not to interrupt the education of the children, also to prepare a list of things she would like him to fetch her from Athens if he should return. At Brindisi Metaxas and the Greek Princes' party boarded a Lloyds ship bound for Piraeus. At Corinth the Princes transferred to the torpedo boat *Ierax* which was waiting to receive them. Welcoming crowds lined the bank of the Corinth canal to cheer the Princes.

In Athens Metaxas went to see Gounaris, who had taken over as Minister of War. Gounaris observed that he was on excellent terms with General Victor Dousmanis, the former Chief-of-Staff. Why didn't Metaxas call round to see him at the Ministry? Metaxas writes: "I understood. I told him I wanted to be called to the colors for the sake of my pension and retired immediately."[43] Then Metaxas went to the telegraph office and cabled his wife: *"Arrivato; niente; dopo regolamento afferi arrivederci; bacci."*[44] In his *Diary*, he noted: "A cold northerly wind. I saw my country again as a stranger with an icy heart. The people are, indeed, great; but the ruling class is contemptible."[45]

He went to see his house (which had tenants in it) and with great emotion he wandered through the rooms and collected his old pistol. He visited his brother in the insane asylum and then went to pay his respects at his father's grave. "I covered him with flowers, my dear father!"[46] He also visited the grave of his father-in-law and the grave of Constantine Eslin, the fiery Royalist who had died in the Athens Municipal Hospital from natural causes while awaiting execution after he had been sentenced to death on his return from exile in Corsica. Metaxas also went to the grave of Ion Dragoumis, who had recently been killed in the steets of Athens by the Cretan

41 *Ibid.*, p. 642.
42 *Ibid.*, p. 462f.
43 *Ibid.*, p. 644.
44 *Ibid.*.
45 *Ibid.*.
46 *Ibid.*, p. 647.

gendarmes; later, Metaxas visited the victim's father, the old ex-Premier Stephanos Dragoumis, to offer his condolences.

He went to the Masonic Lodge and was reunited with his "brothers." He also met many of his old friends: Andreas Livieratos, a prominent leader of the *Reservists*, Demetrakopoulos and Premier Rallis, who embraced Metaxas in the street. He met John Theotokis and ex-Premier Stephanos Skouloudis and had lunch with his old fellow-student Xenophon Strategos: "He is in a much better position than me, as far as politics are concerned. He has worked brilliantly. He has written books: I was absorbed in family life, worries,"[47] Metaxas wrote afterwards. Metaxas also met his beloved John Sayias, the Director-General of the *Reservists*: "We kissed each other profusely,"[48] he noted in his *Diary*. Writing to his wife in Florence, Metaxas conveyed his impressions of his return to Athens:

The people here find me too serious and unsmiling and they ask me why I became like this. I don't know why our country seems small to me; and you can't imagine how painful this is to me. The people, too, are small ... and yet they are nice, sweet. But, my God, weak, without life, without nerve.[49]

From Athens Metaxas went to Cephallonia, his native island, to see his old mother and his sister and to take part in the referendum for the restoration of the King. The Reservists waited all night at the port of Sami to welcome him. The next day, 30 November 1920, he went by horse carriage to Argostoli, the capital of the island, where the inhabitants had prepared a tumultuous reception. Metaxas wrote to his wife in Florence: "The whole city was waiting for me at the bridge with flags, flowers, firing shots in the air, men, women, children."[50]

From Argostoli he went by boat to Lexouri where he was received with music and flowers. After Cephallonia he sailed to Ithaca. Again the islanders came out to welcome him. Metaxas visited the small villages which he remembered from his happy childhood. The descriptions of his journey to his wife are often masterly:

Thus in two days I traversed all Cephallonia and Ithaca; lands amazingly beautiful, but with a corpse-like beauty. Nature is all dead: there is hardly a tree. Enormous rocky mountains, towering high, all stone, suddenly falling into the sea, a deep green sea because of its depth, like crystal. The atmosphere transparent, the lines clear, sharp, imposing. There is no tenderness, no sweetness in this nature: something unearthly. Do you remember us reading in Flaubert the Legende of St. Julien? This was my impression. It would be impossible for me to live in this place.[51]

---

47 *Ibid.*, p. 644.
48 *Ibid.*.
49 *Ibid.*, p. 646f.
50 *Ibid.*, p. 654.
51 *Ibid.*, p. 658.

Why did he go to Cephallonia and Ithaca? "Mainly an inward necessity brought me thence to see again the places where I was born and where I played as a young child -- a kind of pilgrimage."[52] On this pilgrimage he often addressed the welcoming crowds:

I thanked them. I told them that our struggles were waged for an idea, the independence of the Nation and the liberties of the people, and not for individuals. King Constantine was the symbol of these ideas ... I spoke to them briefly without any rhetoric and I made a great impression on them. It was the first time I had spoken to a big crowd but I felt no excitement whatsoever, neither was I diffident. ....

I felt no frenzy in me, no egoism, no ambition; and I am certain that it was just for this reason that I spoke well, in perfect tranquillity, because inwardly I, too, felt great tranquillity and complete lack of any ambition. ...

Everything I told them was the truth and came from my soul. I am happy about this, because I remained an honest man; I shall live as an honest private citizen and they will respect me, and we shall be independent.[53]

His compatriots moved him. To his wife he wrote that for the first time he saw "with eyes unclouded by ambition and egoistical designs this small, simple world."[54] Misfortunes had made him wiser but also he owed this new vision to her. "My mother was always drifting in the clouds. Now she is very old. But when she was young her obsession with ambition did us a lot of harm. Let it be, all this is in the past."[55] The "poor and simple" Cephallonians, "who have their conscience clear," greatly affected him and he contrasted them with the Athenians. "Athens and Athenian society is stench and dirt -- wherever we observed it, in Athens or abroad, it carried poison."[56] Metaxas' journey to his native island helped to clarify his mind. For some time he had been moving away emotionally from the murky political climate of Athens. His former ambitions to rally the anti-Venizelists around the King were shattered when the Royalists passed him over and did not offer him the position he believed he deserved in the new Government, (perhaps that of Minister of Defence or at least Chief of the General Staff). Visiting Cephallonia, Metaxas discovered the people, the ordinary people, who suffered most because of the mistakes of the politicians and who clung to their beliefs without any expectations of reward or promotion of any kind. As the new rulers of Athens, who had been Metaxas' friends, had no intention of giving him a position important enough to satisfy his unbridled political aspirations, Metaxas abandoned "ambition," concluded that Athens was "all stench and dirt," decided to be an "honest" man and turned to the ordinary people who, like himself, remained "pure"

52 *Ibid.*.
53 *Ibid.*, p. 654.
54 *Ibid.*, p. 655.
55 *Ibid.*.
56 *Ibid.*, p. 656.

in their ideals but were, like Metaxas, permanently ignored and forgotten. Among these "ordinary people" there were the former combatants, the veterans of the Balkan Wars, who like himself, had fought for their country only to be vilified and persecuted for their loyalty to King and Fatherland.

One thing pleased me. I found the Greek people, that is the little people, by far superior to what I had previously believed, and to what the educated classes usually represented them. The main leaven of this people, a wonderful leaven, are the Reservists. Their organisation will be to my eternal glory which nobody can steal from me since it was recognized by the court decision which sentenced me to death.[57]

Madame Metaxas had apparently cabled to the *Reservists*, perhaps to congratulate them on the results of the recent elections. Metaxas wrote to her: "The *Reservists* here are preening themselves over the telegram you sent them. Honest men! You will like them when you get to know them."[58]

And while Metaxas was explaining to his fellow islanders that he had no political plans or ambitions, before he left Cephallonia he organised a "People's Political Association" at Argostoli, "of a very democratic character," as he wrote, "whose main purpose is to keep a watchful eye on the island's deputies and the local authorities."[59] Metaxas extended his stay in Cephallonia for seven days to avoid the festivities in Athens on the return of King Constantine. "I had no desire to be present at the reception of the King," he wrote.[60] He disliked the overdone festivities of the Royalists and thought little of the efforts of Prince Nicholas (who was a painter) to organise the reception "in a more artistic manner." The Prince was a busybody: "La mouche du coche!" Metaxas commented.[61] When he returned to Athens, Metaxas avoided all members of the Royalist Government and the Palace circle. "I have seen none of the officials", he wrote. "Neither the King nor the Princes. Only the Queen privately, who is crushed by the death of Alexander. She asked me if I would like to see the King and I said no."[62] In order not to meet anyone he repeatedly declined invitations and he avoided seeing even his friend, Prince Andrew.

Madame Metaxas wrote to warn him not to yield to pressure and accept any position with the Government. Nobody exerted pressure on him and Metaxas pointed out to those he met that the Entente would not be best pleased if he were made part of the Government. So Metaxas wrote back to reassure her: *I do whatever I want, whatever we two want, who are one, and not whatever the others want. I am no longer the old*

---

57 *Ibid.*, p. 664.
58 *Ibid.*, p. 665.
59 *Ibid.*, p. 666.
60 *Ibid.*.
61 *Ibid.*.
62 *Ibid.*, p. 677.

Yiannakis, the good boy, who never refused anything to anyone, who sacrified himself. All this is over![63] In his *Diary*, he noted: "I shall keep to the truth: I reject sharing the responsibility for the Asia Minor campaign."[64] The phrase is underlined by Metaxas himself.

In Athens Metaxas arranged to be called back to the Army, promoted to Lieutenant General and retired at his own request. His only interest in the promotion was to increase the size of his pension -- "as for the rank, they can keep it," he wrote to his wife. He also made arrangements for the pension which had not been paid to him while in exile to be paid to him retroactively now, much augmented, as salary. The Royalists, a trifle guilty because they had not included him in the new Government and anxious to get rid of him, complied readily with his demands. The Royal Decrees for his reinstatement and promotion to Lieutenant General and that for his retirement were published simultaneously in the newspapers on 7 January 1921. He noted in his *Diary*: "I have been promoted. I have been retired. I have completed my career! I breathe free air."[65] That day, writing to his wife, he described himself as a "retired general." At this time his income was his pension, the rent from his house in Athens, the rent from two shops and some shares.

He made plans to go into business in partnership with two brothers from Athens, Nikolaos and A. Kanellopoulos. He spoke German, he had contacts in Germany: an import-export agency between industrial Germany and agricultural Greece was bound to succeed, Metaxas thought. Such a venture would require an occasional trip to Germany, and also the permanent presence of Metaxas in Greece. Compared to Florence, Athens was provincial. "But", Metaxas wrote to his wife, "it is our fatherland and the country where we shall base our future and the future of our children."[66] The children's education in Florence would have to be interrupted, but they could start anew. Metaxas wrote to his wife that the German governess they had in Florence should definitely accompany them to Athens so that the two girls could continue their study of German. In Athens he could easily find them a teacher of Greek and they could study the piano at the Conservatory. As their house had been rented, Metaxas was obliged to look around for a new home. The sudden exodus of Venizelists made many houses available at low rent. Metaxas found a suitable home from a fleeing Venizelist at Phaleron, by the sea which was "good for the health," and in a neighbourhood where the public transport was excellent.

Metaxas returned by way of Rome to Florence, where he arrived on 17 January 1921. From there he went to Germany in connection with the import-export business he was

---

63 *Ibid.*.
64 *Ibid.*, p. 663.
65 *Ibid.*, p. 675.
66 *Ibid.*, p. 649.

hoping to set up. Eighteen years had gone by since he had last seen Berlin. None of the turn of the century glamor had survived in the defeated Germany of the present. Metaxas visited his old college, the *Kriegs-Akademie*: "Memories, but no emotion," he noted in his *Diary*. "The weight of the great city is upon me. I'm impatient for the hour of my departure."[67] From Berlin he went to Hamburg. During a walk around the city, a German friend warned him "not to think that the future Germany would be the men he was connected with, but the suffering young men who are returning [from the Front]."[68] Back in Florence a letter was waiting for him from Cephallonia. Already problems had arisen in the "People's Political Association" which Metaxas had recently founded at Argostoli. "Nevertheless we need the Movement," he noted in his *Diary*,[69] and immediately the Metaxas family packed and took the train for the journey home.

In Brindisi on 11 February 1921 Metaxas encountered the Greek delegation, which was on its way to the London Conference. The Greeks and the Turks (both representatives of the Constantinople Government and the Nationalist representatives of Kemal) had been invited to London by the Allied Powers in the hope of ending the state of war in Asia Minor and negotiating a peace settlement. The Greek delegation was headed by Nikolaos Kalogeropoulos, who had taken over as Prime Minister a few days earlier (7 February 1921) following a disagreement between Premier Rallis and his Minister of War, Demetrios Gounaris. Gounaris, the leader of the strongest single group in the Royalist coalition, was considered unsuitable to represent Greece at an Allied conference because of his notorious record of opposition to the Allies during the War. Thus the colorless, ineffectual Kalogeropoulos took over as Prime Minister for the duration of the Conference. (On 8 April 1921 he was succeeded by Gounaris.)

Kalogeropoulos suggested that the Metaxas family travel on the torpedo boat *Narcissus* which had brought the Greek delegation to Brindisi and was returning to Piraeus. To no avail. Metaxas would not compromise his position on any account and he declined. In Athens the Metaxas family settled in the rented house in the seaside suburb of Phaleron.[70] One evening the King and Queen received General Metaxas and Madame Lela Metaxas at the Palace -"a sign of [Royal] favor,"[71] Metaxas noted in his *Diary*. When the news reached Athens that a proposal had been made at the London Conference for the revision of the Treaty of Sèvres, demonstrations broke out in the streets. At the Conference France demanded that Greece withdraw from Anatolia and

67 *Ibid.*, III, p. 60.

68 *Ibid.*, p. 61.

69 *Ibid.*, p. 62.

70 The Metaxas family lived in the Phaleron house for the next seven years. The house, which belonged to the Mertzanof family, is still standing, its present address being Number 23, Makarios Avenue.

71 Metaxas, *Diary*, III, p. 67.

Thrace. While the Conference was in session, the French delegates carried on secret negotiations with the Kemalist representatives. Britain was kept completely in the dark about these negotiations which, in the following October, culminated in the Franklin-Bouillon Pact by which France gave Kemal Cilicia (and a large supply of arms) in exchange for peace on the border of her Syrian mandate and promises of commercial advantage. In secret, separate talks with the Turkish Nationalists, the Italians offered Kemal their diplomatic support and arms from their stores in Antalya in exchange for various kinds of economic concessions. Italy seconded the French demand for Greek withdrawal from Anatolian and Thrace.

Britain desired it to go on record that she had advised Greece to reach an agreement with the Turkish Nationalists, but in private the British politicians encouraged the Greeks to continue the war against Kemal. Britain wanted the Greek forces to remain in Turkey and protect the meager Allied detachments (mostly British) stationed in Constantinople. More importantly, Britain wanted the Turks kept busy in Western Asia Minor until the new borders between Turkey and Mesopotamia were established and the oil-rich regions of Mosul and Kirkuk could be properly defended.

The Greek Royalists who, when out of power, had denounced Venizelos' interventionist policies as adventurous and rash, now "were mesmerized," as Venizelos had been, by the vision of a Greater Greece in the Eastern Mediterranean,"[72] as the historian Stavrianos wrote, and refused to come to an understanding with the Turks. No one had realized this more clearly than Ioannis Metaxas. On 28 February 1921, while the London Conference was still going on, he noted in his *Diary*:

The chauvinism of the present rulers of Greece, which is really timidity, leads to disaster; but this is the final stage [of a process] we should have been expecting. I have well calculated this since the winter of 1914.[73]

At the London Conference the French and the Italians, using the restoration of Constantine as a convenient excuse, came to an understanding with the Turkish nationalists. In secret agreements the French agreed to revise their borders in Cilicia, while the Italians withdrew all their claims in Asia Minor, choosing to consolidate their occupation of the Dodecanese. In the meantime, Kemal, who presented the Greeks as western imperialists, signed a treaty of peace with the Bolsheviks. Despite the brave words of the Greek generals, the Greek position in Anatolia was untenable. Greece had no money to buy arms and ammunition, there were no more classes of recruits to be called up, there were problems with the provisioning of the Army, there were problems in the High Command of the Greek Expeditionary Force and the morale of the Army, many of the soldiers having been under arms since the First Balkan War of 1912, was

72 Stavrianos, *Balkans*, p. 587.

73 Metaxas, *Diary*, III, p. 66.

low. Also low was the confidence of the Greek people, who saw no end to the war which Greece had got herself into.

At the London Conference the Greek Royalists, however, rejected a compromise with Kemal, and the Turks, fully aware of the desperate position of the Greek Army in Anatolia and encouraged by their newly found European friends, were intransigent as well. To the Turks the Greek campaign was an invasion of their country and Turkish nationalism united the nation, which was determined to throw the Greeks into the sea and establish a new Turkey on the ruins of the Ottoman Empire. For the Turks it was a war of *revanche* for the loss of Crete and the Aegean Islands, of Macedonia and Epirus, after the Balkan wars. Turkish refugees from the lost European territories swelled the ranks of the Kemalist armies, determined to get their own back on the Greeks, who had expelled them from their homes and villages and who now had the audacity to invade their country and threaten the existence of the Turkish State.

The Greek Government in Athens was at a complete loss what to do. Greek public opinion was against the war and did not trust either the politicians or the military establishment, which was made up of a mixture of Venizelist and Royalist officers, hating each other and blaming every misfortune on their political opponents. Gone were the days when the Greeks, under the political leadership of Venizelos and the military command of Constantine and his General Staff of brilliant officers, such as the now forgotten Ioannis Metaxas, swept triumphantly through the Balkans. Venizelos was in exile overseas and none of the Royalists wanted to hear his name mentioned. But Constantine was still with them, although much battered and crestfallen by the misfortunes that had befallen his dynasty. Why not reassemble the former General Staff around him, why not resuscitate the brilliant team of Constantine and his German-trained officers, who had given them the glories of the Balkan Wars? Then the Greek politicians remembered Metaxas.

In the evening of Thursday, 25 March 1921, Colonel Athanasios Hexadactylos, who had been a fellow-student of Metaxas at the Berlin War Academy, visited Metaxas at his house in Phaleron and brought him an invitation from Gounaris, the Prime Minister, to meet with him at the house of Protopapadakis, the Minister of Finance, that same evening to discuss the current situation in Asia Minor. Accordingly, at ten o'clock that night Metaxas met with Gounaris, Protopapadakis and Hexadactylos; no one else was present.

On 29 March there was a second meeting, when also present was Nikolaos Theotokis, the Minister of War. Metaxas' detailed account of these two meetings is now in his Archive and was recently published among many other of his papers.[74] These recorded

---

74 Metaxas' memo of these two meetings, written in his own hand, are kept in Metaxas Archives in Athens. They were printed in his *Diary*, Vol. III, pp. 71-101.

conversations reveal the extraordinary confusion that existed in the minds of the Greek politicians and, in contrast, throw light on the clear-headed pragmatism of Ioannis Metaxas, who could analyse and evaluate the muddled perceptions of the Greek Government and offer concrete solutions; his strength of character when faced with formidable pressure also stands out clearly. A consistently veracious man, Metaxas was meticulous in his recording of these scenes in which he played a major part and there is no reason to doubt that he provides an accurate description of the two discussions. His lengthy accounts of these tempestuous encounters were written little by little and took two months to complete. In these two meetings Prime Minister Gounaris and his colleagues in the Government tried to find out from Metaxas his views on the Anatolian campaign and, if possible, to persuade him to join the King on the General Staff at the front. They did not want Metaxas to be on their team and for this reason they did not invite him to join the Government the previous November when the Royalists won the elections. But they knew about Metaxas' military talents and wondered whether and how they could use him. On the other hand they knew Metaxas' opinion about a war in Asia Minor from the old days, when Metaxas, as Acting Chief of Staff, advised Venizelos against such an enterprise and chose to break with the Prime Minister rather than be part of such a monumental folly.[75]

At the first meeting Metaxas was asked of his opinion of the decision of the army leaders to launch a major attack at the Afion Karahisar - Eski Sehir line in Asia Minor with the ultimate target being Ankara itself. Metaxas answered that although he did not have the details of the tactical military situation, it seemed to him that the Greek forces were too weak and too widely spread out on a front of three hundred kilometers and of an even greater depth, in a most difficult terrain through a hostile local population. This was a war, he pointed out, against Turkey, that is, against the whole Turkish nation.

The Prime Minister explained to him that the Turks refused to come to an understanding which would end the war. If the Greeks captured the Afium Kavahisar - Eski Sehir line and then entered Ankara and Konia, the Turkish Commander, Mustafa Kemal, would be forced to sign a peace treaty. Metaxas explained that even if that were possible, something that he doubted, the Turks would withdraw further into the interior of the country, a country of vast distances, and continue the war from there. For the Turks, he told them, this was a war of national liberation and such a war would always find leaders to carry on the struggle until the bitter end. Greece had never possessed the resources for crushing the Turkish State and imposing by force the terms of the Treaty of Sèvres. Indeed, Metaxas had always held this opinion and had explained the situation to Venizelos during the time they were working together and had warned him against such a rash adventure.

75 *Ibid.*, p. 67.

Gounaris said that he was forced to continue Venizelos' policy when in London he had discovered that the Turks were not willing to reach a compromise. Then Metaxas was asked what could be done so that the Greek forces could at least win the battle of Afium Karahisar. Metaxas replied that he could not give them a plan of campaign, which would in any case be useless at this late stage. All three men expressed doubts as to the ability of the present General Staff. The Prime Minister considered Papoulas ineffective as Commander in Chief; he was always asking for reinforcements and seeking for an excuse to give up his position and abandon the campaign. Protopapadakis then proposed directly to Metaxas that he should go to the front in order to advise the Commander in Chief. Metaxas replied that it was true that in the past he had agreed to perform such subservient offices (referring to his position on the General Staff during the Balkan Wars as assistant to Dousmanis, "for which I suffered greatly, but now I am getting on in years and the extent of my generosity has considerably lessened." He therefore angrily rejected what he saw as a demeaning proposal; whereupon Protopapadakis requested him to take over himself as Commander-in-Chief of the campaign. Metaxas was adamant that he could not do this, as he did not agree with the conduct of the war and preparations for the campaign that were going forward. It was now too late to make any effective changes in the structure of the Army and he could not accept the position and carry out the plans of others, plans which he was convinced would lead to certain disaster.

They begged and pleaded with him but he was unmoved:

By accepting the command of the Army without explaining in public how success was beyond all reasonable expectations, I would have been giving the Nation hopes that I do not share; in other words, I would have been deceiving the Nation, which I cannot do as it goes against my conscience.[76]

They entreated him to make this sacrifice for the sake of the Fatherland.

But what you ask of me is not a sacrifice for the Fatherland but a sacrifice of my honor so that I would [by participating in the campaign] cover up the responsibilities of other people. This I cannot do, I cannot sacrifice my honor for your sake; my honor is all that is left to me after thirty-five years of military service.[77]

On 29 March Metaxas was again invited to the house of Protopapadakis to meet Gounaris and Hexadactylos. At first he protested, as he considered their previous discussion to have been final, but they pressed him and he agreed. Gounaris opened the proceedings by announcing that he and his colleagues in the Government had unanimously agreed that a new General Staff should be put together on the lines of the former Royal Military Staff of the Balkan Wars. "On this Staff you should also be

76 *Ibid.*, p. 74.
77 *Ibid.*, p. 75.

present!"[78] Metaxas pointed out that he could never work under Dousmanis. "Then you should undertake the leadership yourself,"[79] responded the Prime Minister. Metaxas: "But I thought the King was the Commander-in-Chief of the Army."[80]

He stressed to them the myriad tasks involved in a campaign and how, by their very nature, the King could not attend to all these in person; this was the responsibility of the Minister of War. There were duties connected with mobilisation, the supply of arms and ammunition, duties connected with the commissariat, and so on ... The King could not act as an adviser to the Minister of War. Then Theotokis observed:

My dear brother Metaxas, I don't know about these things, I only know about one thing. I remember in the Balkan Wars, when I was in Berlin, in the midst of all my anxiety I knew that you three or four men were here and taking care of the War and I was comforted and even when the news was disquieting, I slept peacefully, because I knew you were in charge. Well then, this is what we want to build up again.[81]

The other two men were silent. Then a heated debate ensued. Metaxas accused them of trying to burden the King with all the responsibility for an impossible situation. The Minister of War observed that he could hardly understand all the matters connected with the war. Thereupon Metaxas challenged him to resign.

Gounaris intervened to say that it was not a question of the Minister and his duties. Public opinion, the desire of the people, who wanted to see the King in command, who demanded the return of the old General Staff - these were grave matters that could not be ignored. In any case, he concluded, we are the Government, we decide what should be done. Do you agree to take over the leadership of the General Staff? Metaxas would not budge:

Then the four of them tried with further supplications to make me change my decision, reminding me of the dreadful situation the State was in. I answered that the Government could get out of this dreadful situation in the way I had explained to them ...[82]

Could Metaxas at least suggest someone else to take over as Commandor in Chief? Metaxas declared that Dousmanis was the least suitable and suggested General Strategos.

78 *Ibid.*.
79 *Ibid.*, p. 78.
80 *Ibid.*.
81 *Ibid.*.
82 *Ibid.*, p. 79; for Metaxas' views of the campaign s. page 341.

They all returned to their first opinion that I should take on the leadership myself. Theotokis was most importunate: "Well then, here we are, four men begging you, and you refuse?[83]

They continued to press him.

Metaxas: *Why do you all so much insist that I should be a member of the General Staff?*

Gounaris: *Because the mood of the public is uneasy and your appointment will quieten their fears.*

Protopapadakis: *You cannot imagine how much the people will be reassured when it is known that you are on the General Staff.*

Metaxas: *Why are the people anxious? What are they afraid of?*

Protopapadakis: *The people are afraid that we will lose the war, that we cannot win by force of arms. If you assume the leadership of the General Staff, their belief in victory will return.*

Metaxas: *Therefore, by assuming the leadership it would be as if I were telling the Greek people: "Stay calm, we shall win. I am here and I assure you of this. Now you too can be certain."*

Gounaris and the others: *Exactly!*

Metaxas: *Then it is as if you were asking me to deceive the people, because I am fully aware that we can never attain our purpose by force of arms.*

Protopapadakis: *True, even if we have to deceive the people, this, if need be, should also be done.*

Metaxas: *But on no account will I deceive the Greek people. According to my principles, the truth should always be told to the people. I consider them sufficiently mature to have the courage to hear the truth. Anyway, do not forget that I for many years have come out against any military adventure in Asia Minor. For this reason I opposed Venizelos and I was in active service then. Now that I am retired, should I return to the Army to reassure the Greek people that I am now convinced that what I was telling them previously, which was impossible then, is possible now? What kind of a man do you take me for?*[84]

Again they asked him why he thought the Asia Minor expedition was condemned to failure. Again and again he explained that they were fighting a war whose aim was to destroy Turkey and establish Greek domination in Asia Minor. Even in Smyrna, the Greeks were in a minority, he reminded them, and in the interior of the country the Greeks were very few. The Turks knew what the Greeks had in mind, their national feelings had been provoked and they meant to fight for their freedom and independence

83 *Ibid.*, p. 82.
84 *Ibid.*, p. 83.

for exactly the same reasons that the Greeks had fought against them in the past. The Turks felt that Asia Minor was their Fatherland and that the Greeks were the invaders. The Greek reiteration of their "historical rights" for which the Greeks were fighting, meant nothing to the Turks. The Greeks were not fighting Kemal or a Turkish political party, they were fighting the whole Turkish Nation. Even if the Greeks were to win one battle, that would not make the Turks sign a peace settlement as the Greeks wanted. And Metaxas explained to his companions how vast Asia Minor was and how impossible it would be for the limited Greek forces to conquer it. "Remember how Spain became the graveyard of one of the best of Napoleon's armies,"[85] he reminded them.

Gounaris tried to explain that the Royalists were merely following the policy of Venizelos.

Metaxas: *You could have come to an understanding with the Turks.*

Gounaris: *I wanted to do that, then the Indian Aga Khan intervened and the Turks changed their minds ... I admit I was deceived.*[86]

Metaxas advised them to withdraw to the boundaries around Smyrna delineated by the Treaty of Sèvres and then negotiate an honorable withdrawal.

Metaxas: *This would have been the right policy towards Turkey - friendly co-operation.*

Hexadactylos: *They are slaughtering us!*

Metaxas: *They are slaughtering us because we have set for our target the conquest of their native land. The Turks know that they can never have our friendship, that nothing can change our enmity towards them and they can expect to gain nothing from us. Naturally, these things do not justify the slaughter, but aren't we slaughtering them as well?*

Hexadactylos: *Indeed, we are slaughtering them too. We must exterminate them, that is the only thing the Turks understand!*[87]

After much argument, Gounaris wanted Metaxas to tell them what course they should follow to achieve victory. Metaxas hammered home to them that even if the Greeks were to win a temporary victory, they would lose everything in the end and that would not be a victory at all. "We are trying to achieve a feat beyond our capacity."[88]

At one point Hexadactylos remembered the siege of Jannnina and the *impasse* faced by the Greek Army and how, while in London, he had gone to Venizelos and asked him to send Metaxas to join the campaign because only Metaxas could take Jannina. Metaxas returned that that had been a very different story. In Jannina the Turkish Army

85 *Ibid.*, p. 84.
86 *Ibid.*, p. 85.
87 *Ibid.*, p. 86.
88 *Ibid.*, p. 87.

was unable to receive any supplies and, sooner or later, it had to surrender. In Asia Minor, Kemal was inundated with supplies from the Italians, the French and the Bolsheviks.

Protopapadakis: *But what do you expect, separating your responsibility from ours? If we fail, the whole world will be against you, the Greek people will never forgive you for refusing to participate in the campaign. You will not gain any advantage.*

Metaxas: *I don't seek to gain anything. I desire nothing other than to be allowed to remain true to my principles and my conscience.*

Protopapadakis: *Perhaps one day the people will demonstrate under your windows and demand your return to the Army.*

Metaxas: *In that case, I shall address them and explain to them what their real interests are, and I shall tell them what I am telling you now and even more and in even stronger language and then we shall see where the demonstrators will direct their steps and their fury.*

Protopapadakis: [angrily] *If we fail, you too will go down with us. A revolt of the people will bring back Venizelos.*

Gounaris: [Suddenly bursting out] *Why should I care for my part? I am all alone in the world, I can take any road, no matter where it leads. Alas for you who have families and property to worry about.*[89]

Metaxas: [raising his voice] *Don't disturb yourselves! Venizelos is not coming back. But even if he were to come because the people wanted him, I am not afraid of him. In the last resort, if Greece can only be saved by Venizelos, then let Venizelos come! Should the country go to the devil solely in order to prevent his return?*

Protopapadakis: *By refusing to join the campaign you are harming yourself. Our failure will be the failure of the whole Establishment and you will not gain any advantage from staying out of this.*

Metaxas [angrily]: *Do you imagine that I have been brought so low that I would hope to gain any benefit from the destruction of my country?*

Protopapadakis: *You will see, your fellow-citizens will not even vote for you as a deputy.*

Metaxas: *I don't care about that, I am indifferent.*

Protopapadakis: *You don't care? Is that not your goal?*

Metaxas: *No, not at all.*

Protopapadakis: *Very well then ...*

Metaxas: [gravely] *I shall not undertake any service if I do not agree with the work I am required to do. For this reason I resigned my commission so that I could have this precious freedom.*

---

89 The Prime Minister, who never married, was known for his poverty - at his death he possessed only a very small sum of money, which he left to his cook.

Gounaris: *Yet you are obliged, whether you agree or not, to offer your services without any objections whatsoever when your country needs you.*
Metaxas: *Do you mean the Fatherland?*
Gounaris: *The Fatherland, yes, the Fatherland! It is your duty to obey.*
Metaxas: [Standing up and raising his voice]. *The Fatherland, Mr Prime Minister, is only an abstract idea. It does not take the concrete shape or the voice of this person or of that. It is a concept that speaks to our hearts, to each one of us individually. And each one of us recognises this voice within us. Every individual interprets what this inner voice tells him. And each of us serves the Fatherland in the light of his own perceptions. The Monarchist serves his Fatherland, the Democrat serves his Fatherland, the Kaiser serves his Fatherland, so does Hindenburg, Kautsky serves his Fatherland, and Lloyd George and Henderson and Clemenceau, and the Czar serves his Fatherland, the Bolshevick serves his Fatherland, Constantine serves his Fatherland, even Venizelos serves his Fatherland.*
Gounaris: *Each one acts according to his own perception.*
Metaxas: *Precisely. I, too, serve my Fatherland according to my perceptions and according to my conscience and as I deem the interests of my Fatherland to be, not in the manner that you or anyone else imagine that I should. I know very well what I am doing; I, too, have a perception of what the interests of Greece are, though I do not agree with you.*
Gounaris: *It is not necessary for all of us to agree.*
Metaxas: *Well then, should I therefore, because I was once an officer, be condemned for the rest of my life to be the instrument of other men's plans, when I perceive that it is precisely in the interests of my country that I should not become that instrument, when I, too, have my own ideas and thoughts? Who is in danger? Is the Fatherland in danger? Not in the least! A certain policy is in danger, a policy which Greece need not follow without any danger to the Fatherland. If you like, the Government is in danger, even the present form of government is in danger, but not the Fatherland. Why, then, should I act against my conscience in order to carry out certain policies which I do not consider to be in the best interests of the Fatherland just because you have been demanding this of me? But I am determined that even if all the Greek people joined together to ask of me something that I consider inappropriate, I will not do it and I do not care if all my countrymen condemn me.*
Protopapadakis: *They will certainly condemn you!*
Metaxas: *No matter! I will have a clear conscience because I will have done my duty.*
Protopapadakis: *Your fellow citizens will never forgive you for your refusal.*
Metaxas: *What will they not forgive?*
Protopapadakis: *That you were not willing to participate in the war.*
Metaxas: *I beg your pardon, Mr Protopapadakis! Who has told you that I refuse to participate in the War? I refuse to participate as Commander in Chief of the General*

Staff, I refuse to take the responsibility of the direction of the war, a war which is against my principles because we disagree about everything. But I do not refuse to go to the War.
Protopapadakis: *Well then, you agree to be recalled immediately and to be placed at the head of a division?*
Metaxas: *I accept this straightaway.*
Protopapadakis: *And it is understood that we could remove you from the division and appoint you chief of the General Staff?*
Metaxas: *What are you talking about, Mr Protopapadakis? Are you serious?*
Protopapadakis: *Then what is the point of giving you a division?*
Theotokis: *Come on, my dear friend Metaxas, agree to take over, make this beau geste!*
Metaxas: *My dear friend Theotokis, I am not accustomed to making „gestes". I am accustomed to performing well-calculated and logical actions and to taking the responsibility for them, but for my own actions only.*[90]

It was getting late, well after midnight. The discussion was detiorating. Gounaris often lost his temper. Metaxas also often lost patience with Gounaris, banging the table with his fist, often getting up and pacing up and down, raising his voice to emphasise a point. His contempt and indignation regarding the politicians was apparent. Hexadactylos, the other military man present, was depressed, his head drooping, eyes downcast; Hexadactylos realised that Metaxas was in the right, but lacked the moral courage to support him. At one point Gounaris addressed Metaxas in a loud angry voice.
Gounaris: *After all, you realise that we are gathered here as old friends, but do not forget that we three are also something else that you are not - we are the Government and, because of this, we have certain rights and, if we like, we can call you back to the Army and dare you disobey us...!*
Metaxas: *Yes, you have this right and I shall obey.*
Gounaris: [banging the table with his fist]. *Then what have you been arguing about for so long?*
Metaxas: *You have the right to recall me to the Army and place me in a position appropriate to my rank, that right and no other.*
Gounaris: *Your rank! Your rank! What do you mean? Lieutenant General? Not, of course, Lieutenant General, because don't forget how you attained that rank.*
Metaxas: *You made me Lieutenant General in order that I would leave the Army.*

---

90 *Ibid.*, p. 97.

Gounaris: *Certainly, so that you would leave! Because if you had not left, if you had remained in the Army, you would not have been a Lieutenant General because there were many others senior to you and you would now have been only a Colonel.*
Metaxas: *What are you trying to prove with this?*
Gounaris: *I want to say that if you are recalled now you will not perform the duties of a Lieutenant General but those attached to the rank you would have held if you had remained in the Army.*
Metaxas: *You mean the rank of Colonel?*
Gounaris: *Yes, of Colonel.*
Metaxas: *How, then, do you expect me now to take over as Commander in Chief?*
Gounaris: *In the wars of 1912 and 1913, what was your rank?*
Metaxas: *I was directing operations, I was doing the job of a colonel -- at least, the duties of an officer of higher rank -- and I was then only a captain.*[91]

Then Metaxas embarked upon a vehement tirade, reminding them how his services were always needed but consistently undervalued. Whenever there was a crisis during the war, they all wanted him to lead, but when the war was over, his services always went unrewarded and forgotten. When promotions and decorations were being awarded, the name of Metaxas was not to be found on the list. He concluded: "I tell you plainly, confronted with such a State, I, too, am a rebel! Yes, I am a rebel! Lay one finger on me, if you dare!"[92] Then Metaxas in more measured tones related to them how often his views had not been taken into account by those in power and how many disasters had befallen the country on account of this. At one point, other officers came in to show the Prime Minister various telegrams and other documents, so further emotional outbursts were prevented. Theotokis whispered to Metaxas: "Well then, there is nothing else for me to do but to give in my resignation and you can undertake the post of Minister of War."[93] But he did not repeat this proposal to the Prime Minister. In his long memos, Metaxas vividly described the conclusion of this meeting.

I sat in an armchair and rested my head in my hands. I was exchausted. It was almost two hours after midnight. For four hours I had been continuously subjected to the attacks of four men who had tried to force me to act against my conscience. Every imaginable temptation had assailed me: high office, senior rank, glory; on the other hand, the danger of being considered a traitor to my country, the danger of having the accusations of the whole Nation hurled at my head, the danger of losing even that little respect which I had acquired, the threats of Gounaris, all these things I had suffered ... I resisted them all, but I felt very great fatigue. I also felt the discomfort of being in the company of men from whom I was emotionally alienated,

91 *Ibid.*, p. 98.
92 *Ibid.*, p. 99.
93 *Ibid.*, p. 100.

or rather with whom I discovered I shared nothing in common, men with whom I had earlier been connected. It was a part of my life which was now fading into the past.

When we separated it was 3.30 in the morning. By the time I reached home, dawn was breaking. Deep inside I was content and I could find nothing for which I could blame myself.[94]

Despite his firm rejection of the Asia Minor policy, despite his refuse to assume command of the campaign, and join his old comrades in arms, Metaxas was often prey to misgivings and doubts. On 1st April 1921 he learned that Dousmanis and Strategos had been appointed to the General Staff. He makes no comment on this in his Diary, but it must have recalled old memories. He followed the fortunes of the Anatolian campaign with great foreboding. On 25 April he wrote in his Diary:

Have I acted according to my conscience? Was what I did correct? Was it not harmful, even ruinous for me? Why should not a victory at Eski-Sehir conclude the campaign in our favor? Why, should it not provide us, at least, with a moral basis to withdraw with honor? Why would not that be possible? How many doubts! What hesitations within me![95]

In Athens one day Metaxas watched with distaste and anger as Greek troops marched down Stadiou Street, bound for the front. The men were silent and haggard. To him they resembled victims on their way to sacrifice, even while the crowds cheered them on. Metaxas wrote a furious entry in his *Diary* [referring to the applauding crowds]: "Idiotic bastards! [Literally, "Idiotic cuckolds!" *Μωροί κερατάδες*!] You know how to shout *Zito*! [Hurrah!] but to turn out and fight, that you do not know!" [95] Every day news arrived of Greek casualties, among them some well-known personalities. Metaxas attended the funeral of Rigas, an old comrade who had been with him in Corsica, then visited his widow several times. "Watching her in her distress one's heart is torn apart".[96]

On 29 May 1921 King Constantine, although suffering from uraemia, set off for the Front. General Papoulas was recalled and his place was taken by General Hadjianesti, an honest man, but eccentric and incompetent. One evening Pesmazoglou came to visit Metaxas, bringing the news that Gounaris had said that those who were opposed to him would be lynched if he failed; and if he won, his present opponents would follow him like sheep.[97]

In an interview given by Xenophon Strategos, now second in command on the General Staff in Asia Minor, to a correspondent from the *Smyrna Tribune*, reproduced on 27 June 1921, in the *Kathimerini* newspaper of Athens, Strategos was reported as

94 *Ibid.*, p. 101.
95 *Ibid.*, p. 105.
96 *Ibid.*, p. 108.
97 *Ibid.*, p. 111.

saying "We would rather fall to the last man than abandon the land where Greek civilization was born, the land to which we have come as liberators".[98] Metaxas noted with some irony in his *Diary*: "He will not return; they will fall to the last man; we shall see!"[99]

Endeavouring to detach himself as far as possible from the distressing news from Asia Minor, Metaxas determindly busied himself in putting his life, which had been interrupted by his exile, into some sort of order. He collected his books around him, classified his voluminous correspondence, collected the back numbers of the newspapers in which he was interested and also worked long hours setting his domestic accounts in order. His household consisted of his mother, his wife and two daughters, Alma, the German governess who taught the two girls, Kouratos, his devoted secretary, a cook and a maid servant. He calculated that he was worth one million drachmas, approximately equivalent to ten thousand English pounds at that time. At the family dinner on Easter Day the fare that appeared on the table was simple. "We are not rich" he noted. Apparently the German project for setting up an import-export business came to nothing and he had now to depend on his military pension as a retired Lieutenant-General, some State compensation for his years of exile and the rent from two shops he owned in Athens. Now that he had settled in a rented house in Phaleron he and his wife decided to sell the house in Athens which had been Lela's dowry. It was a sad business, but it had to be done. He noted in his *Diary*.

At 3.20 p.m. I signed the deed of sale and ceased to be the owner of the house where I got married, where I suffered and was happy, where my children were born, where my sister was married ... where I fell in love with Lela and spent with her so many happy hours.[100]

On 26 August 1922 Kemal launched his counter - attack at Afiun-Karahisar. The Greek High Command lost its nerve at the last moment and ordered a retreat which turned into a rout. Constantine, now only a shadow of his former self, vilified from every quarter, returned to Athens. Thirty thousand men perished in the inhospitable mountains of Anatolia. Metaxas recorded the disaster in his *Diary*: "A dreadful catastrophe. This is the tragic end of our military glory. It began in 1908, it reached its zenith in the Wars of 1912 and 1913 and it was buried today. This is the story of my own life".[101]

On 8 September 1922 the evacuation of Smyrna began; the following evening the Turks entered the city and put it to the torch. There was a wholesale slaughter of the

98 *Ibid.*, p. 113.
99 *Ibid.*, p. 116.
100 *Ibid.*, p. 115.
101 *Ibid.*, p. 65.

Greek and Armenian populations and over ninety thousand Christians perished in the holocaust. Thus the Greek presence in Asia Minor, which had lasted for three thousand years, came to a tragic conclusion. With the destruction of Smyrna died also the *Megali Idea*. The trauma inflicted on the psyche of the Greek nation was to remain raw and unhealed for generations to come.

Thus, the Treaty of Sèvres by which the "historical" rights of Greece were recognised by the European Powers and for which Eleftherios Venizelos had dragged Greece into the First World War, dividing the country in the process, turned out to be "a fatal step" towards the destruction of Hellenism in Asia Minor. The Royalists' policy of non-intervention and especially Metaxas' stand in support of a neutral Greece was most painfully vindicated as Venizelos' gamble failed miserably.

The Asia Minor catastrophe shook the nation to the core. The Greek Army and Navy, appalled by the incompetence and "treachery" of the politicians and the military leaders, rose up in revolt; a revolutionary committee was put up which demanded the immediate abdication of Constantine in favour of his heir, Prince George, and the arrest and trial of the members of the Athens Government. The King, abandoned on all sides, sent for Metaxas, who after travelling all night, arrived at Tatoi in the early hours of 14 September 1922. He found the King alone with Doctor Louros, the obstetrician to the Royal Family. There were no ministers present, no Palace staff, no friends. The King asked Metaxas to write his letter of resignation addressed to the President of the Revolutionary Committee, and then to write the King's proclamation to the Nation. In these two documents, although the King admits nothing concerning the various crimes of which he was accused, in dignified words he bade farewell to the Greek people. Metaxas penned these documents in his own hand, without assistance; in them one cannot but admire his lofty ideals, his flair for self-expression and the elegant precision with which he uses the Greek language.

Metaxas remained with the King all day until the heir to the throne, now George II, took the Oath. It was not easy for Metaxas to say goodbye to his old Chief, Constantine. "The new King took the Oath at three o' clock in the afternoon of the same day. Then Constantine bids me farewell. I weep. I remain with him until the last moment"[102]

Metaxas returned to Pesmazoglou's house, then after some time, slipped away to an empty bedroom and slept for two hours. The house was full of people. Metaxas related to them what had happened. The Revolutionaries had ordered the King and also the Princes Nicholas and Andrew to leave the country immediately. Metaxas then returned home. There he was visited by General Papoulas. Then he heard of the imprisonment of the former ministers and General Dousmanis. "There is a danger that they will be

102 *Ibid.*, p. 198.

shot. I am sorry for them."[103] He was exhausted and spent a sleepless night. Some fellow-islanders from Cephalonia kept guard over his house.

13 Metaxas as a party leader in 1923.

In the morning of Saturday, 17 September a new government was formed under Sotirios Krokidas. In the afternoon Metaxas returned to Tatoi to say goodbye to the King. "I tell him that he will not return to his throne but that he will live happily as a private citizen. He accepts the whole situation .... The Queen [appeared] most dignified.[104] Queen Sophia had advised her son to go to Metaxas whenever he was faced with a difficulty. Already George II had many questions to put to Metaxas. Sophia assured Metaxas that Constantine had always trusted him. There was a moving final farewell. "And thus the reign of Constantine came to an end,"[105] Metaxas wrote.

103 *Ibid.*, p. 199.
104 *Ibid.*.
105 *Ibid.*.

On his return home he found dense crowds surrounding his house, waiting for news. Every day people of all kinds continued to visit him. On 3 October a friend warned him of the threats of Krokidas concerning his arrest or even assassination. Three other acquaintances also told him that day of the threats against his life. His comment: "So they are thinking to kill me. What can be done! It is sad, but inevitable".[106]

There were reports that the Revolutionaries had a list of one hundred people they were going to shoot. Some said that Metaxas' name was on the list. The mood in Athens resembled that in Paris during the Terror. Every day reports reached Metaxas himself that his assassination was imminent. "Gonatas [the leader of the Revolution] is stubborn and menancing. They will shoot a lot of people; I am somewhat worried; but I have declared that I shall not run away."[107]

During these dark days, Metaxas announced the formation of his own political party -- the *Komma Elephtherophronon* --, the Free Thinkers Party. On 12 October 1922 the newspaper *Nea Hemera* published, next to his photograph, the political manifesto of the new party. The Revolutionary Committee, in their *pronuciamento*, announced the holding of future elections and Metaxas' intention was to solicit the votes of the Greek people. The title of the manifesto indicates the direction of the new political party: *A platform statement by Mr. Ioannis Metaxas on the Election Campaign, which is the position of the new party vis-à-vis Venizelism and the Old Political World.* In this document Metaxas attacked the ideological and moral bankruptcy of both the Venizelists and the Royalists. The Free Thinkers Party offered a third solution, beyond the passions of the traditional groupings, in a new framework which would bury the shameful past and rejuvenate the country and inspire the new generation.

In the evening of the same day he heard reports of several arrests of his followers and sent a letter of protest to Prime Minister Krokidas. He wrote in his *Diary* : "I am resolved to die for the liberties of the people."[108] On 26 October the charges drawn up by Theodoros Pangalos, President of the Investigating Committee against the Six, were published in all the newspapers. As the leader of the Party of Free Thinkers Metaxas wrote to Krokidas, reminding him of the need for a fair trial and for observing due process of Law. His advice was not heeded and a speedy parody of a trial was staged. A new attempt by Metaxas to save the accused by granting them the right of appeal to the next National Assembly was unsuccessful.

Britain made various attempts to save the condemned men, but in vain. In Lausanne, Lord Curzon warned Venizelos (who was negotiating the peace settlement with Turkey on hehalf of Greece) that any executions of political figures in Greece would create a most unfavorable impression in Europe. But even Venizelos' letter could not soften the

---

106 *Ibid.*, p. 201.
107 *Ibid.*, p. 198.
108 *Ibid.*, p. 202.

vengeful resolution of the Revolutionaries. The life of Prince Andrew, the friend of Metaxas, who had commanded an army in Asia Minor was in jeopardy, but the last minute intervention of the British Admiral Talbot, sent to Athens by Venizelos at the request of Curzon, proved decisive and the Prince was spared.

The Government of Krokidas, washing its hands of all responsiiblity for the death sentences, duly resigned on the eve of the executions. On 28 November Demetrios Gounaris, Petros Protopapadakis, Nikolaos Theotokis, together with Georgios Baltatzis, Nikolaos Stratos and General Georgios Hadjianestis faced the firing squad. Gounaris, weak from sickness, had to be assisted to the place of execution. Colonel Hexadactylos and Admiral Goudas were sentenced to life imprisonment.

On 29 December 1922, only one month after the trial and execution of the Royalist ministers, Metaxas recorded in his *Diary* the death of Constantine, which had taken place in a cheap hotel in Palermo. The news was broadcast on the radio and then the announcer had played the famous old patriotic song "The son of the Eagle ..." Metaxas strongly protested to General Gonatas about the press censorship on the death of Constantine and demanded the return to Greece of the remains of the King.

Ουαί τοις ηττημένοις! Woe to the vanguished! The year 1923 found Greece inundated by refugees and disillusioned with the ideals of the *Megali Idea*; the economy was in ruins, the Army demoralised, the politicians at loggerheads and the administration in grievous disarray. In Lausanne, Venizelos was trying to negotiate a peace settlement and so conclude the most traumatic chapter in the history of Modern Greece. In Athens, Metaxas was working day and night to build up his party with which he challenged both the Venizelist and Royalist factions. The Greek tragedy was destined to pass through many vicissitudes. The political career of Metaxas, which had begun in the aftermath of the Asia Minor disaster, was to lead, after fourteen eventful years, to the 4 August 1936 and the establishment, with the blessing of King George II, of the Metaxas dictatorship.

Bibliography

Primary Sources

I. The Private Papers and Publications of John Metaxas.

The Private Papers of John Metaxas were donated to the General State Archives in Athens by his widow Madame Lela Metaxas. These Papers were then classified with the cooperation of Metaxas' elder daughter Loukia, and the official catalog was published in March 1971. The Metaxas Papers fill no less than 130 boxes and files and are, perhaps, the richest collection of personal Papers left by a political figure of modern Greece.

The most extensive item in the collection is Metaxas' *Ημερολόγιο* [Diary]. Metaxas made his first entry in the *Diary* on 21 September 1896 [O.S.] at the age of twenty-five when, as a lieutenant in the Engineers Corps he was stationed at Nafplion. The last entry was made on 17 January 1941 when Metaxas, now leader of his country, was, at the age of almost seventy, waging a victorious war against Mussolini's troops in Albania. Next to the date of entry Metaxas noted: "82nd Day" -- i.e. since the outbreak of the Greek-Italian War. The penultimate sentence reads: "I worked deep into the night." Metaxas died twelve days later.

Metaxas wrote the first part of his Diary in six thick Notebooks, 11 x 7 centimeters in size, each averaging 400 pages. These Notebooks cover the period 1896-1903 and 1910-1912. During those years Metaxas' style was narrative and descriptive. He wrote the remainder of his Diary in fifteen smaller notebooks, 10 x 14 centimeters in size, each averaging 100 pages. This part covers the period 1918-1941. Here the entries are brief, at times almost telegraphic. The Diary is written entirely in Metaxas' own hand.

Sometimes Metaxas would neglect his Diary for a short period; he would then return to it and write a condensed account of the missing days, either from memory or from brief notes he had made at the time. However, he always recorded the actual date on which he composed the summary.

Metaxas also wrote "Notes" after participating in an important event or conversation which he wished to remember. Some of the "Notes" which refer to events in 1913 he wrote much later, in the fall of 1918. They should therefore be treated with some caution because, written as they were in the midst of the National Schism, they may be colored by Metaxas' powerful emotions. However, his effort to maintain a measure of objectivity is clearly apparent.

No Diary exists for the years 1913-1917. Either Metaxas did not keep one during this period or he destroyed it in 1917 before he was sent into exile, perhaps fearing that it might be discovered and used against him. In 1923, and again in 1933, Metaxas went through his Diary and personal papers and destroyed anything he considered compromising. Then, using Indian ink, he deleted many words and phrases. On 9 November 1937, by then dictator of Greece, he noted in his Diary: "I have done. Perhaps it is better this way. There are many things that cannot be written. A life full of dangers: the others never perceived it, nor will they ever learn of it. And who knows what the fate of this Notebook will be and into what hands it may fall." (Diary. IV, 285). In June 1940 Metaxas, now certain that Greece would not be able to escape the storm of the Second World War, wrote his will and sorted through his papers once more, destroying a great many of them, but retaining the Diary, although he tore out a few pages here and there and deleted some more passages with indelible ink.

The Diary was published in Athens in four large volumes under the title Ημερολόγιο Ιω. Μεταξά [The Diary of John Metaxas], by arrangement with Madame Lela Metaxas. Vol. I covers the period when Metaxas was stationed in Nafplion, the 1897 War and the Berlin years. It was published in 1951. Vol. II covers the period up to 31 December, 1920 [O.S.] and was published in 1952. Vols. I & II were edited by Chr. Chrestides and published by the Estia Press. Vol. III covers the period 1921-1932. It was edited by Pan. M. Siphnaios and published by the Ikaros Press in 1964. Vol. IV covers the period 1933-1941. It was edited by Phaedon Vrachnas and published by the Ikaros Press in 1960. The Diary was re-issued in 8 volumes by the Gkovostes Press, Athens, in 1975.

The Metaxas Diary would have spanned a period of forty-five years (1896-1941), had there not been some important gaps. These are from 1903-1910 and from 1912-1918. Fortunately, we can partly follow his career during these periods, first from his letters to his wife and, later, from the newspaper articles which Metaxas wrote in the Thirties, discussing the events leading up to the National Schism.

The first series of letters which survive from Metaxas to his wife began on 3 August 1912, about one month after his Diary lapsed, and continued with very few intervals up to the end of July 1913. This was the period of the Balkan Wars, when Metaxas was close to the center of power. In this series there are about two hundred letters and postcards: from Athens, when Lela was living on the island of Tenos; from Sofia, where Metaxas went to negotiate the Military Convention of the Greco-Bulgarian Alliance; from London, where Metaxas was a member of the Greek delegation at the Peace Conference; and from the battlefields of Macedonia, Epirus and Thrace.

From mid-July 1914 to mid-September 1914, i.e., the eve and the first phase of the First World War, there is a series of about sixty letters written by Metaxas from Athens to Lela Metaxas, who was then vacationing on the island of Tenos. There is also a series of letters from the beginning of November 1920 to mid-January 1921, i.e., when Metaxas returned from exile after the elections of 1 November 1920 and was writing to his wife, who was then in Italy. Metaxas wrote another series of letters to his wife from Switzerland between July 1930 and May 1931. He was there with his sister, Myrianthi, who was undergoing psychiatric treatment. Unfortunately, all these letters were destroyed by Metaxas when he cleared out his papers in 1940. Madame Metaxas later stated that these lost letters were of a strictly personal nature and of only family interest.

The publishers of the Diary have included most of the surviving letters to Lela in chronological order. They have also included the various Memoranda which Metaxas submitted to either the Prime Minister or the Chief of Staff in 1914 and 1915. These Memoranda are extensively quoted in the present book.

From 1917 onward, Metaxas recorded his reflections in a separate notebook. Some of these Reflections were printed in the Diary; many were also included, together with his speeches, in two handsome volumes, under the title Λόγοι και Σκέψεις, 1936-1941 [Speeches and Thoughts, 1936-1941] (Athens, 1969).

No important documents have been found among the Metaxas Papers to bridge the gap in his Diary from 1915 to 1917, the most stormy period of the National Schism. This hiatus is partially filled by the seventy newspaper articles which Metaxas wrote between October 1934 and January 1935 for the Athens press in a vitriolic debate on the causes of the National Schism with his old adversary, Eleftherios Venizelos. Metaxas' articles were collected and published under the title Η Ιστορία του Εθνικού Διχασμού και της Μικρασιατικής Καταστροφής [The History of the National Schism and the Asia Minor Disaster] (Athens, 1935). But for a full appreciation of the political rift, the ideological chasm and the undying passions of the two great protagonists of the National Schism, Metaxas' articles should be read side by side with those of Venizelos. This has been made possible in a one-volume collection bearing the names of both Venizelos and Metaxas as joint authors and entitled Η Ιστορία του Εθνικού Διχασμού, 1915-1935, [The History of the National Schism, 1915-1935] (Athens, 1953). In this study use has been made of these articles for the first time. The politician-historian Spyros Markezinis, mentions the articles in his momumental and didactic history of Greece, but dismisses them as of little value, written as they were under the influence of the strong feelings engendered by the National Schism. This attitude of Markezinis is consistent with his attempt to present all Greeks as good patriots and his desire to gloss over any incidents which might cast aspersions on the motives and actions of two such prominent figures in the modern Greek pantheon.

Metaxas' elder daughter, Loukia Metaxas, has edited Το Πολίτευμα του Ιωάννου Μεταξά [The Constitution of John Metaxas] (Athens, 1945). This is an outline for a constitution on which Metaxas mused from time to time when dictator of Greece. Loukia Metaxas has also edited Ιωάννου Π. Μεταξά. Εις το Προσωπικό του Ημερολόγιο Επίμετρο [A Supplement to the Personal Diary of John Metaxas] (Athens, 1977). This is a collection of documents and diverse comments on Metaxas, his life and work. These two publications complete the Metaxas canon.

Documents and Official Sources

American-Hellenic Society,

The Greek White Book, 1913-1917. Translated from the Greek and French by Theodore P. Ion and Carroll N. Brown. ["Venizelist"] Revised Edition. (New York. 1918).

The Greek White Book. Supplementary Diplomatic Documents, 1913-1917. Translated from the French by Theodore P. Ion and Carroll N. Brown. ["Venizelist"] (New York, 1919).

Persecutions of the Greeks in Turkey Since the Beginning of the European War. Translated from official Greek documents by Carroll N. Brown and Theodore P. Ion. (New York, 1918).

Report of the Greek University Commission Upon the Atrocities and Devastations Committed by the Bulgarians in Eastern Macedonia. Translated from the French by Carroll N. Brown. (New York, 1919).

Carnegie Endowment for International Peace.

Report of the International Commission to Inquire into the Causes and Conduct of the Balkan Wars. (Washington, D.C., 1914).

Constantine, H.R.H. Crown Prince.
Έκθεσις της Α.Β. Υψηλότητος του Διαδόχου επί των πεπραγμένων του στρατού Θεσσαλίας κατά την εκστρατεία 1897. [Report by H.R.H. the Crown Prince on the actions of the army of Thessaly during the campaign of 1897]. (Athens, 1898).

Great Britain. Dardanelles Commission.
First Report. Command 8490.
Supplement to the First Report. Command 8502. Final Report. Command 371. (London, 1917).

Great Britain. Foreign Office
British Documents on the Origins of the War, 1898-1914. Edited by G.P. Gooch and H.W.V. Temperley. 12 vols. (London, 1927-1938).

Great Britain. Foreign Office
British Documents on the Origins of the War, 1914-1918. Edited by G.P. Gooch and H.W.V. Temperley. (London, 1926-1930).

Greece. Ministry of Foreign Affairs.
Documents diplomatiques, Octobre 1915-Juin 1916. ["Royalist"] (Athens, 1921).

Greece. Ministry of War. General Staff, Historical Division.
Ο Ελληνικός Στρατός κατά τους Βαλκανικούς Πολέμους του 1912-1913. [The Greek Army during the Balkan Wars of 1912-1913.] 3 vols. (Athens, 1932-1939).
Ιστορία της Οργανώσεως του Ελληνικού Στρατού. [History of the Organization of the Greek Army, 1821-1954] (Athens, 1957).

Hurewitz, Jacob C. *Diplomacy in the Near and Middle East. Vol. I: A Documentary Record: 1535-1914. Vol. 2: A Documentary Record: 1914-1956.* (Princeton, N.J., 1956).

Venizelos, Eleftherios *Greece Before the Peace Congress of 1919: A Memorandum Dealing with the Rights of Greece, Submitted by Eleftherios Venizelos.* (New York, 1919).
Greece in her True Light: Her Position in the World - Wide War as Expounded by El. K. Venizelos. Translated by Socrates A. Xanthaky and Nicholas G. Sakellarios. (New York, 1916).
The Vindication of Greek National Policy, 1912-1917. A Report of Speeches Delivered in the Greek Chamber.

August 23 to 26, 1917, by Mr. E. Venizelos and Others. (London, 1918).

Secondary literature

Ahmad, Feroz — *The Young Turks: The Committee of Union and Progress in Turkish Politics, 1908-1914.* (Oxford, 1969).

Alastos, Doros — *Venizelos: Patriot, Statesman, Revolutionary* (London, 1942).

Alexandris, Apostolos — *Πολιτικαί Αναμνήσεις* [Political Recollections] (Patras, 1947).

Argyropoulos, Pericles — *Απομνημονεύματα.* [Memoirs] 2 vols. (Athens, 1970-1971).

Arnakis, George G. — *The Near East in Modern Times. Vol. I : The Ottoman Empire and the Balkan States to 1900* (New York, 1969).

Augustinos, Gerasimos — *Consciousness and History: Nationalist Critics of Greek Society, 1897-1914. East* European Monographs, no. 32. (Boulder, Colorado, 1977).

Bourchier, J. D. — Articles on the Origin of the Balkan League. Times (London), 4, 5, 6, 11, 13, 16 June 1913.

Chamberlain, Houston Stewart
Die Grundlagen des neunzehnten Jahrhunderts (Berlin, 1899).
The Foundations of the Nineteenth Century, 2 vols. (London, 1911).

Charalambis, Gen. A. — *Αναμνήσεις* [Recollections] (Athens, 1947).

Christopher, Prince of Greece
Memoirs of H.R.H. Prince Christopher of Greece (London, 1938).

Clogg, Richard — *A Short History of Modern Greece* (New York, 1979).

Constantine I, King of Greece
A King's Private Letters of Constantine to Paola, Princess of Saxe-Weimar, 1912-1923. Preface by Rear Admiral Mark Kerr. (London, 1925).

Dakin, Douglas — *The Greek Struggle in Macedonia 1897-1913* (Thessaloniki, 1966).

*The Unification of Greece, 1770-192*3 (London, 1972).

Daphnis, Georgios — *Τα Ελληνικά Πολιτικά Κόμματα, 1821-1961* [Greek Political Parties, 1821-1961.] (Athens, 1961).

Dertilis, George — *Κοινωνικός Μετασχηματισμός και Στρατιωτική Επέμβαση, 1880-1909* [Social Change and Military Intervention, 1880-1909] (Athens, 1977).

Djemal Pasha, Ahmed — *Memoirs of a Turkish Statesman, 1913-1919* (New York, 1922).

Dousmanis, Victor — *Απομνημονεύματα: Ιστορικαί Σελίδες τας οποίας έζησα* [Memoirs: Pages of History I have Witnessed] (Athens, 1946).

Ο Συμμαχικός Πόλεμος κατά των Βουλγάρων [The War of the Allies Against the Bulgarians] (Athens, 1927).

Ekthodike Athinon. — *Ιστορία του Ελληνικού Εθνους* [History of the Greek Nation.] 15 vols. (Athens, 1978).

Enepekidis, Polychronis K. — *Η Δόξα και ο Διχασμός, 1908-1918* [The Glory and the National Schism] (Athens, 1992).

Eliot, Sir Charles [Odysseus] — *Turkey in Europe* 2nd ed. (London, 1908).

Forster, Edward S. — *A Short History of Modern Greece, 1821-1956*, 3rd ed. Revised and enlarged by Douglas Dakin (London, 1960).

Gennadius, I. — "The Truth about Constantine and Venizelos" *Current History*, 5 (August 1922), pp. 810-12.

George I, King of Greece — *Επιστολαί της Α.Μ. του Βασιλέως Γεωργίου Α'* [Letters of H.M. King George I, 1903-1913.] Edited by A. Romanos. (Athens, 1935).

Geshov, I.E. — *The Balkan League* (London, 1915).

Gonatas, Stylianos Ep. — *Απομνημονεύματα, 1897-1957* [Memoirs, 1897-1957] (Athens, 1958).

Grogan, Ellinore — *The Life of Lady Ellinore Flora Borsworth* J. D. Bourchier. (London, 1926).

Helmreich, Ernst Christian — *The Diplomacy of the Balkan Wars, 1912-13* (Cambridge, Mass., 1938).

Hibben, Paxton — Constantine I and the Greek People (New York, 1920).

Higham R., Veremis Th. — *Aspects of Greece 1936-40* (Athens, 1993).

Howard, Harry N. — *The Partition of Turkey. A Diplomatic History, 1913-1923* (New York, 1966).

Iorga, N. — *Histoires des états balkaniques jusqu'a 1924* (Paris, 1925).

Ivanoff, J. — *La région de Cavalla* (Berne, 1918).

Jenkins, Romilly — *Dionysius Solomós* (Cambridge, 1940, 1948).

Izzet - Fuad Pasha, General — *Paroles de vaincu; après désastre--avant la revanche* (Paris, 1913).

Kallonas, Demetrios — *Ιωάννης Μεταξάς* [John Metaxas.] (Athens, 1938).

Karras, Nikolaos — *Ο Ιωάννης Μεταξάς* [John Metaxas] (Athens, 1994).

Kerner, Robert J. — "The Mission of Liman von Sanders, I. Its Origin, II. The Crisis, III. The Deadlock." *The Slavonic Review* (June 1927), pp. 12-17, (December 1927), pp. 344-363, (March 1928), pp. 343-580.

Kerofilas, Costas — *Eleftherios Venizelos. His Life and Work* (London & New York, 1915.

Kinross, Lord — *Ataturk: A Biography of Mustafa Kemal, Father of Modern Turkey* (New York, 1965).

Koliopoulos, Ioannis — *Η Δικτατορία του Μεταξά και ο Πόλεμος του '40* [The Metaxas Dictatorship and the War of 1940] (Thessaloniki, 1994).

Kordatos, Yiannis — *Ιστορία της Νεώτερης Ελλάδας* [History of Modern Greece], 5 vols. (Athens, 1958).

Langer, William L. "Russia, the Straits Question and the Origins of the Balkan League, 1908-1912." *Political Science Quarterly* 43 (September 1928), pp. 321-363.

Linardatos, Spyros *Ο Ιωάννης Μεταξάς και οι Μεγάλες Δυνάμεις, 1936-1940* [Ioannis Metaxas and the Great Powers 1936-1940] (Athens, 1993).

Makraki, Lili *Ελευθέριος Βενιζέλος, 1864-1910* [Eleftherios Venizelos, 1864-1910] (Athens, 1992)

Malainos, E. I. *Ιστορία Ξενικών Επεμβάσεων* [History of Foreign Intervention.] 6 vols. (Athens, 1966-1968).

Markezinis, Spyros *Πολιτική Ιστορία της Νεωτέρας Ελλάδος* [Political History of Modern Greece], 4 vols., (Athens, 1966-1968).

Mavrogordato, John "Greece, Constantine, and Venizelos." *Edinburgh Review* 233:475 (January 1921), pp. 146-163.

Mazarakis-Ainian, Alexandros
Απομνημονεύματα [Memoirs.] (Athens, 1948).

Melas, George M. *Ex-King Constantine and the War* (London, 1920).

Melas, Spyros "Ιωάννης Μεταξάς" [John Metaxas]. *Καιροί* (Athens, December 1949).

Metaxas, Epameinondas K.
Ιστορία της Οικογένειας Μεταξά από του 1081 μέχρι του 1864 έτους [History of the Metaxas Family from the Year 1081 to 1864.] (Athens, 1893).

Miller, William *The Ottoman Empire and Its Successors, 1801-1927* (Cambridge, 1936).

Morgenthau, H. J. *U.S. Ambassador at Constantinople, 1913-1916. Secrets of the Bosphorus, Constantinople 1913-1916* (London, 1928).

Mouktar Pasha, General Mahmoud
La Turquie, l'Allemagne et l' Europe depuis le traité de Berlin jusqu'a la guerre mondiale (Paris, 1924).

Mon commandat au cours de la campagne de Balkans de 1912. (Paris, 1913).

Mouzelis, Nicos P. *Modern Greece: Facets of Underdevelopment* (New York, 1979).

Mowat, R.B. *A History of European Diplomacy, 1914-1925* (New York, 1931).

Nea Estia, "Ιωάννης Μεταξάς, Φίλος και Προστάτης των Γραμμάτων και Τεχνών." ["John Metaxas, Friend and Protector of Letters and the Arts."] *Νέα Εστία* Special issue, 15:340 (Athens, 15 February 1941).

Nekludoff, Anatolii Vasilévich
Diplomatic Reminiscences Before and During the World War, 1911-1917. Translated from the French by A. Paget. (London, 1920).

Nicholas, Prince of Greece
My Fifty Years (London, 1927).

Pangalos, Theodore *Τα απομνημονεύματά μου, 1897-1947* [My Memoirs, 1897-1947] (Athens, 1950-1959).

Papacosma, Victor S. *The Military in Greek Politics: the 1909 coup d' état* (Kent, Ohio, 1977).

Paraskevopoulos, Leonidas I.
Αναμνήσεις: 1896-1920 [Recollections: 1896-1920] 2 vols. (Athens, 1934).

Peponis, I. A. *Νικόλαος Πλαστήρας στα Γεγονότα 1909-1945* [Nicholas Plastiras and the Events of 1909-1945] (Athens, 1947).

Pesmazoglou, George *Το Χρονικόν της Ζωής μου, 1889-1979* [The Chronicle of My Life, 1889-1979] (Athens, 1979).

Pipinelis, Panayiotis N. *Η Μοναρχία εις Ελλάδι, 1833-1843* [The Monarchy in Greece, 1833-1843] (Athens, 1932).

Rangabé, Eug. Rizo. *Livre d' Or de la Noblesse Ionienne*. Vol. 2 *Cephalonie* (Athens, 1926).

Rankin, Sir Reginald *Inner History of the Balkan War* (London, 1914).

Sanders, Liman von *Five Years in Turkey* (Annapolis, 1928).

Seton-Watson, R.W. "Italy's Balkan Policy in 1914" *Slavonic Review* 5:13 (June 1916), p. 48-65.

Smith, Michael Llewelyn *The Ionian Vision* (London, 1975).

Souliotis -Nikolaidis, A. *Ημερολόγιο του Πρώτου Βαλκανικού Πολέμου* [Diary of the First Balkan War] (Thessaloniki, 1962).

Steed, Henry Wickham *Through Thirty Years, 1892-1922: A Personal Narrative* (Garden City, N.Y., 1924).

Stoianovich, Traian *A Study in Balkan Civilization* (New York, 1967).

Story, Sommerville, (ed.) *The Memoirs of Ismail Kemal Bey* (London, 1920).

Streit, George *Ημερολόγιον - Αρχείον* [Diary-Private Papers], 3 vols. (Athens, 1964-1966).

Svolopoulos, K. *Ο Βενιζέλος, ο Bourchier και η ιδέα της Βαλκανικής Συμμαχίας. 1894-1913* [Venizelos, Bourchier, and the Idea of the Balkan Alliance, 1894-1913] (Athens, 1975).

Ventiris, George *Η Ελλάς των ετών 1910-1920* [Greece in the Years 1910-1920.] 2 vols. ["Venizelist"] (Athens, 1931).

Venizelos, Eleftherios *Greece Before the Peace Congress of 1919: A Memorandum Dealing with the Rights of Greece, Submitted by Eleftherios Venizelos* (New York, 1919).

Greece in her True Light: Her Position in the World-Wide War as Expounded by El. K. Venizelos. Translated by Socrates A. Xanthaky and Nicholas G. Sakellarios. (New York, 1916).

The Vindication of Greek National Policy, 1912-1917 A Report of Speeches Delivered in the Greek Chamber. August 23 to 26, 1917, by Mr E. Venizelos and Others (London,1918).

Veremis, Thanos. *Οι Επεμβάσεις του Στρατού στην Ελληνική Πολιτική, 1916-1936.* [Military Intervention in Greek Politics, 1916-1936] (Athens, 1977).

"The Officer Corps in Greece 1912-1936." *Byzantine & Modern Greek Studies* (1976), pp. 113-4.

Vournas, Tasos *Ιστορία της Σύγχρονης Ελλάδας, 1909-1940* [History of Contemporary Greece, 1909-1940] (Athens, 1977).

Xanalatos, D. "The Greeks and the Turks on the Eve of the Balkan Wars." *Balkan Studies* 3:2 (1962), pp. 277-96.

Zavitsianos, Constantine G.
Αι Αναμνήσεις του εκ της ιστορικής διαφωνίας Βασιλέως Κωνσταντίνου και Ελευθερίου Βενιζέλου όπως την έζησε, 1914-1922 [Recollections of the Historic Dispute between King Constantine and Eleftherios Venizelos as He Witnessed It, 1914-1922.] 2 vols. (Athens, 1946-1947).

Zorbas, N. K. *Απομνημονεύματα ή Πληροφορίαι περί των Συμβάντων κατά τη διάρκεια της Επαναστάσεως της 15ης Αυγούστου, 1909* [Memoirs or Information Concerning the Events During the Revolution of 15 August 1909.] (Athens, 1925).

Index of Names

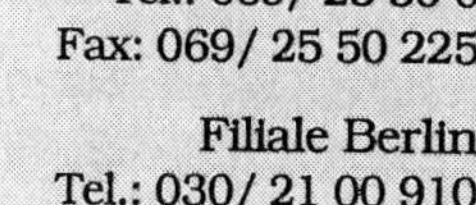